Pursuing Quality of Life

From anxieties over work–life balance and entangling technologies, to celebrations of cool jobs and great places to live, quality of life frames the ways we enhance our lives and legitimate social change today. But how does the idea of quality of life envision the greater good, and what gets lost as a result? This book provides the critical framework for understanding the idea's contexts and tensions that is conspicuously missing in popular discussions, professional activities, and scholarly research on quality of life. With multiple case studies taken across North America and Europe, it provides a sociological perspective on the contradictory ways we talk about and pursue quality of life in relation to technology, consumerism, family, work, public space, rural ways of life, and ultimately the final years of life. Drawing on contemporary and classical social theory, it provides an incisive account of the historical shifts in developed societies over the last half-century that have transformed our views and pursuits of quality of life. Originally a promise to undertake collective effort and pursue social justice at a moment of unprecedented opportunity, quality of life now enshrines a solipsistic ideal with which to accommodate the storms of market forces and political failure.

Leonard Nevarez is an associate professor of sociology at Vassar College. He is the author of *New Money, Nice Town: How Capital Works in the New Urban Economy* (2003).

Pursuing Quality of Life

From the Affluent Society to the Consumer Society

Leonard Nevarez

Routledge
Taylor & Francis Group
NEW YORK AND LONDON

First published 2011
by Routledge
270 Madison Avenue, New York, NY 10016

Simultaneously published in the UK
by Routledge
2 Park Square, Milton Park, Abingdon, Oxon OX14 4RN

Routledge is an imprint of the Taylor & Francis Group, an informa business

Typeset in Goudy by Swales & Willis Ltd, Exeter, Devon
Printed and bound in the United States of America on acid-free paper by Walsworth Publishing Company, Marceline, MO

Library of Congress Cataloging in Publication Data
Nevarez, Leonard.
Pursuing quality of life : from the affluent society to the consumer society / Leonard Nevarez.
p. cm.
Includes bibliographical references.
1. Quality of life—Case studies. 2. Consumption (Economics)—Case studies. I. Title.
HN25.N48 2011
306—dc22
2010037055

ISBN13: 978–0–415–89013–7 (hbk)
ISBN13: 978–0–203–82974–5 (ebk)

SUSTAINABLE FORESTRY INITIATIVE
Certified Chain of Custody
Promoting Sustainable Forest Management
www.sfiprogram.org
NSF-SFI-COC-C0004285
The SFI label applies to the text stock.

For Andrea, Amelia, and John

Contents

Preface

This book critically examines the preeminent framework by which modern societies debate the greater good: quality of life. My project asks the reader to accept a few premises. First, whereas academics, professionals, and everyday people impute different meanings to the idea of quality of life—a state of mental well-being, a set of personal living conditions, features of a physical place, and so on—I ask the reader to give up their attachment to any particular meaning and examine the idea in the semantic breadth and variety that we find in the empirical world of people living and thinking about their lives. Second, it does not follow from the important decisions and actions undertaken in the name of quality of life by individuals, households, groups, institutions, governments, and societies that the idea philosophically precedes its consequence. Far from it—often it is through action that people come to grasp the meanings, motives, and values they associate with quality of life. Consequently, I ask the reader to view quality of life as people understand *and* pursue it, privileging neither one nor the other *a priori*. Third, such understandings and pursuits do not occur in a vacuum. Structured social contexts convey the force of history, economy, and culture on those moments when people consider the issues and choices associated with quality of life; contexts make certain quality-of-life motives and resources easier to draw upon, and others less tangible or accessible. To be sure, ideas have a social force of their own, particularly those as culturally resonant as the one examined in this book, yet they exert that force through the intelligibilities and opportunities that people derive from social contexts. I ask the reader to focus on the connections between social contexts and the idea's semantic formulations; from this perspective, the sociological thrust of my inquiry will become clear.

The initial contrivance of these premises should not mislead readers that my inquiry is just an academic exercise. The problems associated with quality of life are far too pressing, and the deliberation of the greater good within national and international forums is far too imperative, for me not to direct my analysis toward the contours of an agenda for advocacy and reform. To cut to the chase, my position draws from the political and cultural critique associated with the "affluent society," the post-World War II period in developed Western nations when social movements and public intellectuals challenged the economic growth (i.e., *quantity* of life) framework that dominated deliberations of the greater good. Civil rights movements, the welfare state, and environmentalist action are perhaps the most important legacies of this era, and the current precarity of their historic achievements underscores the urgency in my argument. Readers familiar with the academic scholarship on quality of life will also want to know that my view of quality of life emphasizes collective, objective factors that support, but are ultimately external to, individuals' happiness, self-actualization, and other subjective experiences of well-being. This position puts me somewhat at odds with recent directions in quality-of-life research and professional practice, such as the burgeoning field of positive psychology or the cultivation of "creativity" in workplace relations and vibrant cities.

However, I do not seek to give easy assurance to any partisans in the political or scholarly debates on quality of life, at least as the idea is generally understood, for two reasons. First, these debates only add to the cacophony of viewpoints and rhetorics of quality of life that frustrates clarification and illumination of this idea. As economists and sociologists talk past each other, as architects and psychologists neglect each other's insights, and so on, discrete traditions of thinking about quality of life—all valid on their face—have mostly failed to cohere into a singular body of knowledge that addresses the multiple facets and conflicting perspectives of the idea. Of course, it is the scholar's prerogative to put forth certain definitions, select the analytical domain (e.g., health care, economic development, urban planning), and suggest the stakes at hand (a humane health-care system, a more just economic development policy, sustainable cities); this is how most scholarly works on quality of life proceed. Yet in doing so, most researchers and practitioners refrain from considering the idea's articulations by everyday people, politicians, businesses, and communities, dismissing such lay definitions as messy, incoherent, contradictory, and unsuited for the given task. Among other problems, this is hardly the basis to forge widespread consensus on the political questions raised by the idea. Thus, a central task in this book is to provide a conceptual and theoretical toolkit for critically examining the many understandings and pursuits of quality of life. I survey key traditions in the scholarship and professional practices associated with the idea, although not as extensively as textbooks in the so-called quality-of-life research may; instead, I selectively emphasize what I consider the most significant developments and tread lightly on esoteric issues of conceptualization and method. Perhaps more originally, I develop an analytical framework steeped in classic and contemporary social theory to help the reader make sense of the diverse perspectives and dilemmas on quality of life that they may encounter—in the scholarship and in everyday life.

Second, the cacophony of quality-of-life traditions and value positions is itself a social fact warranting investigation. It points to key contexts in which the current regress into quality-of-life idiosyncrasy obscures fundamental questions about how we should live that were clearer and more compelling when the idea made its first historical impact. More to the point, these contexts give rise to—one could even say further—the cacophony. This is as true for philosophers and academics as it is for the layperson, whom we might excuse for not having the time to meditate at length on the diverse connotations of quality life. We should anticipate, then, that a critical inquiry into the cacophony of understandings and pursuits associated with quality of life will point us *away* from the idea itself and toward broader historical developments. Readers seeking the relevance and the 'answer' to quality of life from within the idea's internal formulations may be disappointed, but the need for at least a temporary disenchantment of this idea is acute.

A note about punctuation: Because my topic is the *idea* of quality of life, and because I refer frequently to other people's language and writing to illustrate the idea's various expressions, I use quotation marks in this book according to the following conventions. Single-apostrophe quotation marks highlight quality of life or other ideas in the abstract, usually to scrutinize their properties or usage: 'quality of life' (used interchangeably with *quality of life the idea*), 'high' quality of life, etc. Quotation marks with double apostrophes refer to names and actual expressions: the French government's "Ministry of Quality of Life," Aristotle's maxim that "the quality of life is determined by one's activities," etc. Without quotation marks, I denote the empirical conditions of quality of life (the quality of life of terminally ill patients, for instance) and everyday references to this idea in its taken-for-granted coherence: the research on quality of life, quality-of-life values, and so on.

In writing this book, I owe a debt of gratitude to many people. *Pursuing Quality of Life* originated out of a conversation with David McBride, former sociology editor at Routledge, who thought the broader relevance of quality of life raised by my first book, *New Money, Nice Town*, had not yet been fully addressed. His enthusiasm for my original vision helped steer this book over a very long journey, well after he left the publisher. Steve Rutter, his replacement at Routledge, and editorial assistant Leah Babb-Rosenfeld were very helpful and supportive as the book reached the final stretch. Victor Cohen, Richard Lloyd, Krista Paulsen, and Richard Widick gave comments on some or all parts of the manuscript. Suzanne Bianchi, Claude Fischer, and Janet Gornick graciously shared their data with me. Robert Beauregard, Terry Clark, David Fasenfest, Garry Marvin, Lydia Murdoch, Italo Pardo, Chris Pickvance, Ron Sharp, Daniel Sullivan, and Justus Uitermark offered helpful leads. Laura Fletcher and Victoria Gonzalez provided able research assistance. Pinar Batur, Lisa Brawley, Dick Flacks, Tim Koechlin, David M. Levy, and Juliet Schor offered helpful words of encouragement. These individuals' generosity of time and reflection greatly improved the final book, and they share no blame for the remaining shortcomings.

1 Conceptual Tensions

> Does the ordinary person have a grasp on this notion [of quality of life]? Although it is plausible that he does not talk, nor even reflect, employing such a term, it is also plausible that he does have a grasp on it. To grasp the notion of quality of life, it is simply necessary to grasp the application of qualitative terms to one's life; and such talk of life, or of projects which constitute life, as going better or worse, is common enough .... Thus the notion of (private) quality of life is not in itself theoretical.
>
> (Christopher Megone 1990:29–30)

Any number of examples exposes us to the contexts, complexities, and stakes associated with the idea of quality of life (hereafter, QOL). My first highlights concerns that are common motives for QOL pursuits in developed societies: environmental and economic sustainability, personal mindfulness of the treadmill of work and materialism, the preservation of environmental and urban amenities. I turn to Southern California's Central Coast, a region in the western United States comprising an approximately 200-mile stretch of open space, large ranches and vineyards, coastal settlements abutting the Pacific Ocean such as Santa Barbara, San Luis Obispo, Ojai, and Ventura, and swelling inland cities like Santa Maria, Paso Robles, and Thousand Oaks. Long before the eighteenth-century Spanish conquest, the area was home to the indigenous Chumash. Yvon Chouinard, noted outdoorsman and founder of the Patagonia Company, a Ventura-based designer of internationally popular, environmentally friendly outdoor wear and local champion of green principles, takes the story from here:

> Near the headquarters of Patagonia, on the central coast of California, the Chumash Nation enjoyed a good life for thousands of years. They lived in small villages and possessed fur blankets, intricate baskets and soapstone pots decorated with shells. They painted elaborate abstracts in mountain caves. In every village were game-playing fields and sacred buildings. Almost every day, most Chumash enjoyed a cleansing sweat in the village temescal. In each village was a granary for stockpiling food that would later be distributed to those in need.

> Chumash traded exquisite olivella shells for black pigment, honeydew melons, pine nuts, wild tobacco and various herbs and salt. By the 16th century, theirs was a complex society of hunters and gatherers with a far-reaching, sophisticated trade network … .
>
> Such lives are often called subsistence, which brings to mind the barest, hardscrabble survival. But there is another way to look at them. At Patagonia we choose to call them "economies of abundance." In an economy of abundance, there is enough. Not too much. Not too little. Enough. Most important, there is enough time for the things that matter: relationships, delicious food, art, games and rest.
>
> (Chouinard and Gallagher 2004)

In their exhortation for readers to think and live post-materially, so that they may perceive the existing social and environmental "abundance" and reorient values of human well-being accordingly, Chouinard and co-author Nora Gallagher illustrate how Central Coast environmentalists revere the Chumash for the pre-European ecology they sustained and—in a crucial chain of logic—the 'good life' they were thought to enjoy. Like today's Central Coast residents, the Chumash experienced moderate coastal temperatures rarely dipping outside a range of 40–80° F. One coastal stretch where they concentrated, the South Coast where Santa Barbara currently stands, runs almost parallel with the equator and enjoys a geographical effect in which the sun casts almost no shadows before setting at dusk. In this landscape, the Chumash had little need to wear much clothing, at most donning an animal-skin cape for winter rains. Also, their coastal settlements sat atop the ecological intersection of northern and southern tidal patterns, where biodiversity in sea and on land flourish. This reputedly made their daily work of fishing, hunting, and gathering relatively easy, one reason why, like many California Indians, the Chumash had no collective memory of migration or nomadism. In such a hospitable environment, they could devote much attention to their arts and crafts; basket weaving was particularly refined, and their religious cave drawings (the Chumash had no need for caves as shelter) are thought by some to be among the most colorful and elaborate of any indigenous American population (see Kennett 2005; Librado, Harrington, and Hudson 1977). Little surprise, then, that the Chumash are regular protagonists in the QOL histories and polemics that Central Coast environmentalists tell of their region.

Uncovering Contexts of Local Concern

So did the Chumash enjoy a high QOL? Certainly Chouinard and Gallagher's essay, posted on the Patagonia Company's website, implies this with a subsequent contrast of the problematic present—"We are the world's richest country, yet our quality of life ranks 14th in the world" (Chouinard and Gallagher 2004)—to the Chumash past. Scholars who have sifted through archaeological and historical evidence, which upon closer inspection reveals some less than Edenic aspects (e.g., Chumash groups warred with each other when droughts dried up natural resources), have arrived at similar conclusions nonetheless, deeming the Chumash "distinctive in quality of life terms" (Molotch and Freudenburg 1996:5) and "the wealthiest, most populous, and most powerful ethnic nationality in aboriginal southern California" (Bean and Smith 1978:538; quoted in McEvoy 1986:28).

These assertions rely not only upon data but also an understanding of 'quality of life' that raise questions of conceptualization, operational definition, and inference. What conditions comprise the criteria for QOL: freedom from material want, effort spent on work, the development of arts and technologies, a society's cultural integrity and spiritual seeking, something else? How much of these criteria is needed to demonstrate a 'high' or desirable QOL? What are the analytical interventions and normative claims imposed between objective conditions (of Chumash life) and their subjective evaluation by various beholders (scholars, environmentalists, the Chumash themselves)? Does an evaluation necessarily involve a comparison to QOL for other groups, cross-societally and/or temporally? Does that necessarily make for a sound scientific concept?

Beyond questions like these that many QOL scholars have dwelt upon at length lie less considered ones regarding the social contexts for ideas such as QOL. These questions shape the central analytical framework for this book. *First, in what social contexts—places, periods, institutional settings—does QOL as an idea become salient to people? Second, how do social contexts influence the ways people understand and pursue this idea? That is, how do social contexts lead people to emphasize certain aspects of QOL and neglect others? Third, what sorts of consequences do people's contextual understandings and pursuits of QOL have for how they live and relate to one another?*

Taking up the first question—in what social contexts does QOL as an idea become salient to people?—the Patagonia essay epitomizes how the very interest in pre-modern QOL is a historically recent mode of inquiry. There is almost certainly no record of what the Chumash thought of 'their QOL' at the time. More to the point, anthropological and historical records of many indigenous peoples suggest that the Chumash might recoil at viewing their way of life as a condition or achievement that they possess, looking instead to the animistic blessings conferred by their physical environment and spiritual obligations. More inclined to attribute a way of life to a people, the Spanish conquerors who made contact in 1772 and eventually decimated the population with disease and enslavement saw little worthwhile in the Chumash way of life. From their perspective, the Chumash were so inherently inferior as to require 'salvation' through forced labor in the California missions. In turn, by the nineteenth century many Yankee intellectuals and boosters would find the Spanish devastation of the Chumash repugnant, although their laments for these 'noble savages' reflected their own ambivalence about the march of civilization and their then-contemporary competition with the Spanish-descended Californios more than a genuine consideration of the Chumash's well-being (see Walton 2001; Starr 1990). Tellingly, in all three accounts, evaluations of the Chumash social organization and material livelihood primarily emphasized the actual social relations that the beholders had with the Chumash, including the Chumash with themselves. For the Chumash, their way of life was a sacralized self-understanding of the collective; for the Spanish, a justification for subjugating an inferior heathen race; for the Yankees, a selective and uncritically examined legacy that legitimated their dominance over the Chumash's original oppressors.

Only under modern viewpoints would people conceive of the Chumash's social organization and material livelihood as conceptually severed from the Chumash themselves, objectified into a material thing or condition that one can call QOL. This conceptual innovation has occurred in three overlapping contexts that recur frequently in this book. One is the research-policy field focused on comparative and historical issues of economic development. Shaped by debates since the post-World War II period across the social sciences and policy arenas, this fields sets up 'QOL' as an analytical lens on the productivity of economies, the ecological abundance of regions, and the subsequent possibilities for developing culture. This arena of expertise (in this case, particularly as articulated by human development proponents) serves to legitimate the evidence gathered by scholars of the Chumash as the proper basis for the evaluation and comparison of human societies' QOL.

A second context is the Western environmental movement that expressed the broader post-World War II affluent society critique (further described in the next chapter) and, incidentally, cites local origins in the Central Coast, notably in the 1969 Santa Barbara oil spill and the 1979–81 "Abalone Alliance" mobilization against the Diablo Canyon nuclear plant. The environmental movement shares several premises as the first research-policy context—among them, that QOL is a societal indicator that can be evaluated and compared—but characteristically deploys the idea to challenge uncritical emphases on economic growth. Articulated in a social world where these first two contexts shape the understandings of experts, activists, and laypeople, the Patagonia essay invokes a rhetoric that transforms a largely bygone way of life into a legitimate basis for human action now: reconsideration, reevaluation, change. At the very least, the authors hope readers will never look at a piece of clothing the same way again.

QOL is not articulated in a void of lived experience; on this issue, the essay bespeaks a concrete setting, indeed a geography, for QOL pursuits. Just as Patagonia customers are asked to participate in the "economy of abundance" by purchasing a particular piece of clothing, so too the Central Coast environmental movement (in which the authors can credibly claim membership) enjoins political struggles over ecological issues via market shifts that fuel a certain kind of political mobilization. An example of the "postmaterialist" coalitions that some scholars assert are reshaping the U.S. electoral geography (Judis and Teixeira 2002; Clark and Hoffmann-Martinot 1998), the region's environmentalists have long been effective in making alliances with the educated, internationally traveled, and frequently well-to-do residents ensconced around Santa Barbara, San Luis Obispo, and Ojai to get laws passed that limit urban development and regulate resource extraction (Nevarez 2003; Molotch, Freudenburg, and Paulsen 2000). Perhaps unwittingly, regional environmentalists thereby give support to an understanding of QOL as a scarce resource that people consume individually by moving to or visiting the area. These residential mobilizations reveal the third context for QOL raised by the Chumash example: contemporary economies of uneven spatial development and geographical mobility that put a market premium on places with 'a high QOL.' Well-to-do homeowners and real estate agents may not be cognizant of the Chumash legacy, at least with the kinds of detail and reverence illustrated in the essay, or the progressive political ideals espoused by many in the local environmental movement. Yet as they buy and sell exclusive lifestyles based on the region's location and physical amenities, these groups help materialize—they transform into a social fact of the market—the objectified conception of QOL that environmentalists inherit from the first two contexts.

Shared Languages of 'QOL'

Our second question—how do social contexts influence the ways people understand and pursue the idea of QOL?—points to a set of semantic instabilities that organize the discourse of QOL across the many settings and issues covered in this book. As I elaborate later in this chapter, QOL the idea sustains four pairs of conceptual tensions. First, the idea can connote both an objective condition and a subjective orientation; in the essay above, QOL refers to a material level of welfare provision (e.g., the Chumash economy of abundance) but also a state of cultural-psychological well-being. Second, 'QOL' can be attributed both to a collective (e.g., the Chumash, the U.S.) and to its constituent groups and individuals (e.g., the Central Coast region of the U.S.). The claim that the Central Coast has a "special" QOL not available elsewhere in turn points to a third instability: QOL can reference the production or achievement of a group, society, or environment (e.g., the state of Chumash technology and economy, the aquacultural abundance of the coastal geography) but also the distribution or experience of this accomplishment (e.g., unevenly in the case of the region's exclusive localities and lifestyles). Fourth and finally, QOL can connote both a universal indicator to compare different groups, often to assert one group's superiority (here, the inspiration that the reader is asked to draw from the Chumash economy) and a culturally relative idea that can only be properly understood in a group's meaning system (as illustrated by the anachronism of 'Chumash QOL').

In both the social settings for and analytical reflections on the Chumash example, these contrasting meanings slip from one pole to the other fluidly, as they do more generally within and across other social contexts for 'QOL.' The scholar might be tempted to resolve the apparent confusions through definitional fiat—a typical response within the first two contexts—but doing so only obscures the multiple meanings and stakes of QOL as an idea. Yet even as conceptual tensions pattern the cacophony of QOL concerns and traditions sounded by scholars and laypeople alike, the material thrust of the third context for QOL exerts a particularly powerful and too often unobserved force on the experience of QOL. Here, the well-being that Central Coast residents enjoy is a *subjective* utility, sought out and consumed as *individuals* (and households) in markets that depend upon and further advance the uneven *distribution* of QOL at broader social and geographical levels.

Which leaves us with the third question: What consequences do people's context-specific understandings and pursuits of QOL have for how they live and relate to one another? There are perhaps many to take from the Chumash example, but three foreshadow themes that this book will develop further. First, through the seemingly shared languages of QOL that partake of the conceptual tensions just described, a complex and somewhat contradictory discourse coheres that enlists a diverse set of constituents into the 'advocacy' of QOL (cf. Laclau and Mouffe 1985). In the Central Coast, affluent residents can draw rhetorical support for their lifestyle from progressive environmentalists who might in other settings avoid such regressive allies, as well as from scholars whose concerns for QOL descend from Aristotle. Such a common language of 'QOL' helps participants soften the realities of socioeconomic exclusion and status competition that real-state markets for 'high QOL' frequently entail (cf. Duncan and Duncan 2004). A second point is underscored by the economic project promoted by the leaders of today's Chumash population: a casino-hotel development agenda that many Central Coast residents find distasteful and that slow-growth advocates oppose. Although claims about the public good (along the lines of infrastructural strain, the sustainability of jobs, etc.) are often made to oppose such casino projects, much electoral opposition to this project stems from its potential for aesthetic and lifestyle 'ugliness.' The irony, of course, is that the region's QOL 'history' is thought to begin with the Chumash. As this illustrates, the language of QOL transforms politics into contests over individual preferences, lifestyles, and tastes; it recasts moral questions into aesthetic ones. These two themes point to the third. As the preeminent framework for envisioning the common good, QOL the idea allows advocacy of a great variety of political positions, so long as they are voiced in a language of QOL. What visions of the common good do *not* find fruitful articulation within this idea? Consider who might be excluded from the rhetorical alliances sketched above: advocates of 'low QOL' development, for instance, or political actors who conceive of their causes and opponents in terms of naked, irrational antagonism with other social groups. These are hardly defensible positions in the political arena today. In this way, QOL offers an appealingly civil language with which political participants can promote and contest visions of the 'common good' because the idea, as it is often employed, obscures and politically displaces the social relations—antagonistic, cooperative, or mutually dependent, often all of the above at the same time—that bind members of society to one another. These features of what I will call a *dominant QOL outlook* form the basis for a more nuanced explanation of today's contradictory QOL politics than, say, the claim that QOL advocacy is merely the language of a cultural elite (argued in, e.g., Brooks 2000:46).

Thinking Critically About 'QOL'

Having given the reader a sense of my project, a more formal introduction of the concept and semantics of 'QOL' is in order. QOL seems a deceptively easy idea to grasp. Most usages of the term evoke some aspect of how well one lives. Many people use it interchangeably with 'well-being,' 'the good life,' and 'welfare'; in many cases this is perfectly adequate rhetoric, although the synonyms can suggest particular foci that prematurely narrow our inquiry into QOL the idea. The very phrase 'quality of life' highlights two further connotations. The first is *variability*, which is commonly specified by modifiers such as 'high' or 'better' QOL that are contrasted to 'low' or 'worse' QOL. Occasionally, 'QOL' and its associated concepts are cited to describe static states of 'excellence,' an idea for which the term 'quality' is sometimes used interchangeably (as in a 'quality steak'). In this usage, one either 'has'/'obtains' QOL, or one doesn't. But more often, 'quality' evokes a spectrum or range, as in the methodological sense of observing a phenomenon that 'varies qualitatively.'

This expression highlights the second connotation: QOL is composed of *separate dimensions and domains of life*, and the importance and contribution of each domain to overall QOL cannot be substituted for other domains or reduced to a single gradient. As methodologists might put it, QOL is generally invoked as a scale, a composite measure of some value based in multiple aspects or *dimensions* of life, each of which varies autonomously from one another. Money, time spent with family, physical climate, leisure, and self-determination are commonly identified dimensions of QOL these days. Researchers, philosophers, and other observers with a comparative outlook might invoke more fundamental—and, to some modern eyes, almost invisible—dimensions like freedom from hunger and disease, the productivity of human labor, or the authenticity of ways of life. Dimensions of a scale can be grouped into broader *domains*, an intellectual operation that allows us to reflect on the general order of dimensions, their relative importance, and the relationship of certain groups of dimensions to other groups. Of course, people speak all the time as if QOL were a singular entity. Researchers can measure and analyze QOL as a quantitative variable that varies by numerical degree, while in everyday language people have little problem using the term additively and comparatively, in order to claim this person or group enjoys more QOL than that one, for instance. Generally, these uses of the idea do not belie the qualitative, multidimensional aspects of QOL but merely allow a simpler reference to those aspects.

Fruitful Limitations of the Concept

Different viewpoints on QOL give less or more credence to the many domains and dimensions that can operationally define QOL. At the reductive end of the spectrum, economists often measure QOL strictly in terms of income, while certain fields of psychology understand QOL as personal happiness that can be studied with use of a simple questionnaire, such as the "personal well-being index" scale:

> You will be asked a few questions about how happy you feel, using a scale from zero to 10. On this scale, zero means you feel VERY SAD. 10 means you feel VERY HAPPY. And the middle of the scale is 5, which means you feel NOT HAPPY OR SAD.
>
> (Cummins and Lau 2005:4)

The multidimensional end of the spectrum is illustrated by the work of psychologist and prominent QOL scholar Robert A. Cummins, who in an important meta-study scrutinized over 1,500 studies of QOL for their use of empirical scales to measure and weigh survey responses about "life satisfaction" in various domains. From the 32 scales that met his criteria, Cummins developed a list of all the terms they used to describe particular dimensions of life satisfaction and classified them under seven broader domains—material well-being, health, productivity, intimacy, safety, community, and emotional well-being—that fit his own Comprehensive Quality of Life Scale (see Cummins 1996:307–8). See Table 1.1.

Dimensions and domains can also illuminate the causal dynamics of QOL. Consider perhaps the most prominent feature of the table, the near equivalence of several terms. Now, QOL researchers are no more likely than other people to adopt uniform language when thinking about particular aspects of life, and to some extent the terms differ as to whether they reflect language that is commonly overheard, conceptually inclusive, and/or politically correct (e.g., "wife or husband," "spouse," "living partner," respectively). Yet many apparently equivalent terms in fact connote distinct aspects or contexts of QOL. Consider, for instance, "friendships," "number of friends," "time with friends," "get on with other people," "people to see socially," "social life," "social relations." Spanning the two domains of intimacy and community, these seven terms highlight different sources of QOL: one's own sociability versus external opportunities for relationships. This distinction suggests different stages within the QOL 'process': inputs (the necessary materials or conditions for QOL: education, activities available, residential area, etc.), throughputs (people's transformations of or responses to inputs: housing, vocation, role in family, etc.), and outputs (the results of inputs and throughputs: achieve success, comfort from religion, leisure, etc.) (see Hagerty et al. 2001; Veenhoven 2001).

While QOL scholars are especially inclined to ruminate upon the dimensional diversity and causal mechanics of QOL in such abstract terms, there are

Table 1.1 Domains and Terms of QOL from Comprehensive Quality of Life Scale

Material well-being	*Health*	*Productivity*	*Intimacy*	*Safety*	*Community*	*Emotional well-being*
Car	Health*	Achieve success	Child interaction	Amount of privacy	Acquaintances and contacts	Beautiful things
Clothes	Health/ Functioning	Activities available	Children	Control	Area you live in	Comfort from religion
Economic situation	Intellectual performance	Employment	Contact with family	Control over life	City	Emotional adjustment
Food	Physical fitness	House-work	Family*	Control over personal circumstances	Clubs belong to	Free-time activity
Finances*	Physical strength	Job	Family life*	Financial security	Community	Fun
Financial situation	Personal health	Paid employment	Family relations	How to handle problems	Country	Hobbies
Home		School	Friends*	Legal and safety	District	Leisure*
House*		Vocation	Friendships*	Privacy	Education*	Leisure activities
House appearance		Vocational situation	Living partner	Safety*	Education facilities	Life opportunities
Housing		What accomplishments	Marriage*	Secure from crime	Get on with other people	Non-work
Income		Work*	Number of friends	Security of belongings	Helping others	Overall comfort
Living situation*		Work and education	Parenthood		Location of home	Psychological/ Spiritual
Material possessions			Partner relationship		Neighborhood	Reading
Pay			Partnership		People in community	Recreation
Place of residence			People live with		People to see socially	Relax/Sitting around
Quality of meals			Relatives		Relations with others in community	Religion*

Table 1.1 Continued

Material well-being	*Health*	*Productivity*	*Intimacy*	*Safety*	*Community*	*Emotional well-being*
Savings			Relationship with family*		Services and facilities	Self
Socio-economic			Role in family		Social life	Self-actualization
Standard of living*			Sex life		Social relations*	Self-esteem
			Spouse		Social organizations	Spare time
			Time with friends		Visiting	Spiritual life
			Wife or husband			Sports or games
						Take night out
						Time to do things
						Yourself

* Term appears in ≥5% of QOL scales.
Source: Cummins (1996:309)

effective limits to the idea's conceptual elaboration. Returning to the Comprehensive Quality of Life Scale, we may think of other QOL dimensions absent from the table. In fact, in his meta-study Cummins was left with a large number of residual items that were not found in at least two of the original 32 scales (see Table 1.2).

The infrequent appearance of these terms in studies of QOL could simply suggest these ways of thinking about particular aspects of QOL add nothing essential or crucial in conceptualizing the idea's domains. However, remember that Cummins organized Table 1.1 around the framework of his own Comprehensive Quality of Life Scale; widely adopted throughout the world, this scale seeks to measure 'life satisfaction' and subjective well-being more generally. Accordingly, both tables emphasize an individualistic and subjective view of QOL—hardly the only way to frame the idea. As we will see later, many QOL researchers reject this psychological orientation to QOL, even though it has spurred a tremendous outpouring of research and policy in the areas of clinical psychology, health and medicine, social work, and social policy. Tellingly, Cummins excluded "Police and courts" from Table 1.1, even though it appeared in three different QOL scales, because the term did not fit under the seven domains of his Comprehensive Quality of Life Scale—a revealing example of how paradigms of QOL obscure certain kinds of knowledge even as they generate other kinds.

A *Sociology of Knowledge*

To criticize Cummins for the bias of his 'QOL' formulation would be the wrong lesson to take from this example. For one, methodologists generally assess the

Table 1.2 Residual Terms of QOL from Comprehensive Quality of Life Scale

- Ability to get around
- Ability to manage self-care
- Amount you worry
- Appearance
- Basic child care
- Being a housewife
- Beliefs of the women's movement
- Biculturality
- Body
- Bone marrow transplantation
- Children's education
- Consumption
- Cultural life
- Daily activities
- Democratic standards
- Eating
- Follow politics/voting
- Future
- Government
- Government handles economy
- Grocery shopping
- Health care
- House chores
- Household maintenance
- Housework
- Immigration
- Level of democracy
- Life as a whole
- Life in general
- Life in the country
- Life in USA
- Living arrangements
- Local council
- Local government
- Medical service
- National Government
- Number of others in home
- Personal care
- Place of living compared with hospital
- Police and courts
- Preparing/cooking food
- Pressure at work
- Psychiatric service
- Relationship with sponsor
- Resting
- Shopping
- Singlehood
- Sleeping
- Social work service
- Space outside home
- Television
- Transportation
- Travel
- Trip to work
- Welfare services
- Your transportation

Source: Cummins (1996:309)

internal validity of this or any concept based upon such qualities of coherence, unambiguity, and intellectual precision. Rather, the above illustrates a more general fact that QOL is doubly subjective: based on assessments and judgments of different aspects of people's lives and environments (by which people observe and evaluate empirical QOL), but also—and more central to the point of this book—based on shared understandings and assumptions (by which people recognize what 'QOL' means to them). In and out of the ivory tower, views of QOL are always and necessarily partial, incomplete, and limited. To expand the idea's breadth in order to encompass every possible issue and angle would only make 'QOL' inconsistent, unwieldy, and impractical, if not meaningless altogether. More to the point, the idea's remarkable fecundity in everyday language depends upon its partiality and incompleteness for all situations, which gives this resonant and flexible idea an apparent unambiguity. Because people who 'know what they mean' by the term project their partial and incomplete understanding onto others in dialogue and action, QOL the idea travels far and wide in language and culture, forging new semantic connections and innovating new understandings (cf. Eco 1993).

This semantic promiscuity is especially the case once we leave the ivory tower and the conceptual fixities and epistemological certainty of QOL scholarship. Like so many other ideas of scholarly pedigree (if not origins), 'QOL' has drifted, so to speak, through its lay usage. It epitomizes the "double hermeneutic" that social theorist Anthony Giddens (1984) explains as:

> [t]he intersection of two frames of meaning as a logically necessary part of social science[:] the meaningful social world as constituted by lay actors and the metalanguages invented by social scientists; there is a constant "slippage" from one to the other involved in the practices of the social sciences.
>
> (p. 374; quoted in Meštrović 1998:62)

For this reason, my analysis does not privilege the academic clarifications of 'QOL' as necessarily more interesting or insightful. Instead, by diving deep into messy, everyday language, I hope to draw out more fully the social concerns and social contexts that make the idea resonate.

In this book, I examine QOL the idea as a social fact—a multivalent concept that assumes meaning and relevance, if not logical consistency, *within particular social contexts* for those who invoke it, hear it, or are otherwise subjected to its discursive and material deployments in motivated social action ranging from interpersonal exchanges to governmental interventions. As social fact, QOL the idea generates social consequences that exceed in scale and ramifications the communicative action between those who utter it. Indeed, as it has evolved and been deployed, the idea has given name and shape to social changes of broad import. Scholars may recognize that my inquiry into the idea's social contexts draws on methods characteristic of the sociology of knowledge (Merton 1957). I adopt this approach not to develop universal principles about what affects human well-being—the QOL scholarship has generated enough of these—but rather to stay in the thick of meaning and analyze the relationship between idea, context, and consequences as subjectively understood in specific 'social worlds' today (Reed 2008). Critical insights into these particular social worlds and their connection emblematic of modernity's unfolding trajectories, are, I hope, the intellectual reward of this book.

Tensions of QOL Discourse

To begin this task, I now elaborate on the discursive categories of QOL understandings and pursuits: what earlier in this chapter I called the idea's conceptual tensions. Rather than resolve these tensions by definitional fiat, I offer them here as a framework to make sense of the idea's semantic breadth in QOL scholarship, professions, and context. My discussion draws on examples taken from intellectual debates and social dynamics associated with QOL that will resurface in later chapters.

From Objective to Subjective Condition

A quick glance at almost any collection of QOL terms turns up a fundamental polarity in how QOL can be understood and experienced: as a living condition external to the QOL possessor, or instead as a wholly interior, subjective state of well-being. Disciplinary and professional traditions often divide the labor of observing and evaluating QOL along these two poles. Happiness, optimism, and a sense of belonging exemplify the approach of psychologists, survey researchers, and other scholars whose intellectual orientation emphasizes the direct measurement of people's subjective states. Meanwhile, social workers, social scientists, and planners tend to emphasize objective living conditions such as social ties, the functionality of living arrangements, economic and environmental sustainability, while several approaches have a foot on both sides, such as health researchers who understand depression as a psychological syndrome with some biochemical basis.

Among other things, this conceptual tension offers intellectual precision in theories of how cognitive and emotional states can vary in their correspondence to the quality of external living conditions. Table 1.3, which is widely reproduced in the QOL scholarship, points in the lower-left quadrant to the

Table 1.3 QOL Assessments Based on Objective and Subjective Factors

		Subjective well-being	
		Good	*Bad*
Objective living conditions	*Good*	Well-being	Dissonance
	Bad	Adaptation	Deprivation

Source: Zapf (1984:25); reproduced from Rapley (2003:31)

often-surprising phenomenon of subjective *adaptation* to bad living conditions. In the health care and social work fields, this dynamic is sometimes called the "satisfaction paradox" or "disability paradox," in reference to the commonly observed pattern by which disabled individuals report levels of psychological well-being comparable to non-disabled people (or to their own lives before they experienced disabilities). The adaptation dynamic underscores more generally the ways that people's satisfaction often reflects not only their objective living conditions but also their expectations and aspirations at the time, which they can adjust as they accommodate their personal and social circumstances.

Within the QOL research, the distinction between subjective and objective conditions informs an important scholarly debate regarding whether people can validly and reliably know and evaluate their own QOL. On one side of the debate, the "Scandinavian" approach holds that, given people's social-psychological propensity to modify their aspirations around their present circumstances, the QOL measures they self-report may not be aligned with the necessary frame of reference that scholars and planners need in order to summarize and compare QOL across groups and settings (Erikson 1993). Researchers taking this position accordingly endorse evaluating QOL on the basis of data that are 'objective' in the scientific sense, as in independent of the beholder's perceptions and biases. In the domain of health, for example, these indicators are said to involve 'function-based' understandings of QOL (Haase et al. 1999). In more obviously social domains, objective indicators of QOL may record social activities or material conditions that people rarely associate with QOL in their everyday thinking (GDP, percent of undeveloped land). The Scandinavian approach seeks to circumvent not only the adaptation dynamic but also the problem of cultural indoctrination: people's expectations and aspirations for subjective well-being can be unduly influenced by cultural norms and political manipulation. Particularly when QOL data are gathered by governments with suspect human rights records, these are not trivial matters (Sumner 1996:60–8; Miles 1985:68; Buttel, Wilkening, and Martinson 1977).

On the debate's other side, the "American" approach illustrates the subjective pole in this conceptual tension of QOL the idea. Here, QOL is fundamentally a symbolic meaning based in the observation and evaluation of one's own life, social environment, and experience of personal and social change (Campbell and Converse 1972). In the words of seminal QOL theorist Angus Campbell (quoted in Rapley 2003:10), "quality of life must be in the eye of the beholder." Methodologically, the American approach emphasizes the analysis of subjective data that, importantly, can be gathered using survey methods that boast a methodological rigor typically superior to objective data drawn from the administrative by-products of governments (Miles 1985:67). From the American perspective, the Scandinavian emphasis on objective indicators distorts the measurement of QOL (by introducing extra noise in its observed signal) and misunderstands the concept's very essence.

On the whole, many scholars and practitioners, perhaps most, do not adhere strictly to one side of this debate or the other, opting instead for a more holistic, multidimensional approach when measuring and assessing QOL. Nonetheless, the debate between the Scandinavian and American approaches underscores the vastly different kinds of undertakings and investments needed to alter living conditions in order to enhance QOL. Returning to the satisfaction paradox, if most disabled people eventually adjust their expectations and report sufficient levels of happiness to make life satisfying, the question can be asked, why should society devote resources to improving physical mobility and social access for the disabled within facilities and organizations? Similarly, take the title of a recent non-fiction bestseller, *The Progress Paradox: How Life Gets Better While People Feel Worse* (Easterbrook 2003). If the common refrain that "people were happier" in bygone days of hardship than they are in their better-off present holds water, then Westerners who "don't know how lucky they are" should seek the lessons of positive psychology. By contrast, another popular non-fiction work, *Affluenza: The All-Consuming Epidemic* (De Graaf, Wann, and Naylor 2005) stands on the shoulders of many twentieth-century critics (discussed in the next chapter) in characterizing QOL as a material problem: we feel empty and unhappy because our society consumes too much. If the implications of the Scandinavian approach are taken seriously, then the affluenza argument prescribes substantial changes to our personal and collective living environments as the basis for reform; no attitude adjustment alone will enhance our QOL.

Yet from another angle altogether, there are important ways in which the subjective orientation is inescapably part of QOL. This is because any consideration of QOL, undertaken either by its possessor or outside observers, inevitably imposes subjective meaning onto the external world with the analytical lens of 'QOL.' Even hardnosed realists with no patience for talk of the social construction of science can acknowledge the ultimately symbolic substance of QOL: "To ask 'what is quality of life?' is *not* to ask the same sort of a question as asking 'what is a planet?' or 'what is electricity?'" (Rapley 2003:50). As a problem of epistemology, QOL can hardly be 'objective' in the sense of 'independent of observations,' and intellectual consensus among observers (or what philosophers call intersubjectivity) on the meanings and criteria of QOL may be the best that can be hoped for. (The unavoidable subjectivity of the QOL beholder, I recognize, implicates the author and the project of this book.) Less esoterically, insofar as people adopt and envision 'QOL' as a practical plan for organizing their lives, they necessarily intervene in their external worlds, even if they never make a single change. QOL the idea reorients cognitive and cultural frameworks rather actively through the evaluative undertaking it facilitates. Perhaps the more important question then—one that this book takes up—is *how* people reimagine and reshape their world through 'QOL.'

From Individual to Collective Attribution

One reason why many find it difficult to conceptualize QOL outside of its subjective experience is because the latter is often conflated with a pole in a second conceptual tension. Namely, QOL can be thought to 'belong' to either an individual or a social collectivity. In the QOL scholarship, this tension corresponds to the respective distinction between *private QOL* and *public QOL*. Philosopher Christopher Megone (1990) explains:

> The term 'quality of life' is ambiguous. On the one hand there is the quality of an individual's life, a reflection of how well his life is going; but there is also a broader concept, capturing roughly the quality of living conditions around an agent, where these can be picked out independent of how well the agent's own life goes. These living conditions might encompass the environment and culture in (for example) a given society. It may well be that the two notions intersect, that the quality of an individual's life is affected by the quality of his environment and culture, and that these are in part a function of how well the lives of agents in the society go. But the two ideas, which might be termed private and public quality of life, respectively, are certainly distinct.
>
> (pp. 28–9)

In regards to how people assess and enhance QOL, a number of scholarly and professional fields emphasize one or the other side of this tension. Psychological approaches that study attitudes, sentiments, cognitive dynamics, and biochemical processes necessarily limit their analysis of QOL to the individual level. Certainly, psychology can have implications for groups, institutions, and even societies, but the discipline has no real vocabulary or methodology with which to discuss collective QOL impacts outside of their basis in the mind of the individual. The healthcare system also exemplifies an individual level of analysis, insofar as it treats patients on a one-by-one basis; hence the clarifying modifier distinguishing the field of "public health" from healthcare more generally. Political philosophies that prioritize individual freedom and self-determination can be thought to operate on an individual level of analysis as well. By contrast, an exclusively collective attribution of QOL is illustrated by urban and regional planning, which customarily focuses on sustaining the shared QOL of people living in municipalities and regions; its concerns for environmental impacts and land-use zoning embody a calculus of regulating individual pursuits at a holistic level (although planning agencies can often become politically captured by particular interest groups). Likewise, environmental sciences and management understand the collective QOL of living beings as inseparable from the complexly organized physical ecologies they compose.

When thinking about how intellectual and professional traditions focus on either individual QOL or collective QOL, it is helpful to distinguish the framework or method that QOL analysts employ from the broader ends that they seek to promote. As a mode of analysis, welfare economics provides numerous assessments and proposals for the collective well-being of groups and societies, but the field arrives at these only through the back door of an ontological individualism, summing the individual preferences and decision-making of a group or society's members; such economic data represent what QOL researchers call aggregated indicators. Conversely, urban planners and environmental managers may evoke the spirit of utilitarianism when they talk of balancing competing individual pursuits, but their analysis tackles the *sui generis* level of the system or population first and foremost; their data correspond to what QOL researchers call system indicators (see Miles 1985:71–2).

Are there moral outlooks that adopt an exclusive position on the pole between individual and collective attributions of QOL? Some might see the endorsement of an exclusively private QOL in the tenets of laissez-faire economics. No less a figure than classical economist Adam Smith ([1776] 1904) appeared to enshrine a selfish pursuit of QOL when he claimed that

> every individual ... generally, indeed, neither intends to promote the public interest, nor knows how much he is promoting it. By preferring the support of domestic to that of foreign industry, he intends only his own security; and by directing that industry in such a manner as its produce may be of the greatest value, he intends only his own gain, and he is in this, as in many other cases, led by an invisible hand to promote an end which was no part of his intention.
>
> (Ch. IV.2.9)

However, Smith never intended his dismissal of altruistic economic behavior to harm the greater societal good, which he argued was better served by the invisible hand of the market. Thus, he continued: "Nor is it always the worse for the society that it was no part of it. By pursuing his own interest he frequently promotes that of the society more effectually than when he really intends to promote it."

Conversely, communitarianism has often been described as focusing exclusively on public QOL at the cost of individual liberty. Thus, the Communitarian Network's "Responsive Communitarian Platform" (1990) begins with this preamble:

> American men, women, and children are members of many communities—families; neighborhoods; innumerable social, religious, ethnic, work place, and professional associations; and the body politic itself. Neither human existence nor individual liberty can be sustained for long outside the interdependent and overlapping communities to which all of us belong. Nor can any community long survive unless its members dedicate some of their attention, energy, and resources to shared projects. The exclusive pursuit of private interest erodes the network of social environments on which we all depend, and is destructive to our shared experiment in democratic self-government. For these reasons, we hold that the rights of individuals cannot long be preserved without a communitarian perspective.

Yet while many critics sound alarm at communitarianism's prescriptions and prohibitions on individual liberties (e.g., "people who carry sexually transmitted diseases ... should be expected to disclose their illness to previous sexual contacts or help health authorities to inform them, to warn all prospective sexual contacts, and inform all health care personnel with whom they come in contact"), the platform emphasizes the balancing of individual rights and communal mandates, specifying each against the backdrop of particular contexts: "If we were in China today, we would argue vigorously for more individual rights; in contemporary America, we emphasize individual and social responsibilities" (see also Etzioni 1998). Thus, there is no necessary logical inconsistency in promoting an individual or collective QOL outcome at one end of the spectrum through an assessment of the other.

Conventionally, the QOL scholarship expresses the distinction between individual and collective attribution as operationally defining QOL 'at the level of the individual or the population' (see, e.g., Gerson 1976), but it is helpful to think outside the strict binary of singular/plural. The conceptual tension between individual and collective attribution manifests in a *relational* form when we distinguish constituent units from their collective whole. Depending on the geographical perspective, for instance, a place can be a collective (to its residents) or an individual territory subsumed under any number of larger territories (regions, states, nations, etc.). Markets also illustrate the relational connection between individual and collective QOL. Markets effectively embody collective shifts in buying and selling that are generally external to and constraining upon any single individual, as anyone caught up in a stock-market panic will recognize. Yet insofar as they tend to become pure—the thrust of economic policy over the last three to four decades—markets further *individualize* the structure and lived experience of social relations by encouraging differentiation (through outbidding, underpricing, etc.), discouraging cooperation, and reinforcing the solitary viewpoint of personal preferences rationally executed as the horizons for action.

From Production to Distribution of Well-being

The embeddedness of individuals and constituent groups within larger collectives raises the question of how QOL attributed to the greater whole actually materializes for each member. This points to a third conceptual tension, between the production of QOL and its distribution. At a basic level, this conceptual tension informs the economic problem of allocation. If innovations to improve QOL are available, how do people get them? This question looms large, indeed cruelly, in the arena of healthcare, where resource scarcity makes many medicines, treatments, and ongoing aid prohibitively expensive for people who need them. The problem of allocation similarly hangs over the human development field, where people's basic needs in developing societies depend upon building the infrastructure for essential resources like clean water and healthy food. Invariably, technical problems of allocation turn to moral questions of inequality and social justice. Fundamental ideological cleavages over the fairness and wisdom of different economic systems hinge on the problem of allocation. Thus, in his defense of free markets, Adam Smith ([1776] 1904) acknowledged, "No society can surely be flourishing and happy, of which the far greater part of the members are poor and miserable" (Ch. I.8.35). For remarkably similar reasons, Karl Marx advocated a communist system of production and distribution.

Analytically, the conceptual tension between production and distribution of QOL also highlights issues of cause and effect. Insofar as QOL is influenced by factors external to the possessor, it emerges from the contingent interplay of independent events and activities; given an alternate sequence of historical developments and social responses, the QOL impact might have materialized differently or not at all. As a problem of epistemology, the outside observer must discern the moment when these interplays effectively happen—when, in effect, QOL is achieved or produced. The identification of QOL's production is simpler to grasp when we discuss innovations in technology (e.g., air conditioning is invented) or social organization (a system of courts is established), but even more amorphous and incremental shifts in values (fixed marriages give way to unions of choice) and social trends (women enter the workforce) reach a tipping point after which the observer makes the call that they have 'happened.' Scholarly perspectives that emphasize the production of QOL, therefore, highlight the *potentials* for affecting QOL raised by innovations and developments, often as a shorthand to imply their diffusion through a population: e.g., "1962: the polio vaccine was licensed."

The venerable societal indicator of gross domestic product (GDP) is typically used this way; it most directly indicates the production of QOL (here, a measure of a society's market development) and, through a conventional chain of analytical implications, suggests a QOL impact—a positive correlation with social indicators like education, health, and life expectancy, for instance (Offer 2006:17). Libertarianism illustrates a political philosophy attuned to the production of QOL; by viewing the establishment of legal rights and economic offerings as the basis for QOL, it enshrines equality of access as the fundamental concern of the good society, with little concern for the diverse QOL outcomes that in fact result.

Of course, the materialization, diffusion, and experience of QOL potentials are also historically contingent. Be they cell phones or public schools, some QOL-altering developments are beneficial for some people, but negligible or even negative for others, while their effects never reach yet others. Scholarly perspectives that emphasize the distribution of QOL thus take as a central problem the impacts and diffusion of QOL-influencing developments. In contrast to libertarianism, for instance, egalitarianism illustrates a moral philosophy focused on the equality of outcomes (see Phillips 2006:2–3). Returning to the example of GDP, simple distributive indicators such as GDP per capita can indicate higher/lower ratios of national production to citizen and thus the distribution of opportunities for personal QOL—here, stated in the form of an average standard of living (Nordhaus and Tobin 1973:514). However, opportunities are a necessary yet insufficient condition for actual QOL; this is one reason economists have long examined indicators of income inequality, which more directly depict the uneven opportunities for consumption, to stand in for the intermediate process of distribution.

The conceptual tension between the production and distribution of QOL involves the same properties of relationality manifest in the tension between individual and collective QOL. Consider, for instance, the statistic of household income. Whereas it is a useful indicator of QOL distribution at a macro (e.g., national) level, zooming down to the micro level of the household itself, this statistic indicates only the potential for a standard of living, for reasons that feminists and scholars of families have made clear: consumption within a household often materializes unevenly along lines of power and status between fathers and mothers, sons and daughters, parents and children. For analysts of QOL, then, understanding QOL's distribution requires an adequate grasp of the hierarchical contours of underlying social structures. To the extent that pursuing QOL influences people's life chances, we might anticipate that QOL itself gives meaning and form to such hierarchies.

From Universalist to Relativist Understanding

The fourth conceptual tension within QOL involves the idea's use as an indicator across cultural, historical, situational, and personal contexts. Do particular levels or values of QOL 'translate' over time, social setting, and cultural expression? The position one holds on this question underscores the kinds of analysis that the observer can perform on QOL and the kinds of intellectual, rhetorical, and political claims that can be made about QOL. Most policy and scholarly interest in QOL is motivated by historical questions like 'how far' the good society has come, and comparative questions like how well one person, group, or society is doing in relation to others. Such historical-comparative inquiries require a universal currency of QOL over time and across social units in order to develop valid claims and sound reform proposals. Quantifiable measures of subjective well-being (psychology) and earning power (economics) exemplify the kind of universal indicators that observers can use to gauge the development of QOL over time and across settings. By contrast, a relativist understanding of QOL eschews one-size-fits-all models and takes more seriously what QOL means, and how QOL is experienced, for particular people in specific settings. Relativist perspectives are especially found in anthropology and other social constructionist perspectives that view symbolic systems as emerging out of concrete and, to an important extent, local forms of social organization. In these ways, the conceptual tension between universalist and relativist understandings of QOL echoes the broad paradigmatic divide in the social sciences and humanities between nomothetic and idiothetic approaches; the former focuses on the general, common aspects of human behavior in order to develop grand, overarching theories, while the latter privileges deep, particularistic descriptions of behaviors, groups, and cultures as their participants understand them. Each approach has its shortcomings. By striving to explain the commonalities of human behavior across situations and contexts, nomothetic approaches support essentialist views that neglect the roles of history and culture in diversifying human existence and human meaning. Conversely, the idiothetic premise that human experience can only be understood within its particular cultural contexts undermines the grand theory-building endeavor at the heart of science and—this point especially informs the critique of moral relativism—shields the group or society under question from any evaluation or moral scrutiny by members of other cultures.

Moral relativism is not the only, or even most important, expression of the relativist position; perhaps more germane are QOL perspectives that emphasize the particular circumstances in which the QOL possessor finds him or herself. Consider again the satisfaction paradox: although many medical professionals and most healthy people view severe physical impairment resulting from traumatic accidents as the basis for a lower than normal QOL—for some, even worse than death—in fact "when people experience these events they tend not to regard their lives as valueless or as having a negative value" (Rapley 2003:75; see Koch 2000; Loomes and McKenzie 1990; Jones-Lee, Hammerton, and Phillips 1985). Such subjective adaptation can best be explained from a relativist framework, insofar as the meaning of QOL for disabled people varies based on personal and situational circumstances: personality dispositions, biographical experiences, external living conditions, social support systems, and so on.

Likewise, in its theory of human motivations, conventional economics also adheres to a situational relativism, as economist John Kenneth Galbraith ([1958] 1998) explains:

> Few students of economics, even in the elementary course, now escape without a warning against the error of intertemporal comparisons of the utility from given acts of consumption. Yesterday the man with a minimal but increasing real income was reaping the satisfactions which came from a decent diet and a roof that no longer leaked water on his face. Today, after a large increase in his income, he has extended his consumption to include suede shoes and a weekly visit to the races. But to say that his satisfactions from these latter amenities and recreations are less than from the additional calories and the freedom from rain is wholly improper. Things have changed; he is a different man; there is no real standard for comparison. That, as of a given time, an individual will derive lesser satisfactions from the marginal increments to a given stock of goods, and accordingly cannot be induced to pay as much for them, is conceded. But this tells us nothing of the satisfactions from such additional goods, and more particularly from different goods, when they are acquired at a later time. The conclusion follows. One cannot be sure that the satisfaction from these temporally later increases in the individual's stock of goods

> diminishes. Hence, one cannot suggest that the production which supplies it is of diminishing urgency.
>
> (p. 121)

For Galbraith, this situational relativism is economics' intellectual misfortune. By denying that "anything very useful can be said of the comparative states of mind and satisfaction of the consumer at different periods of time," mainstream economics has failed to challenge the social irrationality and environmental unsustainability of the "affluent society" (which I introduce more fully in the next chapter).

As this discussion suggests, the conceptual tension between universalist and relativist frameworks is particularly acute within psychology and economics—two disciplines that, we will see, have special influence on contemporary scholarship and popular thinking on QOL. On the one hand, most QOL researchers from these disciplines are committed to the generalizing theory-building project that makes scientific claims possible and, in modern society, makes policy proposals legitimate. On the other, deep within their theories of human motives lies a situational relativism that asserts an essential diversity of the meanings, circumstances, and experiences of human QOL. How do these disciplines reconcile this apparent contradiction? Methodologically, their reliance upon quantitative measures and analysis mitigates this relativism somewhat. Subjective well-being can be personally recounted and parsed over on the therapist's couch, but it is more amenable as a basis for universal scientific claims when its meaning is reduced to an intensity that varies from 5 to 35 on a "satisfaction with life scale" (see Pavot and Diener 1993). This analytical maneuver illustrates a more general impulse within psychology and economics—and here, they are not alone—to place the substance and contexts of QOL meanings within a conceptual black box. Thus, economics deems all human values, aspirations, desires, and tastes as "private, individual, unconditioned, and arbitrary" and leaves the matter at that (Cobb 2000:7). The point here is not to assert the superiority of qualitative and hermeneutic analysis or to deny the remarkable predictive powers of psychology and economics. In large part because of their reductive framework, these disciplines have considerable predictive powers and have become hegemonic forms of expertise within modern society. For a critical inquiry, a more interesting issue is how the black box they put over people's pursuits of QOL shapes their social relations and self-understandings.

Plan of the Book

This chapter, I hope, has gotten the reader's feet wet in the productive confusion of QOL the idea, which revolves around an apparent paradox. On the one hand, QOL can be understood in discrete, conceptually modest and empirically delimited ways: it can correspond to personal happiness, or the possibilities for physical health, or the sustainability and amenities of the environment, and so on. This is how researchers and policy-makers tend to approach the subject of QOL, which has led to a robust yet fragmented body of scholarship on the trends and implications of QOL today. On the other hand, the activity of evaluating and enhancing QOL defines 'the good' for modern individuals and societies across a growing range of domains and perspectives. Increasingly, people undertake highly charged dialogues and pursue ways of life around widely exchanged yet slippery understandings of 'QOL.' Such conceptual promiscuity, I believe, is not just a consequence of the idea's flexibility. As this book will document, it also reflects the historical trajectory of social relations over the last half century or so, a fairly recent and brief period of time in which 'QOL' has emerged to challenge yet also embody the problems of modern societies. To shed light on the resonance of QOL the idea in our time, this book provides a critical inquiry into those contexts for the social concerns and pursuits to which 'QOL' gives voice.

In Chapter 2, I examine the *intellectual history* of 'QOL,' first by introducing the historical moment in which it surfaced as a key idea in human deliberation and political initiative: the affluent society of post-World War II welfare states. This moment saw certain thinkers and movements inject 'QOL' the phrase and its associated issues into public discourse as part of a moral and political agenda critical of the political status quo of economic growth and silence on social injustice. Yet 'QOL' did not appear out of a historical vacuum, and this chapter reviews the conceptual formulations that started with classical philosophy and see ongoing intellectual elaboration in QOL scholarship and policy analysis today. The six conceptual traditions I review in this chapter—of Aristotle, utilitarianism, modernization theory, Abraham Maslow, the human development field, and the social indicators initiative—inform today's invocations and pursuits of QOL.

With Chapter 3, I leave the history of letters and scholarship to take up specific contexts in which people understand and pursue QOL today, starting with *technology*. Technology advances the material development of societies and symbolizes the march of civilization to us in a number of ways. Today, under the banner of QOL, many commentators and a number of social movements criticize the unthinking servitude to high technology and material convenience, in contrast to how the latter were celebrated for embodying social progress only decades earlier. Both the celebration and criticism of technology, I explain, reveal underlying social structures of status and class that highlight tensions between the production and distribution of QOL. Although it is perhaps the most popular of symbols for the promise and ambivalence of modern society, in fact technology materially and symbolically sustains broader social stratifications that receive much less critical examination.

Chapter 4 turns to a sphere where today's 'QOL crisis' is experienced acutely, the *family*. The exhaustion of parents, the worries over latch-key children, the difficulty of sitting parents and children around the dinner table at the same time: these experiences illustrate the QOL strains that modern families are subjected to. Conversely, intensive parenting, stay-at-home mothers, and children's growing schedule of extracurricular activities illustrate the ways parents attempt to enhance family QOL, particularly for their children. On the basis of public commentary, it often seems that styles of family-rearing reflect distinct lifestyles and irreconcilable values captured by buzzwords like the "mommy wars." Driving this apparent cultural impasse are the ongoing evolution of the nuclear family as an economic unit, a growing body of expertise on childrearing and maternalism, and a recurring set of cultural and political constraints upon women's freedoms from domestic responsibilities. In many ways, the source of the family's present crisis is QOL the *idea*, which has authorized women's entrance into the workforce, the elaboration of an increasing number of childhood stages, and national policies for family caregiving—three central contexts for contemporary family strains. As the members and life-stages that constitute the familial unit shift the nature and timing of family responsibilities, the family's 'crisis' reveals an underlying micro-relations of QOL conflict.

Chapter 5 turns to the sphere of *work* and asks, when is work the muse of personal QOL? This question may seem odd, given the seemingly universal experiences of labor's toil and workplace conflict. Yet a number of recent viewpoints in managerial practice and social commentary have touted the enhancement of work-based QOL as a solution for advancing personal well-being, workplace productivity, and overall economic prosperity; the no-collar workplaces and the self-employed "free agent" popularized during the late 1990s have made such promises tangible for many. Stepping back from this recent period, I situate the appeal to work as muse of QOL within the late twentieth-century dissolution of collective bargaining, employer loyalty, and bureaucratic organization. As these collective forms increasingly lose their capacity to socialize and reproduce the workforce, the market looms ever larger as the social structure and cultural framework in which workers seek their fate. A high work-based QOL becomes the reward for labor-market winners that legitimates workplace drudgery, abusive employers, and economic insecurity for a far greater number of labor-market losers.

Chapter 6 examines the role of *place*—be it neighborhood, town, city or region—in the pursuit of QOL. Whether viewed in terms of amenities, public space, or place character, place-based QOL is traditionally regarded as a form of collective QOL, in which occupants share the effects of a place's physical environment and social milieu. As public interest grows in the different QOLs that places can offer, however, the pursuit of QOL in place becomes an increasingly individualized undertaking. On the demand side, the opportunity to choose a locality for its QOL reveals the values and viewpoints of the individual migrant. On the supply side, the articulation of various place-based QOLs (reflecting the diversification of socioeconomic, household, life-stage, and lifestyle possibilities discussed in prior chapters) occurs within an increasingly global market for place. Indeed, the pursuit of place-based QOL is one of the quintessentially modern market experiences, with its many modalities shaped by a consumerist search for work (i.e., "best places to work and retire") and leisure opportunities (urban amenities, the vacation home, etc.). The interest in place-based QOL thus illustrates the broader tendency in contemporary QOL pursuits to reify social relations, as people project their dissolving social, economic, and geographical ties with one another onto the experience of 'place itself' and other objects.

Chapter 7 looks at the *politics* of QOL to grapple with the emerging collective visions and advocacies of the good society. Heretofore, scholars have theorized QOL mobilizations as embodying modernization's leading thrusts, be those the market's eclipse of the state or the critical reflexivity that motivates political protest and identity construction. Although these patterns can be discerned in the developments examined in this chapter and indeed the entire book, they hardly advance the rational, deliberative constitution of the political body once associated with modern society. Characteristically, QOL politics surfaces outside the formal political sphere, in the non-deliberative, sub-political realms of community and lifestyle. This mode of politics displaces the social from political deliberation, reifying people's conflicts and reciprocities with one another into the defense of things: ecosystems and animal species, culturally distinct 'ways of life' deserving of legal protections, even the integrity of life itself.

The concluding chapter summarizes the historical drift of 'QOL' from its affluent society articulations to its expressions in today's QOL pursuits. The contemporary discourse of 'QOL' and the social pursuits it authorizes promote an expressive, aestheticized, and individualized modality of social life that takes us far from the weighty questions of collective well-being posed in the initial years of the affluent society. Ultimately, the idea itself cannot explain this shift in moral viewpoint; the institutional disintegration and declining legitimacy of collective institutions that have occurred since the post-World War II period have compelled individuals more and more to take on the work of social reproduction. 'QOL' today reflects this new burden, offering a contradictory language with which people challenge but also accommodate and even enchant the market's penetration of daily life. The memory of the affluent society's political project continues to haunt QOL the idea, but its resuscitation requires a more explicitly social discourse of moral solidarity and political deliberation.

2 Intellectual History

> Finally, the modern liberal no longer identifies production with all political success ... [I]t is no longer unusual to inquire about the quality of life as opposed to the quantity of production. And a younger generation has become concerned with questions of racial equality, the quality of the environment, the role of the great public and private bureaucracies in our lives, and in shaping our beliefs and our prospects for survival, and there has been a simmering of interest in the honesty of artistic and intellectual expressions.
>
> (John Kenneth Galbraith [1958] 1998:142)

From prehistory to modern life, and (within the latter) from highly developed welfare states to the developing societies where life is too often nasty, brutish, and short, on its face the empirical indicator of QOL applies universally to the spectrum of human conditions as a framework for measuring and evaluating how and how well people live. However, its conceptualization and expression, at least in the form of the specific term, "quality of life," is of a far more recent vintage. A detailed history of the term's diffusion in everyday discourse is difficult to assemble, but a suggestive picture can be drawn from a Google Book Search of the exact phrase "quality of life" in popular books and magazines, scholarly journals, and governmental reports; see Table 2.1.[1]

Throughout the twentieth century, "quality of life" appeared most frequently in scholarly works—particularly in the fields of education, psychology, and (by mid-century) sociology—and philosophical and religious essays. Early in the century, for instance, American educational reformer John Dewey (1916) wrote in his *Democracy and Education*,

> To say that education is a social function, securing direction and development in the immature through their participation in the life of the group to which they belong, is to say in effect that education will vary with the quality of life which prevails in a group.
>
> (p. 94)

Then, in the late 1960s, the term started to appear frequently in works written for a policy audience, such as *Police–Community Relations, Urban Riots, and the*

Table 2.1 Publications with the Phrase "Quality of Life"

Period	*Stated in text*	*Stated in title*
1880–89	467	0
1890–99	611	1
1900–09	628	1
1910–19	646	0
1920–29	666	0
1930–39	679	6
1940–49	686	1
1950–59	818	1
1960–69	1,366	25
1970–79	5,530	828
1980–89	6,370	814
1990–99	12,600	1,098
2000–08	11,000	1,827

Source: Google Book Search, conducted January 6, 2009.

Quality of Life in Cities (Strecher 1968); *Quality of Life in the Americas: Report of a U.S. Presidential Mission for the Western Hemisphere* (Rockefeller 1969); and *Quality of Life in the United States: An Excursion Into the New Frontier of Socio-economic Indicators* (Wilson 1969). As Table 2.1 shows, by the 1970s the expression really took off, rapidly increasing in published appearance up into the present. Hypothesizing a cultural lag of, say, five years between the term's diffusion in spoken language and its appearance in published form, it becomes reasonable to mark the proliferation of 'QOL' in public discourse to around the mid-1960s. We face the question: what was the historical context during which "quality of life" began proliferating in public discourse?

The Affluent Society Critique

Historically, this period corresponds to the heyday of the *affluent society*, that social formation in which age-old questions of human scarcity (how will humanity survive and be secure?) are eclipsed by questions of human abundance (what are the opportunities of social affluence?). We can think of the affluent society as a universal sociological category, as the term invites us to do, to describe an advanced stage of societal development in which basic levels of population and economic stability have been established and are explicitly acknowledged within institutions and culture. But more concretely, historians regard the affluent society as a specific political and cultural episode: the flourishing of critical thought and social debate in Western societies from the late 1950s to the 1970s that set the goalposts, so to speak, for the late twentieth-century political consensus that we call 'liberal.' To explore the affluent society further, I turn to its birthplace, the United States, which in this period was the least encumbered among Western nations by the post-World War II task of restoring economies and built environments. Here, consternations over the Cold War, racial injustice, environmental degradation, and the deterioration of old cities grew against a backdrop of unprecedented scientific-technological progress, economic prosperity, and population expansion. Articulating this sense of disjuncture, cultural critics, social movements, and policy-makers viewed the affluent society as a challenge, an unprecedented moment to achieve social progress, that humanity could ill afford to ignore.

The thesis that postwar affluence could undermine democracy, justice, and the American spirit, so long as the U.S. failed to scrutinize and recommit its prosperity, was put forth in several widely read books of the day. Quoted at the beginning of this chapter, John Kenneth Galbraith's *The Affluent Society* ([1958] 1998) countered the prevailing wisdom of growth of any kind with an argument for a new economics promoting a humane system of production, culturally meaningful consumption, and increased public investment in human development and public health. Furthering Galbraith's concern for the rising marketing and advertising sectors, Vance Packard decried their manufacturing of consumer desire through planned obsolescence and other hidden techniques in *The Waste Makers* (1960). The shape and tensions of post-industrial class structure were outlined in Michael Harrington's *The Other America* (1962), Gunnar Myrdal's *Challenge to Affluence* (1963)—which introduced the term "underclass" into social science vocabulary—and David Riesman's *The Lonely Crowd* (1950). Planners and critics proposed the cultivation of vibrant urban spaces, the development of landscape amenities, and other historic opportunities to lift up cities and their neglected populaces (e.g., Jacobs 1961; Whyte 1956; Goodman and Goodman 1947). Perhaps most striking from today's vantage-point, many anticipated a leisure dividend made possible by continuing gains in economic productivity; Americans could soon experience unprecedented freedoms from industrial toil (the focus of the academic volume *Mass Leisure* [Larrabee and Meyerson 1958]), although they might accordingly need to find new foundations for their national character and personal integrity (a concern articulated by Paul Goodman [1960] in *Growing Up Absurd*). In turn, such affluent society statements were part of a larger critical public literature that blossomed in the 1950s and 1960s. Other critical works in this broader genre did not necessarily frame their polemics along the explicit lines of 'affluence,' but authors such as C. Wright Mills (1951, 1956), Rachel Carson (1962), and Herbert Marcuse (1964) inveighed against social problems and political failures that can be viewed within this broader historical formation.[2]

The *affluent society critique* that these writers and thinkers articulated had important consequences. For one, it bestowed further resonance on the social movements of the day, starting with the U.S. civil rights movement. In his 1963 "I have a dream" speech, Martin Luther King's statement that "the Negro lives on a lonely island of poverty in the midst of a vast ocean of material prosperity" put the urgency of African Americans' demands for equality and justice in a material context that white Americans living in post-World War II affluence might better recognize. The anti-war movement, second wave feminism, environmentalism, subsequent civil rights movements (for other people of color and sexual freedom), and the 1968–69 strikes and unrest in Western

Europe also proclaimed the historical ripeness of their cause; having turned the corner on the economic insecurities and military siege that modern societies had mostly known until then, the time for change, these movements asserted, was most certainly now.

Perhaps most significantly, the affluent society critique informed public policy beginning in the 1960s, reaching its zenith within the U.S. during the Lyndon B. Johnson administration. Promoting his "Great Society" initiative, President Johnson advocated a series of ambitious domestic programs targeting poverty and racial injustice in 1964 with an important choice of words: "the great society is concerned not with how much, but with how good—not with the quantity of goods but with the quality of our lives" (quoted in Rapley 2003:4; see also Noll 2000; Cummins 1997). In the Great Society, 'QOL' diagnosed the public-policy challenge and mobilized the response, as illustrated in President Lyndon B. Johnson's 1965 proposal to establish a cabinet-level Department of Housing and Urban Development:

> Let us be clear about the core of this problem. The problem is people and the quality of the lives they lead. We want to build not just housing units but neighborhoods; not just to raise income, but to create beauty and end the poisoning of our environment . . . . The problems of the city are problems of housing and education. They involve increasing employment and ending poverty. They call for beauty and nature, recreation and an end to discrimination.
>
> (quoted in Vitale 2008:33)

Significantly, the Great Society upheld *collective* QOL as the policy problem and the moral stakes of the era. The post-World War II "urban crisis" (and, perhaps to a lesser extent, the rediscovery of rural poverty) threw into sharp relief the nation's collective failure to lift up the most disadvantaged, recognized chiefly as the poor who were geographically concentrated in pockets of economic decline. Seeking to counter electoral resistance based in racial antagonism and American individualism, the Great Society advocates employed a rhetoric invoking mutual responsibility and moral commitment. The unprecedented employment rates, consumer conveniences, educational opportunities, and suburban lifestyles that gave satisfaction to so many, they argued, would stop short of the greater good so long as systematic disparities, unequal opportunity, and injustice characterized the workings of the whole nation.

Eventually, Johnson's Great Society initiative foundered as the Vietnam War escalated, and federal efforts to house and help employ the "other half" stalled under the following Richard M. Nixon presidency (although key environmental legislation did pass under Nixon). As this book will show, the affluent society critique that informed the Great Society still resonates in the U.S. in important ways, but ultimately its influence on public policy was more lasting in Western Europe, Canada, and Japan. As the state's role in securing affluence as collective well-being expanded in these nations, so too did the idea of QOL into their public policies. Notably, at one point in the 1970s, the French government renamed its Ministry of the Environment and Sustainable Development the "Ministry of Quality of Life." Beyond such milestones in naming, of course, QOL has been established as a universal entitlement of all national citizens and provided for (admittedly, not always effectively) via the many public subsidies and provisions in health care, education, family support, youth activities, and so on that are the hallmarks of these societies' welfare states.

In its concern for social and economic justice, its attention to the integrity of the natural environment and human amenities, and its recognition that the historical moment offered unprecedented possibilities for human advance, the affluent society critique proposed a political project that, I confess, I deeply admire. Today, this project is often seen as simply a license to expand the state, but my review of the affluent society critique underscores how its essence lies in its political philosophy, not its institutional expression. Admittedly, the affluent society articulation of 'QOL' underscores a particular and, yes, privileged social position in the historical and cross-cultural scheme of things; their voicing of the problems and possibilities for human welfare is not a 'popular' undertaking in this sense. Yet thinkers and advocates of the affluent society urged their fellow citizens not to lapse into a solipsistic focus on the standards of living, aspirations, and values of affluent people, but for all to acknowledge the connections and solidarities that bind each to the other—relations of inequality and segregation, yes, but also of common incorporation into a socioeconomic system, shared reliance upon a physical environment, and a mutual dependence upon one another if progress is to be made. In this book, I ask the reader to retain the conceptual duality of the affluent society idea, juxtaposing the sociological notion of the 'objective' phase of societal development seen in the West and, most recently, many emerging economies in Asia and Latin America against the historical flourishing of critical exuberance that has almost receded from memory. Today, as citizens scan the horizons for a world after the neoliberalism of the last three or four decades, the affluent society's legacy deserves revisiting.

My value position notwithstanding, it is less controversially the case that whenever people discuss or evaluate QOL today by referring to empirical trends in, say, personal well-being, social inequality, environmental sustainability, or community well-being, they take up a discourse and a practice that were established during the affluent society. In turn, the intellectual ferment surrounding the growing emphasis on QOL in the affluent society period throws into relief—sometimes in harmony, other times in contrast—a number of other intellectual traditions of developing and articulating the idea. Thus, to understand the affluent society legacy of 'QOL' requires further immersion into the intellectual history of this idea. Below, I review six central traditions in order to highlight their influence on how people think about and pursue QOL today, particularly as they relate to the idea's liberal thrust in the affluent society. As is often the case with histories of ideas, my discussion emphasizes scholarly developments that may seem far removed from our day-to-day worlds, such that the reader might reasonably ask whether these 'ivory tower' pronouncements are really germane to lay concerns for 'QOL.' Rather than trot out the truism that ideas have power (which in fact I believe), I would instead invoke the sociology of knowledge insight that ideas do not exist outside of the historical and social forces that shape material life as well. As we will see, a number of these intellectual traditions, presented below in roughly chronological order, are deeply intertwined with their extant historical developments and policy initiatives.

The Aristotelian Tradition

Many scholars attribute the earliest known mention of 'quality of life' to Aristotle. His *Nicomachean Ethics* contains several invocations of QOL, most notably in the oft-quoted phrase, "the quality of life is determined by one's activities."[3] Yet more influential for contemporary understandings of QOL than these explicit references to the phrase is Aristotle's answer to the fundamental question that concerned classical Greek philosophers since Socrates: what is the chief human good? For Aristotle it is *eudaimonia*, a Greek word that is frequently translated as "happiness" (N.E., I.4), although a more accurate rendering—albeit one far less recognizable as the fleeting subjective state that moderns tend to associate with happiness—is human "flourishing." The ancient Greeks held *eudaimonia* to be the highest ideal in a world of primal struggle for daily survival. Cultural historian Darrin McMahon (2006) emphasizes the "less pleasant facts" behind the Greeks' pursuit of *eudaimonia*:

> that thunder or an eclipse could induce terror, that pestilence and hunger periodically wiped out entire communities, that horribly disfigured men and women were a presence in every town, that children were as apt to die before their fifth birthday as to live longer, that bloody warfare was a constant reminder of the fragility of existence. In a world such as that, life was less something to be made than something to be endured. Only those who did so successfully could be deemed fortunate, blessed, happy.
>
> (p. 5)

If *eudaimonia* was a longstanding concern in classical Greek philosophy, Aristotle was the first to assign it a hierarchical status as the most important human good. Further, whereas Socrates and Plato before him viewed *eudaimonia* as godlike, an elusive ideal for mankind, Aristotle saw it as fundamentally human and feasible to achieve (McMahon 2006:45). This is because *eudaimonia* draws upon the distinctive 'function' of the human species, reflective activity (N.E., I.7; X.7). With the *Nicomachean Ethics*, then, Aristotle puts forth the seminal Western thesis that human flourishing, man's ultimate purpose (*telos*), is achieved through the development of reason (Megone 1990).

In the context of classical Greek philosophy, Aristotle's argument is not startlingly original, as it revisits (among other things) Socrates' well-known dictum that the unexamined life is not worth living. If we stand back a minute from the philosophers' arguments, it becomes clear that this credo not only appears throughout Western philosophy as an insight into human experience, it also outlines a recurring biographical arc of how people develop aspirations to improve their individual QOL. That is, it relates the basic process and motivations by which people appraise their own QOL, as anyone who has interrupted the unquestioned trajectory of their life and re-examined their ultimate goals and values might recognize. Yet beyond this, the *Nicomachean Ethics* establishes a more complex legacy for contemporary understandings of QOL.

To begin, Aristotle explains that *eudaimonia*, although feasible in principle, is difficult to attain in reality since the social and biographical conditions in which man can practice his distinctive function are not easily achieved. They include a disciplined life of virtue best practiced through Aristotle's doctrine of the mean (N.E., II.6). In the form of contemplation and study, reason "is thought to reside in leisure from business" (X.7). Reason is not easily exercised by the young, who are too inexperienced and easily led by their emotions to have the proper faculties (I.3). Since Aristotle, like others of his time, thought women and slaves to be deficient in the faculties for reason, *eudaimonia* is effectively limited to a relatively few elite men. Given the possibility, even imminence, of human flourishing that Aristotle's focus on human functioning seems to promise, philosopher Jonathan Lear (2000) observes the paradox:

> those who know most about human life know that what is best is to organize life so as to escape its ordinary conditions—even the conditions of excellence within it. What is best about being human is the opportunity to break out of being human.
>
> (p. 55; quoted in McMahon 2006:49)

Innumerable readers of Aristotle have wrestled with and discarded his ascriptive restrictions of gender and status on who is innately eligible to seek *eudaimonia*. What they have retained—an emphasis on behaviors and undertakings needed to achieve *eudaimonia*—again provides an important biographical narrative of QOL: intellectual scrutiny of QOL is inseparable from its practical pursuit, here depicted as the reshaping of one's life and commitments.

A variety of philosophical and scientific perspectives on QOL and related matters have elaborated the more egalitarian premises to Aristotle's idea of human functioning. On the one hand, this concern has been developed through socially emergent accounts of human behavior from sociology, anthropology, social history, and other paradigms that emphasize the collective and interactional aspects of human groups. Contemporary philosophers like Martha Nussbaum (1993, 1988) have drawn from Aristotle various inventories of social conditions that *societies* must fulfill in order to ensure the individual flourishing of their citizens. Most ambitiously, the philosophical-historical traditions that follow G.W. Hegel and the early Karl Marx in asserting a driving role for *collective* reflection in human progress can trace their origins in Aristotle. On the other hand, Aristotle's focus on human functioning supports more naturalistic perspectives on QOL. I discuss the human development field in some length later in this chapter, but here it should be noted that the field has at least one foot in a biological perspective on human flourishing—perhaps quite rightly, given the ongoing struggle for human survival that people in developing societies encounter in the form of infant mortality, food insecurity, and disease prevention.

A number of scientific perspectives view human flourishing through an evolutionary framework and locate the species's distinctive capacities in its adaptive mechanisms, such as individual psychology and genetic code. Most notably, several schools of psychological research investigate the variability and affective-cognitive factors of happiness (Buss 2000), subjective well-being (aka 'subjective QOL' in Cummins, Gullone, and Lau 2002; see also Diener 2000; Andrews and Withey 1976), life satisfaction (Cummins 2003), optimism (Peterson 2000), optimal experience (Csikszentmihalyi 1990), and so forth. Since the 1990s, the field of *positive psychology* has self-consciously adopted an Aristotelian vocabulary, from *Flourishing: Positive Psychology and the Life Well-Lived*, the name of a recent American Psychological Association volume (Keyes and Haidt 2003), to "The Happiness Formula," the title of a 2006 BBC documentary that relies heavily on the field's scholarship. Positive psychology establishes a natural-scientific framework in which to take up Greek philosophy's concern for the best conditions for happiness and reflection to thrive in:

> The field of positive psychology at the subjective level is about valued subjective experience: well-being, contentment, and satisfaction (past), hope and optimism (future), and flow and happiness (present). At the individual level it is about positive individual traits—the capacity for love and vocation, courage, interpersonal skill, aesthetic sensibility, perseverance, forgiveness, originality, future-mindedness, spirituality, high talent, and wisdom. At the group level it is about the civic virtues and the institutions that move individuals toward better citizenship: responsibility, nurturance, altruism, civility, moderation, tolerance, and work ethic.
>
> (Seligman and Csikszentmihalyi 2000:5)

Positive psychology's own flourishing has not gone without criticism. QOL scholars like Mark Rapley (2003) point out that its psychological view of individual QOL typically ignores social contexts, thereby reifying the external conditions and social relations for QOL and erroneously viewing QOL as a *thing*, and is disconnected from other traditions that view QOL as a collective attribute. Although this charge cannot be levied upon all of Aristotle's inheritors, given his influence upon socially emergent perspectives, the tradition he establishes of theorizing individual QOL underscores the reductionist and ahistorical impulses that tempt all understandings and evaluations of human well-being.

Utilitarianism

As articulated since the affluent society, 'QOL' critiques but also affirms the Enlightenment legacy of thinking about how humans can promote the greater good. This philosophical tension is especially brought to bear upon utilitarianism, a moral philosophy that remains dominant within economics and quite influential in public policy attuned to enhancing human well-being. Drawing on two centuries of economics theory, from Adam Smith through the seminal refinements of Jeremy Bentham and John Stuart Mill, generations of economists and policy-makers have observed that human behavior is motivated by the pursuit of "utilities" or satisfactions such as physical sustenance, sensual gratifications, and the approving regard of others. Further contending that utilities are fundamentally provided through goods and services, proponents of utilitarianism understand individual 'welfare'—i.e., a person's QOL—as the ability to pursue utilities, and have measured welfare as the purchasing power of individual incomes relative to the costs of goods and services. But why do some people desire chocolate and others fruit? Why do some covet Lamborghinis and others Toyota Priuses? The classical and neoclassical economic perspectives' view of the diversity of utilities that people pursue is illuminating. They refuse such relativist questions (seen by Enlightenment thinkers as the province of religious dogma and other transcendent philosophies) and propose that utilities originate in private individual motive; consequently, in the aggregate they are arbitrary in their patterning and essentially unknowable *a priori*.

In welfare economics the central question is how best to distribute the means for satisfying utilities among peoples of diverse tastes, social standings, and incomes. Utilitarianism provides a compelling thesis: since the substance of people's utilities cannot be known beforehand, much less provided uniformly for all members of a society, the "rule of utility" provides an elegant method for conceptualizing, measuring, and promoting human welfare by understanding the good society as that which maximizes the greatest happiness for the greatest number of people. Thus, economists and policy-makers who adhere to a traditional form of utilitarianism regard a society's gross domestic product (GDP), the statistic that captures all the secured prices of goods and services, as "a reasonably good approximation of a society's well-being" (Cobb 2000:7). They furthermore take economic growth and an increasing GDP as evidence that a society is increasing human QOL. However, utilitarianism also suggests, to use a somewhat glib example, that if everyone in a society wants an SUV in their garage, and only two people have the income to obtain an SUV, that society's welfare is still better than if only one person could obtain an SUV. The philosophy provides little means to determine the transcendent ideal for producing and allocating SUVs; it only provides a framework to measure and evaluate "better than alternate societies" in an economy of scarce goods and services (see Hodge 1990:47). A classical utilitarian analysis avoids the logical extension of this example: the 'best society,' one in which everyone gets their own SUV, might also generate collective consequences—i.e., it would have environmental and social impacts—that, among other things, degrade the satisfaction everyone derives from their SUVs. Proponents of an orthodox utilitarianism leave mitigating the collective consequences of individual utilities to the workings of markets, not the alteration of their basic model; hence the somewhat circular thesis that markets provide the means to reforming the consequences of the market. These tenets, needless to say, comprise the dominant philosophy of economic growth in a scarcity-oriented society. If it has been significantly disabused by the affluent society critique, beginning with John Kenneth Galbraith, it remains a powerfully persuasive outlook in most developed nations.

Critiques of utilitarianism as a way to conceptualize and promote QOL are legion, though not all reject utilitarianism's underlying premises. A common one posits that if human welfare is not exclusively or even primarily derived from the income-circulating spheres of work and commerce—two obvious sites being the natural environment and women's unpaid labor in the household—then QOL is imperfectly indicated by incomes, prices, GDPs, and other monetary measures. This critique has led to the development of extended accounting measures of societal well-being that factor in non-market social goods (leisure, civic participation, etc.) and social bads (environmental strain, crime, social inequality, etc.). An example is the Measure of Economic Welfare, part of the United Nations' venerable System of National Accounts, which factors in household production, leisure time away from work, crime, pollution, non-renewable resource depletion, and so on (Offer 2006:21; Nordhaus and Tobin 1973). By design, extended accounting measures are highly amenable to market calculations and activity, since they provide an accounting system that internalizes the costs of production into prices and wages; for this reason, their implementation is generally a key goal for reformist social and environmental advocates (see, e.g., Holliday, Schmidheiny, and Watts 2002; Gore 1992). They do not challenge utilitarianism's paradigmatic premise that QOL is an individual phenomenon, subjectively constructed and measurable (if at least indirectly) by price. Nor does their critique disturb the utilitarian premise that underpins most schools of public policy formulation and evaluation, that a society's QOL maximizes *individual* wants—for utilitarianism, the primary basis for QOL. "'Social welfare' means the aggregate of 'individual welfares' of all members of society," economist Herbert Gintis (1972) explains. "As such, the problem of social welfare reduces to a problem of individual welfare and a problem of aggregation" (p. 574). As these extended accounting measures have proliferated, their reform of utilitarianism's cruder aspects has simultaneously reinforced an overall market framework that explains to whom QOL belongs (individuals), how QOL varies (as widely as subjective preferences are diverse), and how it is ideally secured (through decentralized private pursuits).

If economic growth is perhaps too controversial in the popular thinking on QOL to demonstrate utilitarianism's ethical virtues, consider its value in preserving human life. As advocates for patients' 'right to die' have persuasively argued, some people experience lives so physically painful or stripped of personal autonomy as to be worth less than life itself—the value behind doctors' traditional focus on extending life. "Then we may say that the condition that makes that life less worth living than normal is its low 'quality of life,'" medical researcher Sahin Aksoy (2000:19; quoted in Rapley 2003:74) explains. This is a visceral problem of QOL, almost certainly the one most commonly associated with the idea in the scholarly research literature, as well as one that challenges the traditional mission of healthcare professionals and institutions. I further discuss the politics of the patients' rights movement in Chapter 7, but here I note that a common way healthcare professionals and institutions choose from possible modes of care and treatment is by calculating patients' quality adjusted life years (QALYs), a statistic that "represents life expectancy adjusted for QOL," as Rapley (2003) explains.

> In health economic terms QALYs allow comparisons across medical interventions that differ in their effects on longevity and on different aspects of QOL. Years of life in different states of physical or mental dysfunction or various symptomatic states are assigned values on a scale of 1.0 (healthy) to 0.0 (dead). These values reflect the relative quality of the states and allow morbidity and mortality improvements to be combined into a single weighted measure—QALYs gained. Thus, for example, 10 years of life in perfect health = 10 QALYs; 15 years of life with a mildly compromised QOL (e.g., persistent back pain) may be rated at 0.8 relative to perfect health, with QALY value calculated as the product of the QOL rating of 0.8 multiplied by the years of life = (15 × 0.8) = 12 QALYs.
>
> (p. 143)

For medical professionals, the practical value of the QALY statistic lies in calculating the cost per QALY gained for each possible treatment. With QALYs, healthcare professionals and institutions can quantify the costs of alternate treatments and—in a context of scarce healthcare resources—allocate these resources among patients in a way that maximizes the greatest good for the greatest number. Although for many it raises serious ethical issues (see Cubbon 1991), the QALY "is a measure characteristic of welfare economics in its fundamentally utilitarian nature" (Megone 1990:28). It illustrates how ethical questions (e.g., how should we promote the health of people?) can be transformed into analyses of economic 'efficiency,' a useful technique for institutions and authorities.

As these developments attest, utilitarianism's influence lies greatly in its practicality. It is one thing, for instance, to insist that a healthy environment cannot be reduced to a price, but it is another thing to achieve and evaluate sustainability in a world of human impacts and ecological degradation.

Perhaps markets incorporate information about people's wants and needs more effectively than centralized authorities, or perhaps not—these are the usual sides in economic debates—but certainly utilitarianism resolves thorny problems of resource coordination, collective consensus, and political legitimacy in democratic societies by deferring them altogether.

Modernization Theory

The thesis that boosting GDP advances the social good also comprised a central tenet, arguably the key one, in the post-World War II Cold War for military supremacy and "Third World" allegiance between Western capitalist societies and Eastern communist regimes. Whereas the latter centralized control of production systems in order to administrate economic growth and standards of living, Western capitalist regimes articulated a political narrative of how free labor ('free' here in the double sense of economic exchanges and political liberties) and decentralized markets laid the foundations for national well-being. Never mind that corporate oligopolies and the negotiated labor peace of the post-World War II welfare state undergirded the West's economic prosperity in this period; with the Cold War, the market narrative of economics became a hegemonic worldview within academia, policy circles, and arguably the broader political culture of the West. Other intellectual projects emerged to support this narrative, of which modernization theory is perhaps most relevant to contemporary thinking on QOL. Advanced by several social sciences in the 1950s and 1960s, modernization theory drew upon the example of developed Western nations, particularly the U.S., to generalize the economic, political, civic, and cultural features of modern societies. Most prominently, it theorized a sequence of institutional and cultural transformations that developing nations need to undertake in order to become 'modern,' thereby bestowing a scholarly legitimacy to Western political regimes (e.g., Apter 1965; McClelland 1961; Rostow 1960). As illustrated by the title of economist W.W. Rostow's canonical text, *The Stages of Economic Growth: A Non-Communist Manifesto*, modernization theory's agenda to promote capitalist regimes politically acceptable to Western powers was rather explicit.

Although its emphasis on market development as a means to national 'modernization' lives on in the structural adjustment programs imposed by global financial institutions (the World Bank, Institutional Monetary Fund, etc.) upon developing societies, modernization theory's first incarnation engendered controversy and, by the Cold War's end, lost considerable influence in the fields of international relations and development policy (Gilman 2004; Latham 2000). In the 1970s, a new generation of social scientists revised modernization theory into a more empirically robust and less politically aligned account of social and institutional development. Where QOL scholarship is concerned, the key figure is political scientist Ronald Inglehart, who has developed a *postmaterialist* thesis of modernization theory over the last four decades. As in the original theory, economic development plays a driving role:

"Economic development is linked with a syndrome of changes that includes not only industrialization, but also urbanization, mass education, occupational specialization, bureaucratization, and communications development . . ." (Inglehart 1997:8). However, Inglehart and his colleagues locate the effective force of societal modernization in "deep-rooted orientations among the people themselves" (Inglehart and Welzel 2005:2), which lead initially to popular support for economic growth, welfare institutions, and strong, often authoritarian states that assuage the age-old human concern for physical and cultural security. This institutional development represents the titular stage of "modernization"—Rostow's Cold War market democracies can be situated here, but so too can a number of authoritarian regimes committed to economic growth (the People's Republic of China after Deng Xiaoping is an obvious case)—but it does not yet engender the full flourishing of human freedom and autonomy. Two further, "postmodern" developments signal societal reactions against the scarcity orientation of modern societies: the cultural shift toward postmaterialist values and the democratization of political institutions.

First, through the World Values Survey project that has gathered data from 1981 to (most recently) 2001 over all six continents, Inglehart and his colleagues have discerned stable patterns of materialist and postmaterialist value clusters that correspond to societies in which survival is seen as insecure or secure, respectively; see Table 2.2. Notice that Inglehart defines "QOL" against

Table 2.2 Materialism and Postmaterialism

Materialism	*Postmaterialism*
Survival is seen as . . .	
Insecure	*Secure*
1. Politics	
Need for strong leaders	De-emphasis on political authority
Order	Self-expression, participation
Xenophobia/fundamentalism	Exotic/new are stimulating
2. Economics	
Priority to economic growth	Quality of life = top priority
Achievement motivation	Subjective well-being
Individual vs. state ownership	Diminishing authority of both private and state ownership
3. Sexual/Family Norms	
Maximize reproduction—but only in two-parent heterosexual family	Individual sexual gratification Individual self-expression
4. Religion	
Emphasis on higher power	Diminishing religious authority
Absolute rules	Flexible rules, situational ethics
Emphasis on predictability	Emphasis on meaning and purpose of life

Source: Inglehart (1997:43)

"priority to economic growth," thereby charging the former with the affluent society concerns for collective well-being, e.g., environmental integrity, public health, and amenity development. Meanwhile, the remaining values in the right-hand column emphasize the establishment and flourishing of civil rights and personal expression that locate the postmaterial dynamic at the individual level.

Second, the democratization of political institutions, Inglehart explains, proceeds only after they achieve a measure of success in providing material security for the members of society. As economic development allows people to meet their basic needs, become more educated and affluent, and experience more diverse situations and people—all characteristic patterns of industrial societies—people come to adopt "emancipative orientations"; they increasingly question tradition and authority, demand economic and political choice and personal autonomy, endorse civil rights and ecological integrity for themselves and others, and ultimately promote democratic systems of government (Inglehart and Welzel 2005; Inglehart 1997, 1990; Abramson and Inglehart 1995). The experience of material security sets in motion larger social forces (e.g., elite defection from ruling regimes, mass mobilization outside accepted institutions) that further pressure authoritarian governments to democratize (Welzel, Inglehart, and Klingemann 2003). Material security also promotes interpersonal trust among the members of a society, which serves as a crucial moral foundation for both democratic government and successful markets (Inglehart 1997:172). Once a society prospers sufficiently to give its members a sense of physical and cultural security, postmaterialist values shape the worldview of people who come to take this security for granted—particularly the young, the affluent, and the educated—until their numbers grow to characterize the whole of society, or at least its electoral majorities and key political blocs (Clark and Inglehart 1998:17; Abramson and Inglehart 1995).

Given this elaborate theory of postmaterial values, a great number of contemporary values and experiences of 'QOL' can be meaningfully interpreted through Inglehart's version of modernization theory (see Chapter 7). Yet the Cold War-era genesis of the theory that Inglehart has inherited should not be neglected. Tellingly, he posits a universal model of sequential development culminating in a more or less singular societal type, albeit one that permits the expression of a great deal of cultural and lifestyle diversity. Although the theory accounts for the history of the affluent society's rise in sociological terms, it enfolds this history into a functional outcome of not just economic prosperity but market development specifically. Even with the substantial revision that Inglehart has provided, modernization theory uneasily addresses the contradictory impulses—the environmental degradation, unsustainable consumption of natural resources, and so on—of the market capitalism that it celebrates. In this way, it slights the historically and culturally specific concerns that weighed heavily upon the affluent society thinkers and movements who, in their own ways, also dreamed of the emancipative potentials of modern society.

The Maslowian Tradition

One of the most enduring conceptualizations of 'QOL' arose out of the 1954 publication of *Motivation and Personality* by Abraham Maslow, an historic figure in the psychology of personality development. Maslow's book and its subsequent editions were key statements in humanistic psychology, a field of clinical psychology that flourished in the 1960s and 1970s and, ironically, inspired innumerable self-help groups that eventually discredited Maslow's legacy in the eyes of many mainstream psychologists. The American son of Russian Jewish immigrants, Maslow was tremendously affected by the horrors of World War II and the dim picture of human nature suggested by the Cold War. Through humanistic psychology, he hoped to provide a more affirmative view of individual development than offered by the reigning paradigms of clinical and experimental psychology of his day: Freudian psychoanalysis (in which 'ordinary unhappiness' was the best people could aspire to, so deeply ingrained were the psychosocial dynamics of neurosis) and Skinnerian behaviorism (in which morality was not innate to human behavior but simply a learned personality trait). Maslow rejected the model of value-free science and sought instead to improve society by illuminating the dynamics through which human beings could reach their fullest potential.

Although 'QOL' was not an expression generally used by Maslow, two of his signature concepts have proven especially influential: the *hierarchy of needs* and *self-actualization*. With the first, Maslow contended that beneath the manifest level in which people express culturally accepted desires and attribute motives to their behavior, individuals instinctively move over the course of their lives through an ordered progression of developmental stages or "needs." In sequence from lower-order (or more fundamental) to higher-order (or most evolved), individuals seek to gratify physiological needs (e.g., for food, water, oxygen), safety needs (e.g., security, aversion to the unfamiliar, freedom from fear, anxiety, and chaos), belongingness and love needs (e.g., affiliation, friendship), esteem needs (achievement, success, recognition), and lastly self-actualization needs (for creativity, self-expression, integrity, self-fulfillment). Gratification of the first set of needs frees an individual to devote effort toward the second set, the gratification of which in turn makes possible the gratification of the third, and so on until the final stage. To borrow economists' vocabulary, the hierarchy exhibits an elasticity of needs gratification; individuals and their social affiliations (family, community) allocate more personal resources and effort to gratify lower-order needs and progressively less for higher-order needs. Life-stage is a key factor for Maslow: as an individual accumulates experiences and observations, she or he is more likely to have satisfied prior needs that enable her to advance to higher stages of personal development.

Alongside this scientific account of a universal developmental process, Maslow's theory expressed a humanistic, indeed highly critical, engagement with history. He acknowledged, for instance, that people's ability to progress along the hierarchy of needs is clearly influenced by their social and historical context. War or peace, abundance or famine, the openness of social orders to personal advancement and human connection: these and other factors setting the priorities for human existence transmit the almost arbitrary determination of historical moment, cultural custom, and biographical circumstance. Furthermore, most individuals do not traverse the entire hierarchy of needs in their lives. Lower-order needs may constitute the entire horizon of possibility in less developed societies yet are often moot in more developed ones, while—here lies the paradoxical tragedy of the affluent society—the ultimate stages of human becoming are not commonly achieved in even the most developed of societies. Maslow's insight—a rather emancipative one in the post-World War II era of bureaucratic rationality and outer-directed "lonely crowds" (cf. Marcuse [1941] 1998; Riesman 1950)—was that people need not be slaves to the apparent dictates of social norm and historical moment, especially given the unprecedented historical opportunity presented by the affluent society.

Hence the historical charge behind Maslow's idea of self-actualization. With this idea, Maslow (1987) calls attention to "people's desire for self-fulfillment, namely, the tendency for them to become actualized in what they are potentially. This tendency might be phrased as the desire to become more what one idiosyncratically is, to become everything that one is capable of becoming" (p. 22). At its most evolved state, self-actualization includes a variety of traits such as creativity, an accurate perception of reality, self-acceptance, genuineness of behavior, a strong focus on problems outside themselves, independence from environmental influences and cultural forces, deep sympathy for other humans, and profound interpersonal relationships. Maslow (1987) recognized that his ideas about self-actualization and the processes by which humans are instinctively driven to develop their full potential resembled the biographical arc in Aristotle's theory of *eudaimonia*, but, as he pointedly stressed,

> we have learned from the study of psychopathology and psychotherapy that we must modify considerably our picture of the psychological organism to respect equally rationality, emotionality, and the conative or wishing and driving side of our nature. Furthermore, from our empirical studies of the healthy person we have learned that these are definitely not at odds with each other, that these sides of human nature are not necessarily antagonistic but can be cooperative and synergetic.
>
> (p. 116)

Maslow theorized these dimensions of self-actualization through empirical analysis of select individuals such as his esteemed mentors—an admittedly unscientific sampling method that informed others' critiques of his work. Nonetheless, his concept proved influential in large part because its dimensions corresponded to the values and concerns of many who resisted the stifling, alienating nature of post-World War II society. To name just two dimensions, the tropes of 'creativity' and 'genuineness of behavior' (which today people might articulate through the theme of 'authenticity') have pervaded the language of many groups associated with the affluent society's cutting edges, from the counterculture of the late 1950s and 1960s to the "creative class" of the Internet era. If critics have discounted Maslow's theory for the self-absorption and therapeutic excesses of the many self-help groups it spawned, it is worth recalling the critical impulse behind his claims. Referring to Aristotle's dismissal of slaves' capacity for reason, Maslow (1987) made the now common contention that the Greek philosopher's theory was flawed by its own uncritical observations of "the good man in his own culture and in that particular period of time" (p. 115; for a rebuttal, see Nussbaum 1993). By contrast, Maslow's hierarchy of needs embodies a Kantian model of universal human behavior, drawing on "anthropological evidence to indicate that the fundamental or ultimate desires of all human beings do not differ nearly as much as do their conscious everyday desires" (Maslow 1987:6). The evidence today for his claims may be inconclusive for some, but his theory nonetheless inherits an Enlightenment legacy of critical reflection.

In his final years Maslow recognized that humanistic psychology's goal of helping people reach their fullest potential would require understanding what constituted the "good or healthy society." This, Maslow (1987) concluded, would be "one that permitted people's highest purposes to emerge by satisfying all their basic needs" (p. 31). Although he did not develop these ideas much more than this, in part because his psychological enterprise was at odds with such socio-historical analysis, they highlight another way that Maslow influenced contemporary thinking on QOL. Corresponding to the structured sequence of an individual's instinctual development, Maslow's hierarchy of needs also narrates a history of social progress in which societies focus first on their members' 'lower order' needs from the most immediate necessities (biological needs) to longer-term patterns of survival (safety needs) and on to social reproduction (social needs). Having fulfilled these needs for them members, societies move on toward the 'higher order' needs, first through other-focused affirmation (esteem needs) before reaching inner-focused self-realization, now recast as the ultimate stage of societal potentiality (see also Sirgy 1986). As with the psychological dynamic, Maslow's view of humanity's potentiality brings with it an instinctive motivation, indeed a moral imperative, to achieve its members' fullness.

Human Development

Beginning in the 1970s against the backdrop of the rising geopolitical influence of so-called Third World countries and a growing chorus criticizing Cold War models of national prosperity, a number of scholars advanced alternatives to the priority of economic growth that until then characterized global development policy. Their approaches have been diverse and sometimes incongruent with one another, but on the whole they have articulated visions of individual and national well-being grounded in the acute, specific problems of developing societies. Amidst the economic affluence of developed nations (which by this point had diverted substantial wealth to the proliferation of nuclear weapons and other Cold War infrastructure), the Third World specter of ongoing malnourishment, disease, and other forms of human deprivation gave rise to the *basic needs approach*, a development paradigm that tackles human poverty and national underdevelopment by investing exclusively in the necessities of human survival. Minimal allotments of food, water, and shelter are generally viewed as core basic needs (Streeten et al. 1981). Other basic needs that have drawn attention included healthcare, sanitation, and education. The success this approach has had in shaping foreign aid policy and undertakings rests in the wide consensus and, subsequently, the moral ground it has achieved in the development policy arena. As development scholar Ian Miles (1985) observes, "The concept of basic needs gains this power in part from its very simplicity: few needs are identified, and these therefore elicit general accord," such as the agreement upon the daily per capita caloric intake needed for daily survival that the World Health Organization has established (pp. 153, 156). In the late 1980s, economist Mahbub ul Haq (1995; see also Desai 1991) developed a similarly basic and compelling model of human welfare, in this case an evaluative measure applicable to all societies, with his Human Development Index, which tracked national indicators for life expectancy, adult literacy, and schooling, alongside the standard distributive statistic of GDP per capita. Incorporated into the reports of the United Nations and other global institutions, the Human Development Index's name was given to this growing field of development scholars.

More recently, human development scholars and practitioners have vigorously questioned whether human well-being can be conceived in the material and universal terms of these initial formulations. As the basic needs approach became adopted by a variety of global institutions and policy-makers for a variety of purposes, some commentators criticized its singular focus on delivering bundles of basic goods to the poor, which supports a narrow outlook of "commodity fetishism" that neglects other dimensions of human QOL (see Clark 2005:2–3). As well, the Human Development Index has been called out for not providing a more forceful view of how the meaning and experience of QOL is a collective construction, a neglect that leaves it vulnerable to the same charges of methodological individualism attributable to utilitarianism. Through such critiques, Nobel Prize-winning economist Amartya Sen and other scholars have developed a *capabilities approach* that puts front and center human "capabilities," or "the characteristics of each person that enable him or her to function in the world and lead a full life" (Cobb 2000:10). These capabilities include not just the 'having' of goods and services that the basic needs approach emphasizes, but also the potentials of 'being' (health, social solidarity, etc.) and 'doing' (work, civic engagement, etc.). Although economic growth is an important foundation for human development (Sen 1983), Sen's three-part conceptualization of QOL makes it amenable to articulating affluent society critiques of the kind Galbraith made, as one proponent (Culyer 1990:15) observes: "If you think of 'standard of living' or 'quality of life' in terms of capabilities of functioning then you can immediately see that one may be rich (have lots of commodities) but have a low standard of living."

Significantly, the capability approach in Sen's writings is distinctly attuned to the local contexts of culture, community, and situation through which humans understand the meanings of 'functioning' and exercise their capabilities. Human development scholar David A. Clark (2005) explains:

> In judging the quality of life we should consider what people are able to achieve. Sen then observes that different people and societies *differ* in their capacity to convert income and commodities into valuable achievements. For example, a disabled person may require extra resources (wheel chairs, ramps, lifts, etc.) to achieve the same things (moving around) as an able bodied person. Moreover, a child typically has very different nutritional requirements from a manual labourer, pregnant woman or someone with a parasitic disease. Similarly, the commodity requirements for more complex social achievements (such as 'appearing in public without shame' or 'entertaining family and friends') typically depend on 'cultural' factors such as social convention and custom or status and class, *inter alia* (Sen 1985:25–6; 1999:70–1). In comparing the well-being of different people, not enough information is provided by looking only at the commodities each can successfully command. Instead we must consider how well people are able to function with the goods and services at their disposal. (p. 3)

This emphasis on the social contexts for human flourishing also calls attention to social inequalities and subordinations across gender, race, ethnicity, nation, and other social divisions. For Sen (1993), freedom and individual agency are fundamental aspects of an individual's capabilities; the individual holds ultimate authority in defining his or her own capabilities. Furthermore, the social spheres in which humans pursue their capabilities—markets, work, family, politics, school, and others—embody different norms of fulfillment that are incommensurable with each other. Cobb (2000) makes clear the implication: "Progress in one area should not be regarded as a trade-off for regress in another" (p. 11). With these points, Sen dismisses the claims to political legitimacy made by authoritarian regimes that are committed to enhancing their citizens' standards of living.

As this suggests, a tension between a cultural and situational relativism on the one hand and a universal view of human rights on the other—a tension, it should be stressed, underlying global development concerns more generally—pervades Sen's treatment of the capabilities approach. Perhaps more problematically, because one size of human QOL pointedly does not fit all, the approach's cultural relativism frustrates easy development and implementation of policies to promote human development. Subsequently, in response to Sen's inability to offer a set of definitive capabilities (see Qizilbash 1998; Nussbaum 1988; Williams 1987), other adherents have sought to identify universal capabilities that could better assist development policy and human rights law. Perhaps the best known of these efforts comes from feminist philosopher Martha Nussbaum (2000), who conceives of ten overall categories: (1) life; (2) bodily health; (3) bodily integrity; (4) senses, imagination, and thought; (5) emotions; (6) practical reason; (7) affiliation; (8) other species; (9) play; and (10) political and material control over one's environment. This list "isolates those human capabilities that can be convincingly argued to be of central importance in any human life, whatever else the person pursues or chooses" (p. 74; quoted in Clark 2005:6–7). In Nussbaum's treatment, the capability approach draws on the Aristotelian tradition of assigning value to human functioning and organizing its properties hierarchically (Nussbaum 1993). Gone, however, are the restrictive actual conditions for *eudaimonia* that Aristotle outlined, replaced by the capabilities approach's emphasis on potential conditions. That Nussbaum's universal approach is more practically suited to international and institutional efforts to promote human development is possible; nonetheless, it discards the relativism that gives Sen's capabilities approach its unique moral resonance in developing societies seeking to define a vision of human well-being outside the influence of Western models.

Social Indicators

Part and parcel of the same concerns driving the rethinking of modernization within the human development field, by the 1970s policy-makers and researchers in Western nations had begun seriously pursuing alternatives to the use of GDP, other growth-oriented statistics, and the market-based production of goods and services they measure as the exclusive standards with which governments tracked and evaluated their citizens' well-being (Miles 1985). In his 1973 book *The Coming of Post-Industrial Society*, another important work on the societal transformations ushered in by economic affluence, sociologist Daniel Bell (1999) criticized the U.S. government's conventional data-gathering endeavors that were published annually in the Economic Report submitted by the Council of Economic Advisers:

> [F]or social policy it is highly inadequate, and in some ways even deceptive. The economic report, though presenting data on the incidence of poverty, understandably says little about the social attitudes—apathy, alienation, or resentments—bred by deprivation. It cannot, in its self-limiting scope, deal with the quality or amenities of life, such as better health, the degree of congestion, the availability of social services, and the invasion of privacy. These gaps, and the need to find measures that could chart their extent, have prompted the effort to set up social indicators as a necessary complement of economic measures. Without such social indicators, policy-making becomes increasingly deficient in its ability to judge alternatives.
>
> (p. 329)

Thus, social scientists and policy-makers began to advocate gathering *social indicators* to measure national performance in meeting human needs other than economic growth. The collection and analysis of social indicators data have since proliferated, as marked by the 1974 establishment of the international journal *Social Indicators Research* (subtitled "An International and Interdisciplinary Journal for Quality-of-Life Measurements") and the founding of professional groups like the International Society for Quality-Of-Life Studies. These academic and professional activities are today what most commentators reference when invoking the formal field of the "QOL research" or "QOL scholarship."

The social indicators field sits uneasily alongside other traditions of conceptualizing QOL, since it is not a singular intellectual perspective but rather a broad shift in research priorities. In fact, social indicators data have been used to support the gamut of arguments about the state of human QOL. Depending on how and where it is measured, QOL has been declining (e.g., De Graaf et al. 2005), progressing (e.g., Easterbrook 2003), or fairly constant historically (e.g., Cummins 2003). Researchers and policy-makers frequently disagree on what constitutes the 'quality' of life and thus what aspects of the social and physical world should be addressed when conceptualizing social indicators. In terms of what social indicators can track and illuminate, Noll (2000) contends, "Beyond the general goal of improving the information base of societies there are two basic functions of social indicators: First, monitoring of social change, and second, the measurement of welfare." Such broad 'dependent variables' can be understood easily enough, but interpreting the data gathered to indicate them can raise thorny problems of value orientation and political perspective. An illustration comes from a social indicators' report assembled for citizens and officials in Jacksonville, Florida:

> **Uncertainty of interpretation**. Questions have been raised about the accuracy and clarity of survey data in measuring certain aspects of the quality of life. For instance, if the number answering "yes" to the question about whether race relations are a problem in Jacksonville increases, has the quality of life increased or decreased? Most have chosen the latter interpretation. However, according to an alternative interpretation, recognition of the problem is the first step toward finding a solution, so an increase could be construed as positive.
>
> ***How the issue has been dealt with***. JCCI's volunteer committee members have grappled with this issue each year, but have not yet crafted alternative questions that more clearly measure this aspect of the quality of life.
>
> (Besleme, Maser and Silverstein 1999:15)

As for what factors cause particular social changes and shifts in welfare, policy-makers and researchers continue to debate the relevance of and relationships between physical health, social solidarity, economic development, crime, employment, the natural environment, and other realms of human life. Are all of these 'independent variables' mutually related or equally important? Given the vast array of external factors and human concerns that can be categorized under the conceptual umbrella of 'QOL,' the conventional practice has been to identify a narrow set of QOL domains and select indicators most germane to the specific issues and local contexts—family, community, environment, education, work, etc.—of a study's audience or subjects. As I argued in the prior chapter, this approach drives the intellectual specialization that characterizes the field of QOL research today; although it has much practical and theoretical value for illuminating conditions within given domains, it frustrates the generalizability and comparability of groups and jurisdictions across broader levels and hinders the conceptualization of a more holistic understanding of QOL.

If the social indicators tradition has an ultimate legacy for how people think about QOL, it might be best captured by the scientific truism that "if it isn't measured, it isn't managed." Otherwise, as an initiative within political bodies to put QOL on the radar by measuring it, the social indicators field has had mixed success. Government reports and public deliberations involving social indicators have become newsworthy events that stimulate popular interest in QOL questions and trends. Yet by focusing scholarly activities around data-gathering activities and methodological debates, the research field has given the public few clear, meaningful claims about the trends in QOL. Perhaps this academic quality of QOL research is as it should be, at least to those for whom QOL is an empirical condition 'out there,' about which the data should 'speak for themselves.' Nevertheless, some observers lament a historical failure of action since the heyday of affluent society critique. Notably, in 1969 the U.S. Department of Health, Education, and Welfare released *Toward a Social Report*, a proposal to institute the collection of social indicators at the federal level. The document defined a social indicator as a "statistic of direct normative interest which facilitates concise, comprehensive and balanced judgments about the condition of major aspects of a society" (USDHEW 1969:67). Remarkably, *Toward a Social Report* was released on President Lyndon B. Johnson's last day in office. Subsequent administrations never got much further in implementing its proposals or, in the case of the five subsequent Republican presidencies, even considering them very seriously. Institutional context further illuminates this historic failure of agency. Within the international community of nation-states, the inconsistency with which social indicators have been supported by public policy and data-gathering institutions reveals longstanding differences between 'pro-growth' nations, of which the U.S. is the most prominent, versus 'pro-welfare' nations. Among the latter, social indicators data-gathering and reporting activities were gradually instituted by most European governments as well as the United Nations, the Organization for Economic Cooperation, and the World Bank (these milestones are discussed in Rapley 2003:7; Noll 2000).

Within the U.S., the gathering and use of social indicators data has been adopted most effectively at the local level. QOL is more and more the stock in trade of municipal and nonprofit agencies involved in urban planning, environmental management, and, increasingly, economic development. Also, a vibrant *community indicators* movement has advanced the political incorporation of social indicators data gathered for communities smaller than nations and states—typically towns, cities, and regions (Cobb 2000). Since the mid-1980s, when the community indicators idea first took hold, more than 200 communities are thought to have undertaken such projects. Generally, community indicators projects conceptualize and manage QOL as a public good—i.e., a collective attribute of municipality, region, etc. Particularly as the problems of urban growth have led local policy-makers to adopt agendas promoting slow-growth and environmental amenities, community indicators have been instrumental in associating QOL with community-level action. Significantly, whereas in traditional social indicators projects researchers and policy-makers usually choose the indicators and frame the questions for study at some distance from the constituencies they represent, the community indicators movement generally regards incorporating constituent input as an important corollary if not equal priority to monitoring QOL itself. "For these projects to be successful," sociologist David Levinson (2003) opines, "all sectors of the community must be involved in developing and sharing a common vision of community life .... The process of using community indicators brings people together to develop a shared vision of their community and to set goals for the future" (pp. 272–3).

Social indicators' widespread incorporation at the local level to frame and measure collective QOL makes the absence in the U.S. of a comparable perspective at the federal level seem especially glaring. The U.S. system characteristically institutionalizes this national imbalance in its 'home rule' tradition, under which the federal government constitutionally cedes planning authority to the political unit of the smallest scale (usually the municipality and its planning units) and avoids a centralized role in planning or gathering data for anything but economies (Logan and Molotch 1987:166). Because it constrains effective QOL planning in key ways, the political-legal context of home rule has energized community indicators projects and, indeed, political action by local activists more generally. Ironically, this basis for mobilization often goes unremarked in social indicators research. With its emphasis 'on the data,' the field of social indicators research has so far struggled to call critical attention to the institutional context that frustrates its underlying concerns.

Conclusion

This last discussion illustrates the lesson that conceptual elaboration of an idea's promise, a pattern that recurs throughout the six intellectual traditions recounted above, is altogether different from a critical scrutiny of that idea's historical and social context. These traditions spoke forcefully about the conditions of their time, and perhaps they can hardly be faulted for the direction of historical and social patterns since their influence on the thinking and pursuit of QOL was first felt. Before I turn to contemporary contexts in which people pursue QOL today, it is worth underscoring three themes that surface from this chapter's intellectual history.

First, the sociology of knowledge draws our attention to the social locations and social contexts in which people produce ideas and claims about QOL. The thinkers and writers described here have enjoyed livelihoods and living standards that permit an escape from the scramble for survival and reproduction; the broader picture of human history underscores the uncommon prosperity and privilege that these intellectuals enjoyed. Furthermore, a picture of increasing societal development and affluence is conveyed by the roughly historical sequence in which I have presented the six traditions, suggesting that the personal remove from the scramble for survival and security has over time been extended to broader sections and strata of the societies in which these intellectuals existed. Thus, personal and social affluence are the broadest contexts in which 'QOL' has been articulated and (not always successfully) put forth as a cultural priority. This point does not mean that this intellectual output does not address people and societies across the vast spectrum of material prosperity and cultural diversity, nor that the poor and subordinate do not have original contributions to make to the ideas and concerns associated with 'QOL.' It is only to underscore how the object of this book is the idea, and not the conditions and experience, of QOL itself. As the following chapter will further elaborate, the social relations of power and inequality influence the discourse of human welfare—a key reason why the sociological significance of 'QOL' points outside the semantic contours and intellectual traditions of the idea itself.

Second, returning to those intellectual traditions, it should be clear how strongly developed are the individual and subjective frameworks of 'QOL.' Individual QOL is the primary or exclusive framework for all but one, the social indicators field, which is hardly a singular, coherent paradigm. Likewise, subjective understandings of QOL predominantly inform the first five conceptual traditions. The case is perhaps a little complicated in the human development field, given its priority on material subsistence and physical well-being, but the capability approach's emphasis on the cultural contexts that shape the expectations for individual flourishing returns us again to the dynamic of subjective meaning. Thus, urban planners, social workers, sustainability advocates, and others who emphasize collective and objective QOL concerns find unsure footing in these conceptual traditions. It is telling, if somewhat confusing, that within the community indicators movement "quality of life" designates for some practitioners a specific approach that "focuses most heavily on indicators of well-being," in contrast to 'alternate' approaches that focus on what many might perceive to be obvious and relevant dimensions of QOL, e.g., the environment (here, a distinct "sustainability approach") and public health (the "health indicators" approach) (Levinson 2003:273; Swain and Hollar 2003).

Despite the thrust of these scholarly conventions, it is too simplistic to assign an exclusively individual and subjective orientation to the concept of

QOL by academic fiat. To do so would be to forget the recent historical context in which 'QOL' surfaced as a key public and policy concern: the affluent society of Western post-World War II welfare states. Here 'QOL' foregrounded an undeniably *collective* approach to evaluating welfare; it forcefully raised political and moral issues of how we might live—and, indeed, who comprises the collective 'we'—in a moment when material security offered an unprecedented opportunity for collective action and policy redirection. Further, the new policy focus on QOL emphasized *objective* resources for collective well-being. Granted, such an emphasis was shared by traditional 'quantity of life' indicators like GDP; yet in pointed contrast to these, 'QOL' in the affluent society further underscored a *distribution* orientation by foregrounding the problems of poverty, inequality, and urban crisis, to name just three contemporaneous issues. The discursive shift from the affluent society's collective, objective, and distribution frameworks constitutes a key development in the understandings and pursuits of QOL, as we will see in the coming chapters.

Third, the methodological tone of much contemporary social indicators research, which now supports simultaneously affirmative and negative arguments about the state of QOL, illustrates the ethos of scholarly disinterest that too often distances QOL research from the everyday QOL concerns of laypeople. The problem here is not that social indicators are used to resolve empirical questions independent of observers' own value positions, which is the whole premise of using scientific methods for social evaluation, after all. Rather, the field exhibits a lapse of historical memory when it forgets that its initial focus on QOL was a pointedly normative undertaking. Originally, the social indicators endeavor fundamentally challenged the legitimacy of the institutional and political bias toward economic growth; in their own ways, so too did the Aristotelian tradition, utilitarianism, modernization theory, the Maslowian tradition, and the human development field challenge the prevailing views of human well-being. As affluent society critics like John Kenneth Galbraith and Daniel Bell argued, the conceptual construction of 'QOL' is not simply a methodological problem but also *a question of political legitimacy* when the choices of which social indicators get tracked alter the meanings and interpretations of social change and human welfare. Internationally, collecting social indicators is a charged endeavor that reveals and reinforces the political divides between the United States and E.U., to name just one institutional divide. If these institutional contexts lie outside the analytical scope of what QOL research traditionally focuses upon, they nonetheless shape the ongoing concerns and pursuits that call forth the concept for many. It is now time to step back from the intellectual rigidities of 'QOL' and examine the real contexts in which the idea motivates us today.

3 Technology

> Specialization is how we apply our vast knowledge to many trying challenges of the human race, how we go about improving our quality of life.
>
> (David Shenk 1997:112)

If humanity entered the twentieth century hoping technology would reduce labor's toil, increase leisure, and make life easier, by the century's close Western societies have seen quite different views prevail. More and more, people associate technology with feelings of entanglement, stress, obsolescence, and powerlessness before the sweeping tides of innovation. "I have to take this call": mobile phones and PDAs give us spatial and temporal freedom from the workplace but ensnare us in 24/7 work. "My computer is so slow": enchanted by the promise of steady technological advances, we unquestioningly accept our 'need' for improved models, software upgrades, and new devices. "Let's just get take-out": fast food, ready-made meals, and (for the well-to-do) personal chefs help households shorten their dinner time or give up on it altogether in order to satisfy their incompatible schedules. Technologies intended to simplify our lives often complicate them in surprising ways, as anthropologists (Darrah, Freeman, and English-Lueck 2007) witnessed in the high- and low-tech 'solutions' that working mother Suzanne Jones employed to manage her family's busy schedules:

> By creating an infrastructure of devices to keep track, Suzanne ironically created the work of keeping track of how that infrastructure was used. She kept track of people and activities using a paper annual calendar posted on the refrigerator, a thick paper date book that she carried to work, and a PDA that contained her daily list. She transferred information from the PDA to a slip of paper to use while running errands, and she also used scraps of paper and Post-Its to record notes that she later entered in one of her formal calendars. Suzanne wanted to consolidate lists and calendars but said this would be difficult. She shared the refrigerator calendar with [husband] Humberto; its very conspicuousness guaranteed that she would not overlook a critical deadline or event. While the PDA consolidated

> her "to do" list with other information, such as a calendar and address book, it did not allow her to view how an event fitted into longer units of time, such as weeks or months, thus making it difficult for her to plan. She found the PDA cumbersome to use while dashing between errands; that was why she kept the paper version perched on the dashboard. Because she job shared and divided her week between paid employment and family-related activities, Suzanne also manipulated lists and calendars to differentiate and integrate those domains of her life. For example, she kept extensive work-related information on the PDA, which she filtered from the "to do" lists of family-related errands: "I don't want that invading what my primary goal is."
>
> (pp. 118–9)

From the perspective of such *fin de siècle* anxieties, technology (in its prosaic manifestations, low- and high-tech) is the culprit and emblem of consumer materialism, the earth's physical degradation, and our surrender to ceaseless social and cultural change.

Confronted by the vast scale and sense of helplessness of technological change, many people seek to control technology—its omnipresence, innovations, obsolescence, and solutions for problems they never knew they had. In *Data Smog: Surviving the Information Glut*, journalist David Shenk (1997) offers eight suggestions to mitigate the cognitive strains and cultural overstimulation that information technology has unleashed:

- Turn the television off.
- Avoid news-nuggets.
- Leave the pager and cell-phone behind.
- Limit your e-mail.
- Say no to dataveillance.
- Resist advertising. ("Must we also wear them on our clothes?")
- Resist upgrade mania.
- Be your own "smart agent."
- Cleanse your system with "data-fasts."

(pp. 185–9)

Reducing the use of technology, it is also hoped, liberates people from their unknowing subservience to technological means, thereby restoring free will and human community. As depicted in *Better Off: Flipping the Switch on Technology* (2004), these principles motivate technology scholar Eric Brende and his wife Mary to join an assorted group of Amish, Mennonites, and mainstream defectors in rural Pennsylvania that he calls the Minimites, "in honor of both the history of Mennonite nonconformity and their current predilection to gain a maximum of ends with a minimum of technological means" (p. 43). As the Brendes discover, the price of freedom from modern technology is a reliance on the help of others—perhaps a shocking dependence in today's individualistic world, but also a deeply meaningful surrender to community, mindfulness, and genuine leisure.

In such perspectives, technology's crisis of QOL is invariably 'ours,' attributable to the whole of modern society; thus, activist and psychotherapist Chellis Glendinning wittily titled her 1994 "neo-Luddite" polemic *My Name is Chellis and I'm in Recovery from Western Civilization*. Many commentators see technology as part of larger social structures of economy and consumerism. In a popular book and TV documentary, QOL activist John De Graaf and his colleagues (De Graaf et al. 2005) identify "affluenza" as the "painful, contagious, socially transmitted condition of overload, debt, anxiety, and waste resulting from the dogged pursuit of more" (p. 2). Partaking of a long tradition in affluent society criticism that blames status anxiety and corporate greed, the affluenza argument contends that technology *per se* could make possible a more thoughtful choice between consumption and leisure:

> Our technologically advanced culture offers opportunities for much more meaningful and creative lives than most of us lead. Our amazingly productive technologies could allow all of us to spend less time doing repetitive, standardized work, or whose products bring us little pride, by allowing us to trade increased wages for reduced working hours.
>
> (De Graaf et al. 2005:80)

This last point underscores the Janus-face of technology's connections to QOL (e.g., Cooper 2002:3). When we consider how human life has changed over the course of history, we often think first of the machines and scientific innovations that have eased work's toil, made us healthy, let us communicate and exchange at great distances, and brought the world's ideas and cultures into our homes. For scholars, technology embodies our economic utilities, which motivate us to engage our environments in order to satisfy our needs and wants. On this basis, technology gives us a view on standards of living, the development of human knowledge, the state of social progress, and the broader march of civilization; a society's level of technological development can indicate its ability to meet its members' needs and wants. Such understandings illustrate how we think of technology as the *servant of human society*, and we view our creation of and access to technologies as a QOL good.

Yet at the same time, we often see technology at odds with our QOL. Technology is implicated in a variety of society's ills and annoyances beyond those just cited: job destruction (Rifkin 1995), environmental degradation (Carson 1962), the need-it-by-yesterday pace of modern life (Menzies 2005; Honoré 2004; Rifkin 1987), the loss of privacy (O'Harrow 2005; Garfinkel 2001; Sykes 1999), and a mindlessness brought about by too much choice (Offer 2006; Schwartz 2004). And if we intended technology to serve our interests, its problems stem from unanticipated outcomes as it interacts in complex ways with the ensemble of social and physical elements in our environments, such as physical resources, other technologies, and the diverse motivations of other people. Rational designs yet disastrous consequences: given these elements, it is little wonder that tragic narratives have long framed our musings on technology, from the ancient Jewish myth of the golem to Mary Shelley's *Frankenstein*. Technology supports and enforces durable patterns of human activity—enabling assembly lines, storing foodstuffs, providing anytime-anywhere communication, and so on—that impose themselves on people's lives as external and constraining forces; in this way, we see how *humanity serves technology* (Postman 1992; Heidegger [1954] 1977; Marcuse [1941] 1998).

A sweeping and complicated topic, technology evades a simple discussion because it is enmeshed in the fabrics of human life in so many ways. Too often scholars make "a lightning raid into the wooded slopes of prehistory" (Mann 1986:50) to explain how people live today, only to lose sight of their patently modern nature of their questions. Modestly, I propose that the broad outlines that theory casts upon history are not a fatal problem for social understanding; through such blunt focus we can raise meaningful (and, yes, contemporary) questions about the reality in which we live and take for granted (see Calhoun 1995:4–7). Thus, I focus in this chapter on the competing *concerns* in modern societies about technology's impacts on human QOL. In the first half, I introduce an analytical framework to make sense of the chief ways that technology shapes the 'QOL' people idealize as well as the QOL they experience, via the social relations that technology constitutes. In the second half, I examine two historical perspectives that characterize the competing views of technology's relationship to QOL: the 'promise of technology' and the voluntary simplicity movement. Rather than join in the debate over technology's Janus face, I turn a critical light on this discourse to reveal social relations that construe 'technology' and 'QOL' for other, more purely social if often ignored ends.

Technology and Society's QOL

Ordinarily, people think of technology as physical tools and machinery that put scientific learning to practical purposes. To better grasp technology's scope, we can elaborate and amend on this basic understanding. Although today technology is generally conceived and designed on the principles of scientific knowledge, this is a historically recent mode of technological development that Daniel Bell has described as the codification of theoretical knowledge. By this, Bell means that, in contrast to its prior development by "talented tinkerers" who applied the insights of intuition and trial-and-error independent of scientific activities, technology now follows the lead of scientific principles formulated for their own, knowledge-building purposes, with often little direct connection to the kinds of applied technologies it can stimulate (Bell 1999:116). Technology need not be developed with prior expectations or goals for its uses. More often, it is modified and re-deployed to later goals once its values in new environments are discovered, as the discovery of fire probably first illustrated (Smith 1981:325; cited in Molotch 2003). Nor is technology's medium limited to physical matter. Social organization and symbolic-intellectual forms can also constitute technologies insofar as they can be invented, so to speak, and used to serve human purposes, as, for instance, the corporation and software code illustrate.

It is easy to think of technology as both remote in our lives, in terms of innovations occurring in some far-off engineering laboratory, and at the same time omnipresent via the appliances and gadgets we operate at home, work, school, and other routine settings. This view emphasizes the 'thingness' of technology—it comes from some rarefied other place then is delivered into our lives—and thus obscures the social relationships that technology supports. Especially where QOL is concerned, it is more helpful to consider how technology is *embedded* in social process, organization, and behavior—not merely supporting these in concrete ways, but inexorably part of their very meaning, purpose, and texture. Most centrally, technology is fundamentally embedded into the economy in an anthropological sense: i.e., societies' material modes of production, distribution, and consumption. To explain, I step back from 'technology itself' and elaborate its connections to more general economic processes.

Technologies for Economic Activity

To begin, technology makes possible the *accumulation of material surplus*, the fundamental social and economic process by which a society sustains itself beyond day-to-day, hand-to-mouth conditions. By building up a surplus of goods that can be consumed at a later time (tomorrow, over the winter, when one is sick, etc.), a society frees up its members to perform future-oriented activities: raising families, altering the built environment, practicing rituals of community and religion, crafting material artifacts and verbal/written works, forming social institutions, and so on. Scholars regard the size of a social surplus as a measure of a society's human development; a smaller surplus per member indicates a 'poorer' or more 'primitive' society, while a greater surplus per member indicates a 'richer' or more 'advanced' society. This is one reason why economists' talk of GDP and productivity is so important; for all their abstraction, these indicators provide a snapshot of the most general processes of societal reproduction.

Technology's usefulness in the accumulation of surplus comes from its capacity to boost the productivity of economic activities. At its simplest, technology lets people reduce the inputs of labor and materials needed to grow, build, or otherwise produce the outputs they consume to live; in turn, this lets them accumulate a larger surplus over any given period than they would without the benefit of technological development. Accordingly, one of the currencies of productivity is time. A larger surplus lets a society devote not only more of its resources, but more of its time as well, toward producing the finer things in life: discretionary goods and services, recreations, cultural treasures and elite luxuries, and so on. Crucially, technology is centrally linked to what today we call consumption and leisure; they expend the productivity dividend that comes with technological development from the broadest scale of whole economies to the smallest scale of workplace tools. Hence, QOL concerns about consumer materialism and overwork (the latter discussed in Chapter 5) are ultimately rooted in questions of technoeconomic structure.

Technology is also tied up in another key determinant of economic productivity: the division of labor, or how people divvy up the many tasks needed to produce the goods and services that they consume. At a basic level, the division of labor means people do not each build their own shelters, grow their own foods, make their own clothing, educate their children, and so on. Instead, they look to others to help out with this work, with people specializing in specific activities and eventually occupations. Tools and machinery are often organizing features in divisions of labor, as Adam Smith's ([1776] 1904) famous analysis of the pin factory illustrates:

> One man draws out the wire, another straightens it, a third cuts it, a fourth points it, a fifth grinds it at the top for receiving the head; to make the head requires two or three distinct operations; to put it on, is a peculiar business, to whiten the pins is another; it is even a trade by itself to put them into the paper; and the important business of making a pin is, in this manner, divided into about eighteen distinct operations, which, in some manufactories, are all performed by distinct hands, though in others the same man will sometimes perform two or three of them.
>
> (Ch. I.1.3)

That organizing pin manufacture this way also deskills work and makes it numbingly dull did not escape Smith's attention, or that of the Industrial Revolution's critics who inveighed against technology's deskilling and automating capacities. However, the deterioration and (to cite a popular polemic) "end of work" (Rifkin 1995) are not essential features of the division of labor, which can also enhance the skills of any activity, as we see particularly if we examine non-physical forms of technology. Design and oversight of even the most monotonous assembly lines, for instance, involves engineers, managers, entrepreneurs, and administrators to organize these intellectual activities—in short, the growth of so-called white-collar occupations. Divisions of mental labor put toward understanding the human condition have produced an ever-growing number of symbolic-intellectual forms: the scholarly disciplines and specializations, each of which has generally increased intellectual output and insight (if not practical relevance and popular interest!) than prior divisions of intellectual labor. Technology's incorporation into these intellectual activities, it might be noted, has stimulated the speed and depth of specialization, particularly if we consider information technologies that have permitted ever more sophisticated methods of analysis (statistical, logical, etc.) and ever wider publication and dissemination of scholarship (word processing, the Internet, etc.).

So far we have yet to discuss the concrete ways that the goods and services produced by economies enter the spheres of consumption in everyday life. Consumption issues motivate most of today's criticisms of technology and voluntary simplicity advocates, but it is worthwhile to dwell a bit longer on the primacy of the sphere of production to make two points regarding technology and QOL. First, most people today experience the realm of production as the activity of 'going to work,' which connotes an individualized relationship centered around the skills and labor they offer to employers in exchange for income, benefits, and other job rewards. The connection of individuals at work to broader accumulation processes can seem quite abstract unless their activities involves some administrative function or external outlook. Such an individualistic perspective is not intrinsic to the social accumulation of material surplus, however, but rather a result of fairly recent changes in how and where people labor. Only since the Industrial Revolution have most people left the household economies of agriculture and craft production for the larger-scale industries of manufacturing and resource extraction. Now they report to workplaces set apart from their home lives by distance and a distinct set of impersonal rules and institutional roles. This historical shift of immense importance—one still unfolding in the developing world—gives us the distinction between the *public* and *private spheres* that modern people experience as a matter of course in the physical settings they occupy (e.g., the public settings of work and commerce versus the private domestic realm) and the very symbolic categories that order and give meaning to social relations: public citizens versus private families, public benefits versus private property, and so on (Dizard and Gadlin 1990; Zaretsky 1976). More to the point, the separation of public and private spheres made possible the development and proliferation of impersonal, rationalized institutions like the corporation that could pursue collective efforts and goals beyond the ken of daily cognizance. Thus, it is first and foremost in this context, a legacy of the Industrial Revolution, that the 'workplace' technologies people operate can be put toward abstract goals not of their choosing—like deskilling, speeding up, keeping them on call 24/7, and 'freeing' them from reliance upon neighbors and community—that may conflict with their interests as workers and human beings.

Second, we might take more seriously the influence of the economy's mandates upon technology's diffusion into everyday life. For every computer system advertised with the promise of personal flourishing ("What do you want to do today?" asks the Microsoft Corporation) or every airline's promise of personal escape, far larger markets lie in serving the needs of business and institutional customers. And while images of children imagining their dreams of the future may sell consumer technology, any large employer or community college administrator knows that their workforce viability involves their acquiring the technological skills and workforce discipline needed in an information economy. In short, business demands drive technological innovations and diffusions into consumer realms in ways we often do not appreciate. Today's technologies may reflect a growing importance of consumer markets in electronics, cultural-aesthetic goods, and personal appliances, but these are recent trends in industries and corporations that have traditionally focused on producer goods and business services. We might consider how the celebration of technology reflects these business imperatives.

The March of Civilization

Often associated with the human development that material accumulation enables is the idea that technology promotes the march of civilization. To be sure, like 'QOL,' the meaning and symbols of 'civilization' are vigorously debated in scholarly circles. For those of a materialist bent, civilization involves the establishment of particular social institutions, the number and kind of which are further subject to considerable debate among archaeologists. V. Gordon Childe (1925) identified ten features of civilizations: cities; full-time specialization of labor; social concentration of surplus management into 'capital'; the unequal distribution of the surplus and the emergence of a 'ruling class'; state organization based on residence rather than kinship; growth of long-distance trade in luxuries and necessities; monumental buildings; a standardized, naturalistic artistic style; writing; and mathematics and science. More minimally, A. Colin Renfrew (1972) emphasized three essential social institutions: ceremonial centers, writing, and the city. Many indicators of civilization have sparked scholarly controversy; for instance, writing never emerged among the "civilized" Incas of Peru, but it did appear in rudimentary form in "uncivilized" prehistoric southeastern Europe (Mann 1986:73). Still, whatever the array and number of features, they are thought to promote the physical settlement and social containment of human beings to symbolic and territorial boundaries that constitute civilization.

This process most likely began around 10,000 BC with the discovery of agriculture (Moore 1982; Farb 1978:108–22). Agricultural practices like planting crops, domesticating animals, plowing soil, and (lastly, in Mesopotamia circa 3000 BC) irrigating ditches discouraged the nomadic wanderings of hunter-gatherer societies and introduced permanent human settlements, not so much because they reduced work (more on this topic later) but because they exemplified "labor investment systems" that required cooperative labor only to generate "delayed returns" (Woodburn 1981, 1980; cited in Mann 1986:44). Skipping through human history to Europe's "Dark Ages" (500–800 AD), the development and diffusion in Europe of the water mill, the heavy plow, the three-field system, and the horseshoe created the most productive agricultural system the world had known to that point (see Cipolla 1976:159–60; White 1963:277). These feudal technologies, along with the feudal village and manors that simultaneously coalesced to organize the necessary labor, yielded an intensive productivity that eventually eclipsed the more extensively oriented technologies of other civilizations in their ability to promote human flourishing (Mann 1986:404).

Perhaps this is too esoteric a definition of 'civilization' if it locates a crucial technological milestone in Europe's Dark Ages! For many, civilization refers to the flourishing of arts, sciences, cultural refinements, and human enlightenment more generally—developments emphasized by a humanistic understanding of civilization. Yet inquiring into technology's role in the progress of arts and sciences returns us again to material questions of surplus accumulation and division of labor. Although civilization in this sense is embodied and passed on through the generations in the form of ideas and cultural artifacts, the latter are produced by people with the economic means to undertake such activities. This means can materialize in the form of a widely enjoyed productivity dividend—recall from Chapter 1 the cultural "abundance" of California's indigenous Chumash population—but also the activities of specialists. If developed economies today revolve around science and creativity and turn out an increasing number of occupations in these areas, these are again fairly recent achievements characteristic of a post-industrial society (see Florida 2002; Bell 1999). They beg the question of how societies could sustain the arts and sciences before the post-industrial era, when such activities had not yet become gainful employments. As sociologist David Riesman (1964) explains, the 'work' of civilization was the province of "tiny leisure classes of the past": aristocrats, clerics, and others who were occupationally exempt from menial labor and therefore "exercised their leisure on behalf of the whole society" (p. 168). The extraction and casting of metals, the deep plow, the Industrial Revolution—all are responsible for enhancing the productivity of economic activities and thus sustaining the livelihoods of thinkers, artists, and scientists via the largess of wealthy patrons and social institutions (religious, academic, etc.) who support them.

Producing Society's QOL

Such accounts of technology's capacities—to facilitate the accumulation of material surplus, to increase the productivity of economic activities, to support a division of labor, to develop the material basis for civilization, and to support a cadre of intelligentsia that advance the arts and sciences—illustrate a *collective perspective on QOL* by assigning the benefits of technoeconomic development to the whole of society. In this perspective, an economy or civilization, for instance, 'properly' belong to a whole society. Scholars might correspond this collective framework to something along the lines of what Karl Marx called the social mode of production, in which economies and their technological forces of production draw workers and owners, but also the unpaid and the unemployed, into coherent systems of production and exchange that are legally and politically delimited to a 'society.' To be sure, some cultural work is needed to transform these material systems into meaningful experiences of identification and allegiance for their participants; political-legal regimes and mass media help circulate ideas of symbolic membership in the "imagined community" of the nation-state (Anderson 1991). On the basis of shared nationality, an Italian peasant might claim the musical sensitivities of Giuseppe Verdi as his own, or an American laborer might proudly recognize the "Yankee ingenuity" of Henry Ford. Today's confusions of nation-state authority and legal jurisprudence in a world of global business do not shake the validity of the collective (i.e., societal) view on technology and economy; they only extend its scale to a global society.

These accounts also share an emphasis on the *production of* QOL. The goods and services that satisfy personal and societal needs, the easing of work's toil, the reduction of hours spent in work, the development of arts and sciences: in a production of QOL perspective, all of these outcomes result from useful transformations of physical, social, and symbolic inputs. Notably, collective and production perspectives on QOL inform crudely determinist views of technology's impacts (Fischer 1994). Yet even those analyses that attend more closely to the ways technology mediates productivity, divisions of labor, and other economic dynamics—here free market advocates like Thomas Friedman (2005) and George Gilder (2000) come to mind—pay little heed to the distributional and differentiating properties of technology.

Technology and Unequal QOL

By contrast, an analysis of how technology might unevenly affect human QOL tends to focus more closely on the social and institutional contexts that mediate and differentiate technology's impacts and meanings. These contexts are innumerable, but classic social theory emphasizes two general ones: class and status hierarchy.

Social Relations of Production

Marx initiated a theoretical tradition of viewing class and class inequality as social relations of production, by which he referred to the ways social groups organize the material basis for economic accumulation, particularly the technology, natural resources, factories, workplaces, and business enterprises we now associate with the world of work. Marx theorized that class inequality began with the first division of mental labor from physical labor, as religious and clan leaders exempted themselves from the toil of daily survival while demanding a share of the material surplus that they had no hand in producing. By the time of medieval feudalism, class structure had expanded to encompass a ruling class composed of religious-ideological and political-military elites who together lived off the surplus produced by laborers; hence the adage, "The priest prays, the knight defends, the peasant works" (quoted in Mann 1986:384). The Industrial Revolution transformed the relations of production and simultaneously calcified them in a new way, as the system of private property stripped workers of their communal assets of daily life and compelled property owners into an accelerating cycle of capital accumulation. This dynamic pertains to what people would today call QOL insofar as it confined man to "a particular, exclusive sphere of activity which is forced upon him and from which he cannot escape," which Marx ([1845] 1972) elaborated in a famously utopian passage from "The German Ideology":

> He is a hunter, a fisherman, a shepherd, or a critical critic, and must remain so if he does not want to lose his means of livelihood; while in communist society, where nobody has one exclusive sphere of activity but each can become accomplished in any branch he wishes, society regulates the general production and thus makes it possible for me to do one thing today and another tomorrow, to hunt in the morning, fish in the afternoon, rear cattle in the evening, criticise after dinner, just as I have a mind, without ever becoming hunter, fisherman, shepherd or critic.
>
> (p. 124)

The subsequent "neomarxian" tradition examined twentieth-century developments that Marx could never imagine: why capitalism's 'contradictory' social relations of production did not lead to revolution; how class structure instead expanded with the twentieth-century growth of the middle class; and most recently how new elements of individual autonomy affect one's place in the class structure. Sidestepping the vast discussion related to the first two questions, I offer a brief comment on the transformation of class inequality in today's information- and technology-intensive economy, where entrenched class structure and traditional exploitation seem to have given way to a more open system of mobility and individual entrepreneurialism.

Today, class inequalities are reproduced in large part through people's abilities to tap the institutions—education, social capital networks, rarefied creative fields, and so on—that mediate access to employers and jobs (Bills 2004; Field 2003). Control and innovation of technology are valuable skills provided by these institutions; people's fluency in technical and aesthetic practice, their ability to 'learn to learn,' and their willingness to flexibly adopt new skills and new roles greatly affect the autonomy and expertise they can exercise in the workplace. Comprising a small, privileged fraction of the global labor force, a cadre of elite, self-programmable workers (Castells 1996) undoubtedly enjoys new opportunities for personal and workplace QOL, as we will see in Chapters 5 and 6. However, their rise does not signal an end to the contradictory nature of capitalist class relations because self-programmable workers—specifically, those in information-intensive sectors like technology, business services, and finance—create the tools and provide the services that let employers monitor, deskill, automate, and restructure workforces elsewhere (Head 2003). An immense global labor force working in factories and service establishments encounters the same industrial experience of exploitation that Marx witnessed 150 years ago, albeit under even more technologically intensive conditions, despite or in fact *because* of the empowerment and class mobility that technology promises in some fields. Paradoxically, the fundamental structural impulse in capitalism—to create and manage technology that permits greater extraction of "surplus value" from labor—simultaneously generates a source of autonomous and highly skilled labor that is nearly impossible to automate (Harvey 1989a:186).

This neomarxian account of the contemporary relations of production is obviously relevant to the question of work-based QOL (described further in

Chapter 5), but here it should be mentioned that self-programmable workers are hardly immune to employment turbulence or techno-stress. It may not merit much sympathy, but producing the economy's command-and-control services and creating the technical, artistic, and intellectual forms that consumers crave are demanding undertakings, particularly when these cannibalize one's own job (as witnessed most recently in trading and publishing industries). In a contemporary economy where it seems one can rarely work enough and stay ahead, we might scrutinize the so-called cultural nature of 'our addictions to technology' so often emphasized in self-help literature. Indeed, why do some people and media celebrate the "early adopters" of technologies? Why do some perversely delight in their obsessive use of PDAs, or as it is sometimes called, "crackberry"? The issue for the neomarxian perspective is not simply whether technology tethers people to the workplace, as undeniable as that experience is for many. Rather, we might question how our apparently private values and ways of life discipline us to shoulder the responsibilities of sustaining the conditions for workplace productivity and capitalist profit.

Status Competition

Still, it strains credulity to attribute the stresses and celebrations of technology wholly to capitalist interest. Technology also serves social needs outside the workplace, including the impulse to seek esteem and distinguish ourselves from one another through *status hierarchies*. As sociologists from Max Weber ([1914] 2005a) to Pierre Bourdieu (1984) have explained, the prestige and honor that individuals receive for their wealth, occupations, education, and ways of life are bestowed by others who acknowledge, and perhaps even envy, their membership in specific status groups. Particularly in consumer-oriented societies, status is displayed and conferred in the spheres of everyday life as people compare themselves to others via the goods and services they acquire (Weber [1914] 2005a:161). Possessions are central to the processes of social comparison in large part because they are easily made visible to others; by contrast, other things people might value—an occupation, a way of holding oneself, the associates one keeps—do not lend themselves to such easy and unambiguous display (Schor 1999:45). However, status display is not confined to the acquisition of status symbols; even the disdain of "superficial materialism" can convey a status distinction from groups people regard as 'unenlightened,' 'low class,' etc. As this suggests, status is a fundamental and almost inescapable component of the meanings people draw from human interaction and social structure; as Weber argues, it remains the ultimate source of group life in an increasingly atomized, impersonal modern world.

In the present technology-obsessed culture, it is not surprising that technologies figure so prominently in people's social comparisons, as illustrated by the 'wow factor' that the latest iPhone or the most luxurious Sub-Zero refrigerator provides. Yet technology's role in sustaining status hierarchies also extends beyond such consumer status symbols. Many seemingly innocent QOL utilities that even the most functional, least flashy technologies facilitate—less toil, more leisure, greater social connection—are motivated by broader dynamics in the competition between status groups. This dynamic begins with the fact that status is a socially scarce resource, less because its symbols cost money than because they are *positional goods*; their value comes from their possessors' ability to monopolize them and prevent others from possessing them, and their satisfactions hinge upon their unequal distribution along a status hierarchy. Notably, economists have observed that earning more income does little to boost people's happiness if the larger distribution of incomes goes unchanged. In this 'relative income hypothesis,' subjective well-being is predicated upon consumption norms that expand alongside incomes; if everyone earns more but in the same proportions relative to each other, then their satisfaction stays the same (Hirsch 1976; Duesenberry 1949). Yet in a society where money can buy access to the most exclusive circles and prestigious possessions, any group's monopoly of positional goods is precarious because eventually others obtain them and enjoy the prestige they confer. Rather than let the egalitarianism of the marketplace dissipate their prestige, status groups usually shift their invidious distinctions onto a different, typically more exclusive set of positional goods. Once again, other groups eventually obtain them, and the cycle continues; in this way, elite habits and tastes filter down the hierarchy of status groups, an age-old dynamic of cultural diffusion (Elias 2000).

In this dynamic, technology is both an instrumental medium in the semiotic back and forth of status competition as well as one of its prevailing status symbols. Writing in 1939, long before talk of globalization and the instantaneous communications of today's 'flat world,' sociologist Norbert Elias (2000; see also Veblen [1899] 1994:48) explained:

> From Western society—as a kind of upper class—Western "civilized" patterns of conduct are today spreading over wide areas outside the West, whether through the settlement of Occidentals or through the assimilation of the upper strata of other nations, just as models of conduct earlier spread within the West itself from this or that upper stratum, from certain courtly or commercial centres . . . . It is not "technology" which is the cause of this change of behaviour; what we call "technology" is itself only *one* of the symbols, one of the last manifestations of that constant foresight imposed by the formation of longer and longer chains of actions and the competition between those bound together by them.
>
> (p. 384)

These dynamics of status competition also charge the status accorded to work and its opposite, leisure. This is the insight of economist Thorstein Veblen, who wrote in 1899 that the rewards of the social surplus are purposefully distributed unevenly throughout modern societies, thanks to the status-maintenance activities of their "leisure classes." For an earlier aristocracy whose honor and prestige revolved around the visible distinctions in appearance, manner, and custom between them and the industrious merchant and working classes beneath them, leisure symbolized the "non-productive consumption of time" that only a class who lived off the labors of others could enjoy (Veblen [1899] 1994:43). The demonstration of leisure, i.e., status display, was an ongoing, even strenuous activity for the leisure classes that originally involved immaterial pursuits, such as scholarship, the arts, and the practice of etiquette and discerning tastes, as well as retaining personal servants. As material goods began to proliferate, the possession of goods, both the finer kinds and in general abundance, becomes the accepted symbol of the leisure class: hence the phenomenon of "conspicuous consumption." Too often Veblen's idea of the leisure class is crudely invoked to connote a ruling class, which appears to weaken the idea's relevance to the present moment in which the upper and professional-creative classes hardly lead leisurely lives, so committed are they to their careers. In Chapter 5, I will examine the academic debates and popular worries about whether people are working more or less. Here, I make note of Veblen's more fundamental insight that there is nothing universal or constant across history and societies to the meanings and values of economic activities: work, productivity, leisure, and technology. These emerge and co-evolve as mutable codes and etiquettes by which one group signals its status dominance over other groups.

Distributing Society's QOL

This review of technology's capacities—to mediate divisions of labor, to enable flexible capitalist organizations and labor reproduction, and to support materially and embody symbolically status distinctions—reflects an emphasis on the *individual attribution of QOL*. This does not mean everyone experiences technology uniquely and idiosyncratically. No, individuals share relations to and experiences of technology with many groups beneath the putative 'whole' of society. Rather, the individual attribution framework highlights the differentiating, stratifying thrust of the contexts in which technology shapes people's understandings, pursuits, and experiences of QOL. Accordingly, technology's embeddedness in structures of social stratification also underscores a *distribution of QOL* framework. Advances in technoeconomic organization may expand a society's wealth and drive the march of civilization, but it is an entirely separate matter whether the whole of 'society' or 'civilization' benefits equally.

These frameworks on QOL reveal the fallacy of historicism made by classical humanists who assign the gains in human enlightenment, artistic expression, and political freedom to a particular historical period. 'History' can be invoked as a useful shorthand for the social, economic, cultural, and environmental milieus in which QOL gains appear, but too frequently a historicist perspective ignores that for most of history, it has been intellectual-artistic elites who have introduced, and ruling classes who have hoarded, the fruits of civilization. The work of Thorstein Veblen and Norbert Elias emphasizes how 'civilization,' like 'leisure,' was traditionally charged with the codes of such status hierarchies. These exclusive origins by no means overdetermine how people think today about ideas like 'technology,' 'civilization,' and 'leisure,' but we should nonetheless be alert to the connotations of social hierarchy in the ongoing evolution of these ideas' meanings.

We arrive at a general axiom in a sociological framework for understanding 'QOL.' As both idea and empirical condition, QOL reveals a duality of social relations: the collective accomplishments of a whole society (particularly as constituted within an macro-economy and the imagined community of national citizens) and simultaneously the differentiated, individualized experiences of its constituent units (particularly as shaped by social hierarchies of class and status). The duality is usefully highlighted by the ways technology is embedded in social structure, but technology is not the only context in which to draw this lesson. Indeed, as we consider yet other contexts for QOL pursuit in this book, we should remember that everyone stands in multiple worlds and takes part in multiple forms of social relations. Potentially any or all of these further diversify the experience of QOL, in some cases reinforcing the effects of other contexts, in other cases exerting a dissimilar or even opposing effect. As we will see later in this book, the multiplicity of social relations constitutes a central organizing feature in contemporary understandings and pursuits of QOL.

However, the duality of social relations is evidently difficult to grasp when thinking about technology's impact on QOL. Often commentators adopt collective and production frameworks that, by their very nature, downplay differences *within* social units in order to emphasize differences *between* them. Such perspectives obscure important aspects of QOL's distribution within the population; not all farms or firms are equally productive, nor all members of a society equally cultured. Yet for technological optimists there are rhetorical points to score with collective attributions, for they imply QOL benefits are shared by all the members of the social unit. "Only a few generations back, the typical national economy produced enough surplus value to support little more than handfuls of writers and artists," science writer Gregg Easterbrook (2003) observes. "Today, the western economies support huge numbers of professors, thinkers, writers, and artists who devote themselves to denouncing the system that gives them their sinecure and ease. And that's progress!" (p. 66). Perhaps surprisingly, technological pessimists also frequently subscribe to the collective and production frameworks; witness the handwringing over "our addiction to technology" (e.g., Kronman 2007:257; Norman 1994; Mander 1991).

The Promise of Technology

Moving from sometimes imperceptible contexts of material accumulation and social stratification, I now take up the two sides of technology's contemporary Janus face—technology's service to humanity, and humanity's servitude to technology—by examining popular concerns in the affluent society. Characteristic of my analysis in this book, I do not use these case studies to take positions on one side or the other on the question of whether technology improves or impairs QOL. Rather, I reframe the intellectual debates and empirical patterns associated with these examples to highlight some central contexts of modern life that frame concerns for and pursuits of QOL.

Consumerism and Technology

"All the mod cons": this British expression touting the availability of modern conveniences pithily conveys the sense that goods and services should make people's lives easier and free up time for the activities they really want to do. This promise of technology informs a prevailing social contract within modern societies, whereby people accept the social changes that technology unleashes in exchange for the conveniences and freedoms that technology provides. Rarely articulated yet widely acknowledged, the social contract explains what people expect technology to do for them; it colors the general and specific understandings of 'utility' for the technologies people imagine, invent, and design. The modern notion of 'productivity' embodies this social contract in a very literal way; a group, organization, or society bases its norms and customs of work, technology, prosperity, and leisure by anticipating so much output for so much work. That technology's promise is grounded in cultural norm and social custom, not a universal pursuit of 'efficiency,' is fancifully illustrated in *The Gods Must Be Crazy*, the internationally popular 1980 film from South Africa. Xixo, a Sho bushman, finds a Coke bottle in the Kalahari desert and, unaware of its original purpose, introduces it to his tribe. As he and others discover uses for it (as a rolling pin, a hand-held weapon, etc.), the equilibrium of social relations and economic activities within the tribe is roiled as people become covetous of the bottle, leading Xixo on a journey to save his society by throwing the cursed object off the edge of the earth. The film illustrates technology's embeddedness in social structure, an objective reality of human behavior that is made meaningful to us through cultural norms explaining how we 'should' organize ourselves—into traditional, particularistic forms of families, communities, or by contrast the modern abstractions of classes, formal organizations, citizens, etc.—and why we should accept these social forms.

From here, it is tempting to recite elegies about traditional ways of lives, in which people supposedly valued immaterial things and did not yet succumb to the desire for the material goods they did not need. In fact, some scholars are skeptical that materialism is uniquely modern, arguing that people have long had acquisitive impulses and been enchanted by the dream of possessing certain material goods (Molotch 2003; Twitchell 1999). Nonetheless, it is clear that by the nineteenth century, as new bureaucratically organized production systems offered popular access to mass-produced goods on a scale never before seen, technology's promise lay behind the rise of today's consumer society as both its mechanism and its symbol. More than a little prodding was needed to make this promise a common sense, however. At the turn of the twentieth century, people needed little inducement to buy foodstuffs (even if they did need some coaching to accept industrially produced meat), and farmers needed little encouragement in wanting to purchase a tractor (even if they generally shared ownership of such expensive goods through farmers' cooperatives; see Cronon 1991). However, the desire to acquire goods (and later services) on par with the expectations of manufacturers was rather muted, first and foremost due to necessity. In the West, the middle classes, the largest market for mass-produced consumer goods, were not as extensive as they later became. They lived mostly in metropolitan regions where department stores and other enticing 'cathedrals of consumption' clustered (Benjamin 1999), leaving rural populations without easy ability to view the latest manufactured goods firsthand (at best, a Sears Roebucks mail-order catalog; see Strasser 1989). Significantly, people had little means to purchase commodities beyond their means, since credit systems beyond a local merchant's goodwill did not exist before the 1920s. With the problem of stimulating consumption—how to make people buy more things at a rate commensurate with the needs of a capitalist economy—acute for manufacturers and vendors of consumer goods in the early twentieth century, the U.S. became a testing ground in the stimulation of consumer spending. By the 1920s, formal credit systems began to appear, ranging from the notorious 'hire-purchase' installment plan aimed at working-class consumers (see Vallance 1939) to the more widespread phenomenon of the credit card. After the Great Depression, Keynesianism made the supply-side stimulation of consumer demand a formal priority of government policy.

Still, even with these extensions of consumption opportunity, getting people to buy more stuff ran up against long-standing cultural restraints, including the traditional disinclination to work too much. Philosopher Joanne Ciulla (2000) notes that as far back as Greece of the eighth or ninth century BC, the "display of material goods produced the positive kind of 'envy and strife' that Hesiod had said drove a person to work. In other words, people work more when there are more things available to buy" (p. 47). By 1924, this insight was recognized by consulting-industry pioneer Arthur D. Little ([1924] 2006): "In a town in central New York, girl operatives receiving war wages found four days' work a week sufficient for their requirements until the company brought in some operatives from New York City, whose Georgette waists and all-silk hose soon inspired the girls to work full time." Yet fashion has long been a foundation for social comparisons, given its immediate visibility and easy attribution to its wearer. Further work would be needed to parlay the human propensity for status display into effective demand for new kinds of goods that would essentially be used out of sight of others, in the private realm of the household. In the U.S., a nascent marketing industry employed new and more extensive modes of advertising in the still-emerging realms of mass culture, exhorting a populace still grasping for common identities and values "to validate the new, the heretofore untried, even the unimagined":

> "Revolutionary new" became a standard slogan and people were urged to be pioneers of sorts by being among the first to have this or that new

> commodity. Appeals to adventurousness and status were complemented by suggestions that some products could also offer independence. A new tractor and its accompanying implements could do the work of many hired hands (or sons) come harvest time. The refrigerator ended the need for daily shopping, thus *freeing* the homemaker. More and more commodities were spoken of as extensions—or better, as projections—of self, a self that was adaptable, innovative, exploratory, and autonomous; a self capable of making intelligent choices unburdened by prejudices and habits inherited from the past.
>
> (Dizard and Gadlin 1990:46)

Thus, marketers and advertisers helped cement the promise of technology and particularly American values of social progress and individual prosperity to the promotion of private goods and services that, in some cases, embodied such ideals quite loosely. This thematic association comprises a pervasive motif in corporate advertising that cultural historian Roland Marchand (1985) calls "the parable of Civilization Redeemed" (p. 223).

Since this early achievement, the marketing industry has turned to the human sciences to advance its understanding of consumer behavior and its powers of human persuasion. Marketers have deployed methods from psychology, anthropology, and (discussed further in Chapter 6) geography to illuminate the most specific of human wants. Perhaps unsurprisingly, marketing researchers have sought to contribute to the sciences in return; of note here is how some have developed a scientific account of human QOL that is hardly out of place alongside welfare economics and modernization theory:

> Based on a QOL philosophy, the firm should not formulate marketing objectives strictly in terms of financial-related criteria such as sales, profit, and/or market share. QOL marketing objectives should be formulated along four key dimensions:
>
> 1. Enhancement of a dimension of consumers' well-being by offering consumers an affordable product that facilitates a healthful focal behavior.
> 2. Reduction in "significant" negative side effects to the consumers associated with the marketing and/or use of the organization's offering.
> 3. Reduction in "significant" negative side effects to publics (other than the consumers) associated with the marketing and/or use of the organization's offering.
> 4. Increases in long-term profitability.
>
> (Sirgy 1996:243)

Social critics might reject scientistic rationales for marketers, advertisers, retailers, and industrialists to create consumer demand where none previously existed, but with this example I call attention to how such scientific rhetoric strips away the historical framework in which the parable of Civilization

Redeemed made such an impact. By recasting its historically situated, culturally relativistic undertakings into a universalistic account of human behavior, marketing 'science' encourages in its beholders an amnesia regarding the social contexts in which it originated.

Gender and the Paradox of Domestic Technology

Marketing innovations in advertising reach and rhetorical persuasion notwithstanding, consumerism has found fertile ground in many societies because its outlooks and expressions mesh almost seamlessly with human concerns and social interactions, most notably in the dynamics of status competition. In the twentieth century, status competition informed two further contexts that further shaped the meaning and promise of technology. The first was the massive suburbanization of population and spatial development that began in the middle of the century (see Jackson 1985). New suburban residences promised the middle classes 'safe,' 'wholesome' communities and brand-new houses that needed stocking with consumer goods; both were appealing sources of status distinction in modern societies straining against their nineteenth-century urban environments. Tellingly, market penetration of new appliances and consumer durables generally followed the waves of suburbanization that reshaped the geography of Western nations, as illustrated in Table 3.1, which reports the diffusion rates of key household appliances in the U.S. and UK. The U.S. postwar burst of suburbanization is revealed in the typically high ranks assigned to the penetration of appliances that appeared between 1948 and 1961 (see also Thistle 2006), while the lagged penetration of those same products indicates the period of economic recovery in the UK (and by suggestion throughout Europe). Suburbanization drew upon, and in turn further fueled, the great production and redistribution of wealth in the twentieth century that expanded the ranks of the middle classes in developed nations. The thrusts of public policy, class mobility, regional settlement, and corporate activity coincided to make the new middle classes an overwhelmingly *suburban* middle class, and subsequently "mod cons" became associated in popular consciousness with the demand for new housing and the larger spaces for private household consumption it afforded.

Gender relations within the household are the second context in which the promise of domestic technology unfolded, as men and women's roles altered significantly over the twentieth century, albeit within the enduring framework of male privilege. Domestic responsibilities have long been the obligation, generally unsolicited, of women, yet the housewife who stays home full time in the single-(male)-breadwinner household has never been as common as the 1950s "Ozzie and Harriet" image suggests. For working-class white women and women of color in the nineteenth and early twentieth centuries, the norm was more often formal employment in often unsafe or exploitative workplaces such as factories, offices, and other people's homes (Thistle 2006). However, the symbolism of the housewife arrangement was crucial to the diffusion of

Table 3.1 Diffusion Rate of Selected Household Appliances in the U.S. and Britain

Appliance	*Country*	*Household penetration begins (1%)*[a]	*Additional years to penetration (% households with appliance)*			*Rank*[b]
			of 20%	*of 50%*	*of 75%*	
TV black & white	USA	1948	2	5	7	1
Radio	USA	1923	3	6	8	2
TV color	USA	1961	6	6	10	3
TV black & white	E&W	1949	5	9	12	4
TV color	E&W	1970	4	8	13	5
Video recorder	UK	1979	5	9	15	6
CD player	UK	1984	6	11	16	7
Microwave oven	USA	1973	9	13	17	8
Radio	UK	1923	3	10	20	9
Freezer	E&W	1968	9	14	20	10
Refrigerator	USA	1925	7	13	23	11
Microwave oven	UK	1973		18	25	12
Refrigerator	E&W	1946	15	22	27	13
Electric iron	E&W	1909		24	30	14
Electric iron	USA	1910			34	15
Clothes washer	USA	1916	6	20	34	16
Clothes washer	E&W	1934	23	30	46	17
Vacuum cleaner	E&W	1915	18	40	47	18
Vacuum cleaner	USA	1913		28	48	19
Motor car	USA	1908		16	52	20
Telephone	USA	1890		56	67	21
Motor car	GB	1908	46	57	94	22
Video recorder	USA	1979	7	9		1
Can opener	USA	1959	5	14		2
Electric blanket	E&W	1955	6	18		3
Personal computer	UK	1981	9	20		4
Personal computer	USA	1981		20		5
Clothes dryer	USA	1950	11	22		6
Electric blanket	USA	1948	11	22		7
Air conditioner	USA	1952	12	22		8
Blender	USA	1948	19	22		9
Water heater	E&W	1934	21	33		10
Dish washer	USA	1922	46	75		11
Clothes dryer	E&W	1950	31	44		13
Dish washer	E&W	1957	39			

Source: Offer (2006:174).

Notes

a Electrically wired households, unless indicated otherwise below. The early years of innovation, during which the design tended to be unstable, were usually prolonged, so the first year is taken to be the one in which household penetration achieved 1%.

b Ranking is estimated on the basis of (1) length of time taken to achieve 75% penetration level; (2) length of time taken to achieve 50% penetration level; and (3) length of time taken to achieve penetration level, in that order. An appliance which has reached 75% penetration thus ranks higher than an appliance which has failed to reach 75% or 50% and in some cases 20% penetration levels. For appliances introduced before the First World War, the year of introduction is taken to be the year of first commercial product, with five years added.

domestic technologies. Its cultural ascendancy coincided with the heyday of the Western welfare state, whereby economic prosperity translated into higher earnings for a new middle class and let more married households keep wives in the home. In suburbia, this arrangement became emblematic; the strict demarcation of private and public spheres contrasted with their prior blurring on farms and in cities—two settings where most women typically dedicated at least some of their labor in the goods and labor markets of the public sphere. Notably, the move of women into an exclusively private sphere was endorsed not only by the men who would benefit from their household labor but by Progressive reformers like settlement house activist Jane Addams as well (Ladd-Taylor 1994).

As the housewife was idealized as 'manager' of the suburban home, women were increasingly pitched the promise that domestic appliances would ease the burden of menial and time-consuming tasks like cooking and washing clothes (Shapiro 2004). So insistent was this refrain that, over the last 30 years, scholars have puzzled over whether domestic technologies ever actually reduced women's domestic labor. "Cottage industry is alive and well and living in suburbia," historian Ruth Cowan (1979) argued:

> Several million American women cook supper each night in several million separate homes over several million separate stoves—a specter which should be sufficient to drive any rational technocrat into the loony bin . . . . Out there in the land of household work there are small industrial plants which sit idle for the better part of every working day; there are expensive pieces of highly mechanized equipment which only get used once or twice a month; there are consumption units which weekly trundle out to their markets to buy 8 ounces of this nonperishable product and 12 ounces of that one.
>
> (pp. 59–60)

Many contend that, in terms of labor hours, women's unpaid housework remained *constant* across the twentieth century when the promise of technology suggested such work would have declined (e.g., Bittman, Rice, and Wajcman 2004). For one reason, the introduction of modern domestic appliances encouraged households to raise their standards and expectations of homemaking (Cowan 1979; Vanek 1974). Consequently, domestic tasks grew in number and kind faster even as time spent on each task dropped, leading to the apparent paradox of labor-saving domestic technologies actually sustaining women's workload within their inefficient domestic 'factory' (Edwards and Wajcman 2005).

Other scholars have inquired more skeptically into this paradox of labor-saving domestic technology, urging that we clarify whom we mean by 'women' and untangle them by socioeconomic status. Doing so reveals two countervailing trends that, over the course of a very dynamic period of technological innovation and productivity gains, give the appearance of no shift in women's domestic work hours. A factor *increasing* women's unpaid household work over the course of the twentieth century was the decline of middle-class employment of domestic servants, which subsequently required middle-class women do more unpaid work simply to maintain the same standards of household maintenance. Simultaneously, the diffusion of labor-saving household technologies *decreased* women's unpaid household work, especially relieving working-class women (for whom hiring domestic servants was rarely an option) of unpaid work in the house (Gershuny 2000:66–7, 198–9). Net of women's restriction to the home, then, domestic technology's promise seems to have materialized after all.

Still, as women entered the workforce in growing numbers through the second half of the twentieth century, gender inequities continued to absorb many of the genuine labor-saving effects of domestic technologies. In the next chapter I will elaborate on two reasons: first, although men have taken up more housework, they have resisted doing the amount needed to offset the hours women spend at the workplace; second, women have increased the time they spend on childcare—and men have too, albeit at a significant lag. But beyond these gains and losses in hours spent working, the activities and meanings of housework have shifted as well. Setting aside time spent on direct care for family members, household cleaning accounts for almost all of the time that women have saved on domestic work. "Women's time devoted to cooking remains generally unchanged," finds economist Jonathan Gershuny (2000), who interprets this pattern (following Mattingly and Bianchi 2003; Hochschild 1997, 1989; Berk 1985) as an adaptation of gender ideologies to technological change:

> The household is where we 'manufacture' our identity. The traditional female ideology of creative care and nurturing is best expressed through cooking. House cleaning is mere maintenance, and the better it is accomplished, the less overt and noticeable it becomes. Cooking, however, is an expressive activity . . . . Clearly, women who wish to spend less time in domestic tasks, but still maintain their traditional creatively nurturing role *as* women, and indeed men who seek a new creatively nurturing role as men, will dump the housework, and cook.
>
> (p. 190)

In many middle-class households, the cooking ideals and the broader utilities of domestic technology have moved from a post-World War II rejection of homemade foods to a *fin de siècle* embrace of Martha Stewart-style domesticity (Shapiro 2004).

The debate over the paradox of domestic technology remains alive in large part because values and behavior regarding family and work continue to evolve—topics I address in the next two chapters. But by now we can expect that additional data might fail to resolve this debate so long as we view it solely through a productivity lens. Easing work's toil was never the only value motivating the production, advertisement, and consumption of "mod cons." In the last century, the promise that technology would enhance QOL became tied up in middle-class status display within the contexts of social-geographic mobility and the enduring force of patriarchal norms. Thorstein Veblen ([1899] 1994) viewed the original housewife, the noble lady of the house, as the symbol with which men of the leisure class demonstrated their economic dominance over the industrious classes: "This process of progressive exemption from the common run of industrial employment will commonly begin with the exemption of the wife, or the chief wife" (p. 54). Veblen highlights the status dynamics motivating this so-called traditional household form—dynamics which persist today even as women enter the labor force to pursue undervalued and underpaid work.

Technology vs. Simplicity

In contrast to the promise of technology, recent critiques of the materialistic treadmill of work and consumerism offer seemingly antithetical views of technology's impact upon human QOL. Advocates for "simple living" or "voluntary simplicity" emphasize the element of human choice that has been lost in the unthinking embrace of technology. A rethinking of technology's productivity dividend suggests paths rarely taken in consumer societies; money earned at work could be exchanged back for leisure time, as could technological convenience for the meaningfulness of labor undertaken willingly:

> Today people grow their own vegetables and bake their own bread, even though they can buy them in a store. Despite claims to the contrary, the home-baked bread and homegrown vegetable may not be superior in quality to the ones that people buy, but the very process of making and growing makes eating them more enjoyable. Some types of productive activities give satisfaction even though they are not necessary—or especially because they are not necessary.
>
> (Ciulla 2000:15)

Simple living offers a different vision of freedom than the emancipation from toil and traditional customs with which mod cons were originally sold to us. It recasts the promise of technology as a treadmill of work and consumption, while promising an enhanced QOL in freedom from the entanglements and addiction of modern technology itself.

Voluntary Simplicity

Interest in voluntary simplicity has grown along several fronts since at least the 1960s, when social criticisms of the affluent society's human alienation and environmental costs gave rise to a "back to the earth" movement embodied in numerous rural communes. While most of those disappeared, the ethos of voluntary simplicity saw continuing elaboration in landmark publications like economist E.F. Schumacher's (1973) *Small is Beautiful: A Study of Economics As If People Mattered*, Ernest Callenbach's work of (social) science fiction, *Ecotopia* (1975), and Duane Elgin's (1981) *Voluntary Simplicity: Toward a Way of Life that is Outwardly Simple, Inwardly Rich*. These works also resonated with concerns for social justice under the proposition that voluntary simplicity would free up material resources that developed societies currently devote to their materialism—famously expressed in the credo, "Live simply so others may simply live." Today, environmentalism and a renewed awareness of traditional modes of thrift and prudence (like small-scale farms and, in the U.S., rural Amish and Shaker communities) fuel continuing interest in voluntary simplicity. Within academia and other venues, such as "alternative" periodicals like the Utne Reader, movement intellectuals have put forth a variety of principles and policies. "We should be articulating an alternative vision of a quality of life, rather than a quantity of stuff," contends economist Juliet Schor (2003). "That is a basis on which to argue for a restructuring of the labor market to allow people to choose for time, or to penalize companies that require excessive hours for employees. It is also a basis for creating alternative indicators to the GNP, positive policies to encourage civic engagement, support for parents, and so forth" (p. 80). Consumption taxes have been proposed as means to restrain discretionary spending on non-essential status symbols (e.g., Frank 2003; Galbraith [1958] 1998), while others have emphasized the benefits of shortened work hours and legally protected vacations (Robinson 2003; De Graaf 2003).

Meanwhile, a growing number of people in Western nations have explored and adopted lifestyles of voluntary simplicity. Estimates for the number of simple livers are difficult to come by, but sociologist Amitai Etzioni (2003) identifies three categories of voluntary simplicity adherents. In order of declining magnitude, first, affluent *downshifters* voluntarily give up some material goods, often what others would consider luxuries, as well as consumer habits of perennially buying the 'new and improved' (see also Schor 1999). The most moderate form of voluntary simplicity, downshifting allows participants to maintain an otherwise rich and consumption-oriented lifestyle. It overlaps strongly with popular interests in green products, organic and local foods, and handicraft production (doing one's own knitting, baking, etc.), all of which usually cost more than their mass-produced, mass-distributed counterparts. Although there are interactive, participatory components to the downshifter trend (e.g., bloggers and weekly meetings for "green moms"; see Brown 2008), this group is well supported by the goods and services of a burgeoning voluntary simplicity industry. Innumerable books, magazines, websites, newsletters, workshops, and consultants (or "coaches") offer methods for simplifying clutter, schedules, diets, and homes. A new breed of advertisers, retailers, and 'lifestyle personalities' like MaryJane Butters ("an organic farmer AND the editor of a women's magazine," her website announces) sell products that promote simple living's virtues (reducing household waste, restoring used furniture, etc.) and rewards (knitting circles, etc.). Even venerable enterprises like

North America's *Organic Gardening Magazine*, originally a sober and practical source on agricultural education, have redesigned and branched out to reach a more affluent and less thrifty demographic (in this case, with the failed *Organic Style* magazine [Sloane 2005]).

In the second group of voluntary simplicity adherents, *strong simplifiers* go beyond downshifting and further adopt a strategy of income simplicity: forgoing high-paying, high-status and high-stress jobs; taking early retirement; opting for part-time work; or switching into more personally meaningful if less lucrative jobs. Often strong simplifiers are motivated by dramatic lifestyle decisions—to drop out of the rat race, devote more time to family, and so on—but in many cases these decisions are not fully undertaken by choice. Job loss, home foreclosure, health crisis, a sudden need to care extensively for family members: such unforeseen events can impose the strong simplifier lifestyle as a necessity. They may embrace the philosophies and moral imperatives associated with the history of voluntary simplicity, but characteristically they simplify their income within their pre-existing communities, social networks, and value systems. Such practicality distinguishes strong simplifiers from the third group, "the most dedicated, holistic simplifiers" (Etzioni 2003:11): members of the *simple living movement*. In addition to downshifting and income simplifying, this group joins social networks that support the ethics and infrastructure for a highly principled commitment to voluntary simplicity. Dedicated simple livers may move to smaller or less urbanized communities, live in co-housing arrangements, or jointly own automobiles and other expensive necessities. Perhaps characteristically, movement members take part in "simplicity circles" and other group forums where they exchange practical solutions, share personal frustrations and hardships, and otherwise raise their mutual consciousness about the moral principles, congruent livelihoods (including not working at all), and holistic lifestyles for simple living (Grigsby 2004; Andrews 1997).

In her study of a Midwestern simple-living community, ethnographer Karen Grigsby (2004) argues that adherents to the movement

> are trying to remake the symbolic meanings that construct class/status in such a way that modernist conceptions of desired levels and modes of consumption, wealth, and personal control over the earth's material resources are reevaluated and do not carry the same positive meanings.
>
> (p. 64)

Of course this is true, in different ways and to different degrees, across the three categories of voluntary simplicity groups, all of which share a critique of consumer society's trajectory and a philosophical-behavioral exploration of individual and collective QOL pursuits. Unsurprisingly, the movement has generated countercriticism, particularly within the U.S. Most crudely it has been called 'anti-modern' or 'anti-technology.' The labels sting, mocking adherents' disdain for the promise of technology and their frequent celebration of non-Western philosophies and centuries-old practices of craftsmanship (often derided as "New Age"). Yet designating simple livers as anti-modern is misleading insofar as the movement exists only in a context that techno-economic development has made possible. Consistent with the post-World War II affluent society critique, the voluntary simplicity movement challenges the adequacy of modern society's ideals of 'prosperity' and 'freedom' in a world where the uncritical realization of those ideas has become the problem. Thus the movement embodies the skeptical, emancipative gaze that originally informed modernity's rational ethos, only now it turns that gaze on the contexts of modernity itself, such as science, technology, and material accumulation, in a characteristic example of what social theorist Ulrich Beck (1992) calls "reflexive modernization" (see also Chapter 7). Indeed, with its many references to 'QOL' as the measure of today's affluenza and the promise of simple living, voluntary simplicity perhaps most clearly exemplifies a movement to advocate QOL.

Simplicity as Status Distinction

Another countercriticism observes that simple livers do not depart all that much from the harried, materialistic way of life they challenge. Clearly there is wide variation in the philosophies and strategies of voluntary simplicity, and so this claim overgeneralizes a description perhaps most applicable to affluent downshifters. The paradox of a voluntary simplicity industry supports the charge—one shared, it should be noted, by many hardcore simple livers—that affluent downshifting simply represents another consumer niche within our cornucopian market society:

> Eating locally raised food is a growing trend. But who has time to get to the farmer's market, let alone plant a garden?
>
> That is where Trevor Paque comes in. For a fee, Mr. Paque, who lives in San Francisco, will build an organic garden in your backyard, weed it weekly and even harvest the bounty, gently placing a box of vegetables on the back porch when he leaves.
>
> Call them the lazy locavores—city dwellers who insist on eating food grown close to home but have no inclination to get their hands dirty.
>
> (Severson 2008)

For American editorialist and satirist David Brooks (2004, 2000), voluntary simplicity is another manifestation—alongside communitarianism, slow growth urban planning, the fight against corporate chains, and the derision of all things 'red state'—of the elitist liberal sensibility that he calls "bourgeois bohemian" or "Bobo" for short. As with the satirical thrust of his oxymoronic designation, his concern is for the dissonance between movement ethos and participants' behavior. Although the movement castigates the keeping-up-with-the-Jones mentality that fuels the consumption of bigger, better, and more stuff, voluntary simplicity advocates—or, in another of Brooks' pointed expressions, the "Liberal Gentry"—are still motivated by the dynamics of status competition:

> The Liberal Gentry are trying to elevate themselves not above those who are economically inferior, but rather above those who are equally rich but morally and aesthetically inferior. When you get to the tippy-top of the status stratosphere, you reach an area in which the only way to go higher still is to go down. This is what is called "status inversion."
>
> (Brooks 2003:177)

Brooks's sharp if rather broad swipe involves two specific charges. The first contends that voluntary simplicity's adherents come from the affluent, educated population that has reached the highest tier of the status ladder. Grigsby's research on simple livers complicates this picture somewhat. On the one hand, she finds that the movement's core is composed primarily of members of a middle class that is particularly vulnerable to the economy's job restructuring and increasing work hours. In this way, dedicated simple livers are rationally taking matters into their own hands to reduce their vulnerability to the economy's downturns; if their seats on the frontlines of middle-class risk separate them from more well-to-do downshifters, their ascetic response to material insecurity nonetheless seems to point in the opposite direction from aspirations of affluence. On the other hand, the simple livers Grigsby (2004) studied acknowledged their high levels of education and experience with material well-being, which gives them an "experiential superiority" (p. 64) over the poor and materially insecure, who (simple livers maintain) still misguidedly "believe that if they can attain affluence they will be happy" (p. 59).

Brooks' second charge is that for a movement seeking to challenge mainstream norms of conspicuous consumption, voluntary simplicity is hypocritically driven by a mainstream process of status competition—a positional consumption of anti-consumerism, if you will. This claim makes many movement participants uneasy, but it is less problematic for social theorists who observe that status competition is a common dynamic of social movements. It solves the age-old problem of "collective action": if a movement's achievements will be widely shared upon success and do not include special rewards for its participants' efforts, then what prevents anyone from simply free-riding on others' efforts and enjoying the diffuse rewards of social change (Olson 1965)? For movements, the solution lies in the immaterial rewards that participants receive in the very act of taking part: the sense of urgency, calling, and superiority that comes from the collective identity of movement affiliation and group affinity (Saunders 2008; Eyerman and Jamison 1991; Melucci 1989). As Amitai Etzioni (2003) explains, what critics see as hypocrisy is in fact a necessary function of the movement, whether adherents recognize this or not:

> In such a culture if people *choose* a job or career pattern that is not income-maximizing, they have no established means of signaling that they have

> *chosen* such a course rather than having been forced into it, and thus they have not failed by the norms of capitalist society. There are no lapel pins stating "I could have, but preferred not to." *Voluntary simplicity responds to this need for status recognition by creating the option of choosing lower-cost but visible consumer goods that enable one to signal that one has chosen, rather than been coerced into, a less affluent lifestyle.* This is achieved by using select consumer goods that are clearly associated with a simpler life pattern, are as visible as the traditional status symbols, and often cannot be afforded by those who consume less simply because of low income. For instance, those who dress down as part of their voluntary simplicity often wear some expensive items (a costly blazer with jeans and sneakers), as if to broadcast their voluntary choice of this lifestyle. (Which specific consumption items signal voluntary simplicity versus coerced simplicity changes over time and from one subculture to another.) In this way, voluntary simplifiers can satisfy the higher need of gaining the esteem of others, without using a high—and ever escalating—level of consumption.
>
> (p. 18; emphasis in original)

If the voluntary simplicity movement deploys status competition and positional consumption to delegitimize the entangling materialism of consumer society, from another perspective it does not transcend consumerism at all. This view rests upon the more expansive understanding of *consumer society* that social theorist Zygmunt Bauman (2007a, 1998) offers: a society that enshrines the experience of individual choice. As Bauman argues, a consumer society not only promotes the proliferation of goods and services; more essentially, *it organizes lifestyles and identities around the practice of choice*—of any set of items in the marketplace that people choose, including none at all, so long as they demonstrate their ability to choose. In such a society, 'poverty' is signaled not by lack of income, but rather lack of choice. Choice, in short, is the dominant positional good in contemporary society, and one in which simple livers traffic as well with the emphasis they place on lifestyle *decisions* and *voluntary* simplicity. Furthermore, by constituting their lifestyles and identities through the practice and products of their choices, simple livers exercise an aesthetic sensibility—not necessarily preferences for homemade bread or restored furniture, although those may appeal to many, but the cultivation of tastes for what is (ecologically) superior and (simply) beautiful. It is quite possible that the discussions and debates in simplicity circles over which goods or services best reflect the principles of voluntary simplicity stoke the enchantment of consumerism as effectively (if more sustainably) as any advertisement or shopping binge.

None of this, of course, precludes the broader voluntary simplicity movement from calling attention to society's ecological footprint, role-modeling more thoughtful and satisfying ways to live, or attaining a genuine contentment that eluded them in the mainstream culture of affluenza. And perhaps simple livers' participation in the same individualistic outlook and social comparison that frame the consumer experience of modern society is to be expected. With no substantial support from political debate or government policy, movement adherents must necessarily practice simplicity through individual action in the private sector, even if this risks recasting the movement into just another market served by a hyper-consumerist economy.

Conclusion

At the end of this chapter, technology retains its Janus face, both freeing humanity and entangling us in a web of inescapable dependence. The experience of this duality provokes great anxiety and resistance, increasingly articulated under the banner of 'QOL,' but it is hardly novel in human history. Only half a century earlier, the Janus face of technology was a central theme in the affluent society critique. Critics such as Lewis Mumford (1934) and Herbert Marcuse ([1941] 1998) recognized that affluence and its historical opportunities were only possible through modern technology. While they admired its liberating potentials, they also expressed alarm at the complexity and opacity by which technology had developed under rational industrialism, mass consumerism, and global militarism. Technology, they contended, has ensnared humanity in the 'necessity' of its technical logics and physical proliferation, even as people cling to long-held hopes that it emancipates human life. In some respects, their critique has been only modestly revised in contemporary polemics about affluenza and advocacy of voluntary simplicity; indeed, many critics of technology acknowledge a clear line of descent from the affluent society critique to their arguments. However, an emphasis on technology alone—and, of course, the affluent society critique was much more than that—seduces us with a facile, deterministic approach that ignores the social contexts mediating technology's development and impacts. Technology is embedded within social relations; it cannot simply be withdrawn from by individual refusals to 'use' it.

Fallacies of the determinist perspective, both optimistic and pessimistic, on technology and its relationship to QOL highlight the contours of what I call today's dominant QOL outlook. I will elaborate this outlook in the coming chapters, but it is worth noting in this chapter how, at the dawn of a new millennium, technology is deeply embedded in the physical, organizational, and cultural structures of a society that directs technoeconomic development to proliferate and multiply individual choice across the board—in goods, services, occupations, cultural identifications, social experiences, and personal lifestyles. Despite the affluent society's warning against the seductions of technological expedience and material consumerism, capital has only further reorganized the industrial foundations for optimal consumer gratification (through the globalization of production and the disciplining of global labor) and advanced the desocialization and commodification of economic transactions across the board. Increasingly, as people labor with each other impermanently and find themselves unable to reform the structural conditions of work (see Chapter 5), the sphere of consumption—of material sustenance, yes, but also of daily life, lifestyle, and identity—moves to the foreground of daily experience as the privileged realm of meaning and authenticity. Sociologists and historians remind us that the sphere of consumption has not always enshrined individual choice as the *sine qua non* of meaning and authenticity. In traditional status groups, the 'choice' of what to consume is collectively determined and in this sense unfreely chosen by their members; affluent society critiques of the conformist world of suburban mod cons and stay-at-home mothers remind us of the collective impulse motivating so many status strivers in the post-World War II era. At the present, however, capitalism seems to have established individual choice in the sphere of consumption as the normative experience, and if technology is hardly the sole culprit, it has been a handmaiden to this achievement, both as medium and symbol.

Too often, today's movements advocating disentanglement from technology and materialism fail to transcend the ideological horizons of the market society they decry. Granted, some voluntary simplicity advocates have proposed reforms that would collectively restrain individual choice (e.g., consumption taxes to discourage discretionary, status-maintaining spending) and call into question the prevailing social contract of technology (e.g., laws mandating paid vacation to return technology's productivity dividend to its true contributors). Yet technology is also 'resisted' through lifestyle-based activities that, despite the best intentions, are actually quite compatible with the thrust of consumer society. Specifically, the emphasis on lifestyle and value shift privileges the realm of consumption as the realm of human agency; it too often neglects the economic relations of production where shared fates are rarely elective. Even criticisms of workplaces that tether people with the demand that they be on call 24 hours a day are typically cast in the rhetoric of private life, urging change in 'values' and 'our culture' rather than demand change to the collective terms of work. (As Chapter 5 will show, even today's solo "free agent" experience of work was a coordinated accomplishment.) In these ways, the refusal these movements advocate, although hardly bought and sold in conventional markets, nevertheless support the market's hegemony as the experiential framework for contemporary life.

Nonetheless, other contexts also highlight the individual framework that characterizes the dominant QOL outlook. To that end, I now turn to a social unit whose 'crisis' today is paradoxically couched in terms of its collective integrity: the family.

4 Family

> ... and who is society? There is no such thing! There are individual men and women, and there are families [...].
>
> (Margaret Thatcher 1987)

The list and sequence of events vary, but parents may recognize the feel of the long sprint in this typical day. The alarm clock rings, and mother or father begins preparing breakfast before rousing children from their beds. Perhaps the other parent is in the shower by this time; single parents have taken theirs earlier, maybe the night before. With a constant eye to the clock, parents pick clothes and put them on children, brush their teeth, and assemble lunches and school materials. A TV or radio provides the soundtrack to the frantic ritual, distracting kids and parents alike. Is there a dog or cat that hasn't been fed yet? Mother and father review the schedule of afterschool activities, jot down a grocery list, at which point one of them (usually the father, data show) leaves for work. For the other parent, quick: get the kids in the car, on their bikes, or out the door to await the school bus or walk to school. Are they gone? Take a breath—then pick up in the children's wake, jump in the shower, get dressed and into the car/bus/subway for work. During the commute, more mental notes are taken (does laundry need to be done? how can the little one be fooled into eating her spinach?); with a mobile phone, domestic multitasking might be done, such as scheduling appointments for doctors/teacher meetings/playgroups. At the workplace, the frantic pace of the morning abates, but as parents pick up and even enjoy the flow of work, the home life interrupts with calls from kids ("Can we give my friend a ride home from football practice?") and e-mails from spouses ("I'm running late; can you pick up the kids/take-out dinner?"). By the early afternoon, one of the parents (generally the mother, evidence suggests) is pulled out of work and back into active family service. Serving as family chauffeur, the parent picks the kids up from school and takes them to music lessons/sports practice/playgroup/a shopping run. If another child is in tow, they play sedentarily or start some homework until the first child's activities has ended. For the umpteenth time, the clock is consulted. Done? Get the kids back in the car/bus/subway and home for dinner, which might be already prepped for a quick cook or brought home in the form of take-out dinner. Their partner has yet to return, so the parent serves the children dinner and joins them for an unleisurely bite. ("You want chicken nuggets instead?") Dinner is over, and children are urged and cajoled to do their homework or take a bath. The table is cleared, but the food is still out; the partner comes home, and the adults gulp down dinner while keeping a distracted eye on the kids. ("Get off the Internet and do your homework!") Dishes are cleared, other housework done, and babies put to sleep; a co-worker phones to review tomorrow's presentation or request a shift-swap. Meanwhile, older children do their homework, watch television, scan the Internet, and text their school friends, often simultaneously. Noshing on leftovers, parents attend to work matters—replying to e-mails, reviewing reports, ironing work shirts—then retreat to the bedroom to debrief each other on the day's events and sort laundry, watch TV, or flip through a magazine. Finally they succumb to exhaustion, only to wake the next day too soon and start the long sprint over again.

If today's parents sense there are simply not enough hours in the day to do all they need to do, they may be right. Extensive research documents the strain of *work–life balance*, the consequences of which for a family's collective QOL are many. Family time together is scarce and weighed down by tasks and necessities; love and affection are filtered through the commitments and expectations of work, school, and afterschool activities. For mothers, especially in the U.S., this burden is exacerbated by social pressures to embrace a style of *intensive parenting* (Hays 1996) symbolized by badges of honor like "soccer mom" and "minivan mom":

> The new definition of good motherhood was, in the popular imagination, the state of being "almost always on-duty." Yet the duties of parenthood had now reached epic proportions. It wasn't enough, if you were "at home" or working part-time, to be there to pick your kids up at school if you wanted to clock in virtuous mommy hours. You had to do homework with your children, bake for their bake sales, and volunteer in their schools. You had to give quality *and* quantity time—and, if you wanted, at the same time, to set your child on the path to a productive future, you had to model productive behavior, and keep yourself in a state of constant busyness. Your love for your child was judged not just by the amount of time you spent with him or her but by the amount of time you spent *doing for* him or her.
>
> (Warner 2005:116)

To meet these expanding familial demands on time, energy, and money, today's mothers and fathers modify their parenting behavior in remarkable ways. Many organize their households into split-shift or "tag-team" families, where at least one parent works a non-day shift so that both can attend to children while bringing home two incomes. In the U.S., this group includes over one-quarter

(27.8 percent) of dual-earner two-parent households (Presser 2004:51); data for other countries show lower but growing rates of split-shift families (e.g., 15 percent of all dual-earner couples in France [Lesnard 2008]). "In terms of parent–child," sociologist Harriet Presser (2004) reports on split-shift families, "two-parent families often look much like one-parent families, and single-parent families much like no-parent families" (p. 65). The risks to family QOL for these households are high, as split-shift spouses are more likely to experience separation, divorce, and other impacts on marital quality (Fenwick and Tausig 2004; Presser 2003; Deutsch 1999).

Beyond such drastic rearrangements, working parents everywhere are devoting more time to the direct care of their children. In a landmark study of two-parent families in the U.S., sociologist Suzanne Bianchi and her colleagues report that in 2000, working mothers ratcheted up their time spent "primarily" tending children to 11 hours a week—"virtually the same" number of hours that non-employed, stay-at-home mothers put in back in 1975. The researchers also noted that U.S. fathers are making more time for childcare; in 2000, they spent on average 2.4 hours per week on interactive activities with their children, up 30 minutes from only five years before and 80 minutes since 1965 (Bianchi, Robinson, and Milkie 2006:77, 64). These trends are hardly limited to America; economist Jonathan Gershuny (2000) and sociologist Anne Gauthier and her colleagues (Gauthier, Smeeding and Furstenberg 2004) have observed similar patterns, albeit at different levels and with different gaps between mothers and fathers, in 18 other Western nations.

Where do working parents find this new time for their children, particularly when more women are formally employed than ever before? One source comes from married fathers who assume some of mothers' past housework, particularly cooking and housecleaning; U.S. fathers on average took up 5.3 more hours per week of core housework (i.e., the kind traditionally accorded to women) from 1965 to 2000, even as domestic technologies made housework more productive, while married mothers dropped 15.1 hours of such housework. Whereas married mothers today do twice the core housework than married fathers, this discrepancy has shrunk from almost eightfold in 1965 (Bianchi et al. 2006:64, 93). International evidence suggests married fathers in other developed nations have also taken up much of their working wives' housework, although again gender parity remains far off (Hook 2010). Perhaps more uniquely to the American context, additional time for children is further taken from mothers' free time and parents' social lives. In 2000, married mothers in the U.S. on average had 31.7 hours per week of free time, a drop of 4.4 hours since 1965, although married fathers kept their free time roughly constant (34.5 hours) over this same period. Married fathers and mothers alike spent about 3 hours less per week visiting in friends' and relatives' homes; married mothers also lost 1.9 hours in reading, 1.3 hours on hobbies, and 0.9 hours in organizational activities; and married fathers lost nearly 3 hours of reading (Bianchi et al. 2006:97). A final source is time spent with spouse. From 1975 to 2000, married parents in the U.S. spent on average 20 percent less time with their spouses, with or without their children present. (This statistic captures the split-shift families, among others.) Even more, parents' time alone with each other, those waking hours available for reconnection and intimacy, dropped over 25 percent in the same period, from 12.4 to 9.1 hours per week (Bianchi et al. 2006:104).

For an inquiry into the aspirations and crises of family QOL today, a key issue is why its pursuit should warrant such a sacrifice of individual well-being. If it seems that parenting has always entailed parents subordinating their own QOL to children's needs—to eat well, have clean clothes, and be safe—observers today may well wonder how those needs have now come to include playing league sports all year, visiting best friends who live a 20-minute car ride away, and earning higher SAT scores through private tutorials. Considering how the historical record indicates a quite different legacy of sacrifice—*children* sacrificing for the well-being of the whole family—the experience of a family QOL 'crisis' clearly points to social contexts of the here and now. Importantly, 'family QOL' and its changing ideals highlight the internal relations that constitute the familial unit. First, the family's *structured relationships* provide an experiential prism for QOL: parents to children, mother to father, mother to child, child to child, individual members to the whole, and so on. The rise of non-traditional families only adds new possibilities: step-parent to step-child, half-sibling to half-sibling, child to single parent's companion, etc. Within these relationships, affective bonds, individual interests, and power dynamics make certain hopes and opportunities for family and personal QOL materialize, or, just as often, dash them altogether. Second, within the finite lifespan of any one familial unit, the nature of its relationships changes as members progress through the course of their lives. Thus *life-stage* is another variable of QOL; the nature of familial dependence, the burden of responsibilities, and the opportunities for autonomy shift among members as they age alongside each other.

In this chapter, I develop an analytical framework with which the reader can put contemporary concerns about family QOL in social and historical context. I emphasize a micro-relational perspective to highlight the evolving tensions between collective and individual perspectives of the family. Below, I offer a brief historical account of the family in its evolving economic context; history's unfolding has given rise to new family strains but also, as we will see, a seminal tradition of thinking about 'QOL' in general. Second, I turn to the present moment to examine family policy in Western welfare-state societies. Here, "welfare" refers not specifically to state support of needy families (a particularly American way of understanding the term) but more broadly to political philosophies and policies that define and promote the well-being of all citizens, families being just one of the citizenry's many configurations. Not just the sources of family crisis, but also the individualization and apparent 'privacy' of its experience vary across different welfare regimes. Finally, I review three emblematic expressions of contemporary family QOL crisis—latchkey children, the "mommy wars," and overscheduled children—that illustrate the increasingly contradictory development of the social contexts impacting family life, particularly in societies like the U.S. and UK where the market especially infiltrates family life. If by the chapter's end I refrain from asserting some common conclusions about the QOL strains that contemporary families feel, that is quite the point, as a critical inquiry into 'family QOL' begs the question: Whose QOL: fathers, mothers, children, some combination thereof, and/or the entire family?

A History of Family Welfare

For a starting point on family QOL, I return to the central societal dynamic, discussed in the previous chapter, of accumulating an economic surplus. Before offspring are born and families extend generationally, daily survival must be accomplished; accumulating a surplus for later consumption allows the progression beyond hand-to-mouth subsistence that is the precondition for raising children and creating culture, two fundamental expressions of humanity's mark upon the future. The activity of surplus accumulation is, as we have seen, necessarily a collective one, and the 'family' is its primary unit of economic participation and social reproduction. Within an economic context, then, the family is *the smallest organization of social reproduction*—a social molecule in the generation of society's QOL. Examining the historical evolution of the family and its ideals for QOL raises two key issues for QOL. First, how has the familial unit evolved as an organization to secure material well-being? Second, how have concerns for, indeed the very consciousness of, family members' individual QOL emerged?

Evolving Relations of Family Life

Locating the family at the origins of society's *raison d'être* highlights the overwhelming pattern reported by scholars of ancient civilizations and hunter-gatherer groups today, that families constitute the experiential totality of 'society' in the least developed societies. (Below, I use the present tense to describe traditional family forms to underscore the fact that they continue to be observed today in many parts of the world.) Of course, 'family' in these primordial settings refers not to the nuclear family but the extended clan united by kinship and intermarriage. Well before landed connotations of 'property' arose from the advent of agriculture and the settlement of civilizations, the clan assumed a normative-legal role as the organizing basis for the intergenerational transmission of assets and craft skills. In pre-agricultural societies, the clan generates surplus by gathering and hunting; it also distributes surplus by sharing food and resources with one another, albeit unevenly via gender and status hierarchies. Large families provide more hands to do the work, a fact made urgent by the likelihood of infant mortality; before the twentieth century, up to half of the world's children did not survive childhood (Sulloway 2001:14060).

But what about love? Raising children, caring for the elderly, economic cooperation, defending one another from the elements and predators, and other prosaic household activities may very well be conducive to affection, but historically the pursuit of romantic and filial 'love' that modern observers understand as a primary motive for forming families has not been the impetus behind traditional family forms. These families envision and pursue their collective well-being through patriarchal hierarchy, arranged marriages, and primogeniture (the privileging of elder children, usually males). Such patterns are 'rational' within agricultural economies "where wealth is stable and based on limited land, and where talent does not matter much," observes natural historian Frank Sulloway (2001). "Leaving the bulk of parental property to a single offspring avoids subdividing estates and hence reducing the social status of the family patronymic—something that was particularly important in past centuries among the landed aristocracy" (p. 14059). In some societies, polygamy, infanticide (especially of females), the compulsory marriage of widows to their husband's male relatives, and other enforcements of family structure that might repulse modern observers have also been 'rational' strategies of resource conservation and labor reproduction (see, e.g., Lancy 2007:275; Therborn 2004). In all varieties of traditional family life, then, ascribed relationships provide an emotional life that is not inimical to love of mate, parent, and child, but which is nonetheless *devoid of individual choice and freedom from familial obligation.* Wives and children might protest their ascribed fate, by withholding affection or competing with siblings, but to leave the family would threaten their very social existence.

The decline of agriculture and rise of industrialization move the family further toward its modern form and meaning. For children of the emerging middle classes, trade, finance, and other industries that require skilled labor offer livelihoods other than agriculture and land; this erodes the patriarch's power to control his offspring's lives and breaks down the economic primacy of the extended family. For peasant families drawn into industrial economies, able men and women move with their children out of the traditional 'community' of family and land, and the prospect of geographical mobility further reduces the size of family units. These changes enable, and in turn are further fueled by, the growth and penetration of the market economy into ever more areas of everyday life, making paid work outside the home more compulsory, and the social status of such work more attractive. Historically, this march toward the nuclear family did not proceed smoothly, to be sure. Wrenching economic and social changes, such as the Industrial Revolution and the Great Depression, often drove families in the opposite direction, turning to extended kin for material support. The inverse relationship between family size and economic prosperity, observed generally in developed and developing world alike, underscores the centrality of material well-being as an organizing principle of the family (Dizard and Gadlin 1990). That the overall trend has been toward smaller families suggests this pursuit has been successful in the long view of history.

Personal Flourishing vs. the Family

It is in this context that the emancipation of family members from the grip of 'family' norms and the patriarch's power occurs. The story begins, first, with the fate of wives and daughters. As standards of living rise and the market extends into goods and services formerly provided by kin, the companionate family, centered in the husband and wife who freely choose one another based on romantic love, appears as the prevailing norm of family formation. Sociologists Jan Dizard and Howard Gadlin (1990) point out:

> Until quite recently marriage was a declaration of autonomy. Autonomy was understood to mean, more or less, freedom from direct parental supervision. Marriage took the young man and young woman out of their respective parental orbits, allowing them to embark upon their own life. The promise of autonomy is no doubt one of the important contributing factors to the steady decline in the average age at first marriage that started in the nineteenth century and continued steadily until the 1960s. . . . Until very recently, there was no social space between the parental home and marriage for young people, especially women.
>
> (p. 51)

Independence from the property-based household economy gives a new role to emotions and affection. Love, guilt, appeasement—these evolve from unplanned by-products to formal methods of parental control once children can find alternate livelihoods outside the home. Historically, such familial transformations did more than enhance families' subjective QOL or give rise to expectations that families should even have a subjective QOL based on the emotional quality of members' relations with one another. For women and children particularly, these changes offered the first substantial experience of *psychological autonomy*—the very premise behind our understanding of subjective, individual QOL both within *and* outside the family context.

Industrialization's separation of home from workplace further advances the psychological autonomy of wives and daughters. In agricultural economies, the household—the home and farm, or just outside in a village common, a feudal strip, or a vassal's estate—is usually the 'workplace' where produce is grown, animals are kept, foods are prepared, and goods are bartered. Although there are certainly gendered spaces within the agricultural household, the social roles, spatial boundaries, and cultural meaning of the public and private spheres are blurred to a large degree (Blau et al. 2002). Perhaps the public marketplace might be deemed too public for 'proper' women to be seen there, but only families of means can generally observe such patriarchal restrictions. In the eighteenth- and nineteenth-century settlement of the New World, economic necessities and demographic conditions gave women an extra leg-up on self-determination compared to their European counterparts. "Settler women had always had important economic functions, and an extra scarcity value," sociologist Göran Therborn (2004) explains. "Social control of them had almost always been more difficult than in the villages of Old Europe" (p. 30).

With industrialization, 'work' begins to connote an unambiguously public setting outside the home, occupied by strangers whose commonality comes from their status as workers (Zaretsky 1976). Now a truly gendered division of labor emerges, as the workplace becomes culturally associated with men's presence and fathers' new roles as economic 'breadwinners.' Historically, this masculine association was always more imagined than real, since many women worked outside the home; in the U.S., 18 percent of women in 1900 were in the paid labor force (compared to 85 per cent of men). Yet work in the public sphere was most accepted for single women; upon marriage, retreat to the household became normative if not possible for families of all means (Blau et al. 2002; reported in Gornick and Meyers 2003:26). Still, at the risk of offering too rosy a view of industrial employment, women's participation in work outside the home gave them an important dimension of autonomy (Shammas 2002; Ehrenreich and English 1973). Daughters and wives left the home geographically, socially, and culturally, becoming exposed to new ways of life that tradition-minded families continue to lament in the present era of the developing nation sweatshop (Therborn 2004:22).

The geographical separation of work from home, and accordingly of public from private, remains a dominant feature of modern life, but the undercutting of patriarchal control that it promised did not go unchallenged. Beginning in the nineteenth century, precisely when gendered divisions of labor were in flux, wives and daughters in Western societies became subject to new ideologies of domesticity that naturalized women's place in the private realm of home and family, away from men's dominance in the workplace and public life. Class lay behind the ascent of these ideologies of domesticity in two ways. First, the ability to keep women at home was strongest for families of means. For instance, in the 1900 figures cited in the previous paragraph, although only 5 percent of wives in the U.S. in 1900 were in the paid labor force, the rate rose to 25 percent for African-American wives, whose race consigned them to the bottom of the social hierarchy in that era (Blau et al. 2002; reported in Gornick and Meyers 2003:27; for similar 1960 figures, see Thistle 2006:43). (This figure almost certainly undercounts the employment of African-American wives in this period, for whom domestic employment was generally informal and thus underreported.) Second, the ideology of domesticity informed and mobilized the middle-class ascendancy in politics and culture, particularly in Anglo-American societies (Sealander 2003; Walkowitz 1992). Sociologist Sharon Hays (1996) explains, "The new ideology of domesticity . . . served as a central symbol for the distinctive identity of the American middle class, providing them with a claim to moral superiority over both the frivolous rich and the promiscuous poor" (p. 33). Venerable status distinctions and social emulations underlay an important historical shift: by the second half of the twentieth century, middle-class women in North America and Europe began supplementing or altogether replacing their housewife role with formal employment, around the same time that the rise of the welfare-state finally made it a viable option for working-class women. "Basically, working-class families emulated the middle-class norm of housewifery at the very moment that middle-class women began to distance themselves from it," observes sociologist Gøsta Esping-Andersen (1999). "The 'Ozzie and Harriet' model seemed to depict the standard American middle-class family; in reality, it was more of a working-class phenomenon" (p. 28).

These developments—the companionate family, the separation of work from home, and the diffusion of class-based lifestyles down the status hierarchy—established a complex legacy for how wives and daughters viewed their personal QOL within the family. On the one hand, these developments outline the history of economic change that continues to lead women, by necessity but also by choice, to support families in the formal workplace and to find a sense of vocation and public identity therein. On the other hand, they gave rise to still widespread norms that enshrine women's place in the domestic sphere. If over the last half of the century women were increasingly relieved of much of the non-caregiving work formerly assigned to the stay-at-home wife, more and more their "natural" role has crystallized around tending children—maternalism—even as they stream into the workforce in ever greater numbers.

The Discovery of Childhood

The contemporary ideology of maternalism as women's calling depended, however, upon the historical appearance of the stage of life now called childhood. That childhood 'appeared' may seem counter-intuitive; we might imagine that children have always been children, physiologically immature and materially dependent upon parental caregiving. Yet this common-sense idea implies a set of premises that have not been the historical case: that children have parents or other family to raise them, that children's character is something that parents actively manage, and even that children enjoyed a period of life free from adult responsibilities. Those premises inform a nineteenth-century Romantic vision of childhood, "which viewed children as symbols of purity, spontaneity, and emotional expressiveness, who were free from adult inhibitions and thus required parents who would ensure that their innocence was not corrupted" (Mintz 2004:76; see also Cross 2004; Zelizer 1985). Yet such ideals have hardly been the reality in economies of agriculture and physical labor, where children offer sources of household labor and are typically put to work by seven or eight years of age. Not only infant mortality but parental mortality and orphanage are facts of life in this world. Besides the diseases and poor health that afflict the general populace, mothers die frequently during childbirth, while fathers regularly disappear due to war or immigration. Even in the best of health, families might not stay intact for long. Historically, children might be sent out at infancy to live with a wet nurse (a norm of eighteenth-century France: Badinter 1981), or in their pre-teen years be indentured as apprentice or servant (common in seventeenth-century colonial Virginia and Maryland: Mintz

2004:37), or as adolescents emigrate to industrial cities or the New World, all of which often compelled them to 'grow up' at a very early age. The gradual and uneven unfolding of historical conditions promoting family stability and economic prosperity affected children's QOL in two ways, enhancing their material well-being, of course, but also prompting new beliefs about how children might be a special kind of creature who deserve their 'own' way of life.

Public schools in Europe and North America emerged over the nineteenth century, although many families did not send their children to them regularly. At the century's end, most children only enrolled in primary school; graduating from high school and (in the U.S.) college did not become normative until well into the twentieth century (Fischer and Hout 2006). Alongside laws targeting child labor, mandatory school attendance represented a key nineteenth-century reform that reflected and promoted middle-class ideals of childhood. Historian Steven Mintz (2004) explains, "For the urban middle class, increasing economic affluence allowed parents to provide an extended, protected childhood; but for the labor classes, a sheltered childhood was impossible" (p. 134). Imposed upon working families with little recourse, these reforms restricted their economic abilities and often endangered their stability with the threat of the state breaking up destitute families (Sealander 2003). Nonetheless, the reforms made a significant impact. In the U.S., for instance, the reported number of working children aged ten to thirteen dropped from 186,358 in 1900 to under 30,000 only 30 years later (Zelizer 1985:57). Held back from the workplace and enrolled in schools, children's economic importance for families diminished, but their sentimental significance for parents and the culture at large grew.

Undoubtedly a key factor in the new cultural interest in childhood was the remarkable drop in family size in industrialized societies; in the U.S., for instance, the average number of births dropped from seven to ten at the beginning of the nineteenth century to just three by the end (Mintz 2004:77). At one level, the correlation is quite simple. When parents raise more children, they have less time to devote to each child separately. Conversely, fewer children allow more time for parents to observe their offspring and individualize their parenting strategies; fewer mouths to feed increase the resources and parental investment each child receives. Maybe less visibly, the birthrate drop also reduces the potential 'co-moms' that can help raise children. Studying the American family, sociologist Frances Goldscheider and her colleagues (2002) report that in 1900, 40 percent of mothers with children under five had an adolescent daughter or their own mother at home to help, but by 1990, only 25 percent did. Historian Peter Stearns (2003) concludes that by the early twentieth century in the U.S. (and presumably after World War II in Europe and Japan), "parents confronted children, particularly babies, more directly, with less assistance and fewer intermediaries, than had been the case in the 19th century. This could easily contribute to a sense that children had problems—partly reflecting the fact that parents had more problems with them" (p. 45).

The explosion of childhood development expertise gave further shape to children's new preciousness and problems in two ways. First, signaled by the 1904 publication of *Adolescence* in which psychologist G. Stanley Hall conceptualized the namesake stage between childhood and adulthood, experts began identifying and institutionalizing ever more stages of childhood. Moving away from a time when children's relations within the family and to social institutions were based on general competence and fitness for the work at hand, age-grading in the twentieth century lent greater force to the segmentation of children's life-stages. Needless to say, expert deliberation and cultural debate over the age-appropriate development of children continue into the present; one wonders what Hall might think of parents today mulling over the developmental needs of "tweens" (ages ten to thirteen) or the desirability of "redshirting" (holding back a year) four- and five-year-olds entering kindergarten (see Weil 2007).

Second, the new chorus of child development experts charged mothers and fathers with new concerns and duties for proper childrearing, and by so doing inserted their authority in place of traditional sources (parents' own family, word of mouth, religious leaders) on how children should be raised. At times experts in fact reinforce the common wisdom; up through the 1960s, for instance, the psychological establishment contended that "over-involved" and "coddling" mothers were endangering their children's mental and emotional well-being. But the figure who most famously challenged this wisdom helped establish the field of childhood development as a science of children's preciousness: Benjamin Spock, who iconoclastically called in *Baby and Child Care* (1946) for mothers to embrace their maternal affections. Criticized by some for the 'permissive' parenting he seemed to endorse, Spock's ideas of maternal responsibilities nevertheless laid the basis for the attachment parenting philosophies that characterize much of the mothering wisdom today. In *Infants and Mothers*, Dr. T. Berry Brazelton (1983) proposed new standards of maternal involvement from a biological perspective, assuring readers that "mothering is instinctive" (p. 42). In *Baby and Child*, Penelope Leach (1986) urged mothers to be the "ever-present, always-present person" to their children (p. 122; quoted in Hays 1996:56). Hays (1996; see also Warner 2005) summarizes the collective contribution of these child experts:

> All in all, Spock, Brazelton, and Leach demand what I have called intensive mothering. First, they assume that child care is primarily the responsibility of the individual mother. Second, the methods they recommend are child-centered, expert-guided, emotionally absorbing, and financially expensive. Finally, they clearly treat the child as outside of market valuation: children are sacred, innocent, and pure, their price immeasurable, and decisions regarding their rearing completely distinct from questions of efficiency or financial profitability.
>
> (p. 54)

In sum, developmental experts' ongoing 'discovery' of childhood has influenced the ways parents in Western societies envision and pursue family QOL in at least three key ways. First, from merely keeping children alive so they could labor for the family, parents have largely shifted their priorities toward how to best manage an increasingly complex and ever-lengthening period of children's lives before adult responsibilities. Developmental experts' powers of persuasion have not merely been rhetorical here; their rational authority over the mission and techniques of schools, the legal system, child welfare agencies, and other institutions since the late nineteenth century have enforced dramatic changes in the daily lives and material welfare of families, particularly middle-class ones (see, e.g., Mintz 2004; Stearns 2003; Zelizer 1985; Wohl 1983). Second, across the changing and often contradictory advice on keeping or breaking with hard-nosed child-rearing traditions, expertise has continually held mothers and fathers accountable for new sets of sentiments, duties, and skills beyond those they might acquire by personal inclination or first-hand observation. By so doing, experts have put parents on the sometimes frenzied hunt for knowledge about "what to do" (and in the process created a market for their expert product). Third, childhood development expertise has encouraged parents to equate the family's collective well-being with their children's 'own' QOL and, accordingly, to push parents' individual well-being to the background. The growing chorus advocating intensive *mothering* places the burdens of family members' individual QOL even more squarely on women's shoulders: whereas fathers promote their families' well-being through work and other public actions, mothers' primary contribution are seen to reside 'naturally' within the private household.

Contexts of Family Caregiving

As I turn to the 'crises' of family QOL in Western societies today, the analytical framework I have developed (which conceptualizes family as a historically evolving unit of social reproduction constituted by structured internal relationships) and the history I have recounted (which reveals the emancipation of family members from the collective grip as well as the growing emphasis on women's place in the domestic sphere) underscores the central tensions between familial caregiving and women's flourishing. Interestingly, the relationship between these two arenas of social life is a key theme in the QOL scholarship, although it takes different forms in different economic contexts. Human development practitioners who look at developing societies have asserted that women's autonomy can enhance families' material well-being, particularly when mothers defy patriarchal authorities to distribute resources equally among children or engage in agricultural/service work that has market value. In industrial and post-industrial societies, by contrast, conflict often frames the relationship, as women's autonomy in the public sphere can challenge the economic function and power inequalities of the patriarchal nuclear family. This echoes a familiar contention of feminism's "second wave," which upheld women's emancipation as the freedom to live outside the heterosexist, patriarchal family structure. The U.S. women's movement especially emphasized the right to equal pay and opportunity in the workplace, crystallized by the failed Equal Rights Amendment; such assertions prompted a political and cultural backlash that castigated the claims of workplace equality as 'anti-family,' a stigma that has stuck tenaciously to the women's movement. Presently, in a world where lesbian and gay couples raise children and defend their families from discriminatory 'pro-family' legislation, many feminists have reconsidered the movement's initially critical stances toward women's family aspirations while retaining *self-determination* as an orienting principle.

For my purposes, self-determination provides a useful lens with which to observe how family QOL is understood and pursued in Western societies today. Touching upon several intellectual traditions of 'QOL,' in particular the Maslowian tradition and the capabilities approach, it highlights important stakes for well-being and happiness in modern families, such as mothers and fathers' aspirational harmony, children's developmental potential, and families' ability to devise meaningful work–life arrangements for themselves. Significantly, self-determination resonates with the contemporary 'post-feminist' value of women's individual "choice"—choice as to whether (and, if so, when) women work, raise children, get married, and so on. As a sociological lens, self-determination calls attention to the structured range of choices that parents have to promote their families' QOL. Given my analytical focus on the family's internal relationships and the historical centrality of women's evolving roles within the family, I contend that an inquiry into 'family QOL' must attend particularly to the structured range of choices that *women* have, and to the specific settings and stages in which women are given or denied particular paths for their flourishing. With this emphasis, I do not mean to discount the ways that men have questioned traditional definitions of fatherhood, increased the time spent with children and domestic work, or otherwise moved toward households based on "equally shared parenting" (see Vachon and Vachon 2010; Deutsch 1999). Yet as the data overwhelmingly show, men make these strides out of a familiar position of patriarchal privilege in industrialized societies—namely, their normative role as economic breadwinners in formal workplaces outside the home—and still lag substantially behind the family caregiving and domestic work that women put in. The situation of single mothers, a sizable group that unfortunately this chapter too often references via the proxy of married mothers' QOL strains (single fathers are an almost statistically insignificant group, their unique burdens and challenges notwithstanding), only further underscores how the meaning and experience of 'family QOL' today still rest primarily upon the unwanted dilemmas and aspirational subordinations faced by women.

Defamilialization

As feminists remind us, it is not helpful to think of women's choices in terms of family *versus* work, since women's labor, generally unpaid at home and underpaid in the workplace, has always been a determining factor in families' economic well-being. Furthermore, we need only think of the many working mothers today who prefer less time at work and more time at home with family to appreciate how many women actively seek a place in their lives for caregiving (see Bielenski and Wagner 2004). It is not then that the unpaid work of family caregiving deprives women of their self-determination because of its emotional, other-directed aspects. Rather, self-determination is lost because traditional and patriarchal family systems reserve the work of caregiving exclusively for women as a compulsory occupation. Feminists' insight is that this reflects a collective, political choice. *Familialism*, a concept scholars use to characterize the policy regime that "assigns a maximum of welfare obligations to the household" (Esping-Andersen 1999:45), reinforces the burden that tradition and patriarchy lay primarily on women's shoulders. A feminist politics of family caregiving, by contrast, advocates for *defamilializing* women's household work by removing the obligations of social reproduction from the household and lessening all family members' dependence upon their families. Such a politics is hardly 'anti-family'; instead, it merely allows mothers to move "away from 'living for others' towards 'a bit of life of our own'," thereby extending a privilege fathers have historically enjoyed (Beck and Beck-Gernsheim 2002:55).

Initially, the defamilialization of family caregiving proceeds as women assert their public place via formal employment. In the U.S., for instance, by 1950 only 33 percent of women worked outside the home, largely in a few exclusively female occupations; by 2000, women's numbers in the workforce had risen to 74 percent and expanded across the spectrum of occupations (England 2001:247; see also Smith and Bachu 1999). Similar stories can be told, give or take a few years and a few percentage points, for all developed industrial societies; indeed, women's entrance into the workforce is one of the central demographic trends, perhaps the most important one, from the last century. Women's work can serve different QOL objectives. Within families, women can pool their earnings with husbands and other household earners for the family's collective well-being. However, the ability to earn also provides an important source of individual power within the household that lessens their material dependence upon fathers, parents, boyfriends, etc. Not surprisingly, divorce rates have risen in tandem with women's entrance into the formal workplace—a symbol of women's growing resistance to patriarchy for some, but also an indicator of families' economic fragility.

More recently, women's access to higher education, long an avenue for women's self-determination, has shaped the collective march toward defamilialization. Women's access to education possibly represents the women's movement's most successful achievement; in most developed nations presently, women are not only gaining more educational opportunities but surpassing men's attainments as a group. To cite the U.S. again as an example, women surpassed men in high school graduation by 1970, and in college graduation by 1980; by the year 2000, American women earned 57.2 percent of all BAs (Fischer and Hout

2006:13, 15; Hacker 2003:81). Higher education increases one's earning power and social status, enhances the likelihood and prospects of full-time employment, and expands one's personal horizons, all of which have important consequences for the households that educated women form. The latest data show that women with college degrees are less likely to divorce, but more likely to postpone marriage and childbirth, than women without them (Fischer and Hout 2006:70–1). The latter trend in part reflects the incentives, experienced by men as well, of pursuing full-time careers and higher earnings, particularly in "front-loaded" careers that reward the state-of-the-art education, long work hours, and freedom to commit themselves to work that younger adults without families can offer (see Florida 2002:154–5; Sennett 2006).

However, gains in the workplace and educational attainment have generally not relieved women of their household responsibilities, which remain normative in patriarchal societies. Indeed, in many regards working mothers were historically the first to encounter the problem of work–life balance, at least in its manifestation as "time crunch," that parents of both genders now regularly experience. Certainly divorced and single mothers feel this crunch most acutely, since few of them can escape the need for full-time employment or have a partner to share household duties with. For many scholars and policy-makers, however, the problem of work–life balance was first scrutinized within the married dual-earner household. In *The Second Shift*, sociologist Arlie Hochschild (1989) examined full-time working mothers in two-parent households who come home only to put in a "second shift" of child-rearing and household work that their husbands do not share. Controversy surrounded Hochschild's book because it reported what some observers construed as 'anti-family' views: in contrast to their presumed maternal dispositions, many women reported they actually found emotional refuge in their high-pressure jobs from the daily chaos and emotional labor of family! Remarkably, such sentiment still makes news today, as in this front-page *New York Times* article:

> Before Lucia Skwarek, a portfolio manager and mother in New York City, gets on a plane bound for business in Moscow or Milan, there are not only meetings, but play dates to schedule. When she is done wooing investors for her hedge fund and parsing a pile of e-mail messages, though, Ms. Skwarek looks forward to a little "me" time.
>
> "I can go home and deal with two screaming 6-year-old twins and a grumpy preteen," she said. "Or I can go to the Four Seasons in Mexico City and drink Cognac in the bathtub."
>
> Hers is the guilty pleasure of the traveling working mom. After slogging through airports, sitting through PowerPoints and networking through lunches, there is, at the end of the day, a small taste of freedom. And as hard as it can be to balance the demands of business trips and family life, for the relatively small group of employed mothers who travel, it can be delicious.
>
> (Foderaro 2006:1)

Since the publication of Hochschild's book in 1989, married fathers have offset women's housework to a significant degree (Hook 2010; Bianchi et al. 2006), but high-earning women also have other options besides a full-time second shift. In what sociologist Saskia Sassen (2006) calls "the professional household without a 'wife'" (p. 181), high-income dual earners outsource the more menial tasks of housework and childcare, so that maintaining work–life balance can focus on "quality time" with children. Meanwhile, childless women, single and married, defer motherhood for a substantial length of time, possibly indefinitely, while handling as much paid work as men can. The fiscal incentives for deferring motherhood are suggested by 2000 data from the U.S. that show the 25–44 cohort of unmarried adult women in the workforce inching closer to the earnings by men of the same age than prior generations of women: $942 to every $1000 men made on average (Hacker 2003:172–3). Such earning profiles give career women significant new choices about children. And, should parenting be taken up, technologies of birth control and fertility enhancement let women move childbearing back to later stages of adulthood. Once again, this tends to result in fewer offspring and thus greater parental investment—possibly to include intensive mothering—in individual children (Gauthier et al. 2004; Becker 1991).

National Contexts of Family Policy

If this discussion suggests that the dilemma between work and family is always stacked against women's meaningful self-determination, such that the pursuit of work invariably takes away from family QOL, this sobering conclusion presumes that caregiving is always women's *individual* responsibility. In fact, women's strides toward defamilialization can take two possible routes, toward the market but also the state, and each has very different material consequences and political implications. A world in which individuals and families turn to the market to secure their well-being does not necessarily transform gender inequalities within the household; wives and daughters are generally still held accountable for family caregiving, only now through their income-generating abilities. At best, this scenario promises mothers a scarcity of hours in the day with which to balance work and life, while at worst—when women's pay and job prospects lag behind men's—it reinforces mothers' economic incentives to accept their household confinement. Consequently, many feminists further call for the *decommodification* of caregiving, a politics that addresses the social inequities imposed by women's unpaid household work by shifting that burden toward the state (Dale and Foster 1986). For our purposes, decommodification highlights how policy contexts influence the private lives and QOL aspirations of mothers, fathers, children, and families.

Specifically, the social services and income supports associated with the modern welfare state affect how the equality between mothers and fathers is achieved—on the backs of parents in the home, via the services available in the market, through the state's provision of public services, or (most likely) some combination thereof. By 'welfare state,' I refer to the modern nation-state that redistributes wealth in order to provide citizens proactive assistance or at least fall-back support—the distinction is significant, as we will see—to ensure a minimum standard of living.[1] Gøsta Esping-Andersen (1999, 1990) offers a robust typology of three "welfare regimes" in developed capitalist democracies. First, encompassing the U.S., the UK, Canada, Australia, and New Zealand, the *liberal welfare regime* is 'liberal' in its economic philosophy, emphasizing the individual as the primary recipient of social welfare and the labor market as the chief mechanism for distributing welfare. Liberal welfare regimes tolerate a wide degree of social inequality, and the state tends to limit public services as back-up support for narrowly-defined groups (exemplified by means-tested eligibility for family poverty relief). Second, the *social democratic welfare regime* is illustrated by the Scandinavian countries, Sweden, Norway, Denmark, Finland, and Iceland, all of which are well known for their generous social benefit levels and relatively egalitarian social class structure. This regime emphasizes universal entitlements, considering citizens of all economic and social categories eligible for the same pensions, services, benefits, and protections. As much as possible, it takes welfare services out of the market and makes them the responsibility of the state. Third, corresponding to Continental Europe and Japan, the *conservative welfare regime* is 'conservative' in that the design of welfare policies reflects traditional influences such as Catholic/Confucian doctrine, Christian Democratic parties, or histories of authoritarian governments or monarchical étatism. This regime endorses a policy of familialism, viewing the single (i.e., father) breadwinner family as the normative caregiver and distributing state benefits accordingly. Corporatist occupational groups like industrial workers and civil servants play a driving role in the conservative welfare regime by negotiating and monopolizing the benefits and insurance that the state provides (the private sector generally plays a smaller role).

Within any of these three regimes, nations can differ widely in the standards of living enjoyed by their citizens—within the liberal welfare regime, for instance, compare Canada's universal health care to the U.S.'s lack thereof—and even the most progressive welfare-state can gender policies in inadvertent and often inequitable ways (see Sainsbury 1999). Nonetheless, policy analysts generally agree that Scandinavia's social democratic welfare regimes, which prioritize maximizing the workforce participation of all citizens, go furthest in giving women the right and opportunity to work full-time while supporting families; thus in 1998, Denmark, Sweden and Norway boasted the highest rates of female employment, over 70 percent, among the 15 European Union members and Norway (Bielenski and Hartmann 2000:2). Generous income transfers are distributed to each worker, not simply the main (male) householder, and are flexibly organized to accommodate the diverse employment needs of working mothers. Chief among these are maternity and parental leave benefits, which are reviewed for 12 European and North American nations in Table 4.1. Mothers in Scandinavian nations receive the longest paid maternity leaves in Europe, from 29 weeks in Finland to 42 in

Table 4.1 Family Leave (Maternity and Parental Leave Provisions)—Approximately 2000

Nation	*Maternal leave benefits (paid)*	*Parental leave benefits (unpaid and paid)*
	Nordic countries	
Denmark	18 weeks. 100% of wages up to flat-rate ceiling of DKK2,758 [US$321] per week, equal in practice to about 60% prior wages. Owing to collective agreements, many employers "top up" so 80% of parents receive 100% wage replacement.	Paid leave: Parents may share 10 weeks of parental leave. Benefit level same as maternity leave. Extended to 12 weeks if father takes 2 weeks. As with maternity, 80% receive full wage. Following parental leave, each parent entitled to 26 weeks of additional child care leave (13 weeks if after first birthday). Benefit level is 60% of parental leave benefit level; sometimes supplemented by local authorities. Available until child's ninth birthday.[a]
Finland	18 weeks [105 days]. Benefit based on graduated replacement rate: approximately 70% at low income, 40% at medium income, 25% at high income (equal, on average, to approximately 66%).	Paid leave: Parents may share 26 weeks [158 days] weeks of parental leave. Benefit level is 66% of earnings, flat-rate if not employed. Following parental leave, family entitled to 108 weeks home care leave, on the condition that the child is not in public child care. Benefit paid at a low flat-rate of approximately FIM2,900 [US$475] per month. Available until child's third birthday.[b]
Norway	Paid leave: Parents may share 52 weeks of leave at 80% of wages, or, alternatively, 42 weeks at 100% of wages. (9 weeks exclusively for the mothers, 4 exclusively for the father). Benefits subject to maximum income of NOK290,261 [US$26,876] per year. Benefit can be paid while parent is employed 50%–90% time, and leave time is extended accordingly. Available until child's third birthday.[c,d]	
Sweden	Paid leave: Parents may share 65 weeks [15 months] of leave. Benefit level is 80% of earnings for 52 weeks [12 months]; flat rate for remaining 13 weeks [3 months], at approximately SEK1,800 [US$187] per month. Earnings-related benefit subject to maximum income of approximately SEK270,000 income [US$28,000] per year. Benefit can be paid while parent is employed part-time, and leave is extended accordingly. Available until child's eighth birthday.[e]	
	Continental countries	
Belgium	15 weeks. 82% of wages for first 4 weeks [1 month], plus 75% of wages thereafter. Benefits during first month not subject to ceiling; thereafter, benefits subject to maximum income of approximately $95/day.[f]	Paid leave: Each parent entitled to 13 weeks [3 months] full-time leave or up to 26 weeks [6 months] of half-time leave. Parents taking leave receive flat-rate benefit payment of BF20,400[US$551] per month. Available until child's fourth birthday.

France	16 weeks for first 2 children, 26 weeks for third and subsequent children. 100% of wages, up to maximum of FF387 [US$59] per day.[g]	Paid leave: Parents may share 156 weeks [3 years] of leave. No benefit paid for first child; benefit level is flat-rate FF3,024 [US$462] per month for second and subsequent children. Benefit can be paid at reduced rate while parent is employed part-time. Available until child's third birthday.[h]
Germany	14 weeks. 100% of wages.[i]	Paid leave: Parents may share 156 weeks [3 years] of leave. Benefit is flat-rate of DM600 [US$309] per month for 2 years or up to DM900 [US$464] per month for 1 year. Benefits are income-tested, but majority of families qualify (during the first six months, then the income limits are lower and about half qualify). Benefits can be paid during part-time employment of up to 30 hours per week. Paid leave can be used until child's second birthday; third year of leave may be used until child is 8 years old.[j]
Luxembourg	16 weeks. 100% of wages.	Paid leave: Each parent entitled to 26 weeks [6 months] full-time leave; one parent can receive flat rate of LF60,000 [US$1,471] per month. Benefit can be paid at half rate if parent works part-time. One parent must take parental leave directly following maternity leave; other can take leave until child is 5 years old.
Netherlands	16 weeks. 100% of wages, up to daily maximum of 310 guilders [US$154] per day.[k]	Unpaid leave: Each parent entitled to leave of the equivalent of 13 weeks [3 months] at their usual hours of work per week. Standard take-up is 26 weeks [6 months] at 50% working time. Available until child's 8th birthday.
	English-speaking countries	
Canada	15 weeks. 55% of previous average insured earnings, up to a maximum benefit of C$413 [US$350] a week. Family supplement for low-income earners (less than C$25,921 [US$21,967]) raises replacement rate to 80%.[l]	Paid leave: Parents may share 35 weeks of parental leave; combined maternity [15 weeks] and parental benefit cannot exceed 50 weeks. Benefit rate is same as for maternity (55% up to a maximum of $413 [US$350] a week.) Parents can continue to work, earning the greater of $50 [US$42] per week or 25% of their weekly benefit rate without affecting their parental benefits. Available until child's first birthday.

Table 4.1 Continued

Nation	*Maternal leave benefits (paid)*	*Parental leave benefits (unpaid and paid)*
United Kingdom	Statutory Maternity Pay (stricter eligibility): 6 weeks at 90% of wages, plus 12 weeks at flat rate (£60.20 [US$92]) per week. Maternity Allowance (broader eligibility): 18 weeks. Paid at lesser of 90% of wages or flat rate (£60.20 [US$92] per week).[m]	Unpaid leave: Each parent entitled to 13 weeks full-time leave per child. No more than four weeks can be taken in any given year. Available until child is 5 years old.
United States	No national policy of paid maternity leave. Some benefits paid under temporary disability insurance (TDI) laws in 5 states: California, Hawaii, New Jersey, New York, Rhode Island. Approximately 23% of the US population resides in these states. Maximum duration: 26–52 weeks; average duration: 5–13 weeks. Maximum weekly benefits: $170–$487; average weekly benefits: $142–$273.	Unpaid leave: Each parent entitled to 12 weeks family and medical leave (if employer has 50+ employees and work history requirements fulfilled). Available until child's first birthday Several states extend federal leave; generally, state laws broaden coverage (including smaller employers) and/or increase duration. California enacted paid parental leave in 2002. Pays approximately 55% wage replacement for six weeks, subject to earnings cap.

Source: Gornick and Meyers (2003:125–8).

Notes: All durations are expressed as weeks, to help with interpretation. Where authors converted from days, years, or months, original duration is given in square brackets. All currency amounts expressed as 2000 US dollars, adjusted for purchasing power parities.

a Danish parental leave reformed March 2002. Entitlement increased to 32 weeks (to be shared between the parents) at same pay as maternity; 80% of employers still top up. Other changes increased the flexibility of parents' take-up options.

b Finnish parents can replace the home care leave payment with payment for a private child care provider.

c Norwegian cap equivalent to approximately 1.9 times average annual earnings among working-age mothers (part-time and full-time combined).

d Norwegian parents can use cash benefit to pay for private child care (for children aged 1 or 2) if child is not in a public slot. In addition to paid parental leave, each parent is entitled to one year of unpaid leave.

e Swedish cap equivalent to approximately 2.2 times average annual earnings among working-age mothers (part-time and full-time combined).

f Earnings ceiling in Belgium as of 2002.

g French replacement rate is 100% of net wages (after social insurance contributions are deducted).

h French parents working 50% time receive 66% of full benefit; parents working 50–80% time receive 50% of full benefit.

I German maternity leave is paid about 25% by health insurance and about 75% by employer.

j German parental leave law as of January 2001.

k As of January 2001, the Netherlands government offers subsidies to employers who provide paid leave, to defray some of the costs.

l Canadian maximum pertains to benefit level, not maximum covered earnings. Maximum benefit of US$350 a week converts to approximately US$17,500 per year, or equivalent to 55% of about US$32,000 in earnings. Also, the national government pays benefits, but rights to take leave are established at the provincial level.

m As of 2003, both maternity leave benefits in UK extended from 18 to 26 weeks.

Sweden and Norway. *Fathers* receive shorter but (for this group) still generous paternity leaves, granted with pay and other incentives to motivate their enrollment and facilitate new mothers' re-entry into the workplace shortly after childbirth (Gornick and Meyers 2004). Since the 1970s, Scandinavian nations have offered a remarkable array of family caregiving services like child care, residential services, and home help for the elderly; their public provision works to reduce the inequality of care that working mothers and their families receive. Sweden and Denmark lead Europe in the provision of kindergarten for children aged one to two, a policy designed again to ease mothers' quick re-entry into the workplace (Gornick and Meyers 2004; Williams 2000:49; Gustafsson 1999; Papadopoulos 1998:49). Furthermore, only in Scandinavia are kindergartens and other childcare services made available 24 hours a day, to accommodate working women's irregular schedules (see Bihan and Martin 2005).[2] With Scandinavian mothers enjoying greater flexibility in arranging and sequencing their familial caregiving, the social democratic welfare regime's "stress on individual rights and, even more importantly, on promoting women's employment (since the 1960s) has *de facto* replaced the conventional male-bread winner model with the double-earner, dual career family" (Esping-Andersen 1999:18).[3] More than in the other two welfare regimes, the social democratic package of family support and services liberates mothers from confinement to the household and its obligations as well as dependency on a male-breadwinner. As a result, Scandinavia has not only high rates of single-mother-led households, but also some of the highest fertility rates (albeit still below the natural replacement rate) in Europe (Kravdal and Rindfuss 2008; Esping-Andersen 1999:67; see also Drew 1998).

Other forms of public caregiving assistance are common across Europe, even in conservative welfare regime nations. Most of Continental Europe publicly provides or subsidizes "over-threes" kindergarten for children aged three to six, with enrollment in France, Belgium, and Italy at over 90 percent. Then there are policies regulating the length of the work week, which safeguard the time parents can devote to taking care of children and home; the normal work week in Europe ranges from 39 hours per week in Finland to 35 in France. Laws mandating paid vacations are not only a cherished entitlement for workers but give parents caregiving flexibility when children's school terms end. Most of Europe and the UK as well offer at least 20 days (i.e., four weeks) of paid vacation, while France, Denmark, Finland and Sweden offer most or all of a fifth week (Gornick and Meyers 2004).

In contrast, the liberal welfare regime offers little public caregiving assistance, with the U.S. staking a position at the bottom of the spectrum. Consistent with economically liberal philosophy that minimizes state regulation of employers' contracts with individuals, the U.S. has the longest workweek (normally 40 hours) and the fewest weeks off per year; famously, it is the only industrialized nation (at least among the nations discussed here) with no mandatory vacation policy. Paid vacation days are typically a private benefit and, in medium to large employers, range around 10 to 17 days for most workers, depending on years of service. Surveying the comparative national data, social scientists Janet Gornick and Marcia Meyers (2003) conclude:

> American parents have good reason to feel that they are squeezed for time. Nearly all fathers and a substantial share of mothers in the United States are employed. Those who are employed are averaging long weekly hours in the workplace; and compared with their counterparts in other countries, many of them are spending extremely long hours at work.
>
> (p. 59)

Alongside this general time crunch, families with children get modest public support for childcare. U.S. maternity and paternity policy falls under the 1993 Family and Medical Leave Act, which grants 12 weeks of *unpaid* leave a year for new births, adoptions, and family and personal health emergencies. While employers must preserve the jobs that employees leave behind, would-be mothers who fear tacit reprisals and demotions by employers in professional and high-mobility sectors may postpone or defer pregnancy instead (see, e.g., Spalter-Roth and Erskine 2006). Nor is pre-school a public entitlement in the U.S. with the exception of the Head Start program, which is reserved for children of families living at or below the poverty line (Gornick and Meyers 2004; Gustafsson 1999). Otherwise, daycare for children (certainly outside traditional school hours) is a private, market-based service, which stratifies its affordability along socioeconomic lines. For American working families with children under age 13, childcare in 1997 cost an average of $286, which made for 9 percent of average family earnings and of course more for lower-income families (Giannarelli and Barsimantov 2000). Although compared to most other nations, private childcare on the whole can be relatively inexpensive in the U.S.—at the low end, it costs about 6 per cent of average family income (Esping-Andersen 1999:56–7)—the primary reason is the nation's large pool of low-wage workers, which yields a large number of informal, unaccredited daycare and domestic services. This hardly bodes well for the overall quality of private childcare in the U.S., a factor that prompts many parents to take on more childcare work for themselves than they might otherwise prefer (Hofferth 1996).

Working Mothers' QOL Compared: France and the U.S.

If Scandinavia provides the outlying and, for some, optimal case of state support for family caregiving, a comparison of France and the U.S. illuminates other QOL trade-offs that women today make in different policy contexts. Although France belongs to Esping-Andersen's conservative welfare regime, in fact "the male breadwinner ideal is weaker in France than in Germany or Austria for example," sociologist Marie-Thérèse Letablier (2004) notes. "Since the nineteenth century, women have been protected by the state in France, both as workers and as mothers" (p. 191), and the state has developed many policies to accommodate women's entrance into the workplace. France boasts some of the highest rates of dual-earner families and the lowest gaps in working time between men and women. To support this norm of full-time work among mothers and fathers, the state supports a range of childcare options, from public enrollment in highly-coveted collective *crèches* to subsidies for personalized care by a registered "childminder" or (via a parental leave allowance) a parent him- or herself, although these are unevenly available across region and socioeconomic status.

In important ways, the respective emphases in the U.S. and France on market provision versus state support for family caregiving reflect the orientations of those nations' women's movements. The American movement, despite failing to get the Equal Rights Amendment passed into law, has achieved remarkable success in asserting women's equality in the workplace. Tellingly, the one indicator of women's equality where the U.S. matches other industrialized nations is married or cohabitating mothers' share of total parental earnings: about 28 percent, which suggests a sizable fraction of full-time employed mothers (Gornick and Meyers 2004:62). U.S. mothers' contributions to household earnings are the envy of many in Europe, even in non-Nordic countries where opportunities for women's employment are greater (Bielenski and Wagner 2004:145). However, this is perhaps an ambivalent achievement, considering the U.S.'s weak public support for caregiving; the trend reflects families' financial necessity as much as women's political accomplishment. Significantly, the U.S. women's movement is relatively uninvolved with the nation's work/family movement, which consequently has failed to connect its concern about families' time crunches to the gendered organization of work and caregiving. By contrast, France's women's movement has put expanded caregiving options and related policy changes at the forefront of efforts to get recognition for mothers in the workplace.

A case can be made that the French and American women's movements advocate women's self-determination through the respective lenses of ascription and achievement. Philosopher Sylviane Agacinski (2001) describes the French feminist principle of sexual *différence*; the source of conflict between the sexes, it also holds the basis for men and women's ultimate harmony:

> The political nature of the male/female relation . . . does not derive solely from a natural difference but from conflicts of interest and mutual dependence. Men and women depend on each other for the satisfaction of their desires as well as for procreation. Many other disputes follow. We aren't likely to ever get beyond them, and we shouldn't complain about them.
>
> In certain respects, it might be considered that the ideal of the reduction of difference or, as it's called, the "*disappearance of genders*," would constitute a totalitarian fantasy in aiming for a uniformization of individuals. There is nothing worse than the dream of a society of like individuals liberated from conflicts by their very likeness.
>
> (pp. 23–4)

Agacinski's allusion to the American women's movement's emphasis on equality in the workplace is clear, as is the gender essentialism and normative heterosexuality in her view of *différence*. She does not speak for the entire range of perspectives in the French women's movement, but many scholars have noted that equality of representation in the public sphere has not been the movement's primary goal (e.g., Nadeau and Barlow 2003:59; Fagnani 1998; Jenson and Sineau 1995).[4]

After six years of living and raising children in France, *New York Times* columnist Judith Warner confesses she came to see the wisdom of the French model—not for the "perpetual game of kittenish femininity" it encourages in French women, but for the light it casts upon the market individualism of American women's post-feminist "choice":

> It seems to me that the French, where mothers are concerned, have wedded their society's belief in *différence* to a realistic and humane view of modern women's lives. We Americans, on the other hand, have wedded an abstract belief in equal opportunity to punitive notions of women's "choice" and women's "compromises." The result is that once children come into the picture, women retain the right to compete in the marketplace, but lose the right to any kind of decent quality of life.
>
> (Warner 2001)

Such 'realism' concerning French women's maternal roles is further colored by a national culture that places the emotional needs of parents, not children, at the forefront of family life. In the French version of familialism, children are a central concern of the state, and their care is not left to families alone. "Strong public support of [French] families helps parents to balance their daily lives," observe sociologists Laurent Lesnard and Alain Chenu (quoted in Bianchi et al. 2006:201). "Contrary to liberal-oriented countries, children are not only a private matter and consequently, children are less central to couples' daily lives." Supported by a hierarchical educational system and a family tradition that values strong, non-indulgent parenting, French mothers do not feel the pressure to embrace the time- and energy-consuming maternal devotion that drives American mothers to lead what French women see as "dogs' lives" (Warner 2005:19).

Overall, the French women's movement envisions self-determination through a 'realistic' lens of gendered heterosexuality and familialism that the American women's movement has generally challenged. On the basis of the resistance to "American" approaches to gender equality expressed by renowned French writers like Agacinski, Françoise Giroud, and Elisabeth Badinter, it is unlikely that French feminists will embrace the American movement's ideal of self-determination as equality in the public sphere. At the same time, neither France nor other European nations are veering away from high rates of women's employment. "Employment first" is a key policy principle motivating efforts to prevent poor families' social exclusion and to raise overall employment rates to 70 percent (Giele and Holst 2004:11). A key distinction between France and the U.S., then, is France's societal expectation that women should be protected as workers *and* mothers—an expectation that the women's movement has supported to a large extent. By providing vigorous women's policies like maternal leave, the state does not challenge this expectation but actively promotes it, in contrast to the primacy of the market to which the U.S state and women's movement leave women and families.

But What About The Children?

By this point, some American readers may be confused that a nation like France outperforms the U.S. in promoting a welfare policy called 'familialism.' After all, few Americans can hear a political speech, watch a daytime talk show, or read a newspaper editorial without encountering a loud burst of pro-children rhetoric. The end goal of the American dream, it is often said, is a life for children that is better, more fulfilling, and more prosperous than the one their parents have known. Such child-centered optimism is even incorporated into standard American survey questions like this one from the General Social Survey: "When your children are at the age you are now, do you think their standard of living will be much better, somewhat better, about the same, somewhat worse, or much worse than yours is now?" If the 'point of it all,' from family and work to lifestyles and communities of choice, is not enhancing children's QOL, Americans might reasonably be puzzled what 'it' might be then. The concern and even outright panic with which Americans think about their children, however, have hardly translated into American children's overall well-being. Comparing the U.S. to nine European nations (the UK, France, the Netherlands, Belgium, Germany, Norway, Sweden, Finland, and Denmark), Gornick and Meyers (2004) observe,

> children in the U.S. are more likely than children in the other welfare regimes to be poor, to die young, to lag in school, to spend excessive hours in front of the television, and to become pregnant as teenagers. In the U.S., children's well-being, captured at the average, is alarming—in absolute terms and, even more so, in cross-national terms.
>
> (p. 63)

This paradox by which American children are seemingly valued without limit in family rhetoric, yet are more at risk in reality, directs our attention to the contexts in which we think about the QOL of children today. Below, I illuminate these contexts by examining the debates over children left unattended after school, the mommy wars, and the "overscheduling" of children. These debates rage especially in North America and the UK, and they go some way to illuminate the constraints and dilemmas thrown up by these nations' market-based systems of family welfare.

The Latchkey Kid

The chorus of alarm over children left unsupervised at home, otherwise known as latchkey kids, has risen steadily since women entered work in greater numbers in the 1970s. A widely reported study by sociologist Sandra Hofferth (reported in Berger 2000) noted a substantial rise in latchkey children between 1984 and 1990, when unsupervised U.S. children aged 5 to 12 increased from 1.8 million to 3.4 million. Associated with this trend were fears of modern perils facing youth. Psychologist Deborah Belle, author of *The After School Lives of Children: Alone and With Others While Parents Work*, contends, "Parents can reasonably worry about their child's . . . experimenting with drugs, sex, and shoplifting. . . . These things happen to boys and girls throughout adolescence, and the incidents may increase when there's no supervision" (quoted in Karasik 2000).

However, the very name of this phenomenon reveals much older concerns over unsupervised children:

> Negative associations with this term were carried over from the eighteenth century, when "latchkey" referred to the method of lifting the door latch to gain access into homes. By the turn of the century in the United States, latchkey kids were called "dorks" because they had their own door keys to get inside their homes. During the 1940s, keys around a child's neck signaled poverty, neglect, and lack of motherly love and affection.
>
> (Robinson, Rowland, and Coleman 1989:2)

Ironically, nineteenth century reforms made latchkey children even more common by making mothers' paid work all the more necessary for working-class families and compelling them to leave children unsupervised after school hours—presuming, of course, their children were enrolled in public school at all. In America's swelling industrial cities, large numbers of idle working-class children, particularly immigrant and African American, fended for themselves for portions of the day, a situation that stoked popular fears about juvenile delinquency and ethnic gangs. Films featuring "Our Gang" (a.k.a. the Little Rascals) and the "Dead End Kids" (a.k.a. the Bowery Boys) comically depicted widespread anxieties about unsupervised children of the early twentieth century (see Park 1925). When suburban exodus began in earnest after World War II, sustained by middle-class families seeking more wholesome environments for their children, cities' subsequent depopulation and deterioration gave urban families more reasons to fear for their children's safety during unsupervised hours, even in their homes. Today, the suburbs and exurbs no longer seem to guarantee a carefree and safe childhood. Residing in smaller families and larger house-lots than prior generations did, children frequently live near no one in their age range for miles (see Lareau 2003:45). Visiting a park or attending an activity often requires a drive of some distance; in auto-centered neighborhoods, this increases traffic and thus parents' hesitation to let children play outside the house or ride bikes. Media attention to child snatchings, abuse, and other violent crimes also fuels parents' anxieties, even in neighborhoods with low crime rates (Jacobs and Gerson 2004a:36; Kurz 2002; Warr and Ellison 2000).

The concern over latchkey kids thus reveals particular social and cultural contexts, some venerable and others evolving, that shape understandings and pursuits of family QOL today. First, it has its basis in patriarchal ideologies that view mothers as home-bound caregivers of first and last resort. Children are mothers' charges, these ideologies contend, and responsibility for unsupervised children's well-being lies with the decisions mothers have made to leave them for work. Of course, stay-at-home fathers could supervise children, and many do, but the novelty and stigma of this arrangement—evoked by the humorous yet feminizing designation "Mr. Mom" (why no comparable "Mrs. Dad"?)—suggest that social disapproval is primarily targeted at mothers. Indeed, data for U.S. men associate the addition of children to their households with an *increased* likelihood that these fathers will be employed, work full-time, and earn more income (Gornick and Meyers 2003:36; Lundberg and Rose 2000). Men's obligations to children's QOL still reside normatively in the sphere of work.

Second, the latchkey kid, by definition confined to home, implies that families have no resort to childcare by extended family or daycare centers. Anxieties over unsupervised children thus reveal the context of the liberal welfare regime, which absolves the state and workplace of caregiving responsibilities to all citizens and leaves parents to promote their families' welfare through their earnings. As we have seen, the U.S. makes the commitments of parents' work especially demanding by failing to provide national vacation policy or regulation on work-week hours (the latter irrelevant for a parent with more than one job anyway). This context helps explain the occasional concern expressed by employers bemoaning the "three o'clock syndrome" whereby working parents "victimize" the workplace with their caregiving burdens:

> It occurs as uneasy parents interrupt their work to call home and check on their kids. During this time, businesses report productivity slowdowns, increases in assembly-line accidents, and absenteeism. There may be as many as two or three calls each afternoon. Sometimes the calls come in from children checking in with their working parents.
>
> (Robinson et al. 1989:8)

Third, socioeconomic inequalities make a mother's formal employment an avoidable situation for some families and an inescapable reality for others. Often our intuition about this comes from the first half of the twentieth century, when working-class families had to cobble together non-market daycare alternatives (extended family, friends, babysitting pools) or leave their kids unsupervised for some hours of the week. However, by the twenty-first century it has become an oversimplification to associate latchkey children with the working classes. For one reason, working-class households are now more likely to keep mothers at home, presumably for the sake of the children; on the whole, they also find fewer hours of work than their middle-class counterparts (Jacobs and Gerson 2004b; Gershuny 2000; see also Chapter 5). For another reason, daycare affordability has become a source of economic uncertainty for families well up the socioeconomic hierarchy. Reliable, quality private caregivers who can watch children at all hours of mothers' employment are an especially high-end service, the availability of which is further shaped by location, social capital, and other factors beside household income. This underscores the special burdens facing single mothers; unless they can afford on one income a daycare provider who can attend their children at all hours (or find alternative non-market arrangements), their kids will almost certainly spend some hours unsupervised.

Fourth, these contexts are mediated through the life-course of the family; parental caregiving preferences fluctuate based on the ages of children and mothers, mothers' prior pursuits in the labor market, the number of children in a family, and the spacing apart of their births. In the post-World War II era, scholars theorized a three-phase model of mothers' life-stages: work until first childbirth, then 10 to 15 years caregiving in the household, followed by a resumption of formal work (Myrdal and Klein 1956). Formulated at a period when middle-class norms of women's place in the home were strongest, recent trends have somewhat deflated the model's robustness. Nowadays, would-be mothers are still likely to work full-time before having children, but higher educational achievements and career investments make workplace commitments strong for many middle-class women, who increasingly give birth at later ages than prior generations. Citing 2000 data, sociologists Claude Fischer and Michael Hout (2006) comment that "it impresses us that the United States has so many supermoms. American mothers with three preschool children at home participate in the labor force as much as European women who have just one preschool child at home" (p. 303 fn16; see Stier, Lewin-Epstein, and Braun 2001). Finally, at whatever stage of life they may return to work, socioeconomic factors like household income, job security, and daycare affordability continually test mothers' ability to stay there. Indeed, many mothers choose at some point to stop working or cut down on hours in order to take care of their children in the ways they see fit.

Fifth, such employment irregularity explains to a large extent the persisting inequalities of pay that women earn compared to men (Gornick and Meyers 2003; Budig and England 2001; Crittenden 2001; Waldfogel 1998, 1997). Across the socioeconomic spectrum, mothers who earn less than what they consider necessary to pay for a suitable daycare service (their "reservation wage," in economists' vocabulary) feel compelled to withdraw from the workplace—to part-time status, or out altogether (on the case of poor single mothers, see Edin and Lein 1997:76). And when they finally do return full-time to the workplace, many can anticipate bringing a résumé marked by episodic employment and insubstantial experience in any single workplace. This constraint helps explain the latest pattern in American women's labor force participation: having increased steadily over the twentieth century, American women's collective hours in paid work have recently peaked and started dropping as mothers reduce their work hours in order to take care of children (Bianchi et al. 2006; Gornick and Meyers 2003). Publicized in front-page newspaper headlines of newspapers (like the *New York Times* from March 2, 2006: "Stretched to Limit, Women Stall March to Work" [Porter 2006]), this latest trend among other things signals the importance of women's labor market patterns in explaining the inequality of women's and men's pay.

As this brief sketch suggests, families typically do not adhere to one household type or even one earnings profile over their life course. Yet the complexity and variety of possibilities are still framed by an overarching *neo-traditional* model of household arrangement, as wives subordinate career advancement to their husbands, particularly when children are young (Moen 2003). Below, the proportion of dual-career household adhering to the neo-traditional model is reported for the U.S. in the third column of data in Table 4.2 and for Europe the second column of data in Table 4.3. Note that these data correspond to a single point in time, and the likelihood that households will assume different arrangements at other stages suggests these tables underestimate the

Table 4.2 Two-parent Households—U.S., 2000

	With children under 6	*With children under 18*
Dual earner	53.8	60.8
Both parents full-time	30.5	37
Mother part-time, father full-time	19.1	19.1
Father part-time, mother full-time	2.1	2.6
Both part-time	2.1	2.2
Father sole earner	37.3	29.1
Mother sole earner	4.6	5.8
Neither	4.2	4.2
Total	100	100

Source: adapted from Bianchi *et al.* (2006:206).

Table 4.3 Households of Men and Women Married or Living Together— Europe, 1998

	No children	*Youngest child under 6*	*Youngest child 6 or over*
Both partners full-time	40	24	32
Man full-time, woman part-time	15	24	23
Only man economically active	27	47	35
Both partners part-time	2	1	2
Other patterns	16	4	8
Total	100	100	100

Source: adapted from Bielenski and Wagner (2004:159).

Note: "Europe" here refers to Austria, Belgium, Denmark, Finland, France, Germany, Greece, Ireland, Italy, Luxembourg, the Netherlands, Norway, Portugal, Spain, Sweden, and the United Kingdom.

neo-traditional model's prevalence. This fact suggests many mothers experience a different calculus of work–life balance, one that leans more heavily toward the domestic sphere, than full-time career mothers like those portrayed in *The Second Shift* (who, it should be noted, can still expect "a ghastly eighty hours per week in work at home and for pay" [Thistle 2006:138]). The latch-key-kid arrangement may put children at risk—the jury is still out—but in these contexts it also represents a strategy by working parents to shoulder the costs of families' private welfare when mothers face persisting labor market disadvantages.

The Mommy Wars

As discussed earlier in this chapter, in recent decades working mothers have increased the time they spend caring for their children. However, so too have non-working mothers, who unsurprisingly devote more time now in this area than any of their predecessors, according to time-use researchers. In 2000, U.S. stay-at-home moms spent an average of 15.6 hours a week on childcare—4.6 hours more than working mothers (Bianchi et al. 2006:77). The upward trends in childcare illustrate how the standards of mothering—for working and stay-at-home mothers, married or single—have changed dramatically since the 'housewife' of mid-twentieth century lore (who to some observers today must seem like she had a far easier time raising children). Yet the fact that mothers of all categories are on average giving their kids more time than they themselves or any prior generation received is often overshadowed by the attention given in North America and the UK to the "mommy wars" between mothers who work full time versus mothers who stay at home. Sustained in numerous talk shows, articles (e.g., Darton 1990), and books like *Mommy Wars* (Steiner 2006), this conflict pits mothers against one other based on apparently antithetical priorities; non-employed mothers stay home full-time to maximize quantity and quality of time with their children, while working mothers find personal fulfillment in their careers and give their children a happy caretaker, a productive role model, and extra family income (see Hays 1996:145–6). One mother (Evans 2006) depicts the antagonism she witnesses in the mommy wars as each side views the other through the prism of their own choices:

> "You must feel guilty," the stay-at-home mom sneers, pulling out her switchblade, taking another jab.
>
> "You must be so bored," the working mom says, spitting in disgust.
>
> Spit. Jab. Spit. Jab. Spit. Jab.
>
> (p. 63)

Many observers give credence to the notion of a value conflict between working mothers and stay-at-home mothers because it resonates with other discourses of "culture war," most notably surrounding the ideology of maternalism that modern women and men have wrestled with (Blair-Loy 2003; Faludi 1991). Interestingly, despite the traditionalism that stay-at-home mothers seem to symbolize, many of their advocates invoke the 'post-feminist' value of choice when they assert a right to decide their own lifestyle and recast their contributions to their children through the legacy of the women's movement. "Here is my admittedly utopian definition of feminism: self-determination for women," writes one stay-at-home mother (Shea 2006). "I am doing exactly what I want to be doing in this fleeting chapter of my life that includes my daughter's childhood" (p. 112). "The feminist in me is grateful to every mother who remains in the workplace, but it's partly because I am so fiercely, proudly feminist that I want to raise my own kids," explains another stay-at-home mom (Clifford 2006). "Sexist messages still abound, and I want to make sure that, day in, day out, *I* get to counter with [my husband's] and my view of things" (p. 82). This post-feminist rhetoric neutralizes criticisms of maternal selflessness; fusing the latter with an assertion of self-determination, it proposes an ideal in which family QOL is accomplished by harmonizing children's development with mothers' self-actualization. The micro-relations of conflict and power that underlie family QOL seem to disappear in this view.

Still, there are reasons to question the idea that different values pit stay-at-home against working mothers. The divide between mothers is illusory, or at least overstated, if it suggests that mothers opt for all or nothing, that is, working or staying at home for the duration of their offspring's childhood. As we have now seen, in fact most mothers find themselves in both camps over the course of their lives, staying home with children at some points and then working (at least part-time) at others. The number and age of children, maternal leave policies, childcare availability and affordability, career opportunities and prospects, the stability of a breadwinner's job—such variables change frequently and alter the costs and benefits for women and families if mothers stay at home or seek employment. The lack of control over families' material situations is an experience shared by mothers on both sides; respectfully acknowledged, it could perhaps lay the grounds for a mommy war détente (Warner 2005). Yet even that common ground assumes the framework of individual choice: not in the post-feminist terms of decisions made of free will, but rather the need to take initiative for one's family's well-being in a context of social and economic uncertainty. Choice in this latter sense is unequal; periodically threatened for the mommy war partisans, it is structurally lacking in a broad swathe of households including single mothers, who cannot freely choose one option or the other, and (with substantial overlap) poor families, who live with the consequences of unemployment or, more often, underemployment in a political economy that compels families to earn their well-being in the labor market.

The mommy wars in turn point to the anxieties of middle-class striving in today's information economies. The heat generated around the mommy wars' ultimate question—whose QOL do mothers serve, families or their own?—distracts attention from the unnoticed fact that all categories of parents, fathers included, currently spend more time attending to their children than prior cohorts ever did. Why? In a world where the route to children's prosperity and well-being seems more and more unclear, middle-class families perceive that rewards lie for those adept in intellect and sociability with resource gatekeepers. So assured, they concertedly cultivate an ever-expanding range of skills and behaviors in their children, the rewards for which are emphatically extrinsic. Preschool language classes enhance early cognitive development; team sports teach responsibility and cooperation; prosaic lessons in how to address adults respectfully enhance children's ability to network later in life. Parents organize their quality time with children to lay a firm foundation of parental attachment, if not more specific developmental goals: attending children's events, practicing skills in athletics or second languages, and so on. Through such instrumental, rationalized child-rearing, middle-class children are hardly 'left to be children' in the ways they themselves were, or the way children still are in working-class and poor families, where parents typically lack the time, resources, or history of successful interactions with gatekeepers to motivate such an undertaking (Lareau 2003; see also Hays 1996).

Supervising a Carefree Childhood

In 2007, a British non-fiction bestseller entitled *The Dangerous Book for Boys* (Iggulden and Iggulden 2007) stoked a national fascination for the games, skills, and adventures that preoccupied boys of an earlier era when unscheduled play and modest standards of household consumption (certainly no video games!) compelled children to engage the environments and materials of their everyday lives with imagination and creativity. The book quickly became a bestseller in the U.S. as well, suggesting a transatlantic nostalgia for a simpler, 'less overprotective' childhood that seems unimaginable now—at least to many parents. Its readers might not realize that *The Dangerous Book for Boys* draws upon a longer cultural ambivalence over the twentieth century about the burdens shouldered by modern children. Historian Peter Stearns observes that the growth of the latchkey children arrangement accompanying women's mass entrance into the workforce could have "increased the possibility that children might be asked to do things around the house. Latchkey kids, for example, might need to start dinner or maintain other activities until the parent got home." Instead, for the most part, American parents generally bent over backwards not to saddle children with extra chores or household responsibilities, observes Stearns (2003):

> But what is really remarkable, given the rise of single parents and working mothers, is that the overall level of chores did not go up, according to all available evidence. There was some significant impact on younger kids, but this was balanced by the continued decline in commitment to chores by older children. Parents—even single mothers—worked hard to avoid a

> real redefinition. They went to great lengths to prepare meals before they themselves left the house, requiring a child at most to dish stew up from a hotpot. Weekends became times for frenzied parental activities, cleaning the house with at most an hour or two of help from a younger child. Stress may have existed for children, given parents' absence and mental preoccupation, but the actual chore level reflected parental guilt, rather than parental imposition.
>
> (p. 158)

Thus, a carefree childhood, long a mainstay of middle-class family ideals, has become another parental obligation, joining the list of conditions that mothers feel they should create and sustain for their children. Of course, not all parents share this view, as attested by too many refrigerator calendars crammed with extracurricular activities that children must attend and be driven to. The recent growth of expert pronouncements urging mothers and fathers to scale back their "hyper-parenting" (e.g., Honoré 2008; Rosenfeld and Wise 2000) may even give the impression of another culture war dividing families today. However, both advocates and opponents of hyper-parenting share anxieties about the risks awaiting children caught in the drift of modern life, from diminished cognitive potential (for proponents of early education) to a sedentary, passive orientation to play (an implicit motive behind *The Dangerous Book for Boys*).

In the environment of social and economic uncertainty that faces families today, what seems untenable, yet ultimately unmanageable, for middle-class parents is the possibility that children might develop on their own, independent of parental influence. In fact this too is a legacy of the liberal welfare regime, in which all are individually responsible for their own, well-being. In such a setting, children learn to expect individual autonomy, perhaps because no institution—no state, educational system, religion, or familial tradition—makes a serious, consistent counterclaim on their *collective* duty and welfare. This point surfaces in the observations of Benjamin Chabert, a French teenager who spent a year in the U.S.:

> Two things surprised him about life in America. Academically, his American peers were way behind. Benjamin knew more about English grammar than they did. That's not surprising given the drill-type education French children receive and the number of hours they spend at school—up to forty per week. On the other hand, Benjamin said, American teenagers were much more "socially mature" than his French peers. Most of the high school students he met had part-time jobs and earned their own pocket money. They came and went as they pleased between home and school, setting their own schedules and taking responsibility for their lives. Most expected to be driving at age sixteen and to own their own car soon after.
>
> (Nadeau and Barlow 2003:177–8)

Certainly there are sources of peril awaiting children today in a society like the U.S., where they are more likely than the Baby Boom to have no brothers or sisters, have a working mother, see their parents divorce, spend significant amounts of time without adult supervision, have sex during their mid-teens (particularly for girls), and hold a job before their high school graduation (Mintz 2004:4). Potentials for risk but also for individual autonomy and flourishing: these, as we will explore throughout this book, are the guideposts through which people generally pursue QOL in the liberal welfare regime.

Conclusion

This chapter's tour of the contexts for family QOL and its many crises highlights a number of themes that will inform my analysis in the coming chapters. Family illustrates how the provision and conception of QOL for any social unit should be assessed for both the whole *and* each member. Such a micro-relational assessment takes into account the particularities of the unit's composition and internal history—in the case of family, each member's role (mother, father, child, etc.), household type (composed along single- vs. two-parent family, dual-provider/neotraditional/single breadwinner arrangements, etc.), and the life-stage of each member as well as the collective (punctuated by the number and timing of children, parents' labor history, and so on). The analytical attention to life-stage that family highlights turns out to be an especially important lesson in this book. Life-stage reveals the social unit's internal history, embedded within social contexts, along which members' understandings and pursuits of QOL arise and evolve; where a critical inquiry into 'QOL' is concerned, life-stage belies the fallacy of unchanging aspirations, obligations, and values that pervade popular thinking on QOL (illustrated in this chapter by the mommy wars). In turn, families are very much evolving, historical creatures of society. Especially significant for our critical inquiry is how today's understanding and pursuit of individual flourishing emerged out of the primal act of self-reflection and individualization—that is, of family conflict—in which women struggled against patriarchal subordination and children sought a life distinct from the ones their parents ascribed. Altogether, these themes suggest that below the taken-for-granted exterior of any social unit lie relations of conflict and power that enforce an uneven distribution of QOL aspirations and opportunities.

Notwithstanding British prime minister Margaret Thatcher's proclamation to the contrary at this chapter's beginning, forces of society and economy have always powerfully shaped the familial unit as well as ideas of 'individual QOL' and 'family QOL.' One significant force is scientific authority, exemplified by the many child development experts who generate new wisdom on what children's well-being involves and how parents should act to promote it. In one sense, modern experts have merely taken the place of traditional authorities (patriarch, church, community) who similarly intervened in households' affairs and obligated parents' conformity to their dictates. However, today's experts differ by their rational authority that motivates the adherence of families and other social institutions. Drawing on the Enlightenment of science as critical wisdom, such rational authority articulates an account not of its own self-interest or other imminent social relations but of extrinsic concerns, be those the 'greater good' or simply the 'good of the children.' Another key institution that family highlights is the state, or more specifically the constellations of policy and underlying philosophies that comprise different welfare regimes. These provide the institutional frameworks through which families secure their material welfare and conceive their QOL aspirations—as single-breadwinner households, individuals enshrined (and compelled) by the market, or universally entitled citizens.

These themes gives an analytical edge to our recurring question, whose QOL? And whose 'QOL'? The exclusive assignment of caregiving work to mothers; the separation of the public sphere of the formal workplace from the domestic sphere of home and family; policy choices in the Anglo-American world that compel families to secure their well-being through the market—these social arrangements have shaped the world in which many parents simply cannot find enough hours in the day to raise families, earn income, and find a life of their own in an equitable and meaningful way. What is so potent, and for critical thinkers so chilling, about Thatcher's quotation (truly one of the great political expressions of economic liberalism as a way of life) is how it asks us to ignore the contexts for the QOL we experience and naturalize the initiatives and accountabilities of individual men, women, and families for their own well-being. As I will further argue in the coming chapters, such blindness to history and social contexts comprises a key feature of the dominant QOL outlook. That said, the market framework of the liberal welfare regime gives Thatcher's dictum the force of reality. The necessity of labor-market competition and the sources of economic uncertainty that we will encounter in the next chapter make such familial effort compelling, if not quite rational from all angles.

5 Work

> We are dealing with a cultural evolution … . How long do you think we can have a free and democratic society if we insist on maintaining totalitarian systems in our companies? We must have freedom for individuals and organizations to grow and to realize their potentials.
>
> (Delmar Landen, head of organizational development at General Motors, 1981)

Conceivably, examining the connection of work to personal QOL suggests an easy case for their zero-sum relationship: the more we work, the less QOL we have. Work's toll on our bodies, consumption of our waking hours, and contamination of our solace are historic burdens that persist into the present day. Who cannot recognize to some degree the experience described in the 1730 British poem, "The Thresher's Labour" (quoted in Jordan 2003:80)?

> LET those who feast at Ease on dainty Fare,
> Pity the Reapers, who their Feasts prepare:
> For Toils scarce ever ceasing press us now;
> Rest never does, but on the Sabbath, show;
> And barely that our Masters will allow.
> Think what a painful Life we daily lead;
> Each Morning early rise, go late to Bed:
> Nor, when asleep, are we secure from Pain;
> We then perform our Labours o'er again:
> Our mimic fancy ever restless seems;
> And what we act awake, she acts in Dreams.
> Hard Fate! Our Labours ev'n in Sleep don't cease;
> Scarce HERCULES e'er felt such Toils as these!

To these venerable burdens, the contemporary worker can add three others symptomatic of the "new world of work" (see Cooper and Burke 2002). First, the erosion of stable employment has reached remarkable levels; a 1999 report estimated that by that year, the typical American had already worked for nine different employers (Clark 1999; reported in Schwartz 2004:35). Anxiety over job loss, underemployment, and other forms of work insecurity (or "precarity," to invoke the mobilizing theme for European labor activists; Ross 2009) takes its toll upon blue- and white-collar workers alike, manifesting as personal stress and emotional turmoil shared by workers' families and communities. Second, many are putting in more hours than ever, often just to keep themselves and their households financially afloat. In her 1991 book *The Overworked American*, economist Juliet Schor (1991) quotes a 59-year-old blue-collar worker whose plight will be all too familiar to readers today whose pensions and individual retirement accounts deflated in the recent economic downturn:

> Just at the point in my life where I was hoping I could ease up a little bit on the job and with the overtime, I find that I have to work harder than ever. If I'm going to have enough money when I retire, I have to put in five good years now with a lot of overtime because that is what they will base my pension on. With all the overtime I have to work to build my pension, I hope I live long enough to collect it.
>
> (p. 32)

In the previous chapter, we encountered the third burden of contemporary work: the work–life imbalance experienced by households as parents and other adults of employable age commit to increased hours in the formal workplace. Altogether, these conditions constitute the *crisis of work-based QOL* that has gripped public imagination in recent decades.[1]

Yet we also know and sometimes even glimpse around us how for some people work can be the *muse to personal QOL*, providing them outlets for creativity, autonomy, and self-actualization that in turn inspire them to greater degrees of morale and productivity that benefit the workplace. The factors that give work its "challenge"—the feature that 20,000 information technology workers cited most frequently (67 percent) in an *Information Week* poll on what matters most in a job (Florida 2002:90)—are the focus of an extensive body of research investigating the synergy between work and QOL. The stakes of this investigation seem nothing less than a human renaissance, the restoration of longstanding values and ways of being that were lost to the daily grind of industrial work. This quest reflects a Romantic vision of work that draws upon the craft and professional traditions. With their intellectual and artistic stimulations and their control over work's pace and organization, craft and professional vocations approach the loftiest Aristotelian ideals of 'leisure' as an activity that involves reflection, learning, and the practice of a skill:

> Craftspeople and professionals have much in common as ideal types of workers. First, they do not make sharp distinctions between work and leisure—both reflect a continuity of life and work. Second, their work is a direct extension of what they are. They are what they do and are proud of it. Third, because of their commitment to their work, they are often respected by others in society. Fourth, and most important, both are

> independent. No one tells them what to do when they are engaged in doing the work at hand.
>
> (Ciulla 2000:69)

In these contrasting views of work, QOL is typically regarded as an individual property. Philosopher Joanne Ciulla provides a simple yet elegant utilitarian framework for understanding the gamut of individual orientations, from bane to inspiration, toward work-based QOL. Although the goals people have for work are subjective and can reflect an almost infinite variety of wants and needs, we can begin to think about them by distinguishing between intrinsic and extrinsic rewards: work can be its own reward, or it can be the means to other goals, respectively. Four overarching values frame the pursuits of these intrinsic and extrinsic rewards: meaningful work, leisure, money, and security (Ciulla 2000:16). These generic terms mean different things for different people in different settings, obviously, but their ability to cover the many incentives and experiences of work-based QOL is impressive. Meaningful work and leisure pertain to the control one exerts over one's works activities and, in this sense, are fundamentally intrinsic aspects of work. By contrast, money and security are more obviously extrinsic rewards of work, as they provide means for personal goals pursued outside the realm of work. Since hardly any job can satisfy all four goals equally, they must be *balanced through personal choices* in the kinds of work people pursue; the priorities individuals assign to one or more of these values inform the subsequent trade-offs they might make in their choices about work. For instance, being a musician may be the most meaningful occupation I can imagine, but since my aspirations far exceed my ability (sadly, a result of my childhood resistance to music lessons), I accommodate this constraint on my pursuit of this goal and pursue a different kind of balance with the opportunities and abilities that I do have. Maybe I pursue the second most meaningful occupation I can think of; or prioritize the leisure, money, or security I can find in yet other occupations; or maybe combine these two alternates somehow.

As economists recognize, prioritizing and pursuing individual preferences do not mean the choices people have are ideal. In the realm of work, the supply of jobs does not always suit all job-seekers' preferences, nor do they necessarily have the needed aptitudes and skills for the work that is available. Yet even taking a 'bad' job, one that threatens to crush the spirit, can be understood through this framework as a personal trade-off of sorts, particularly if we recall the cognitive dynamic of adaptation by which people report positive subjective well-being in negative objective conditions (see Chapter 1). Bad jobs offer little in the way of meaningful work, but to the extent we take them, we effectively pursue a different kind of work-based QOL that revolves around the secondary values of leisure, money, or security. Furthermore, "These values carry different weights at different times in life," as Ciulla (2000:16) observes, thereby highlighting the organizing role of the life-course in the work-based QOL people pursue. As a failed musician but, more significantly, a new parent,

I choose to prioritize my goals for work in the order of leisure (to have time to care for my children at home), security (to obtain consistent health insurance for my family), and money (to provide for as many of the remaining necessities to raising children as possible). Thus, I might relegate meaningful work to the bottom priority, seeing my choice as a necessary and meaningful sacrifice that comes with raising a family (see Bellah et al. 1996:69). Alternatively, I might view my private 'career' as parent to be the most meaningful work I have ever undertaken. Different stages of life bring different constraints; traditional parenting norms often limit women's career opportunities and raise men's earnings expectations at the time they bear and raise children, for instance, while a non-traditional, part-time path to college and graduate degrees can prevent working-class individuals from optimally timing their careers in high-paying 'front-loaded' sectors in medicine and law. Thus, specific life-stages mediate the external impact of gender, class, race, and other social forces and make more or less feasible certain pursuits of work-based QOL.

While Ciulla's theory helps us understand how people approach personal work-based QOL in modern societies, it begs an important question. Do the four values of meaningful work, leisure, money, and security and the trade-off calculus by which they are pursued comprise a universal framework of work-based QOL? As the last two chapters have illustrated, the individual QOL perspective that underlies Ciulla's utilitarian calculus of personal trade-offs represents a historical development. Accordingly, this chapter develops a historical account of work-based QOL, both as a lived experience and (a far more recent endeavor) an idea for evaluating work. Whereas the prior chapters addressed work's historic roles in generating technological productivity (Chapter 3) and giving economic form and function to the family unit (Chapter 4), in this chapter I discuss the QOL that people obtain in formal work activities and settings. Although I focus on the workplace extensively here, the reader should keep in mind those external connections to work discussed earlier, which illustrate how work itself is rarely the only factor in work-based QOL. Below, I review the evolution of industrial work to examine how work has impoverished the personal QOL of so many, and how they have consented to this, before examining some recent thinking on how work can actually enhance personal QOL. Although many people may never personally experience work as the muse of their QOL, we will see how the contemporary discourse surrounding this ideal draws *everyone* into the stark new world of work shared by the less fortunate "working slob."

A Brief History of the Daily Grind

Antipathy to work seems a timeless human experience. "As punishment for his ambition, Adam was sentenced by the Lord to work the earth with the sweat of his brow," observes psychologist Mihaly Csikszentmihalyi (1990). "The passage of Genesis (3:17) that relates this event reflects the way most cultures, and especially those that have reached the complexity of 'civilization,' conceive of work—as a curse to be avoided at all costs" (p. 144). Insofar as human proclivities (i.e., what we want to do) and aptitudes (what we can do well) diverge from the tasks of material survival (what we must do), the opposition between work and personal QOL is no doubt an ancient experience. But which social settings systematically oppose work to personal proclivity and aptitude? Many scholars would point to the division of labor, the crucial historic achievement by which societies flourish materially (see Chapter 3), as the original force setting work against personal QOL. By specializing task and skill, the division of labor limits the free play of human curiosity and technical ability. Invariably, once leaders, managers, and other 'higher' specializations of mental labor appear on the historical scene, emotional labor is also exacted when subordinates must appease their superiors with word as well as deed. In the modern industrial context, most workers, perhaps all of them, subordinate their personal goals and even more—their ego, social esteem, life-chances—to the execution of the collective goal in assembly lines and bureaucracies (Marx [1844] 1978; Weber [1920] 2005c).

We get ahead of ourselves. Returning to prehistoric life, there is evidence that many traditional groups and societies saw the division of labor that would hurdle them into modern civilization as a bad deal—the argument anthropologist Marshall Sahlins (1972) makes in his seminal work, *Stone Age Economics*. Examining contemporary hunter-gatherer bands as a proxy for prehistoric societies on the cusp of the Neolithic Era, Sahlins contends that these primitive groups, whom he calls "the original affluent society," generally reject the simple divisions of labor required by agriculture for fear of losing their leisure-filled lives. In one Tanzanian group, for instance:

> The Hadza, tutored by life and not by anthropology, reject the Neolithic revolution in order to keep their leisure. Although surrounded by cultivators, they have until recently refused to take up agriculture themselves "mainly on the ground that this would involve too much hard work." In this they are like the Bushmen, who respond to the Neolithic question with another: "Why should we plant, when there are so many mongo-mongo nuts in the world?"
>
> (p. 27; quoted in Gershuny 2000:52)

Skipping ahead to medieval Europe further supports Sahlins' claim that rest is abundant in traditional societies. Historian Ian Blanchard (1994) describes a typical year experienced by British men over a millennium of feudal agriculture:

> [In England the] male participants in the familial labour force were engaged almost exclusively in field-work with its characteristic pattern of work intensity. Each year after the long Christmas recess their work steadily built up to a climax in late February and March when they laboured mightily in preparation of the tilth. A dry spring augured particularly heavy and protracted work . . . . Thereafter Easter ushered in

> a period of relative calm until the fruits of their labour were ready to be garnered and harvest time once more witnessed a phase of intense male labour. In July they mowed the meadows. In August they aided the women to bring in the grain crops and in September they prepared the winter crop land. Then peace once more prevailed. Periods of great work intensity, in spring and late summer, thus alternated with periods of relative idleness, but overall the menfolk of the family enjoyed a relatively light work load, labouring only some 128 days a year.
>
> (pp. 12–3)

Considering the generally dim view that modern people hold of life in the Middle Ages, the idea that peasants spent about three-fifths of the year not working comes as a shock—a reaction that contemporary proponents of shortening the work-week have used to good effect; see Figure 5.1.

Figure 5.1 Flyer from the Take Back Your Time Day campaign (2003)

Illustration by Jennifer Akre.

Yet a closer investigation of this quotation also reveals that rest in traditional societies rarely held the connotations of 'leisure time' with which people now associate it. Obviously, without clocks and the measurement of work in terms of hourly wages, the measurement of time spent at work and rest was hardly possible, much less pressing (see Urry 2000:108–10; Thompson 1967). But more generally, before contract-based economies, peasants rarely understood their work as a personal exchange of labor-time for income or other rewards. In the agricultural past, they experienced rest much as they did work: an external, unalterable constraint built into the temporality of the day (before electricity illuminated the nights), the seasons, and the rituals of religion and community (which in many societies mandated the first periods of leisure, i.e., "holidays"; Blanchard 1994:19; Heschel 1952). Rest was frequent and no doubt frequently enjoyable but rarely understood as a reward for individual effort. Furthermore, with class position enforced by military force, consumption habits fixed by tradition and sumptuary law, and no real consumer goods to speak of, feudal peasants gained almost nothing by laboring more. Thus, the pre-modern world was hardly one in which work and rest were meaningful, actionable choices undertaken through a personal calculus of values toward work.

Achieving the Trade-offs of Work

In Europe of the Middle Ages and the developing world more recently, peasants' venerable schedules of work and rest, sustained by custom and law, would be transformed only through the wrenching social and cultural changes set loose by capitalism and the Industrial Revolution. Characteristically, these changes introduced systematic variations into the human experience of meaningful work, leisure, money, and security. Accordingly, their legacy is not just industrial drudgery and toil but also the very experiential framework by which people now conceive the QOL 'trade-offs' of work.

Take, for instance, the security of employment, a condition that medieval peasants most likely would know as an unfree life of feudal agriculture; for them to view 'security' as a choice would be meaningful only once the opposite, *insecurity* of work, became common—which it did on a mass scale via the historical trends of enclosure and proletarianization that gave us the condition of 'free labor.' Or, take the pursuit of money. For feudal peasants, accumulating wealth could threaten expropriation and physical force by landholding vassals and exile from their peers; one could really only pursue money, at least without fear for one's personal well-being or community existence, in the urban, contract-based economy of capital and wages, where money served as a medium of exchange. For the great masses of modern society, the pursuit of money thus required immersion into the social infrastructure of wage labor and industrial labor demand—the same setting in which "all that is solid melts into air," in Karl Marx's evocative phrase. Or, consider leisure. Only after the Industrial Revolution separated the sphere of work geographically and experientially from the home would 'getting a life,' to invoke the contemporary phrase for the uses of leisure, involve leaving the physical space and social order of the workplace. Sociologist and affluent society critic C. Wright Mills (1951) draws a direct line of descent from the factories of Marx's time to the white-collar offices of the post-World War II era:

> Alienation in work means that the most alert hours of one's life are sacrificed to the making of money with which to 'live.' Alienation means boredom and the frustration of potentially creative effort, of the productive sides of personality. It means that while men must seek all values that matter to them outside of work, they must be serious during work: they may not laugh or sing or even talk, they must follow the rules and not violate the fetish of the 'enterprise.' In short, they must be serious and steady about something that does not mean anything to them, and moreover during the best hours of their day, the best hours of their life. Leisure time thus comes to mean an unserious freedom from the authoritarian seriousness of the job.
>
> (p. 236)

Finally, consider the meaning of meaningful work. Crucial here is the rise of modern work ethics exhorting us to a lifelong 'calling' of hard work, as Max Weber documented in *The Protestant Ethic and the Spirit of Capitalism* ([1905] 2005b): as religious doctrines regarding the age-old concern for attaining one's salvation evolved, a work ethic emerged in Western Europe and the United States to uphold a secular calling through ceaseless industriousness in the realm of work. Of course, for the industrial proletariat, designating their toil as 'meaningful'—much less as a personal 'calling'—could seem patently absurd, but the work ethic nevertheless undermined the broader cultural support for workers' resistance to surplus drudgery:

> As Max Weber (in Michael Rose's apt summary) was to point out, looking back on the job already performed, the work ethic 'amounted to an attack' on the 'traditionalism of ordinary workers' who 'had operated with a fixed image of their material needs which led them to prefer leisure and to forgo opportunities to increase their income by working harder or longer.' Traditionalism 'was disparaged'.
>
> (Rose 1985:30; quoted in Bauman 1998:11)

Importantly, for capitalists and workers alike, the Protestant work ethic legitimated an individualized framework toward work and the personal goals it might advance. Certainly workers might share proletarian sentiments that frustrate their bosses' exhortations to embrace hard work, but increasingly they shared the same dreams of rising consumption and entrepreneurial opportunity (cf. Thompson 1967). In a context where industrial divisions of labor alienated workers from an autonomous engagement with their labor and its products, the work ethic promoted an instrumental outlook in which work became valued for its personal extrinsic rewards, be that salvation or more secular dreams of material acquisitiveness.

The Good Ol' Days of Work

Given industrial capitalism's role in the history of work's degradation, it may be surprising to readers that many commentators regard its crystallization in the mid-twentieth century Western workplace (after the Depression in the U.S., after World War II in much of Western Europe) as the heyday of 'good work.' Such surprise indicates fading memories of the *standard employment relationship*, which sociologist Gerhard Bosch (2004) defines as a "stable, socially protected, dependent, full-time job … the basic conditions of which (working time, pay, social transfers) are regulated to a minimum level by collective agreement or by labour and/or social security law" (pp. 618–9). A fixed workday, employment insurance, other benefits, standardized job descriptions and schedules for promotion, sick days and paid vacation, to name just a few features, enhance workers' personal and family QOL in obvious ways. Perhaps less obviously, the standard employment relationship provides a predictable and legible schedule for the life-course, providing workers "a set of bureaucratic guidelines to organize their experience for the long term," observes sociologist Richard Sennett (1998:66). By being able to anticipate even meager promotions, benefits, and pensions, workers can plan for extrinsic rewards of work: mortgages can be taken out to buy homes; children's education saved for, retirement plans made, the latest consumer goods purchased. Significantly, these benefits do not lessen the alienating qualities of work; instead, they anchor a cultural and political framework through which workers accept and endure their daily grind. If 'meaningful work' seems nearly impossible to find in bureaucratized, Taylorized industrial capitalism, under the standard employment relationship workers can nonetheless derive QOL from their work's extrinsic rewards and the meaningful sense of accomplishment that comes with fulfilling ethical commitments to family and other moral communities.

The standard employment relationship highlights the evolving relations between corporate bureaucracy, workforce, and state over the twentieth century. As a rule, workers in this period did not gain job security and steadily rising earnings out of corporate altruism; instead, employers conceded these when they sought to plot out the corporation's long-term growth and depended upon a labor force versed in specific skills and workplace norms. In America, this mutual dependence between employers and employees was presaged by corporate-initiated 'welfare capitalism,' manifested in the company town built by the Hershey Chocolate Company in 1903 (in a Pennsylvania town called Hershey, no less) and, even more famously, the five-dollars-a-day wages that Henry Ford paid his Highland Park, Michigan, auto workers in 1914. Competitive pressures and, later, the Great Depression forced most companies to abandon such welfare capitalism policies, but following great political effort and no small amount of employer–labor turmoil, governments began guaranteeing workers' welfare by recognizing unions' right to collectively bargain for such concessions or publicly providing them outright via the nascent welfare state.

These developments laid the ground for the great labor peace in affluent societies between World War II to the mid-1970s. The standard employment relationship was crucial to this peace, as it was widely recognized as embodying a social compact under which workers consented to employers' control over the process and products of work—i.e., to the alienating work that Karl Marx railed against—in exchange for job security, internal promotion (within the corporation or unions), and regular increases in earnings and consumption that would be pegged to the fortunes of employers (Greenhouse 2008; Reich 1998; Esping-Andersen 1990:187). In white-collar sectors, the standard employment relationship was symbolized in the 'organization man' (Whyte 1956), a now-derogatory phrase that evokes the homogeneous workplace cultures imposed by employers. In one of the more famous examples, the IBM Corporation controlled white-collar workers' work lives through dress codes (the "white shirt, dark suit, and sincere tie" [Smith, Berry, and Pulford 1999:24]), company songs, and extracurricular activities in offsite settings (golf courses, cocktail parties). Conformity to workplace norms of propriety was also expected outside of work in the private lives of employees and their families. In exchange for consent to this employer intrusion into daily life, white-collar workers received an enviable set of material rewards—good salaries, new homes, and access to good schools in the greenfield suburbs surrounding corporate branches—but also an important source of personal status as well (Packard 1959). Importantly, accounts from the post-World War II era reveal a this-but-no-more ethos informing the social compact between labor and employers: worker autonomy and reform of the production line were beyond the pale. Thus, sociologist David Riesman (1964) observed that "a group of union leaders in one of the more open-minded unions" that he studied for his seminal book *The Lonely Crowd* felt "it was impossible to get either unions or management in the least interested in making work more humanly satisfying" (p. 171).

Contemporaneous with the cultural tumult of the affluent society, the standard employment relationship was never whole-heartedly embraced by the era's critics. Notably, in his famous polemic *Growing Up Absurd* (1960) Paul Goodman derided the petty ambitions and bureaucratic assent with which it presumed to inspire post-World War II youth. Meanwhile, civil rights advocates stressed how only certain segments of the labor force were sheltered by the standard employment relationship. Befitting the single-breadwinner norms of the time, men monopolized the group of 'workers' privileged by the welfare state, and then generally only men of dominant racial and ethnic groups. Women and racial-ethnic minorities were regularly denied membership into the major unions and white-collar firms; they rarely received the protections of collectively bargained contracts. In the U.S., southern states lobbied heavily to exclude tenant farmers, sharecroppers, and migrant labor from New Deal legislation, an effort that disproportionately impacted non-whites (Domhoff 1996; Schwartz 1976). Needless to say, undocumented workers remain excluded from most of the welfare state's shelters today. Arguably, the authors of the twentieth-century standard employment relationship had rational, if not purely economic, reasons for restricting its eligibility among workers of Western societies. Excluding large parts of the labor force created the tight labor markets that gave organized labor political leverage and made collective negotiations with adversarial employers feasible by limiting the number of parties at the table (Olson 1965); as the last chapter indicated, this political economic balance of power continues to characterize conservative welfare regimes today. Yet if it was not a widely shared reality for most in the post-World War II era, the standard employment relationship nonetheless mobilized workers in these 'secondary labor classes' as a cultural value symbolizing nothing short of the fundamental redistributive promise of the affluent society. Not surprisingly, its protections and entitlements were central goals sought by the civil rights and women's movements of the 1960s and 1970s. In many Western nations, the political standing for the standard employment relationship fell apart just as these movements started to make gains toward its extension.

Pursuing 'Quality of Working Life'

Deindustrialization, the growth of service sectors, globalization, new applications of information technology—these and other economic trends eroded the growing market share and rates of productivity that had previously given corporations incentive to abide by the standard employment relationship. Currently, even as 'pro-business' advocates and lobbyists vigorously attack the standard employment relationship, employers nonetheless face an unprecedented insecurity in a turbulent global economy that portends the end of stable corporate bureaucracy. This chapter cannot address the vast debate about whether corporate collusion or economic constraint drove the retrenchment from the affluent society entitlements that shapes politics in today's liberal welfare regimes. Suffice it to say, these ongoing changes have dramatically impacted the well-being and sense of security that many workers enjoyed earlier in the century. Yet if the global economy's consequences for material QOL seem on the whole negative to most commentators, the cultural meanings of work-based QOL have expressed these consequences rather ambiguously.

The Quality of Working Life Initiative

Remarkably, it was only by the 1970s that 'QOL' as a term used in policy and popular language really began guiding the evaluation and reform of work explicitly. To some degree this is simple historic coincidence, since in this period the term proliferated in many other arenas of public discourse (recall Table 2.1). Still, the curious fact is that as the standard employment relationship began its slow demise, 'QOL' emerged to mobilize a rather substantial challenge to corporate organization of work; even more curiously, this challenge emanated largely from *within* the corporate fields of labor relations and business management. Over the 1970s and 1980s, a "quality of working life" (QWL) initiative took hold in Western European and later North American firms in response to workers' discontents over low levels of meaningful work, task variety and significance, organizational feedback, knowledge of results, and other potentially satisfying features of work that employers had rationalized away. This corporate movement acknowledged that workers understood the alienating quality of industrial work in antagonistic, even radical terms; one proponent situated the "revolt against work" in Western Europe amidst "the French worker-student revolt in 1968, the Italian 'hot autumn' of 1969, and general leftist tendencies in numerous countries" (Jenkins 1983:9). With the 1972 establishment of an International Council for the Quality of Working Life (Kolodny and van Beinum 1983:vii), human resources and management professionals officially hoisted the QWL banner, studying and advocating redesigns in the structures of occupations and organizations to promote the goals of enriching workers' jobs, increasing their interactions with fellow workers and management in meaningful ways, and establishing opportunities for educational and consulting opportunities within the workplace.

The extent to which the QWL initiative viewed work-based QOL as an organizational problem warranting deep and extensive reform can be gleaned from a representative paper of the era (Davis 1983:80–1; see also Boisvert 1977:156).

Excerpt from Louis E. Davis, "Learnings from the Design of New Organizations" (1983)

The important general criteria for high quality of working life, based on a variety of studies, are:

- security;
- equitable pay and rewards;
- justice in the work place [sic];
- relief from bureaucratic and supervisory coercion;
- meaningful and interesting work;
- variety of activities and assignments;
- challenge;
- control over self, work, work place [sic];
- own area of decision making (or responsibility);
- learning and growth opportunities;
- feedback, knowledge of results;
- work authority—authority to accomplish that for which one is held responsible;
- recognition for contributions—financial, social, and psychological rewards, status, advancement;
- social support—can rely on others when needed and be relied upon, can expect sympathy and understanding when needed;
- futures that are viable (no dead-end jobs);
- ability to relate one's work and accomplishments to life outside the workplace;
- options or choices to suit the individual's preferences, interests, and expectations.

In the typically terse and abstract language of this literature, the inventory above underscores how the initiative's proposals to shake up alienating organizational structures and constraining job roles were potentially radical in their scope. To some skeptics, they were hopelessly unrealistic insofar as they naively challenged a key tenet of the twentieth-century social compact, the rationalized authority of corporate bureaucracies (Esping-Andersen 1990:198).

The QWL initiative was historically significant for its attention to the quality of blue-collar work; manufacturing workers have long suffered alienating work and organizational rationalization, and the movement took aim at these accordingly. Yet with its origins in human resource offices and management schools and its growing emphasis on workplace productivity as an end goal, the QWL agenda drew mixed responses from labor. Some union leaders worried that the movement undermined their collectively-bargained contracts over the pace and process of work, if it was not in fact a covert attack on the unions' authority to represent rank and file's demands. A few QWL advocates acknowledged that by giving workers opportunities to have their say, make an impact in some situations, and thereby "identify with management goals," QWL reforms could indeed obscure managers' adversarial stance toward labor's demands (Jenkins 1983:23). Other union leaders, notably Irving Bluestone (1983) of the United Automobile Workers, saw harmony between the QWL initiative and unions' advocacy for a less alienating workplace, expressing interest in how the movement could make work more interesting and rewarding for workers—so long as management separated any QWL reforms from the provisions of collective bargaining.

Meanwhile, the QWL initiative gained traction among corporate management through the late 1970s and early 1980s. A quick scan of its literature of this era shows many an executive questioning or challenging the reigning Taylorist paradigm of hierarchical control over specialized and isolated rank and file (see, for instance, the quotation by General Motors' Delmar Landen that opens this chapter). Corporations grew warmer to QWL reforms when manufacturers, particularly in the U.S., sought to meet the challenge posed by Japanese competitors, who attributed their higher productivity to flexible assembly lines, just-in-time inventories, and "total quality management" that gave workers greater input and participation in shaping the nature and organizational context of the work process. Faced by the threat of economic failure, Western firms incorporated the Japanese-inspired paradigm shift to varying degrees, giving rise to the "flexible production" system that has become normative (if not fully adopted) for complex, information-processing organizations today (Amin 1994; Piore and Sabel 1984). In turn, the QWL initiative gained prominence as Western corporations adopted (or at least gave lip service to) aspects of the flexible production system, which resembled a kind of organizational 'democracy' for many movement adherents. In many cases, corporations got behind QWL reforms that unwittingly presaged later trends in precarity by introducing risk, uncertainty, and nonstandard work arrangements within the bureaucratic workplace. By advocating QWL as a means to enhance workforce competitiveness, workplace reforms gained a legitimacy among corporations that its earlier focus on QWL as an intrinsic goal for discontented workers did not.

Discovering the Work–Life Nexus

Despite these points of tension, the view of QWL that human resource professionals, corporate management, and labor representatives alike articulated is, from today's perspective, revealing for what it fairly ignored: *workers' life outside the workplace*. The 1970s and 1980s QWL literature gave relatively little attention to time scarcity or work–life balance, either in general or with specific regard to those workers charged with household caretaking, usually women. On those occasions when QWL researchers addressed family contexts of QWL, they tended to emphasize the effect of male breadwinners' employment and occupational status on family stability, marital satisfaction, and child relations. Women's QWL was rarely discussed as a condition of the formal workplace. In 1974, a year when some 45 percent of women were formally employed (Smith and Bachu 1999, Figure 1), sociologist Lee Rainwater (1974) would write in a central QWL research volume:

> Each of the major family roles (male adult, female adult, child) can be thought of as having a work component. The husband/father is expected to be the provider; that is straightforward enough. But much social policy ignores the fact that being a housewife is also a job . . . . If we took seriously the homemaker role as a job, we might consider a system of unemployment insurance for homemakers (to be paid by their husbands), and we would take as a goal of public policy the creation of opportunities for women to find and keep jobs as homemakers—that is, the facilitation of family stability and [for unmarried mothers] of remarriage.
>
> (p. 367)

The issue here is not that QWL advocates expounded male chauvinist beliefs (they were hardly alone in this regard) or that pinning a view of QWL to the single-breadwinner model that invariably privileges men is outdated (this premise still informs employment policy in much of Continental Europe and Japan). Cutting Rainwater some slack for adhering to what were unfortunately mainstream values for his time regarding women, what this exceptional reference in the QWL literature to women underscores is how the movement otherwise viewed caregiving and family as concerns outside the domain of QWL.

To appreciate how much the work-based QOL discourse has changed since the QWL initiative, compare the bullet-point criteria quoted earlier with this contemporary perspective, put forward in a conventional article on employers' QOL policies published in the influential management journal *Human Relations*:

> We define quality-of-life issues as any that impact a person's perception of his/her overall life quality. One such example is work-family balance . . . [O]ther issues might include states of being (e.g., satisfaction and balance in various life domains, physical and mental health, and well-being), having resources (e.g. time, money), and doing activities (e.g. work, recreation and leisure, service to others).
>
> (Dallimore and Mickel 2006:63)

This illustrates that, whereas the QWL initiative that thrived in the 1970s and 1980s centered on the intrinsic reward of work's meaningfulness, management and labor discourse regarding QOL and work has since begun *focusing on rewards expended outside the workplace*: leisure (i.e., time), money, and security. As the influence of the QWL initiative declined, not much attention in the scholarship and advocacy of work-based QOL has been paid to what was lost in the conceptualization of work-based QOL.

The context for the QWL initiative's decline as well as these shifts in thinking about work and QOL is the dramatic workplace transformations wrought by globalization and later the so-called new economy. The Japanese model of 'organizational democracy' so admired in the 1980s needed the conditions of secure employment and firm stability for shop floor expertise and labor-management rapport to develop. Such security and stability were precisely what started to disappear in the late 1980s. Workforce downsizing, automation and deskilling enabled by information technology, organizational restructuring, corporate relocations, entrepreneurial spin-offs, and other forces of economic turbulence laid waste to any semblance of organizational durability upon which any firm would invest in QWL-enhancing redesigns. The new business wisdom advocating entrepreneurial innovation and short-term profit pushed corporations, indeed entire industries, in the opposite direction. The effects on workforce stability were dramatic; a widely-cited 1999 article from *U.S. News and World Report* reported that 17 million people would voluntarily switch employers in that year alone (Clark 1999; reported in Schwartz 2004:35). The shift in work-based QOL literature—from changing the corporation to supporting workers' private lives and subjective well-being—reflects this new reality. Bereft of a stable workplace in which to pursue organizational reforms for QWL, workers have little basis to anticipate anything but pursuing enhancements of their personal work–life nexus for as long as their jobs might last.

QOL at Work Today: Are You Kidding?

With the standard employment relationship still a fresh memory for many Western workers, the pace of workplace change accelerated through the

1980s and 1990s with a revolution in information technology and later the boom (and eventual bust) of the new economy. As in prior eras of intense economic restructuring, public fears of the 'end of work' surfaced during this period. "Now, for the first time, human labor is being systematically eliminated from the production process," claimed social critic Jeremy Rifkin in *The End of Work* (1995). "Within less than a century, 'mass' work in the market sector is likely to be phased out in virtually all of the industrialized nations of the world" (p. 3). Economic indicators have since shown such pronouncements to be overwrought for the most part. Globalization and technology may have destroyed work as many once knew it, but jobs have hardly disappeared on the whole; rather, they rematerialize in other sectors and new, often lower-paying and less sustainable forms of employment (Carnoy 2002). Indeed, there exists such a diversity of employment modes today that to analyze them in a single profile is an exercise in scholarly hubris. If one had to discern a common thrust to the changes in work-based QOL, we might look to the extension of the employment insecurity that was once the province of secondary labor classes (i.e., women, ethnic-racial minorities, and youth) further up the workforce hierarchy. Otherwise, a multiplicity of work modes is, in many regards, *the* key point to consider when examining QOL at work today. Consequently, we might also be skeptical about the sweeping claims in debates over whether this new world of work is a boon for or bane of work-based QOL. As we will see, the individualistic connotations of 'QOL'—autonomy, self-actualization, and the like—provide unsteady goalposts now that the target of work-based QOL has moved away from the organizational context of work itself.

New Freedoms, New Burdens

Conceivably, the *erosion of the traditional breadwinner occupation* over the last three decades could unleash personal freedom for many. It is no stretch to assert that women's growing participation in the labor market symbolizes at least some element of meaningful achievement for women in their personal freedom and their advocacy of social change. As Chapter 3 showed, countries where breadwinner occupations hold a privileged place in welfare policy tend to be patriarchal and conservative in political culture and private life, and women in these countries tend to hold paying jobs much less frequently. Conversely, in the U.S. and other nations with more deregulated labor markets, the growing opportunities for part-time and freelance employment suit the preferences of many working mothers and other workers to carry out both formal work and family caregiving. Granted, when family welfare is an individual responsibility, women's work preferences and the opportunities to fulfill them are not necessarily pursued under optimal conditions, but it is unclear, on this count at least, whether the workplace has failed women as a site of personal fulfillment (see Chapter 4). One 37-year-old American mother of three seeking to re-enter the workplace puts the point succinctly: "We got equality at work. We really didn't get equality at home" (quoted in Porter 2006).

Likewise, the *impermanence of employment* may offer new opportunities to pursue QOL through work, if not a fixed workplace, by freeing workers from intolerable bosses, unwanted office politics, and bureaucratic constraints upon workers' initiative and creativity. In *Free Agent Nation*, Daniel Pink articulates a class manifesto of sorts for the independent contractor, temporary employee, and "permalancer" "who operates on his or her own terms, untethered to a large organization, serving multiple clients and customers instead of a single boss" (Pink 2001:25). The impermanence of employment gives free agents an opportunity to turn the tables on employers, as it were, and exploit them as temporary stops along a self-defined journey of personal interest, skill development, and work-life flexibility. Many of Pink's critics responded with concerns that the free agent-ethos he endorsed promoted a calculating and mercenary outlook and loosened traditional commitments to employers, communities, or even families. Several commentators worried whether public morality would dissolve into a market ethos of short-term self-seeking and commitment avoidance (Sennett 1998; Bellah et al. 1996; see also Hirschman 1970). Both sides of this debate missed the mark in one important respect. Its moralistic tenor (particularly in North America) and frequent references to the bureaucratic, 'organization man' office as the traditional experience of work underscored their distinctly middle-class perspective. The debate largely overlooks the longstanding precariousness of the lower classes or, for that matter, the freedoms from institutional 'commitment' enjoyed by the very wealthy.

Commentators also dispute the effects on QOL for the growing number of workers *holding two or more jobs*. Daniel Pink (2001) again illustrates the optimistic view, arguing that for free agents, this mode of employment offers a rational strategy of risk avoidance:

> [. . .] Freedom and security are not necessarily trade-offs. Not only is it more interesting to maintain a portfolio of clients and projects than it is to answer to a single boss, it may be safer. The more clients you can assemble, the more projects you can land, the more nodes you can add to your personal network, the more secure you will be.
>
> *Freedom, once a detour from security, is now a path toward security.*
>
> (p. 94; emphasis in original)

As with other 'freedoms' in the new world of work, the question to be asked is, whose QOL? Pink presumes a knowledge-based, innovative economy where symbolic analysts' skills and social contacts are dulled and diminished by serial, routine exercise under a single employer; in this world, multiple, episodic employment along a career trajectory of "horizontal hypermobility" enhances not just workers' own QOL but the bottom lines of firms and sectors as well (Florida 2002:104; Bahrami and Evans 2000). However, holding more than one job promises a far less innovative, far more exhausting work experience for those tied to physical workplaces outside the home. Academia is a well-studied case in point. Representing the largest growth sector of college personnel, adjunct faculty with PhDs in hand or almost completed must often eke out a full-time living by teaching a class or two here and there at more than one institution (Jacobs 2003). Because their workload imposes considerable travel and preparation time, such faculty are more likely to seek new employment and hold more jobs over the course, all of which detracts from time needed for research and family (Conley 2005:37). Further, these risks are disproportionately concentrated among particular groups. Because they constitute the majority of part-time faculty, women especially face the risk of falling behind men in the academic advancement track (summarized in Perna 2005; see also Aronowitz 2001).

Needless to say, the focus on knowledge workers understates the economic risks faced by low-wage, low-skill workers in personal service sectors, the group most likely to hold two jobs (see Castells 1996:208; Reich 1992:176). Among other things, parents in this category are often rendered effectively absent and leave their children at risk from unsupervised activities (Presser 2004; Edin and Lein 1997:133). Yet perhaps remarkably, some neoliberal advocates argue that holding the two or more jobs needed to put together a livable family income promotes low-skilled workers' personal and family QOL goals, at least relative to the dysfunctional effects of chronic underemployment. In this argument, parents and siblings who are employed and bring home earnings from any form of legitimate work help low-income households get ahead while role-modeling 'middle-class' values to young people who are vulnerable to temptations of welfare support or the underground street economy (see also Wilson 1997).

The Problem of Overwork

Then there is the *number of hours* people work, or overwork as it were—perhaps the most visible symbol of changing QOL in the new world of work. Far from the post-World War II vision of mass leisure, many Westerners perceive only less leisure, more work, and less in the way of effective choice about how the two are distributed. As Chapter 4 showed, Americans lead the way among developed Western nations in terms of having the longest standard work-week, no mandatory vacation policies, and high rates of women in the formal workplace. To the extent that other Western nations follow the lead of the United State's liberal welfare regime, these developments bode poorly for work-based QOL across developed societies. But are Americans working more than they used to? This is the contention of the "Take Back Your Time" campaign, which seeks to promote minimum paid-leave laws and raise public consciousness about the costs of overwork (De Graaf 2003; Robinson 2003). The campaign takes its cue from Juliet Schor, whose book *The Overworked American* laid out the case for the ever-growing work week and year. From 1969 to 1987, American workers took on 163 more annual hours on the job; this "extra month of work," Schor (1991) contends, "is attributable to both longer weekly schedules and more weeks of work" (p. 29). Other scholars, most notably sociologists John P. Robinson and Geoffrey Godbey (1997), have parsed the work-hours data differently to advance a contrary thesis: from 1965 to 1985, Americans' workweeks have in fact declined about six or seven hours. However, Americans tend to think they work longer hours than they actually do, a pattern Robinson and Godbey attribute to the subjective experience of 'time-deepening' that technology, multitasking, and rising expectations of personal productivity impose upon us.

Is overwork a reality or myth? Like the earlier (and in retrospect quaint) debate over whether work was 'ending,' the seemingly intractable debate of whether people work more hours gains some clarity when we abandon the search for a single trend and look to differences within the workforce. Historically, overwork has been the burden of the working classes—hence the importance of organized labor's victories in establishing the five-day work-week as a tenet of the standard employment relationship. In the contemporary period, however, we find evidence across developed nations of an unprecedented class reversal in who works longer hours. Analyzing time-budget data from 12 Western countries over the 1961–99 period, Jonathan Gershuny (2000) reports that overwork has become the province of the higher classes. Over the last century, this trend reflects the compositional shift within the ranks of the affluent, as those whose wealth derives from active employment have been eclipsed those whose wealth came from property and investments. He explains:

> As the general technological level of the society rises, there emerge requirements for very high levels of skill or productive competence, whose possessors can extract a 'rent' that rivals or exceeds that of the possessors of material capital or the inheritors of the feudal class, and positions toward the top of productive organizational hierarchies increasingly become sources of honour. And as production processes become more complex, more paid jobs may require skills which command such rents. So a growing proportion of the richest and most honoured members of the society have paid work in production institutions; and the specifically idle rich become a diminishing minority in industrializing societies . . . . Those of superior social status increasingly achieve this status by working longer hours.
>
> (pp. 71–2)

Today, among all workers, those in professional, technical and managerial occupations are most likely to work "long work weeks" of 49 or more (Rones, Ilg, and Gardner 1997; cited in Florida 2002:367 fn. 8). Meanwhile, subordinate groups face the undesirable situation of having too much 'time off,' i.e., finding too little paid employment. Again, generalizations are tricky; after all, in this lower tier we find those workers who are unwillingly compelled to hold more than one job. Yet below that time-impoverished stratum lies the 'underclass' of workers with the weakest attachment to the labor force, for whom unemployment brings hours of forced idleness, while above it lies the dispossessed proletariat, restructured out of the industrial occupations that gave their ranks meaning and mobility and in many cases saddled with the liabilities of narrow skills and 'inflexible' job-search expectations.

Why high-income earners overwork is also the subject of debate. One view focuses on the driving role of personal consumption. Many commentators attribute overwork to the 'needs' for greater earnings in order to satisfy material acquisition and status-seeking impulses. "Work-and-spend is a middle-class affliction," Schor (1991) argues in a claim that has become a point of faith for voluntary simplicity movements and popular polemics against overconsumption. Others look to the rising costs of middle-class fixed expenses—mortgages, insurances, education—that commit many parents to long hours at work. "Americans are not going broke over lattes! Americans are going broke over home mortgages and health insurance," contend researchers Elizabeth Warren and Amelia Warren Tyagi (quoted in Mieszkowski 2003; see Warren and Tyagi 2003). Yet consumption does not exhaust the reasons for overwork. In *Married to the Job*, psychologist Ilene Philipson (2002) observes that in nine years of conducting group therapy with career women, "no one I have seen in psychotherapy has ever discussed consumption in connection to what propels them to invest in their jobs. Rather, they are more likely to speak of emotional longings—for recognition, self-esteem, a sense of belonging, or purpose—that they seek to fulfill at their workplaces" (pp. 11–12; see also Hochschild 1997). Philipson reminds us that work remains a source of positive meaning in workers' QOL pursuits, even when it strains their private lives.

The Labor-market as Cultural Framework

The historical appearance and intellectual heat of these debates reveal a broader context: as the modes of employment multiply, *a collective ideal of modern work declines*. Increasingly, citizens of developed societies share fewer experiences and expectations, of the kind symbolized (if never universally fulfilled) by the standard employment relationship, about what work should provide people and what they should offer in return. It is not unreasonable to conceptualize the decline of this common ideal as the further demise of what Marx called class consciousness; while people are still social, empathetic creatures who relate to each others' predicaments, aspirations, and sacrifices through group affiliations, they do so less and less as collective producers, as workers. Organizational deinstitutionalization is a key factor here; when corporations go "flexible" and welfare states retreat from regulating work conditions, the market individualizes the experience of work as workers negotiate their earnings, hours, and benefits. As the virulent resistance in Continental Europe to 'pro-business' attacks on the 35-hour workweek suggests, these cultural and institutional shifts are probably strongest in the Anglo-American liberal welfare regime. Here, after nearly a half-century of union decline, corporate restructuring, and welfare-state retrenchment, workers really are 'on their own' in stark new ways where establishing the conditions and rewards of their employment is concerned (Craver 1993; Renshaw 1991).

The paucity of cultural references to shared class identities sets the stage for more personalized frameworks of public morality. Zygmunt Bauman (1998) helps us think about this in his discussion of an aesthetic, consumerist orientation in the new world of work. In a "world where aesthetic criteria rule supreme," people reject the ethical meanings of work, such as calling, duty, or entitlement, and view occupations and industries through the prism of 'interesting' versus 'boring' jobs. Boring jobs are understood to

> be chosen willingly only by people as yet unprocessed by the society of consumers and unconverted to consumerism, and thus satisfied with selling their labour in exchange for bare survival (first-generation immigrants and 'guest workers' from poor countries, or the residents of poor countries drawn into factories set by the immigrant capital traveling in search of cheap labour could be said to fall into this category). Others need to be forced into accepting jobs that offer no aesthetic satisfaction. Rough coercion once hidden under the veneer of the work ethic now appears barefaced and unconcealed.
>
> (p. 34)

Interesting jobs, by contrast, maximize and validate the currency of personal choice; they represent one of the highest status symbols in a society where work is compulsory (indeed, a cultural obsession) but ethical views of work have receded from view. Bauman's theory underscores how work and class, still viable sociological categories for analyzing our structural relations with one another, are increasingly lived and understood as individualized pursuits. Absent the sense of shared fate and collective identity expressed by collective frames of reference—the bureaucracy, class solidarity, the welfare state—people in a consumer society relate to fellow workers as impermanent third parties in job trajectories of serial hiring and firing. As the once-urgent question of how employers might enrich work and make the collective workplace more humane appears less practical and more utopian, they turn their attention to strategizing their own QOL goals for work, be they intrinsic rewards like autonomy and personal development, or less Romantic extrinsic rewards like earnings, perks, and job prestige.

Quintessentially, the labor market frames this individualized understanding and experience of work-based QOL. Economists view labor markets as social structures that aggregate job seekers and job opportunities; through the balance these two achieve, labor markets stratify job seekers in terms of potential competitiveness and likely reward. However, labor markets are more than arenas for job competition. As internal labor markets—i.e., the union protections and corporate promotions that once shielded breadwinners from the economy's turbulence—lose prominence within the new world of work, economic competition for jobs becomes more diffuse and more pronounced within the world 'outside' work. Penetrating the spheres of daily life such as family, education, and community, labor markets reinforce particular ideas, stories, and values about how to succeed. These comprise a culture of competitive, individual *homo economicus*, but all is not rational, Hobbesian struggle here. There is an affirmative vision as well: as a cultural framework of how people relate to one another, labor markets enshrine, indeed celebrate, the experience of choice. Where the evaluation of QOL is concerned, if we cannot definitively resolve such debates as whether it is consumer materialism or the workplace that seduces us to overwork, the labor market's centrality as a cultural framework makes those debates somewhat moot. As both scholarly ideal and lived experience, the labor market encompasses work's diverse appeals and trade-offs, the winners and losers of work-based QOL, expressing them all within a *single, universal currency of individual choice* as people pursue employment under conditions not always of their making.

Work as the Muse of QOL

This discussion provides the analytical basis from which to scrutinize the contemporary perspectives on how work can enhance QOL. Despite the battering that workplace restructuring has given personal QOL in the last few decades, work continues to entice and seduce many people, possibly more than ever before in human history. This is only partly attributable to popular endorsements of 'being your own boss' that promote entrepreneurialism and self-employment as the paths to self-actualization; many people still look to doing work and being in the workplace as ways to enhance their QOL. Below, I discuss three notable perspectives from the business and popular literatures that illustrate current ways people relate to work as the muse for QOL. These Romantic visions of work throw into sharp relief the changed contexts for pursuing work-based QOL.

The 'Cultures' of Companies

If it has become a truism that "corporations have personalities just like humans do," as Google's chief of philanthropy (quoted in Solomon 2008:13) recently commented, this reflects the influence of a management paradigm that originated in the late 1980s, when both business experts and investors began urging corporations to distinguish themselves from competitors within their markets through corporate image and brand. Extending that strategy into the realm of human resources, management literature has increasingly endorsed the cultivation of company culture, that is, a company's signature competencies and "values" (to use another unfortunately ambiguous term in the business context). Today, it is a regular commandment within boardrooms and employee lounges that firms articulate a company culture, make it coherent, and bring employees on board with it. Company culture gurus Terence Deal and Allan Kennedy (1999) illustrate the thinking behind this strategy:

> A robust culture in a cohesive enterprise is committed to a deep and abiding shared purpose. Its robustness is highly dependent on a unifying

> cultural tapestry woven over time as people cooperate and learn together. It is woven from the interplay of a set of interlocking cultural elements: History yields values. Values create focus and shape behavior. Heroic figures exemplify core values and beliefs. Ritual and ceremony dramatize values and summon the collective spirit. Stories broadcast heroic exploits, reinforce core values, and provide delightful material for company events.
>
> (p. 3; quoted in Philipson 2002:113)

Where is the company culture strategy implemented? Most visibly, it appears in retail and entertainment sectors, where employees are rewarded for demonstrating and advising customers on the branded experience or lifestyle being sold. Examples are fairly easy to identify: the 'magical' enthusiasm of Disney employees (or "cast members" within the corporation), for instance, the do-it-yourself home 'handyman' of the Home Depot staff, or the precocious sexuality and ennui of young Abercrombie and Fitch salespeople. But the display of company culture goes beyond consumer marketing, so that even business-to-business firms that might be obscure to the average consumer have also seized on the enhancement of their company culture as a means to 'add value.' As management experts Tom Peters and Robert Waterman explain in their genre-defining book *In Search of Excellence* (1982), employee identification with an authentic culture is the crucial first step to boosting corporate morale, innovation, and productivity:

> In the very same institutions in which culture is so dominant, the highest levels of true autonomy occur. The culture regulates rigorously the few variables that do count, and it provides meaning. But within those qualitative values (and in almost *all* other dimensions), people are encouraged to stick it out, to innovate. Thus, "IBM Means Service" underscores the company's overpowering devotion to the individual customer; but that very formulation provides remarkable space. Everyone, from clerks on up, is prodded to do whatever he or she can think of to ensure that the individual customer gets taken care of.
>
> (p. 105)

The company culture strategy not only offers existing employees opportunities to find genuine meaning in their work through the exercise of organizationally-specified 'autonomy,' it also shows its most positive side to potential employees as they consider new employment opportunities.

Often undertaken with great hoopla and at great expense, the company culture strategy paradoxically emerged around the time that corporations began seriously attacking rising payroll costs and eliminating or "rationalizing" positions across occupational strata, including management. Commentators have noted the contrary logic to these dual trends—one cost-generating, the other cost-cutting—but through trial and error firms can reconcile this contradiction by effectively selecting and cultivating employees who 'get the culture,' that is, who share the values and work-styles that firms want to emphasize to their specific markets. Research has yet to vindicate company culture as a surefire path to increased profit, but the question is largely immaterial for the strategy's impact on the workforce within the company: to promote employee self-discipline. When workers get the culture and embody its values of, say, 'integrity' (for highly regulated, politically active companies; on the case of General Electric, see Welch 2001:381), 'innovation' (in firms where the competitive advantage is impermanent), 'commitment' (where management expects long work-hours), 'having a life' (read: non-competitive pay for an overeducated workforce), or whatever messages are emphasized, they relieve employers of the need to invest in traditional sunk costs for the "Fordist" corporation, like managerial bloat, workplace surveillance, and other techniques of labor control.

Reflecting on these developments, sociologist Paul Du Gay (1996) contends that the company culture strategy signals the end of the corporation's ability to provide workers its own social world, its own total institution (cf. Goffman 1961). Precisely because firms can no longer systematically devote resources to employees' formal training and socialization, nor promise much in the way of internal promotion or job security, much less offer employee housing or after-hours entertainments, companies increasingly seek the 'fit' of their employees to organizational culture. As befits the lean "post-Fordist" firm, promoting company culture is a passive and cost-effective managerial strategy of workforce motivation and, in an important chain of logic, of workplace productivity. As the management tome *Corporate Cultures* tells managers, "A strong culture enables people to feel better about what they do, so they are more likely to work harder" (Deal and Kennedy 1982:6; cited in Ciulla 2000:132). Maybe management doles out an expensive party here or a time-wasting game room there, but those only symbolize the culture and entice employees into it. The labor and resources needed to adhere to company culture are put forth primarily by employees who either get it or learn quickly; those who fail to do either call attention to themselves as not having a long future with their employer. For this reason, firms can periodically cut back on the workplace perks and amenities and still expect workers to adhere to the culture.

Yet the company culture strategy empowers workers as well, by acknowledging and rewarding the personal sensibilities of workers who 'get it.' Workers who recognize the company culture within their own individual aspirations and experiences find new self-worth as valued contributors to a *gemeinschaft* of management and employees. Indeed, workers who *really* get the culture in a bold and 'entrepreneurial' way can put the fire to managers' toes, perhaps even becoming candidates for their jobs—all towards the end of motivating employees toward increased corporate performance and productivity. Like many forms of self-discipline, the company culture strategy masks its coercion with a discourse expressing something altogether different: in this case, *a new template for work-based QOL*. Here, workers discover where they fit based on their own personalities and values—their 'soul,' so to speak. The contrast to conventional Taylorist forms of hierarchical command is significant, as one British manager explains:

> You won't win by a stick. You won't win by a carrot. You'll only win by really making your people feel "I want to do this", not "have to", not "being attracted", but "I want to". And that's really the key.
>
> (quoted in Du Gay 1996:131)

Such cultural fit is certainly not loyalty. Recasting the serial hiring, quitting, downsizing, and firing in the new economy's labor market as a touchy-feely narrative of self-actualization, the strategy of company culture makes sense only because the corporate promise of internal promotion and job security is more or less gone.

For critics, including many workers subjected to this managerial strategy, company culture illustrates a rather plastic, superficial understanding of 'culture.' 'Integrity,' 'innovation,' 'commitment'—these and other buzzwords rarely smooth over the alienating features of work for many employees and merely add a note of high absurdity to the job. Management credibility frequently falls apart when employees are somehow expected to ignore prior cultures that accompanied earlier changes in management and strategy—a point that is regularly played for laughs in pop-culture references like the cartoon strip "Dilbert" and the television sitcom "The Office." For most workers, the psychic reward of sharing the company's culture is perhaps small compensation for the loss of benefits and security or the ever-looming specter of performance evaluations.

Flow

My second example illustrates how the discipline of psychology views the harmony between work and QOL. In his 1990 book *Flow: The Psychology of Optimal Experience* and many other writings, Mihaly Csikszentmihalyi, a key figure in the field of positive psychology, has explored the ways that people experience "flow," his concept to describe subjective conditions of enjoyment and concentration. Studying a broad range of satisfied doers, such as artists, athletes, intellectuals, and craftspeople as well as everyday job holders, Csikszentmihalyi (1990) identifies eight dimensions of flow:

> When people reflect on how it feels when their experience is most positive, they mention one, and often all, of the following. First, the experience usually occurs when we confront tasks we have a chance of completing. Second, we must be able to concentrate on what we are doing. Third and fourth, the concentration is usually possible because the task undertaken has clear goals and provides immediate feedback. Fifth, one acts with a deep but effortless involvement that removes from awareness the worries and frustrations of everyday life. Sixth, enjoyable experiences

> allow people to exercise a sense of control over their actions. Seventh, concern for the self disappears, yet paradoxically the sense of self emerges stronger after the flow experience is over. Finally, the sense of the duration of time is altered; hours pass by in minutes, and minutes can stretch out to seem like hours.
>
> (p. 49)

Combined, these features make the rewards of work intrinsic; work feels like an end in itself (what psychologists calls an autotelic experience), the key characteristic of flow (Csikszentmihalyi 1990:67).

Csikszentmihalyi acknowledges that flow thrives in particular historical and organizational settings. He writes of several communities living outside of industrial civilization for whom the work of daily subsistence—milking cows, tending to gardens, and so on—triggers the conditions for flow. Flow became threatened with the onset of industrial civilization, which introduced routinizing divisions of labor and bureaucratic practices that made work less complex, as well as emphasizing material pursuits that encourage people to wish they were doing something else. Unsurprisingly, the division of labor stratifies the experience of flow across the workplace, as Csikszentmihalyi (1990) observes:

> As one would expect, managers and supervisors were significantly more often in flow at work (64 percent) than were clerical workers (51 percent) and blue-collar workers (47 percent). Blue-collar workers reported more flow in leisure (20 percent) than clerical workers (16 percent) and managers (15 percent) did. But even workers on the assembly lines reported they were in flow more than twice as often at work as in leisure (47 percent versus 20 percent). Conversely, apathy was reported at work more often by blue-collar workers than by managers (23 percent versus 11 percent), and in leisure more often by managers than by blue-collar workers (61 percent versus 46 percent).
>
> (p. 159)

Yet if contexts affect flow, reform of the contemporary workplace is ultimately not the psychologist's goal. "Happiness, in fact, is a condition that must be prepared for, cultivated, and defended privately by each person," Csikszentmihalyi (1990) observes. "People who learn to control inner experience will be able to determine the quality of their lives, which is as close as any of us can come to being happy" (p. 2). His passages here suggest the route to happiness involves meditation or a philosophical journey through a lifetime, but his recommendations are much more mundane. "The best moments usually occur when a person's body or mind is stretched to its limits in a voluntary effort to accomplish something difficult and worthwhile. Optimal experience is thus something we *make* happen" (Csikszentmihalyi 1990:3). As a condition for work-based QOL, this voluntarism can involve exercising real choice—finding a better job, for instance—or coaching oneself to think differently about the present work situation, either by identifying what is most appealing or simply resigning oneself to pursuing recreation in a personal hobby outside of work.

Characteristic of the field of positive psychology, Csikszentmihalyi's ideas about flow rest upon the Maslowian premise that humans can enhance their individual QOL through control over their consciousness, even though he emphasizes mental activity over developmental end-state (Snyder and Lopez 2007:138). Positive psychology's contrast to industrial psychology, an older field of psychology that emerged in the mid-twentieth century alongside the corporate formation of human resources divisions, is telling; notably, positive psychology de-emphasizes social contexts and workplace relations, while giving more attention to individuals' cognitive process. This is a fortuitous shift in emphasis, considering how the stable workplace has become ever rarer; with it has gone the organizational setting for the practice of industrial psychology in its traditional sense. By contrast, positive psychology offers a portable form of industrial psychology, well suited for those who experience job change, workforce turnover, and workplace transformation as the norm. In this context, Csikszentmihalyi's (1990) recommendation that the individual "find rewards in the events of each moment" (p. 11) is eminently practical because it does not require the interventions of managers. It is also telling that Csikszentmihalyi emphasizes the opportunities for flow in pastimes and hobbies outside of work. His theory equalizes vocation and avocation to existential alternatives in individual decisions to pursue flow through change, accommodation, or rejection of workplace conditions. Achieving flow no doubt enhances the experience of work, yet the psychological perspective that surrounds the understanding of QOL's muse uncritically rearticulates the dilemma ('trilemma,' really) of voice, loyalty, and exit that constitutes choice in insecure workplaces (Roth 2006; Hirschman 1970).

Creativity

In many ways, the managerial strategy on corporate culture and workers' pursuit of flow come together in the third and most recent perspective on work as the muse to QOL. In *The Rise of the Creative Class* (2002), planning professor Richard Florida makes the case for the importance of creativity in today's economies, workplaces, and communities. Creativity, he posits, characterizes work for artists, thinkers, designers, and others in the "super-creative core" who produce "new forms or designs that are readily transferable and widely useful" (Florida 2002:69). Observing their work process, Florida identifies ten dimensions of creativity. Creativity involves the playful combination of data, perceptions, and materials; it requires self-confidence by creators to take risks; it is not hoarded by geniuses but rather can be exercised by everybody, given the right circumstances; it proceeds via the stages of preparation, incubation, illumination, and verification/revision; it draws on personal experience across many realms; it demands diligent and substantial effort; it involves inestimable stretches of time; it often makes for an obsessive and solitary life; it motivates primarily through its intrinsic rewards; it draws heavily on interpersonal collaboration; and it flourishes in open and tolerant social environments (Florida 2002:31–5). These features of creativity also inform, albeit in less open-ended and more hierarchically constrained (yet often better paid) ways, the discretionary, non-routine decision-making of lawyers, doctors, managers, and other "creative professionals." Florida contends these two occupational strata comprise the "creative class," the ascendant value-creating tier of the new economy.

Florida's ten dimensions of creativity may seem to resemble Csikszentmihalyi's eight dimensions of flow, and not only because they share a presentation-ready, bullet-pointed format. The theories of flow and creativity depict the possible harmony, even synergy, between work and QOL. In a world where people are encouraged to 'do what you love,' Csikszentmihalyi and Florida offer intuitively appealing accounts of what this romance with work might look like. There are instructive differences between their two perspectives, however. Like flow, creativity is ostensibly ubiquitous among the population, even if social context matters very much for its economic value, but Florida emphasizes the setting and pace for creativity in ways that Csikszentmihalyi does not. Typically, the proper organizational forms are non-hierarchical, non-specialist milieus for social interaction, in which creative workers come together for productive collaboration and inspirational chit-chat, then break off for intense effort or recreational distraction (i.e., "incubation"). For Florida, parsing the philosophical distinctions between the social and personal, and between work and play, is not only beside the point; rigidly structuring and enforcing such opposites via job descriptions, work schedules, office layout, or productivity measurements can only retard the spontaneous and unpredictable unfolding of creativity. Tolerance of the autonomy of creative workers, with their 'undisciplined' process and infusions of personal (sometimes quite countercultural) 'lifestyle,' is thus fundamental to effective management in the creative economy. Importantly, corporate tolerance conveys to current and potential employees that the workplace respects their freedom to work passionately and productively as only they know how.

Harnessing creativity might seem like a nightmare to corporate managers, yet Florida's book, published at the tail-end of the "irrational exuberance" of the late 1990s economy in North America and Western Europe, drew wide interest among management gurus, academics, urban leaders, and a popular audience fascinated by bohemian dot-commers and artists-cum-entrepreneurs, technology and media industries located in revitalizing downtowns, and telecommuting professionals living in quiet towns and countrysides off the go-go grid. Given his expansive definition of the creative class, Florida's argument can hardly stand or fall with the subsequent deflation of the dot-com sector, despite what critics have argued. The iconic "supercreative" worker epitomizes broader trends in talent-heavy, IT-intensive fields many media, cultural, financial, and consulting firms as well as educational and research institutions.

Particularly outside the academic field, these sectors are often immersed in the lifestyles and activities that lure young creative talent (from recent college grads, to childless or nanny-equipped thirty- and forty-somethings) to cities or other amenity-rich places. Whether ensconced in band practice at a seedy rehearsal studio or hacking away at a laptop in a cushy IT office, the creative worker is motivated primarily by 'fun' and 'interesting' work—the criteria of flow are not irrelevant here—with extrinsic rewards a distant second (see also Lloyd 2003).

Inevitably there is overgeneralization in this ideal type, but there is also a social basis that we might recognize from the last chapter. Namely, this idealized creative worker occupies the most adaptable life-stage and is rarely encumbered by family dependents or other commitments that might preempt long hours of devoted and not necessarily well-paid creativity. She usually comes recently graduated from college and versed in the latest creative skills; even if she skips higher education, her youth leaves her steeped in the latest tastes, lifestyles, and sociabilities that marketers and consultants value highly. In these ways, the creative worker's life-stage and lifestyle preformat her for flexibility and creative savvy in the contemporary workforce; if her creative proficiency and financial rewards are not necessarily assured, employers' preferences are in her favor. Significantly, en masse she and her peers raise the bar in the labor markets for creative jobs and add liabilities to older employees, those who give priority to family or other commitments that prevent long hours of creativity, and others upon whom the economy forces an involuntary 'inflexibility' (Sennett 1998). The parallels to the selection and cultivation of employee fit with company culture described earlier are noteworthy, but Florida makes clear that such managerial concern can be 'flexibly' externalized out of the firm onto external features of the labor market itself: industries and cities, but also 'value-adding' life-stages and lifestyles.

As with most of his subsequent writings, *The Rise of the Creative Class* is not a self-help book for creative-class readers (most of whom are doing quite well, if Florida is to be believed) so much as a prescriptive manual for employers, municipalities, and other groups and institutions seeking to tap the wellsprings of economic growth and cultural vibrancy which the creative class brings. Its technocratic agenda is revealed by the absence of substantial discussion of employer-creative employee conflict (from which managers might reasonably infer: They want to live the bohemian life, and we want them to work hard—everyone wins!), as well as the focus on universal features of the creative milieu that make for tidy takeaway lessons. Missing from Florida's theory is how particular company- and employer-specific contexts for creative work offer their own intrinsic rewards. These contexts, by contrast, are the primary emphasis in cultural analyst Andrew Ross's (2003) *No Collar: The Humane Workplace and its Hidden Costs*, a participant-observation study of the NYC-based interactive agency Razorfish. Documenting this company's employees' creative energies, playful workplace, and long hours (the phrase "seventy-hour workweek" recurs frequently), Ross adds to the growing consensus on the relationship of work and QOL in the new economy that Joanne Ciulla (2000) pithily summarizes: "One of the great paradoxes of employer–employee relationships is that it's just as easy to exploit someone's contentment as it is to exploit his or her misery" (p. 159). Much of the reason is consistent with Florida's creative-class model. Exciting work and freedom of lifestyle expression are powerful motivations for Razorfish's creative workers, who find great fulfillment (and forgo the industry's top earnings) in a company that they insist is "as good as it gets in corporate America" (Ross 2003:13).

As that quote suggests, however, employees' scan of their job prospects reflects a different understanding of the creative milieu than what managers might draw from Florida's argument. Although the company partakes of the company culture management jargon, creative workers are quick to sniff out the inauthentic; as an employee tells Ross (2003):

> when culture comes from the corporate office, that's what I call The Culture. It's different from the thing that happens among us vibrant, interesting people when we interact with each other. Our own vibe of "anything can happen" is more of a reflex thing, and it's what nourishes us.
>
> (p. 99)

Ross shows how the new economy's 'great places to work' do more than simply pull together the universal elements of flow or creativity. Purposefully or unwittingly, they organize an *affective milieu* in which work becomes seen as intrinsically rewarding. In the new economy, emotional engagement is one of the big pay-offs sought by creative workers and, indeed, other kinds of workers as well. It can compensate for the incessant performance reviews, absurd management, unanticipated demands, and very long hours of many jobs. Often, emotional engagement recasts such workplaces cons as pros; stated differently, from the affective milieu, local ideals and experience of work-based QOL can emerge (Sharone 2004). However, this affective milieu is specific not only to particular companies, each of which brings a different history and cast of characters, but more precisely to employee subcultures that develop independently of employer intent. Razorfish employees define and experience their creative labor *vis-à-vis* employee solidarity (fellow workers are "fish," in the firm's parlance), the quality of work (a "cool job"), managerial authority (the need for "permission"), clients ("mega-companies"), other places to work (not as "cool"), and other subcultural expressions. Their idiomatic language reflects the substantial time, skill, and emotion that employees have invested in the workplace; such investments are hardly portable across the labor market, which sheds light on the bitter betrayal felt by Razorfish employees who were laid-off or, even worse for many, whose jobs were restructured into the kinds of 'normal' roles and tasks that allay investors' anxieties.

The Movable Feast of Work-based QOL

Industrial sociologists and anthropologists have long documented the workplace cultures of affective solidarity through which workers understand their toil, turmoil, and satisfaction at the workplace. Ross's contribution here is not new in that regard, but it casts doubt on the value of Florida's technocratic takeaway; his lack of attention to the workplace's affective milieu is one reason why his theory of the creative class, for all its insights into the quality and organization of work, provides such an antiseptic view of workers' lives. The affective milieu for labor, creative or otherwise, represents a 'sunk investment' in workers' QOL that the firm cannot externalize—an inflexible value-added in a flexible economy. By contrast, the technocratic emphasis on creativity, like the discourses on company culture and flow, serves the managerial interest in easing workers into a new world of impermanent employment, unstable earnings, and work-life imbalance. Here, a 'great job' is shorn of the concrete human relationships and collective negotiations from which workers have customarily derived their QOL at work: the traditionalistic solidarity of community and labor, the hierarchical but reliable bureaucracy, the historic post-World War II social compact between capital and organized labor, or the mundane office or factory where personal relationships, office subcultures, and emotional satisfactions are found. These managerial discourses *reify* work-based QOL, recasting real social relations into a discrete, portable *thing* (cf. Marx [1867] 1906:83)—a goal of meaningful work that workers can define individually, trade off against other personal preferences, and pursue through the many jobs they take and leave over the course of their 'careers.'

To be sure, many workers do find QOL in just the ways described by the theorists of company culture, flow, and creativity. But those who can truly find work-based QOL *on their own*, independent of the *specific* occupations, workers, bosses, or workplaces they find themselves among today—recall that in the new world of work, all of these can disappear tomorrow—are highly valued in contemporary labor markets. We can imagine at least two classes under this umbrella. First, workers whose in-demand skills lead employers to concede various elements of a great job (considerable occupational autonomy, a flexible schedule, freedom in location of work, etc.) represent the most advantaged stratum of elite workers on the labor market (Nevarez 2003). Second, workers who authentically adhere to the culture and norms demanded by employers (to work long hours, demonstrate the appropriate flexibility, etc.) are prized for the self-discipline they contribute and model to others—modern-day monks of the new economy. These two labor-market categories can overlap, of course, the obvious example being managers themselves, whose horizontal mobility (via headhunters, serial entrepreneurialism, or just plain gumption) and ideological malleability form the basis for much of their organizational value. Hence the innumerable proclamations of CEOs and vice-presidents who "love to come to work each day"—perhaps we should not question the authenticity of their statements, considering the depth to which they have internalized the ethos of the new world of work.

Conclusion

So has QOL increased or decreased in the new world of work? Insisting that the answer is one or the other, or even somewhere between, has sustained a number of debates, as various titles from the literature on this topic suggest: *The End of Work*, *Free Agent Nation*, *The Rise of the Creative Class*, *The New Ruthless Economy* (Head 2003), *White-Collar Sweatshop* (Fraser 2001), and so on. However, entering into any of these debates on its face neglects what by now is an axiom of our critical inquiry: sweeping claims about trends in QOL are difficult to sustain. To some degree, this reflects the diverse QOL preferences that people pursue. Some workers will be driven to overwork for external rewards, particularly money, for instance, while other will seek internal rewards like the self-worth, gratifying collaborations, and emotional relationships that work and the workplace can offer; diverse circumstances, experiences and opportunities explain these distinct motives, as do differences in personal dispositions. However, economic restructuring is increasingly the more significant context for the diversity of work-based QOL pursuits. In the new world of work, gains and losses in workplace QOL occur simultaneously as the common, normative experience of work recedes from view. With stable institutions like big business, unions, and the welfare state no longer regulating employment and reproducing venerable collective categories—manufacturing laborers, part-time employees, salaried employees—workers increasingly thrive or fail by the individual assets and liabilities they bring to a dynamic, all-encompassing labor market.

One need not be a radical Marxist to grasp that this dynamic and individualized playing field benefits employers, even if it is not wholly capital's own creation. Alongside the longstanding interests of employers in 'flexible' employment strategies—preventing collective bargaining, outsourcing and deskilling occupations, and restructuring the remaining jobs with the responsibilities and expectations that were restructured out of previous occupations—the resulting diversification of employment relations provides an advantageous terrain for labor control. If that paradoxically requires certain employers to offer real workplace autonomies or personal freedoms here and there, it asks workers generally to surrender to the individualized relations of the labor market and give up collective demands for organizational reform. This labor-market orientation, in which the QOL rewards experienced by the few entice many others to give up the political possibilities of collective solidarity, informs the dominant QOL outlook we will encounter in the following chapters; as well, it reminds us of the critical value of paying attention to the QOL ideals and concerns of society's elite few and reigning status groups, unrepresentative though they may be of how most people live.

Given these troubling contexts, should we give up on the idea of work-based QOL? Do its troubled history and managerial resonances mean the idea is nothing but an ideology for a dominant class? I think not. To give up on 'QOL' as it relates to work is to ignore its legacy of mobilizing criticism and reform.

Notably, today's multiplicity of employment relations reflects a larger historical pattern of individualization that has been driven not just by corporate abdication from the standard employment relationship but genuine advances in human emancipation as well. Emblematically, women joined the workforce en masse over the last half of the twentieth century, to a large degree, in unapologetic pursuit of freedoms and flourishing that were denied at home (Beck and Beck-Gernsheim 2002). In the U.S., the civil rights struggles of racial-ethnic minorities and later gays and lesbians explicitly sought freedom and dignity of employment, seeking to realize the promise of the affluent society. Furthermore, Ross's (2009) assessment of the free-agent ethos applies to the broader impulses for work-based QOL reform:

> [I]t would be misguided to dismiss the hunger for free agency as a mere product of market ideology; the flexibility it delivers is a response to an authentic demand for a life not dictated by the cruel grind of excessively managed work. Autonomy is a critical goal, and while its attainment is more approachable for the self-employed, there is no reason why it cannot be nurtured inside organizations where the work process has been genuinely humanized.
>
> (p. 47)

Yet the integrity of QOL the idea does not preclude its conceptual ambivalence. The irony of history is that women and minorities made gains in a labor market increasingly driven by new exertions of labor control and surplus extraction—this was, after all, the era that gave us deindustrialization, the rise of the service sector, the IT revolution, the deregulation of finance capital, and other political economic developments we now associate with 'globalization.' In an important sense, women's entrance in an increasingly individualized world of work set the pattern for the personal 'emancipations' that subsequent classes of workers would pursue: 'free agents,' the 'creative class,' secure workers who can afford to become 'affluent downshifters' (see Chapter 3) or take cuts in pay in order to prioritize their choice of lifestyle and community (Nevarez 2003), and so on. QOL the idea's overdetermination as an individual measure of emancipation and flourishing gives us a weak foundation for challenging the labor market's commands in the new world of work.

6 Place

> As the benefits to clustering increase and the world becomes spikier, more people may feel compelled to join the ranks of the mobile in order to prosper economically. This does not mean that we are all doomed to be global nomads forever. It does mean that to reach our potential and find happiness, we must recognize the importance of place, know how best to weigh our options, and be willing to move when necessary.
>
> (Richard Florida 2008:89)

When we think about how our material QOL is linked with others', places often comes to mind, be they neighborhoods, municipalities, regions, or nations. More clearly and concretely than for technology, family, or career, we grasp how place provides the collective infrastructure for QOL—services, amenities, landscapes, and other features that are external to various users (residents, workers, shoppers, commuters, tourists, and other place occupants) and shared by them all—connoted by the idea of "public QOL." This term begs analytical precision; sharing place-based QOL depends on the particular place feature in question, its context, and typical experience. Maps and city charters lend the impression that place features are accessible to all within its territory, but distance often determines practical access (hence the real estate broker's motto: "Location, location, location!"), while markets, laws, and other systems of distribution effectively limit access further (as beachgoers will recognize when private residences enclose prime beachfront). Nonetheless, from the basic idea that place features are external to and shared by place occupants come the premises that place represents a social good; that the extent and kind of its benefits indicate a place's QOL; and that the latter's maintenance and enhancement are political matters. Sociologist Daniel Bell (1999) elaborates:

> Social goods are not divisible into individual items of possession but are part of a communal service (e.g., national defense, education, beautification of landscape, flood control, and so on). These goods and services are not sold to individual consumers nor adjusted to individual tastes. The nature and amount of goods must be set by a single decision, applicable

> jointly to all persons. Social goods, therefore, are subject to communal or political, rather than individual, demand.
>
> (p. 304)

Today this normative view of place as a social good surfaces in the current "politics of place," in which residents, businesses, and interest groups debate the public benefits and costs of big-box stores, housing subdivisions, polluting facilities, highway exits, and other controversial land-uses that portend broad consequences for their locations (see, e.g., Halebsky 2004).

In the post-World War II heyday of the affluent society, critics and policy-makers regarded place as a key site for political investment in collective QOL; recall, for instance, the central invocation of 'QOL' in the establishment of the U.S. Department of Housing and Urban Development, President Johnson's response to the post-World War II urban crisis (see Chapter 2). From these liberal origins, urban policy uses of 'QOL' have shifted dramatically. Sociologist Alex Vitale documents in *City of Disorder: How the Quality of Life Campaign Transformed New York Politics* (2008) how the idea now also connotes a highly sanitized, middle-class vision of civil order. Increasingly, 'QOL' motivates and legitimates the zero-tolerance punishment of homelessness, graffiti, informal street vending, and other feared precursors to full-blown crime and disorder, as this San Francisco newspaper column illustrates:

> I don't know how San Francisco can be tipped back, but I know it will take discipline and intelligence. Sorry, but drunks cannot rule the streets, throwing over news boxes and urinating on any hotel they find. Schizophrenics shouldn't dominate conversation in the public square with curses and threats … . In a city built on quality of life, how can we dismiss something as a "mere" quality-of-life crime. The quality of life is strained to the broken point.
>
> Imagine downtown San Francisco without the human degradation. What a town that would be, one fit for leaving a heart in. Instead of just leaving.
>
> (Morse 2001)[1]

Thus from a post-World War II ideal to lift up the most disadvantaged, place-based QOL has become a rationale to suppress and criminalize the homeless, immigrants, non-white youth, and other marginal groups who seek their livelihoods or lifestyles in public space (Vitale 2008; Duncan and Duncan 2004; Duneier 1999).

Yet 'place-based QOL' connotes an evidently different set of ideas and activities once we leave the urban scene of "broken windows" (the name of the aforementioned police enforcement strategy [Kelling and Coles 1996]). Popular interest in visiting or moving to places "with a high QOL" is reflected in the proliferation of city ratings and best-places lists in websites, magazine special editions (*Money* magazine is a well-known example), and popular guidebooks that rank different places for general interest, particular demographics (e.g.,

Best Places to Raise Your Family), or specific activities and interests (e.g., *The 100 Best Art Towns in America*) (McCann 2007; Rogerson 1999). These and other *place media*—think of travel channels on cable television, or of regional lifestyle magazines on waiting-room tables—have raised popular awareness about the QOL to be found in different places and about the many dimensions of place-based QOL in general. For *QOL migrants* who follow the pursuit of QOL in place to its logical next step, the decision also reveals the play of biographical narrative:

> Take Stuart Leventhal. A venture capitalist who now lives in Park City, Utah, Leventhal grew up in the Silicon Valley city of Palo Alto in the 1950s. When he left Palo Alto for good in 1998 for the mountaintop community outside Salt Lake City, Palo Alto no longer resembled the quaint, safe college town that it had once been. Sitting in a Starbucks several blocks from his new home, Leventhal recalled, "You didn't lock your doors. As a kid you just ran around and no one worried. I wouldn't want to be a kid growing up there now. There's too much pressure in the valley now . . . .
>
> "Here it's different. The quality of life we have here is fantastic—it has all the activities you would ever want. A day in the life of a child here is great. Here you get to structure your life the way you want it to be. This place is a time warp. Go twenty miles from where we are and the big talk is crossbow hunting season. You go here for the kids because things haven't changed so much."
>
> (Kotkin 2000:47)

This chapter takes up such diverse examples in the popular thinking about place and QOL to show how people increasingly pursue and consume place-based QOL *individually*, solitarily and in households, to express values and lifestyles through a social space and derive the personal satisfactions therein. With this thesis, I do not mean the simple claim that individuals benefit from the social good-ness of place. Rather, I intend, first, to reverse the causal arrow implied by the social good of 'place-based QOL' and show how QOL inheres not in any place itself, but in the individual's subjective gaze, as anchored in specific geographical, historical, and biographical contexts. Second, I explain how, for all the different landscapes and QOL appeals that the user can discover, a consumer framework shapes the pursuit of place-based QOL, subverting the political ideals implied in the value that place is a social good. Third, I examine how place itself, in this case the "quality-of-life district," sheds light on political economic contexts for the interest in and pursuit of place-based QOL today.

Conventional Perspectives on Place-based QOL

It has been customary, when thinking about our relationship to place-based QOL, to start at the level of place itself. Entire professions and perspectives involve managing and enhancing the collective QOL associated with municipal territories and physical landscapes: urban planning, environmental management, and so on. In the QOL scholarship, debates on a host of social problems, from obesity to child-snatching, pose questions about how the properties of place affect our QOL: How auto-dependent and pedestrian-unfriendly are the places we live? How safe are our neighborhoods for children and the elderly? How well do we know and interact with our neighbors? These examples illustrate the common tendency toward *place determinism* when thinking about place-based QOL—the idea that place itself necessarily influences the QOL that users find therein.

Traditions of Place-determinism

Place-deterministic views of QOL generally foreground three categories of place features: amenities, public space, and place character. *Amenities* represent the most tangible aspect of place. In the language of real estate agents, an amenity denotes landscape features and physical assets that please the eye aesthetically (for instance, viewsheds of open green space) or offer an enjoyable experience (pedestrian-friendly sidewalks, concert halls, etc.). Planners and policy-makers expand the idea to encompass less visible public infrastructure and services (public schools, water or sewer systems, mass transit, etc.), as well as privately-consumed place features (backyards, architectural codes that give visual coherence to neighborhoods, etc.). These references presume that amenities enhance QOL, but of course they can also degrade QOL, as illustrated by the "negative amenities" of crime, locally unwanted land-uses (theme parks, nuclear power plants), non-useful features (lack of parking), or even people whose activities diminish a place's value to their neighbors. Consistent across all these examples is the idea that an amenity comprises an intermediate-level mechanism between individuals and place; by adding or subtracting value, an amenity produces an outcome that is larger than the individuals who experience it and is attributable to the place that contains it. This is the sense in which we say amenities support public QOL.

When pressed, place analysts and planners generally acknowledge that the QOL value of amenities and, indeed, most place features is ultimately subjective; what enhances QOL for some people or in some situations is neutral or even impairs QOL for other people or in other situations:

> Although some differences in the quality of life between types of communities can be assessed more or less objectively, the relative importance of these differences to people is a matter of value. Small towns may afford more access to clean air, hunting, and fishing; cities, to Chinese restaurants and specialized medical services. These differences, however, do not automatically make small towns—or cities—better places unless one or another system of values is adopted.
>
> (Hummon 1990:49)

This issue informs debates surrounding the construction of "McMansions" (privacy and spaciousness for owners, or the degradation of neighborhood aesthetic and planning integrity for everyone else?) and skateboard parks (a positive source of recreation for youth, or a generator of disorder and delinquency?), to name just two examples. Furthermore, certain amenities may hold particular appeal for certain groups. In a recent study, sociologist Terry N. Clark (2004) found that an increase in local amenities like Starbucks, Whole Foods stores, juice bars, used bookstores, museums, operas, and research universities (which benefit neighbors culturally with arts and educational programming) correlated positively with population growth of college graduates and patent holders. Clark's study did not directly observe these groups actually using such amenities, but urban leaders hoping to grow the local creative economy have taken that lesson to heart in any case. There are degrees of subjectivity that the analyst of place can stress, and the preceding quotation highlights a rather superficial if common one: the idea that QOL is filtered through personal dispositions and tastes. Recalling Bell's social good dictum that "goods and services are not sold to individual consumers nor adjusted to individual tastes," most planners and policy-makers square this superficial view of subjectivity with an objective (i.e., independent of particular values or preferences) focus on the QOL appeal and effects of place itself. In practice, then, amenities are often designed, built, managed, and promoted as if their QOL appeals are environmentally contextless and geographically unspecific; that is, their effects on QOL derive from their internal workings and are, in this sense, potentially relevant to any number of places. Not that a public park or coffee-shop works well in any and all settings, due to contextual idiosyncrasies of neighborhood design and market demand, but the operative elements of an amenity—a lawn, a playground, a latte machine, and so on—are thought to produce a QOL effect irrespective of surrounding context.

A second place-deterministic view of QOL emphasizes *public space*, the infrastructure of sidewalks and streets, parks and greens, plazas and town squares, civic commons and civic centers, that constitute the physical settings for face-to-face communion. As conveyed by modifiers like 'vibrant' and 'thriving,' public space is often thought to enhance a place's QOL by offering the small intrinsic pleasures of walking and people-watching as well as promoting lofty ideals of tolerance, citizenship, and the spontaneity of informal social order. Public space is found almost anywhere strangers gather and mingle among one another, but for many analysts it is synonymous with the city. Urbanists of the classical persuasion generally view cities as the stronghold of public space—so-called New Urbanists include many old, economically self-sufficient towns here—and regard public space in the suburbs as characteristically weak, since daily rounds there are largely confined to detached dwellings and auto-centered circuits. The assessment of New Urbanists Andres Duany, Elizabeth Plater-Zyberk, and Jeff Speck (2000) is typical:

> Dollar for dollar, no other society approaches the United States in terms of the number of square feet per person, the number of baths per bedroom, the number of appliances in the kitchen, the quality of the climate control, and the convenience of the garage. The American private realm is simply a superior product. The problem is that most suburban residents, the minute they leave this refuge, are confronted by a tawdry and stressful environment. They enter their cars and embark on a journey of banality and hostility that lasts until they arrive at the interior of their next destination. Americans may have the finest private realm in the developed world, but our public realm is brutal. Confronted by repetitive subdivisions, treeless collector roads, and vast parking lots, the citizen finds few public spaces worth visiting. One's role in this environment is primarily as a motorist competing for asphalt.
>
> (p. 41; see also Jackson 1985:272; Sennett 1977)

Urbanist Jane Jacobs (1961) is the key thinker theorizing public space as a contextual dynamic of social interaction that cannot be reduced to its physical infrastructure (see also Whyte 1980). Unplanned gatherings, informal activities, and face-to-face exchanges flourish when fueled by critical mass (in population, land-uses, nearby destinations and businesses) and a visually appealing yet sufficiently transparent physical milieu. Putting restrictions on the times, settings, and types of activities that users spontaneously initiate is famously *verboten* for Jacobs. The recent popularity of many privately-managed "urban entertainment districts" complicates her claim (see Zukin 2010), but even planners of these privatized spaces tend to take Jacobs to heart in recognizing that attracting and sustaining *more*—more people, public art, storefront businesses, streetside vendors, etc.—is crucial for effective public space. The limits of Jacobs' contextual, anti-reductionist perspective on public space become apparent when we consider how planning advocacy groups like the Project for Public Space have blossomed in the last decade or so. Although these groups proselytize the Jacobs gospel of carefully cultivating the environmental and interactional intangibilities of public space, their *raison d'être*—consulting on the design and management of public spaces for municipal and private clients—can effectively treat public space as a physical thing, another amenity to be constructed and made available for public consumption. The reason is not hard to discern: local boosters and private developers seek to build and enhance public spaces for residents, visitors, shoppers, and others who would otherwise visit other destinations and patronize other public spaces. Thus, if public space is geographically specific to place at the scale of its immediate surroundings, from an economic development perspective, the 'sense of place' it provides can be rather generic and insensitive to local context.

A more concrete 'sense of place' comes from the third place-deterministic tradition of QOL, which emphasizes *place character* or what sociologist Krista Paulsen (2004) theorizes as the "set of patterns in meaning and action that are specific to a distinct locale" (p. 245). This amorphous idea is illustrated in the second edition of *Cities Ranked and Rated*, for which travel publisher Frommers evaluated 375 American and 27 Canadian cities in ten categories. In this typical publication of the best-places genre, Frommers defined "quality of life" as a residual category that captured important place features that were excluded from the other nine categories (economy and jobs, cost of living, climate, education, health and healthcare, crime, transportation, leisure, and arts and culture):

> We have determined a combined score for each metropolitan area based on the perceived overall quality of life . . . . By their very nature, the factors determining this score are difficult to quantify. They are based mainly on perception, personal experience, and anecdotes from others who have spent time in these places. Features considered include the following:
>
> - *Physical attractiveness*: This includes both the physical setting and overall appearance of the area itself. Included is the attractiveness and functionality of the downtown core. We believe these factors influence initial impressions and long-term satisfaction in an area. The effects of a pancake-flat, windswept, nondescript landscape with dirty air and little vegetation are far different from that of attractive, well-kept, tree-lined streets with good buildings and a pristine mountain, valley, river, or lakeside setting. Cities such as Boulder, Colorado; Corvallis, Oregon; and Burlington, Vermont, do well in this regard, while some larger cities such as Pittsburgh, Pennsylvania, and Chattanooga, Tennessee, are improving.
> - *Heritage*: A city that knows its roots and tries to preserve its physical and cultural heritage is usually more physically attractive as well as genuine in character. These cities are almost invariably better places to live. Metropolitan areas with well-preserved historic districts and public buildings include Charlottesville and Winchester, Virginia; Boston, Massachusetts; Portland, Maine; and Santa Fe, New Mexico.
> - *Overall ease of living*: The most subjective element in this subjective category, ease of living incorporates crowdedness, attitude and friendliness of people, and simplicity of infrastructure. In essence, it considers the "stress factor." Issues with places such as Los Angeles, San Francisco, and New York are obvious, and these cities score poorly, while cities in the South—even the workaholic New South—tend to score high.
>
> (Sperling and Sander 2007:117–8)

Admittedly, this is an idiosyncratic definition of "QOL" in which amenities play an important role, particularly in the physical attractiveness criterion and the issue of "simplicity of infrastructure" under overall ease of living. Public space is also implied as physical setting ("well-preserved historic districts and public buildings") and property of social concentration ("crowdedness"). Still, amenities and public space do not exhaust the connotations of Frommers' "QOL" category; place character can be gleaned from the remaining emphases on "[a] city that knows its roots," that can be characterized by a distinct "attitude," and that maintains a custom of "friendliness." Tellingly, a place could exhibit the opposite traits—e.g., a lack of historical consciousness, a custom of unfriendliness—and still exhibit a distinct character. What the concept of place character requires is simply that a place has its 'signature' customs, values, and ways of life. To the extent that place character orients the identification or first-hand experience of places, we may further say that that place character sustains a 'sense of place' (Molotch et al. 2000).

The Problem of Placelessness

The opposite of place character is implied by the assessment that a place has no distinct character or, in the common parlance, that it is *placeless*. Yet a review of this idea reveals the semantic instabilities with which this idea and, by extension, the prior three traditions strain against their place-determinism. First, placelessness generally describes a uniformity in landscape and ways of life among places, such that one placeless place is effectively no different than another; thus, the idea moves away from place itself to highlight the beholder's comparative view. Second, placelessness typically evokes a historical narrative on the transformation of place from premodernity to modernity. Third and relatedly, placelessness characterizes the sources of place distinction and character as indigenous in nature. Premodern places may have actually resembled each other quite a bit, but we rarely deem them placeless because we regard their community structure, economies, and built environments as having local origin. In this sense, placelessness connotes not only uniformity but also inauthenticity, which points to the concept's fourth dimension, its critical value position. Few observers cite placelessness to praise it; most invoke it to lament the ways that modernity has brought an end to geographic isolation and supplanted local influences, as industry, states, mass media, and the military incorporate localities into regional, national, international, and eventually global circuits of mass-produced commodities and culturally homogeneous broadcasts (Relph 1976; Mills 1956). Placelessness is frequently associated with U.S. suburbs; not only do they all seem the same, but their form reflects a cultural export of non-native (British) origins that has been subsidized by the federal government, enshrined in national planning discourse, and advertised as nothing less than the mass-produced "American dream" (Kunstler 1998; A. Wilson 1991; Fishman 1987; Jackson 1985).

But does placelessness impair place-based QOL? An answer requires separating the condition from its causes. Among the latter, urban sprawl is especially singled out for increasing auto dependency, which reduces physical fitness and increases congestion and pollution, and for reducing the density and face-to-face nature of social interactions, which can increase loneliness and impair mental health (see e.g., Plantinga and Bernell 2007; Morris 2005). So, too, capital-intensive commercial development of the kind that promulgates shopping malls, corporate franchises, and big-box stores can threaten the sustainability of local economies by undermining local businesses and reducing the economic multipliers of local earnings. Yet viewed this way, placelessness is actually the outcome of market forces and corporate power (Knox 2005; Ritzer 2004, 1993). If we set those aside, the question then becomes, is our QOL impaired by the inauthenticity of the places we live in, and the interchangeability of our built environments, local commerce, and ways of life? The impact of these on objective QOL is unclear, but many urbanists insist there is a cultural effect: placelessness provides a dreary, disposable landscape for daily life, one that is hardly conducive to human imagination, self-actualization, collective ennobling, and the march of civilization. New Urbanist James Kunstler (1998) stresses this view in his depiction of U.S. architectural trends since World War II:

> We reject the past and the future and it shows in our graceless constructions. Our houses, commercial, and civic buildings are constructed with the fully conscious certainty that they will disintegrate in a few decades. There is even a name for this condition: the *design life*. Strip malls and elementary schools have short design lives. They are not expected to endure through the span of a human life. In fact, they fall apart in under fifty years. Since there is no expectation that these things will last, nor that they will speak to any era but our own, we seem to believe there is no point in putting any money or effort into their embellishment—except for the sort of cartoon decoration that serves to advertise whatever product is sold on the premises. Nor do we care about the age-old solutions to the problems of weather and light, because we have technological artifacts to mitigate these problems, namely, electricity and central heating. So the windows don't open in many new office buildings. In especially bad buildings, like the average Wal-Mart, there may be no windows. Yet this process of disconnection from the past and the future, and from the organic patterns of weather and light, all done for the sake of expedience, ends up diminishing us spiritually, impoverishing us socially, and degrading the aggregate set of cultural patterns that we call civilization. We register these discontinuities as *ugliness*, or the absence of beauty.
>
> (pp. 89–90)

Cultural Geographies of QOL Aspirations

The New Urbanist polemic does not sit well with many commentators, for whom its bold claims about the modern degradation of place-based QOL seem so steeped in particular tastes that they illustrate only an impartial, elitist vision of the 'good place.' Presaging this charge over 40 years ago, sociologist Herbert Gans (1967) forcefully argued against placeless diagnoses for suburban QOL:

> Critics of the suburbs also inveigh against physical homogeneity and mass-produced housing. Like much of the rest of the critique, this charge is a thinly veiled attack on the culture of working and lower middle class people, implying that mass-produced housing leads to mass-produced lives. The critics seem to forget that the town houses of the upper class in the nineteenth century were also physically homogeneous; that everyone, poor and rich alike, drives mass-produced, homogeneous cars without damage to their personalities; and that today, only the rich can afford custom-built housing.
>
> (p. 171)

Yet such impartiality, when acknowledged explicitly (as New Urbanists generally fail to do), is precisely the point in *subjective perspectives* on place, for which any characterization of place-based QOL directs attention to the user's viewpoint as much as, if not more than, the place in view. Among these subjective perspectives, Gans proposes an approach that foregrounds the social activities and cultural values of place users. Far from impoverished, suburbs effectively reflect and advance the widely held values of suburban residents; private space dominates the landscape because suburbanites emphasize the family and socializing activities that occur therein (Gans 1962). His point is perhaps obvious, but it goes a long way to debunk the myth of 'cultural homogeneity' that often accompanies the alarm over suburban placelessness. In an ethnography of the original cohort of residents in Levittown, America's first suburban subdivision, Gans (1967) found this group to be considerably diverse along lines of class (from working to upper middle class), ethnicity (except African Americans), religion, and social interest (for contemporary evidence of suburban diversity, see Frey 2003). They indeed tended to "go their own way" by socializing in homogeneous groups (in block settlement, neighboring, and couple visiting), but this reflected Levittowners' need to establish a stable social life within a settlement of diverse newcomers by finding people with common interests and values. In this regard, the suburban impulse toward homogeneous socializing, Gans (1967) observes, does not essentially differ from what happens in cities:

> Critics assume that urban children experience heterogeneity, but middle class parents—and working class ones, too—try hard to shield them from contact with conditions and people of lower status. Upper middle class children may be taken on tours of the city, but to museums and shopping districts rather than to slums . . . . [Nor is it] at all certain that mere visual exposure—to Negroes [sic] or anyone else—encourages learning of pluralism and tolerance. Children pick up many of their attitudes from parents and peers, and these are not necessarily pluralistic.
>
> (pp. 169–70)

If the suburbs reflects suburbanites' QOL pursuits, then so too do New Urbanist landscapes that enshrine 'collective QOL.' In *The Best Laid Plans: How*

Government Planning Harms Your Quality of Life, Your Pocketbook, and Your Future, libertarian pundit Randal O'Toole makes this point quite sharply, contending that New Urbanists and others who insist upon promoting neighborhood density, public space, or other supposed enhancements of place-based QOL idealize a lifestyle that reflects a particular taste and, in this sense, is no less 'selfish' or private in principle than that of the most auto-dependent suburbanites. Preferring such places is certainly their prerogative in a free market society, the libertarian argument goes, but what right do they have to force their values on 'the rest of us' through more broadly imposed growth restrictions and regional planning codes?

Foregrounding place users' subjective outlooks highlights the important fact that the values and activities people exhibit *in* place need not be oriented *toward* place. Thus, O'Toole (2007) contends, "no invention has enhanced the quality of life of the average American as much as the mass-produced automobile" (p. 203).[2] His claim offends New Urbanists who recite the litany of woes that the private auto has unleashed on cities and neighborhoods, but as a statement of his own QOL values, it illustrates the point that many people's QOL pursuits emphasize private QOL over the public ones represented by place-based QOL. O'Toole (2007) clarifies he is no asocial Robinson Crusoe, only that the "communities" that sustain his well-being do not correspond to places:

> I myself belong to communities of road cyclists; people who love trains and restore historic rail equipment; and owners of Belgian Tervuren dogs, among others. Very few members of any of these communities live in my town, yet I feel a strong sense of community with them all. If people were restricted to forming communities only with their geographic neighbors, their lives would be far shallower and narrower. Since they are no longer so restricted, they do not feel a need to form a strong sense of community with neighbors with whom they share few interests.
>
> (p. 61)

In subjective traditions, then, the idea of 'place-based QOL' shifts from an external infrastructure anchored in place itself to a geographic expression of human worldviews. Accordingly, New Urbanist endorsements of public space and other place-determinist views of QOL have no monopoly on conceptualizing place-based QOL; landscapes composed of "single-family homes, churches, satellite dishes, and malls" (Kotkin 2003:34) also offer their users a place-based QOL—merely a different kind, and one in which users may be unattuned to the collective infrastructure of place.

From the assertion that different people have different subjective QOL orientations, including a total disregard of place, comes the conclusion in subjective traditions of place-based QOL that the broader cultural geography of place reflects and organizes the diversity of QOL concerns. Perhaps the most common theoretical account of this thesis comes from the *demographic* perspective that emphasizes how individuals and households seek out places that best fit their livelihoods and aspirations. In this vein, much has been written about the geographic mobility of human capital in the new economy. As early as 1989, urban researchers have described European and North American knowledge workers as "very sophisticated consumers of place" (Knight 1989:237). More recently, urbanist Joel Kotkin (2000) has argued that highly educated and usually childless workers seek smaller, compact cities (your Portlands and Austins) as well as revitalized neighborhoods in larger cities (Wicker Park, Silverlake, and so on); employees of high-tech R&D and manufacturing firms set in sprawling campuses prefer to raise families in socially homogeneous neighborhoods along the metropolitan periphery (Irvine County, California; north-central New Jersey, etc.); foreign immigrants look for older cities and suburbs with low economic barriers to jumpstarting their new-world fortunes (your Houstons and San Gabriel Valleys); and established entrepreneurs and self-employed symbolic analysts opt to work from home in rural homesteads off the beaten path (your Vermonts and Montanas). Through such sorting, the pursuit of individual livelihoods and lifestyles en masse give rise to "boutique cities," "nerdistans," "casbahs," and "valhallas," respectively. Yet new economy enclaves do not exhaust the range of place types or the QOL they afford in the demographic perspective. David Brooks suggests an even broader outlook in *On Paradise Drive* (2004), his paean to modern America's rich cultural mosaic: "as we take our drive through America, we will see that people congregate into communities not so much on the basis of class but on the basis of what ideal state they aspire to, and each ideal state creates its own cultural climate zone" (p. 18). Note the causal narrative implied by this emphasis on individuals and households scanning the terrain for locational opportunities that optimize their preferences. Zooming out from specific "cultural climate zones" to the larger scale, the demographic perspective explains cultural geography as a market of place seekers and suitable locales.

Contexts for Place-based QOL

Subjective perspectives on place-based QOL provide a useful corrective to place-deterministic accounts. The conceptual tension between the production and distribution of QOL (see Chapter 1) illuminates their insight: places may have an latent potential to generate QOL, but the realization of QOL by human beings implies a different set of dynamics (see Gerson 1976). To put the point more simply and maybe controversially: places do not really 'have a QOL.' They encompass social relations and material landscapes that shape the QOL perceived and experienced by humans, but as passive objects of evaluation, places do not automatically impart their QOL salience; hence the possibility that people who experience virtually the same objective place conditions (including the same person at different points in time) may experience and assess a place's QOL differently. 'Having QOL' ultimately entails evaluating ways of life, a subjective intervention into objective conditions that implicates the *beholders* of place—in particular, their analytical criteria for assessing QOL, the values and aspirations that inform these criteria, and the social contexts in which they consider QOL. Thus, we should not emphasize the QOL of a place so much as instead the points of departure for its pursuit: subjective orientations (preferences, lifestyle affinities, etc.) and the social actions that these motivate.

By contrast, to articulate or act upon the idea that 'places have QOL' *reifies place-based QOL*, projecting onto an inert territory a nexus of social relations and social powers that in many cases transcend place itself. Yet subjective perspectives can also reify place-based QOL, particularly those that posit essentialized affinities between place features and social groupings: coffee-shops and creative workers, suburban cul de sacs and middle-class families, Walmarts and America's "country folks," vibrant public space and "community." Such analytical correspondences between landscapes and demographics too often neglect the social contexts in which people pursue QOL through place. I now turn to those contexts that have shaped subjective orientations toward place-based QOL.

To Pursue Place

Consider the following anachronism: would royalty of old have thought of their private gardens or castle walls as 'QOL-enhancing amenities'? More likely, they would view the stimulations, securities, and other satisfactions provided by their environment as their social birthright, understood through a feudalistic view of the explicit social hierarchy of the day. Today's vocabularies of pursuing QOL—at least the enhancing kind—from a place reveal a uniquely modern sense of autonomy from and agency toward our environment; they frame our relationship to place as one in which we effect our social interests. Like self-actualization or a rewarding career, 'enjoying place' presumes that human livelihoods and fortunes, which in this case include encountering or living in a place, are under human control to a significant degree. Such an orientation toward place as an achieved objective emerged historically on a wide scale with urbanization, and quite likely the experience was not wholly positive for most. "City air breathes free," peasants shackled by agricultural feudalism were said to exclaim, but leaving their place of origin would almost certainly subject them to anomic dislocations from kin and custom. The compulsion of human necessity—in this case, to find employment and support one's family in the wake of enclosure movements and rural economies' collapse—put great masses of people on the unprecedented and probably unwanted march to shaping their own destinies in the industrial city. Needless to say, the grim perils that we associate with urban life in the Industrial Revolution attests to the less than ideal circumstances in which most sought well-being there. The prospect of living in the industrial city and mingling with strangers in urban public space triggered anxieties catalyzed by real and imagined perils of overcrowding, disease, anonymity, moral degradation, immigration, diversity, crime, vice, and fraudulence (the last a special obsession in Victorian Britain [Murdoch 2002]).

Furthermore, the collective infrastructure for QOL that we associate with place itself hardly existed in this period. Before the late nineteenth century, cities rarely had the municipal capacity to support urban planning, public parks, or other public amenities and infrastructures. In Europe and North America, the development of such governmental capacity followed from "reforms" that generally promoted middle-class values and amenities at the expense of egalitarian ideals of citizenship: vaccinations and public parks 'for all,' but also settlement houses and orphanages for the lower classes (Wohl 1983). Outside the nascent municipal state, market opportunities to enjoy the features of place depended even more directly on class position, which influenced the tastes and proclivities for, but also economic means and free time to pursue, particular settings and activities for leisure. Historians record a number of mass leisure destinations enjoyed by the proletarian classes: penny arcades and (by the twentieth century) movie houses, amusement parks, and the raucous taverns, music halls, and gambling houses located in districts of questionable repute. The better-off could avail themselves of 'their own' set of urban amenities, such as department stores and other cathedrals of commerce (cf. Benjamin 1999), or destinations for cultural enlightenment like museums and opera houses. The moral disapproval of middle-class spokespersons for mass leisure destinations speaks to the cultural circumscription of working-class QOL in this era; proletarian opportunities to enjoy amenities and public space were few in number, viewed as morally suspect, and regulated by political and cultural institutions (Hannigan 1998; Nassaw 1993; E. Wilson 1991).

Hence the historical significance of the suburbs, that emblem of a domestically oriented, amenity-enhanced place of residence: they exhibited the new middle classes' power to shape the form, amenities, and infrastructure of place in *explicit reflection of their status ambitions*. Nineteenth-century concerns for the benefits of nature, the geographical-infrastructural conditions of public health, and cities' 'inhospitality' to women and children's morality coincided with new social capacities in technology, construction, and planning to create a landscape of harmonious physical and social conditions. In 1838, John Claudius Loudoun (2006), the British landscape gardener and architectural writer, wrote of the suburbs' QOL benefits (note his social engineer's vocabulary of cause-and-effect):

> [A]ll, in the way of house accommodation, that is essential to the enjoyment of life, may be obtained in a cottage of three or four rooms, as well as in a palace; and we shall prove, in this work, that a suburban residence, with a very small portion of land attached, will contain all that is essential to happiness, in the garden, park, and demesne of the most extensive country residence . . . . The master of a suburban residence, however small his demesne, may thus procure health and enjoyment at the same time, with more certainty than the possessor of a larger property; because his

> grounds lie more in his hands, and he can superintend every change himself. His wife's exercise consists in the personal management of her household affairs; and her enjoyments are the same as those of her husband . . . . One immense advantage of a suburban residence over one isolated in the country consists in its proximity to neighbours, and the facilities it affords of participating in those sources of instruction and enjoyment which can only be obtained in towns: for example, public libraries and museums, theatrical representations, musical concerts, public and private assemblies, exhibitions of works of art, &c . . . . The suburbs of towns are alone calculated to afford a maximum of comfort and enjoyment at a minimum of expense . . . .
>
> (p. 17)

The values of domesticity, neighborly interaction, and moral enlightenment that Loudoun emphasizes reflect a variety of extant sources, from Victorian concerns for women's 'proper' roles to growing nostalgia for the 'loss' of traditional rural community; importantly, all became most salient against the backdrop of industrial urbanization (Marsh 1982; Williams 1975; on the U.S. case, see Schmitt 1969). But the materialization of these values in the form of residences, amenities, landscapes, and other place features was not given; these had to be built at great expense and technological power out of an untamed landscape on the urban periphery. Thus, the suburbs achieved, on a massive (and, by the twentieth century, mass-produced) scale never seen before, the seemingly universal principle that place is an instrument of QOL aspirations. Today, as the suburbs themselves become the subject of controversy over sprawl and placelessness, the taken-for-granted human capacity to conceptualize and construct physical space to serve our interests remains the fundamental premise of QOL concerns.

Place Reflexivity and the QOL Gaze

Today, place no longer serves as the primordial community that sociologists of old variously called *gemeinschaft*, primary groups, or mechanical solidarity. Randal O'Toole's "communities" of road cyclists and Belgian Tervuren dog-owners exemplify the sociological axiom that modern individuals transcend the territorial and social structures of place to associate and self-identify through occupations, institutions, interest groups, cliques, subcultures, social networks, and lifestyle affinities, now online as well as off (Wellman 1999; Webber 1963; Wirth 1938; Lynd and Lynd 1929; Zorbaugh 1929; but see Calhoun 1998). The relevance of this expanding matrix of potential affiliations is heightened under the contemporary development that theorists following sociologist Ulrich Beck call the *individualization of social structure*, in which people assume responsibilities for their own social reproduction as social institutions lose their collectivizing force (cf. Beck 1992; Giddens 1991). For most, the migration from the primordial community to the industrial city marked the first untethering of our collective fates. By the late twentieth century, collective institutions like the state, the corporation, the union, and the nuclear family had largely lost their social reproduction functions; as a result, people have little choice but to reproduce their social position through each biographical event and major decision they undertake. Consciousness shifts accordingly. With place reduced to one of many factors, alongside the kinds surveyed in the prior chapters, that shape our lives, livelihoods, life-stages, and lifestyles, consciousness of place—and of family, work, and other venerable institutions (see Chapters 4 and 5)—becomes more *reflexive*. Freed from its primordial grip, place can now be categorized, strategized, and used to achieve social concerns, values, and identities.

Reflexivity toward place can be instrumental in nature—"Where can I find a good job? Should we move before the kids finish high school?"—but it is hardly limited to this. Place especially highlights how individuals enchant and aestheticize their values, goals, and progress through the world. This is most evident in tourism, as sociologist John Urry (1990) explains with his theory of the *tourist gaze*, a subjective perspective on place that foregrounds the structured orientation through which tourists perceive the subjective 'appeal' of particular landscapes and destinations. Across the vast array of tastes and interests that various destinations can stimulate, the tourist gaze "depends upon what it is contrasted with; what the forms of non-tourist experience happen to be . . . particularly those based within the home and paid work" (p. 2). This means tourist destinations are not intrinsically interesting, culturally exotic, family fun-filled, or romantic. Rather, tourists actively and often imaginatively discern those place qualities when they perceive their own lives to be routine, culturally homogeneous, unsupportive of family unity, or romantically uninspired, respectively. In its emotional and aesthetic modes of place consciousness, the tourist gaze constitutes an irrational reflexivity. From such imaginings of place, drawn from affective orientations often based in whim or titillation, may come sentiments of 'love' for a place and idealizations of the 'beautiful' destination or landscape.

Tourism is perhaps the archetypal modern encounter with place. Like mass migration, education, and non-leisure forms of travel, it teaches us about various places and 'expands our horizons' (i.e., provides a comparative orientation) on place in general. Unlike these venerable experiences, tourism frames this awareness of place as a consumer experience (Urry 1995). Until recently, tourism emphasized mass consumption; popular destinations, oceanliner cruises, and group vacations illustrate how the tourist gaze is traditionally a standardized one often made in the co-presence of many other beholders (see, e.g., Aron 1999; Savage et al. 1992). More idiosyncratic, 'postmodern' forms of tourism have since arisen with ecotourism, tours of urban decline or wartorn regions, and other kinds of visits motivated by dissatisfaction with the pre-packaged, superficial nature of mass tourism and a search for an 'authentic' landscape or ways of life. In this postmodern sense, *residential mobility* stands upon but goes further than contemporary tourism, offering arguably the most intensive and personalizable modality for the encounter and consumption of place. Moving from one place of residence to another deepens the comparative experience of place, exposing the migrant to subtler, less visible aspects of place than might be gleaned by visiting only. Residential mobility also constitutes social reproduction in an individualized world; in both the decision to move and its consequences (new job, neighborhood, friends, romantic relationships, etc.), it epitomizes the ways social reproduction and personal well-being are accomplished with each significant biographical event one undertakes. Economists and other social scientists often assume that residential migration involves the most of rational decision-making dynamics, given the considerable fiscal and social investment this act entails. Yet the prior discussion suggests we might be skeptical that rationality alone informs the decision to move; the assumption surely underestimates the number of moves made based on apparent whim ("I knew I'd have to live there one day the first time I visited . . .") or 'irrational' constraints ("I would do anything to get out of this place . . . .").

Can we conceive of a *QOL gaze* among the possible modes of place reflexivity? Extending Urry's idea of the tourist gaze allows us to consider a vast array of QOL attractions through the standpoint of the beholder's extant daily rounds. Places 'with a high QOL' are attractive as possible places to live because they imaginatively resolve the anxieties people attribute to their current contexts; limiting ourselves just to residential contexts (for work, see Chapter 5), these may range from security concerns about crime, congestion, neighborhood change (or *neighbor* change, as in fears of ethnic diversity and foreign immigration), and even the fear of terrorism (on this, see the case of Argentina in Otero et al. [2006]); to 'post-material' concerns for placelessness, environmental unsustainability, and the affluenza of neighbors and peers. In the developed world, the (imagined) rural way of life has especially imprinted ideals of place-based QOL by offering a countervailing vision to the ills of the industrial, urban living situations that most modern people have known. Surveying the American context, historian David B. Danbom (1996) argues:

> agrarianism fills a vacuum that, in other Western societies, is filled by developed ideologies critical of industrial capitalism and its values. Agrarianism can fill that vacuum so comfortably because it is so American. It goes back at least to the Founders, and it is so tied up with such sacred values and mythic concepts as individualism, liberty, equality, community, and family as to be virtually invulnerable to effective criticism.
>
> (p. 17)

Still, in other countries where such "developed ideologies critical of industrial capitalism and its values" can be easily found—England (Murdoch et al. 2003), France (Nadeau and Barlow 2003), Canada (Bonner 1997), among others—the rural exerts a similarly strong influence on visions of the good place.

As these examples suggest, in no case need the beholder accurately assess the QOL of the places he or she lives and works in. Indeed, Urry's attention to the user's contrasting standpoint provides new insights on the 'authenticity' of QOL that people seek from places. For instance, we might anticipate that those who, following the New Urbanist philosophy, regard the walkability of urban downtowns and village centers as salient emblems of a 'place with high QOL' are likely to include a disproportionate number of middle-class residents of sprawling metropoles whose daily dependence on their private cars makes lack of walkability the norm. Yet by the same token, transportation-poor residents of those same sprawling metropoles, for whom walking represents an everyday condition that simultaneously symbolizes their stigma in a sprawling, car-centric metropolis, might not see walkability as especially enhancing their QOL. ("Only a nobody walks in LA," a 1982 pop song observes.) Given the opportunity to acquire the reliable private automobile that suburban living demands, for such residents a move *to* so-called auto-dependent suburbs might represent a more urgent QOL aspiration.

Consumer Orientations toward Place

The QOL gaze and place reflexivity more broadly are well served by consumer research, services, and businesses that codify affective and aesthetic orientations toward place into systematic criteria that help people decide which places to consume. Among these technologies to calculate place-based QOL, we can first include the best-places literature and related place media that put categorizations and evaluations of place to the service of our subjective considerations. Business clients may seek out consumer research firms that sort geographic populations into demographic clusters, social groups, and life-stage groups with characteristic wants and needs. Thus, from the Claritas group, pioneers in the field of commercial "geodemographics," comes the statistically quantified, zip-code disaggregated finding that in exurban areas, some younger populations "fashion fast-paced lifestyles centered on sports, cars, and dating," while some older groups "lead low-key, home-centered lifestyles, with social lives revolving around activities at veterans clubs and fraternal organizations" (Claritas Inc. 2008). The cutting edge in technologies to calculate place-based QOL criteria might be Richard Florida's recent collaborations with leading figures from the field of positive psychology (including flow expert Mihaly Csikszentmihalyi) to identify the psychological affinities between personality dispositions and place types. In his book *Who's Your City: How the Creative Economy is Making Where to Live the Most Important Decision of Your Life*, Florida (2008) argues that people characterized by one of five personality dimensions (openness to experience, conscientiousness, extroversion, agreeableness, and neuroticism) thrive in one of three kinds of regional clusters:

> The first cluster I call outgoing regions. Scoring high in extroversion, regions in this cluster are low in neuroticism, conscientiousness, openness, and very low in agreeableness. Topping the list here are Chicago and Minneapolis, along with a mix of old industrial regions such as

> Pittsburgh, Cleveland, Milwaukee, and Detroit, and Sunbelt Centers such as Salt Lake City, Fort Worth, San Antonio, Orlando, and West Palm Beach . . . .
>
> The second cluster I call conventional or dutiful regions. Regions in this cluster score high on agreeableness and conscientiousness as well as extroversion, but low in openness and neuroticism. The regions that stand out here are mainly in the Sunbelt: Atlanta, Phoenix, Charlotte, Raleigh, Greensboro, Memphis, Nashville, Tampa, Fort Lauderdale, Jacksonville, Miami, as well as Indianapolis and Portland, Oregon . . . .
>
> Experiential regions form the third cluster. Places in this cluster score highly on openness and neuroticism, but low in conscientiousness, extroversion, and agreeableness. Regions in this group include large creative centers such as New York City and its environs, the San Francisco Bay Area (San Francisco, San Jose, and Oakland), LA and San Diego, Boston, Seattle, Washington, D.C., and Baltimore, Denver, Austin, and Dallas, but also Las Vegas, Buffalo, Louisville, and New Orleans.
>
> (pp. 198–200)

In critically reviewing these consumer offerings, I am not so much concerned with challenging their claims (that certain kinds of QOL are found in certain cities and regions or best suit certain types of people) or questioning the pedigree of their scholarly perspective. Rather, they highlight a central context for contemporary place reflexivity: the growing number of and interest in such services and research enroll us into a *consumer orientation toward place*. Economic scholar Clifford W. Cobb's (2000) observation of the best-places literature is instructive:

> City and quality of life rankings by commercial publishers … use utilitarian criteria to determine the "most livable" city or the "highest ranked" state. They use arbitrary formulas combining components as diverse as income, pollution, accidents, number of women-owned businesses, and library books per capita. By that means, they compare the QOL of particular locations, as if they were adjuncts of the real estate business. In effect, these ranking exercises treat the attributes of a good life as a location to be purchased.
>
> (pp. 8–9)

So, too, for other technologies to calculate place-based QOL: by digesting the QOL options that places provide and offering cognitive templates for our decision-making, they recast beholders into buyers and sellers of place.

As a cultural framework, the consumer orientation to place promises a remarkable kind of moral emancipation. Consider how these technologies promote a heightened sensitivity to place preferences and a comparative, abstract orientation toward place-based QOL. "When one likes a town because it is small, one does not have to think about or come to terms with the particularity of the town because what is attractive about it only incidentally belongs to it," sociologist Kieran Bonner (1997:167) has observed in his study of Canadian exurban migrants. The QOL gaze also exerts the same effect 'back home,' where people's conceptions of what they want from a place escape the moral gravity of current livelihoods, relationships, and daily rounds; the *gesellschaft* of place-based QOL is not subject to the frictions of distance and wealth that normally ties them to existing *gemeinschaften*. Bonner (1997) further asserts, "Thinking about a place in this way allows one to keep one's options open—a method for keeping the possibility of mobility alive" (p. 167). Richard Florida's advice at the beginning of this chapter urging us to "be willing to move when necessary" suggests how radically the consumer orientation toward place-based QOL strives toward rootlessness, although the most significant outcome for my purposes here is not the actual migration across geography (about which, see next section). Even if one never walks out the front door, the ability to evaluate and try on places (at least in imagination) becomes practically infinite.

The 'freedom' afforded by this consumerist orientation toward place-based QOL contrasts remarkably with the affluent society premise that places as social goods are "not sold to individual consumers nor adjusted to individual tastes" (to reference Daniel Bell's earlier definition). Left-wing critics of the New Urbanism have pointed out the political contradictions when place-based QOL is allocated by the market. Despite its goal of resuscitating the collective integrity of QOL, the ways that most people actually experience the New Urbanism—as urban design amenities found primarily in exclusive model settlements or gentrifying urban neighborhoods occupied largely by tourists, well-to-do homeowners, and their (frequently non-resident) service staff—suggest the New Urbanism is effectively rendered into a scarce real estate good that relatively few can afford (Ross 1999). But beyond this market allocation, the consumer orientation privatizes place-based QOL as a moral conception, reimagining the rights to and entitlements of place as fundamentally individual and private, not shared by the local community as a whole. This view is delivered by Claritas and other consumer research firms that aid retailers and businesses seeking to locate new establishments, tailor promotions, and otherwise geographically segment their markets. Undertaken in advance of the eventual consumers they promise, their locational research sets in motion the circuit of place valorization that amenity-minded researchers close: marketing data help business find and urban boosters rebuild for the 'right' kind of users, until finally scholarship pronounces the geographic attraction an objective fact. Arguably the dominant paradigm of urban development in North America and Western Europe today generalizes the creative-city emphasis on QOL into a generic strategy of urban competitiveness (cf. Florida 2005a, 2005b). "QOL," "livability," and other keywords legitimate the redevelopment of public spaces, the construction of amenities, and the enforcement of a civil order that is thought to enhance creative lifestyles and workstyles (McCann 2007; Rogerson 1999). Beneath the glitter of attractive public spaces and amenities, all is not gold, however; creative-city strategies characteristically ignore the costs to collective QOL—the social inequalities exacerbated by the creative mode of production (Peck 2005; Marcuse 2003). The political implications of this consumer orientation to place are stark. If we "know how best to weigh our options" using abstract, individualized calculi of place-based QOL (to cite Richard Florida's opening quotation again), do we not approach the sovereign individual of neoliberal visions?

QOL Migration

My discussion of humans' growing subordination of place's primordial power and, moving into the present, the rise of place media and other technologies for place reflexivity points to broad contexts in the contemporary pursuit of place-based QOL. A separate question is, what is it that makes possible the ultimate individualized pursuit of place-based QOL: the *QOL migration* in which an individual or household relocates full-time to a place primarily for its 'high QOL.' For the rest of the chapter, I examine the case of the QOL migrant in order to develop further insights about the contexts of our relationship to place. In this section, I focus on the demand-side factors that shape our migrations. Next, I examine the political economic contexts that fuel the geography of QOL migration.

Freedoms to Move

The long-term move to a new residence explicitly to enjoy its place-based QOL is a rarefied event. To appreciate the unequal distribution of QOL migrations, consider first the distinction between migrations of necessity and migrations of choice (cf. Brown 2002:15; Petersen 1964). Only the latter freely initiates and undertakes the move; only here would we find the QOL migrant, among other groups. Winnowing the group further, it is likely that to be able to prioritize place-based QOL over other locational features—job opportunities, proximity to friends and family, housing cost—and secure a new residence on this basis requires a substantial degree of economic stability. Unlike the lucky ones who enjoy "another day in paradise" by accidents of birth or geography, QOL migrants agree to take on the costs of moving, traveling, and obtaining a new residence—usually all by themselves, when housing or moving subsidies are unavailable. The normal real estate scarcity in places known for their high QOL promises such costs will be considerable.

Evidence that self initiative and material security, two basic elements of the QOL migration, are hardly the norm for residential migrants comes from the U.S., a valuable case-study since its citizens move more frequently than others elsewhere in the developed world. Sociologist Claude Fischer (2010) has parsed data from the U.S. Census Bureau's Current Population Survey and found that by 2008, some 12 percent of Americans moved from one full-time residence to another during the year. Although not an insubstantial rate, it is a modest one that in fact continues a declining rate of migration over at least the prior six decades, since the Census Bureau began tracking such figures; see Figure 6.1. Fischer (2002) emphasizes how economic instability figures in most residential migration; compared to Americans as a whole, those who move are more likely to be renters, aged 18 to 24, service workers, less educated, and/or poor. With instability comes lack of choice, as these groups typically face circumstances of personal constraint—in the tenure stability of one's residence and the freedom to avoid the migratory decision—that make migration more likely an act of necessity.

Real estate agents and place media work hard to distinguish their local areas in the minds of buyers and associate certain neighborhoods or municipalities with different kinds of QOL, but a QOL migration takes advantage of a broader geographical scan that comes with a long-distance move. How far away, then, do people normally move? In fact, most American migrants move locally, i.e., from one residence to another within the same county (Fischer 2002). Local moves typically include households seeking to upgrade their housing due to common life-cycle milestones like marriage or children, but even households who discretionarily move into the McMansion worthy of the most delirious affluenza dream are often effectively limited in their locational scan, drawing on local networks of work and institutions (e.g., schools) and the moral solidarity offered by family, locality, or tradition to mitigate the instability of uprooting (Cox and Mair 1988; Logan and Molotch 1987:40).[3] By contrast, more educated individuals and households are more likely to move over long distances, i.e., to a residence in a different county (Fischer 2010, 2002; Schachter 2001). Only this last pattern indicates the level of material stability necessary (if insufficient) for a bona fide QOL migration.

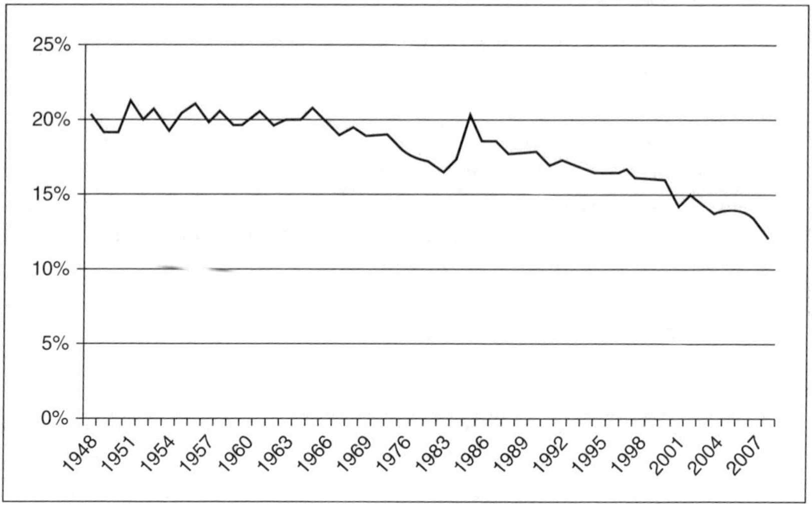

Figure 6.1 Residential mobility of Americans, 1948–2008

Source: U.S. Census Bureau, as reported in Fischer (2010).

In turn, this raises a question that pervades much discussion of place-based QOL: does seeking out a 'place with a high QOL' reflect class privilege? Popular discourses of place-based QOL would suggest so; the geographical aspirations peddled by high-end travel and regional lifestyle magazines presume economic means and a 'refined' taste in place. However, we might exercise prudence in asserting this correspondence as a general principle, since the affluent and the educated are less likely to move than are the less affluent and the less educated. Indeed, on the whole, moving up economically in America has not meant moving out; "increasing longevity, greater affluence and security, and the widening range of daily mobility" (the last especially evocative of American suburbs' auto-centrism) have made Americans more rooted than at any time in the recent past (Fischer 2002:193). Second, when the well-to-do and educated do move, they often do so for reasons other than place-based QOL—to take a job for the money, notably. And third, the less affluent also prioritize and sentimentalize place in their QOL aspirations. Significantly, non-white Americans have over the last 50 years become more likely to move long distances, as they take increasing part in the class mobility that in the twentieth century entailed a move out of the city to the suburbs (Fischer 2002:189; see also Frey 2003). They have also been most likely to be affected by the new century's sub-prime mortgage crisis as first-time home-buyers with a suburban house in foreclosure (Rivera et al. 2008). Perhaps this may be another symptom of Americans' affluenza-based fiscal overextension, but it underscores how 'democratic' the QOL gaze is in contrast to how limited are the financial means and freedom of choice necessary to a long-distance QOL migration.

Other Modalities of Pursuing Place-based QOL

Full-time migration is not the only way to exercise the QOL gaze, *seasonal migrations* being a case in point. Over various lengths of time and frequencies of migration, many people shift residencies between different locations, for different reasons. Geographer Kevin McHugh and his colleagues (McHugh, Hogan, and Happel 1995) propose a life course framework to help make sense of the possibilities for seasonal migration. The examples they give in Figure 6.2 are by no means exhaustive, but they highlight important categorical axes in the possible motives for occupying multiple residences: life-stage, frequency of migration (from weekly to infrequent circulations), and production- versus consumption-related reasons for moving (see also Roseman 1992; Smith 1989). This last axis corresponds overlaps largely, if not definitively, with migrations of necessity versus choice; cycling between residences for work illustrate production-related reasons, while cycling between residences for family and, significantly for this discussion, for place-based amenities exemplifies consumption-related reasons.

Seasonal migrations underscore by similarity and contrast the modes of place reflexivity that inform the QOL migration. Consider the relocations made by owners of vacation homes and recreational vehicles (RVs), two

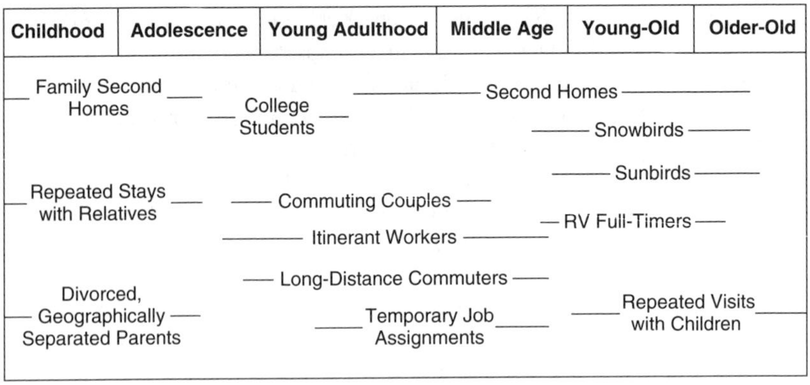

Figure 6.2 Examples of multiple residence by life course phase

Source: McHugh , Hogan, and Happel (1995:253).

popular forms of seasonal residences. Their use often centers around the amenity of climate, as symbolized by the elderly "snowbirds" and "snowflakes" (long-term and short-term visitors, respectively) who flee polar latitudes for equatorial latitudes in the winter, and their summer counterparts, "sunbirds" migrating in the opposite direction (Coates, Healy, and Morrison 2002; Mings 1997; Hogan and Steinnes 1994). Yet in contrast to a permanent move, vacation homes and RVs offer a more episodic mode of QOL consumption that requires less fiscal investment and personal commitment to a destination. Purchases of vacation homes that require long-distance travel are growing, but most vacation homes still lie within a day's drive from primary residence and "fall within the weekend leisure space of the urban sphere" (McIntyre 2006:10); in this way, owning a vacation home is on the whole a "moderate, rather than a life-changing lifestyle choice" (Quinn 2004:123). Furthermore, the very seasonality of part-time residences gives their occupants an added measure of individual agency over place and its QOL—they can always go home or (for RV users) go somewhere else—that full-time migrants surrender. Furthermore, vacation homes and RVs offer a relatively fixed environment of domestic amenities and activities (for RV users, this includes the RV camp) that may overshadow the engagement with the surrounding locality, particularly over repeated visits (in vacation homes: McIntyre, Rogenbuck, and Williams 2006; but see Stedman 2006) or peripatetic road trips (for RVs).

Needless to say, opportunities for seasonal migration depend upon the costs of fuel, time off from work, and other scarce personal resources, such that would-be owners of vacation homes or RVs may weigh these discretionary seasonal recreations against a wide-screen television, swim club membership, all-terrain vehicle, or other big-ticket items consumed back home. Such a utilitarian trade-off of forms of QOL, of course, characterizes the individualized understandings and pursuits of QOL more generally. In the case of place, perhaps a couple views their long-distance commute for several days a week as a way to 'enhance QOL' in terms of their individual career aspirations and household wealth, or as personal 'dues' they need to pay before they can reward themselves with a more harmonious balance of personal QOL and place-based QOL. The ability to trade off place against other forms of QOL and the decision not to do so are thus what distinguish the bona fide QOL migrant.

'Getting Away from it All'

My analysis of the relationship between place and QOL has so far focused on the subjective, demand-side contexts of beholders' gaze and choice in order to correct for the fallacy of place-based QOL. The entanglements of technology, the suburban overscheduling of family life, the seductions of work: people may seek to resolve QOL anxieties like these and others discussed in earlier chapters through place, but their salience does not emerge innately out of specific places or place more generally. 'Place-based QOL' is called into existence as people alight their QOL gaze upon geographical contrasts to home-based QOL and act to consume that geography. Those individual and household 'preferences' for place that economists and demographers enclose in conceptual black boxes in fact embody modern geography's remarkable story, one in which people exercise increasing power and reflexivity, in historically contingent ways, over place and other primordial spheres of social life.

That said, the supply side of places 'out there'—more accurately, the political and economic relations embodied in contemporary geography—also influences today's understandings and pursuits of place-based QOL. To further illuminate the case of the QOL migrant, I draw in this section on the evidence from *rural amenity destinations*, an ideal-type locale insofar as work opportunities are a second-order draw at best for migrants. As we will see, however, even the purest of QOL destinations does not escape service to today's flexible economy.

Privileged Assertions of Local 'QOL'

Social scientists have recorded what has been variously called the "rural renaissance," "rural population turnaround," or "turnaround migration," whereby cities in developed nations saw population declines while many rural areas (and, more importantly, suburbs) registered increases from the 1970s to early 1990s (Brown et al. 1997; Champion 1989). Britain has been singled out as the "vanguard" in the counterurbanization of Europe (Champion 1994:1504; cited in Murdoch et al. 2003:45), while population growth has affected many rural regions of the U.S., even as many cities have recently slowed down or reversed their population losses (Glaeser and Shapiro 2003). Scholars debate just how much urban–rural migrants have been drawn by 'QOL,' in all its ambiguities. Some evidence (see, e.g., Keeble and Tyler 1995; Clark and Cosgrove 1991; Williams and Jobes 1990) indicates that rural economies in many regions have restructured to the point that urban migrants are finding substantial local job opportunities. Still, the draw of country living specifically for its place-based QOL is undeniably significant for many migrants. Notably, 50 percent of respondents in a 1999 British Social Attitudes Survey indicated they would like to live in the countryside; of them, 90 percent said the countryside offered a "healthier environment to live in" (Murdoch et al. 2003:46).

Whatever rationale urban-to-rural migrants give for their move, it is clear their arrival impacts the public QOL in rural amenity destinations considerably, often disproportionately to migrants' actual number. In such places, old-timers' livelihoods are usually based on the primary sector, sleepy Main Street businesses, or large employers on the outskirts; the original architecture, lack of corporate chains, and other rural and small-town amenities that urban and suburban emigrants prize are often preserved accidentally, as economic stagnation and geographic isolation effectively freeze the locality until its 'rediscovery.' Into these settings, the infusion of new residents and their money threatens to raise taxes, exacerbate socioeconomic inequality, increase pressures on undeveloped open space, strain physical infrastructure, and impose other negative externalities. Old-timers see their way of life challenged indirectly (e.g., "rural gentrification" caused by rising property values and costs of living) and directly (by challenging the political deference traditionally acceded to old industries and landholders) (Moss 2006a). Marfa, Texas, a small town (2000 pop. 2,121) in the West Texas desert with a growing art/tourism economy, illustrates such changes:

> It's a familiar pattern. Western havens like Aspen, Colo., Taos, N.M., and Missoula, Mont., were Marfas once, playgrounds for coast-hugging hipsters who could slip into jeans and the rustic camaraderie of the outback. But those towns are full up now, victims of their popularity. Now the sagebrush Medici come to Texas, piloting the corporate Gulfstream into tiny Marfa Municipal airport and bellying up to the jes-folks atmosphere of Joe's Bar, where the Bud Light costs $1.75. The town remains an aesthete's dream, devoid of Olive Gardens, Best Buys, and any sign of the suburban middle class. Rather, Marfa is the honest texture of adobe and fine art set against a big sky. It's the simplicity of line and the haunting emptiness of the land.
>
> But this isn't what Marfa means to everybody in Presidio County. Most residents don't own much in this southwest corner of George Bush's Ownership Society. The county is 84 percent Mexican-American; 36 percent of its residents live below the poverty line (the U.S. average is 12 percent). Marfa itself is 70 percent Hispanic.
>
> Today, on Marfa's main street, tony art galleries and wine shops are driving away traditional cafes and shops, whose local owners can't afford the new sky-high rents. Everywhere you go the townsfolk, independent Texans to the core, lament the changes to their community. The term "ChiNazi" [in reference to Manhattan-based sculptor Donald Judd's local Chinati Foundation art museum] is used locally to describe anyone from

> out of town who arrives with artistic ambitions and a superior attitude. Observes one local cattle rancher, who asked to remain anonymous: "We're filling up with triple A's—artists, assholes and attorneys."
>
> (Nelson and Corley 2005)

It may seem that newcomers pursue place-based QOL in amenity destinations by effectively sacrificing it for old-timers, but the language of QOL complicates matters. Typically, those with socioeconomic advantage invoke place-based QOL as their privileged claim. The issue here is not that newcomers always seek to "raise the drawbridges" behind them and halt local growth after their arrival. Some evidence suggests that in destinations where recreational opportunities like skiing and fishing are the draws, QOL migrants (including a good number who find work in these sectors) tend to value their development and the subsequent sacrifice of rural character more than old-timers (Smith and Krannich 2000). The more general dynamic appears to be that the well-to-do advocate for local development that enshrines their preferred amenities. As illustrated by residents' efforts in the pastoral exurbs of Westchester County, NY, to halt the arrival of Latino immigrants, affluent old-timers also invoke 'defense' of the local QOL to challenge newcomers. "Some unarticulated racist practices take the form of calls for the enforcement of housing codes and other safety measures on the part of residents who normally take no special interest in the health and safety of renters," write geographers James and Nancy Duncan (2004). "In fact, the word 'renters' along with other words and phrases such as 'quality of life issues' have become codes for complaints about the increasing visual presence of poor Latinos in Mount Kisco and other towns in Westchester County" (pp. 219–20).

Competing for QOL Migrants

These patterns bring us full circle back to the hypothesis that class privilege explains the pursuit of places for their high QOL. While education and wealth have long been predictors for political activism and voluntary activity in "environmental" causes broadly speaking (Jones and Dunlap 2010; Franzen and Meyer 2009; Morrison and Dunlap 1986), the class skew in the advocacy of place-based QOL arises within a particular geographical context: the stratification of localities and their populations based on their abilities to *control capital investment* (Logan and Molotch 1987). In the present era of urban entrepreneurialism (Harvey 1989b), local growth coalitions of businesses, government, and boosters compete with their counterparts from other places to attract and retain population and business, and to profit from this growth. This competition manifests geographically in the form of metropolitan sprawl, placeless commercial development, and a physical environment of "new and improved" for the places that 'win'; for the losers, there are economic decline, declining revenues and services, and geographic marginalization. Within the locality, growth is an ambiguous gain that residents often experience as a loss, since it strains the collective infrastructure; often entails costly subsidies, tax abatements, and other fiscal concessions that drain municipal coffers; and otherwise impairs the local environment for residents' daily rounds (Molotch 1976).

How does the relationship of class privilege to the 'defense' of local QOL emerge? In some cases, growth coalitions may profit from protecting and promoting local use values for sought-after place users, like gated community residents or tourists. Alternately, residents with ample resources, cosmopolitan networks, and political savvy can sometimes outmaneuver business communities desperately focused on growth 'of any kind' (Stone 1993). As uncommon as such challenges to "value free development" are, they do not really challenge the rules of the game. Local defenders of use values have only seized the control of capital investment that motivates the competition for growth more broadly. This political economic context, more than class privilege in isolation, helps explain the power of the affluent to wield political rhetorics like 'QOL' to their advantage.

Importantly, the competition across geography for capital investment sets the stage for the rural amenity destination, as QOL migrants—on the whole, a cosmopolitan group with the means to invest their sentiments, energies, and often considerable income into their new locality—become the latest currency of capital investment for places. Their population growth is a feather in the cap of local boosters and, just as importantly, a lucrative source of profits for developers, real estate, and other sectors dependent on local growth. Other old-timers may not be ready to recognize this new wisdom, but QOL migration and the development industry have effectively trumped them, incorporating their isolated rural localities into the same competition for capital investment that larger cities and leafy suburbs have enjoined. Although we might question whether QOL migration can sufficiently sustain local economies amidst rural restructuring and deindustrialization (a debate that generally accompanies the rise of any emerging sector), 'place-based QOL' fits easily into the zero-sum geographical competition for another finite source of growth.

The Quality-of-life District

Each round of capital investment transforms the broader geographical horizon over which would-be QOL migrants cast their gaze. For many residents, the burdens (real and imagined) of continuing development may suddenly tip over the point of acceptability; the desire to 'get away from it all' may become too compelling. This QOL gaze is focused by media and popular discourses like the critique of placelessness that narrate how and *where* QOL has 'deteriorated,' and of course the many celebrations of potential destinations where QOL can be 'regained' (cf. Brown 2002). Yet as we have seen, many people may feel the same QOL 'push' out of their current locale that QOL migrants experience, and many people have similarly cultivated place-based QOL aspirations, but a proactive, full term relocation over long distance is not in the cards for most. What biographical circumstances makes this kind of QOL migration possible, especially when the destination's economic base is relatively undeveloped?

Perhaps the most general economic factor that shapes residential choice is access to a livelihood. For most households, this means access to employment: where they work, how far away from work they live, and how they get between the two limits their ability to disperse geographically and underscores their dependence on local labor markets (Cox and Mair 1988). Under such constraints, most households can at best move to the exurbs, where they exchange the comparatively rural QOL for a longer commute back into job centers (see Bonner 1997). Telecommuting is invariably cited as auguring greater geographical freedom, but so far as an actual workplace policy it has yet to have that effect—and certainly not for the vast workforce whose primary work platform does not involve information technology. When they offer it, employers generally view telecommuting as part of a larger flexibility package alongside, for instance, shorter workweeks of longer workdays. Such opportunities do not permit most telecommuters to move away so much as flexibly manage their daily rounds of work, school, errands, household upkeep, and family life within their existing circuits (see Kossek, Lautsch, and Eaton 2006). Meanwhile, freelancers who constitute the many "people who work from home on computers" are often tied to their localities even while they are liberated in their home offices, since the need to drum up multiple jobs (often involving a face-to-face meeting or same-day delivery of physical documents) makes living in the geographical thick of their clients an effective residential decision (see Pink 2001).

For most individuals and households seeking to maintain the standard of living of their former residences without its familiar stresses, moving over a long distance to a rural amenity destination requires having a livelihood independent of a local economy. Not surprisingly, retirees, investors, and others who live off non-labor income are the most common category of QOL migrants; where they move, often "the mail box is the largest source of income" (Rasker and Alexander 2003:2; quoted in Moss 2006b:11; see also Longino and Bradley 2006). Otherwise, as an IT executive in a small coastal California town explains, "[i]t's a fairly gutsy thing" to move beyond commuting distance from the labor market where one's work history and contacts are tied up (Nevarez 2003:65). Maybe migrants use their business and industry experience to start a business serving the rural amenity destination: traditional professional services like law and accounting, web design and IT systems administration, or personal "lifestyle coaching" (a possible option for former managers and personal assistants). Depending on the size of local markets, which is always questionable further off the metropolitan grid, newcomers may have difficulties in sustaining employment at the level they anticipated. The symbol of the "ski bum" illustrates how some switch over entirely to local job markets with a corollary drop in standard of living in order to preserve their QOL preferences.

From the beginning of this chapter, our venture capitalist who still works for a living from Park City, Utah, underlies the more general economic context that makes QOL migration possible. Namely, QOL migrants wield sufficient influence in the labor market that employers and clients accept the inconveniences and unavailabilities caused by their geographic distance and full-time telecommuting. Characteristically, such relocations are ventured by entrepreneurs, high-level executives, and other *elite workers* whose reputations, contacts, skills, and leverage gives them important measures of indispensability and autonomy in their industry (Nevarez 2003:51; Keeble and Nachum 2002). In recent decades, many employers in IT and other talent-intensive industries have come to anticipate such geographical defections by elite workers. To retain them, they spin off satellite branches or ad hoc projects in *quality-of-life districts*, remote enclaves where the competitive 'value-added' is primarily satisfying elite workers' lifestyle demands. In a crucial sense, elite workers who undertake QOL migrations do not really leave the labor market back home, since the locational concessions they wrest are made back in their industries' centers, with almost no influence from the local economies of their QOL destination.

These are but the most common biographical arcs of the QOL migrant, and certainly more could be said about the economic geographies that they traverse. For my purpose here, this brief discussion sheds light on how flexible capitalism incorporates our apparently idiosyncratic locational choices. Many may want to live in a place with a high QOL, but those who successfully advance through the sequence of labor market contingencies sketched here are most likely to arrive in the quality-of-life district, at least with their initial amenity and lifestyle aspirations intact. This is an institutional privatization of public QOL, and its consequences are very public, indeed political. For one, QOL migration accommodates and, indeed, relieves the perceived strains of unchecked growth and work-life imbalance back in economic hotspots (Nevarez 1999; see also Keeble and Tyler 1995). For another, the allure of the quality-of-life district undermines the moral commitments 'back home' in our old workplaces and localities. The lucky ones who move somewhere they can surf on their lunch break goad the rest of us into further embracing the risks and responsibilities of the market, hoping for such a place to get away from it all, while our previous localities and their remaining populations are left with the ongoing crisis of cultural (if not physical) rootlessness and place abandonment.

Conclusion

In 1970, the Girard Bank, a leader in the Philadelphia business community that was then experiencing the full force of the urban crisis, commissioned historical novelist and occasional sociology lecturer James Michener to identify the key challenges facing the region and the nation. He wrote *The Quality of Life* (1970), an 85-page essay of cogent, well-reasoned discussion of the issues he thought most worth tackling in an era overwhelmed by upheaval and protest. The title underscored the stakes of the problems Michener outlined; although he worried little for America's economic prosperity and military security, he feared their unquestioned priority could only cheapen the QOL Americans enjoyed and ultimately poison the decency and civility that characterized the best ideals of the nation. Among all the issues he addressed, including race relations, the environment, education, and youth, Michener devoted his first chapter to "Saving the City." His proposals to achieve this sound radical for their ambition and scope from the vantage point of today's U.S. urban policy climate: strengthening metropolitan government, ending the municipal fragmentation and retail exodus that shrink city coffers, sustaining the higher wages typical of urban labor markets, creating a urban transit system that does more than facilitate suburban commutes, tackling crime, maintaining cultural amenities, and reversing the population shift.

I mention this anecdote not to dwell on causes and policy solutions for the urban crisis, but instead to highlight how unlikely, even antithetical, Michener's argument that resolving the urban crisis would enhance QOL seems in light of contemporary pursuits of place-based QOL. By linking 'QOL' to a set of proposals that would surely require individual sacrifices in tax revenues and suburban convenience, Michener urged his readers to acknowledge their mutual dependency and shared interests with their fellow metropolitans across socioeconomic, racial, and geographic divides—in short, to understand the Philadelphia region as a moral community. Yet today, in the name of 'QOL,' people, policies, and economies tend in the opposite direction with regards to place: emphasizing individual preferences, shirking collective obligations, and seeking 'common ground' in segregated particularities of lifestyle and life-stage. Disappearing from place-based QOL pursuits and the dominant QOL outlook more generally is the affluent society promise in which our well-being can be achieved through collective deliberation on the greater good and political regulations of market forces that dissolve our commitments to one another. In this sense, the urban crisis persists today, even as some cities recover and as decline turns upon many suburbs and rural regions (see, e.g., Frey 2004; Hudnut 2003).

This chapter highlights how residential mobility colors our cultural imaginations of place-based QOL today, even if the reality of QOL migrations as an empirical trend is often overstated. The sense of agency over environments and social affiliations; the weighing of utilitarian, affective, and aesthetic concerns for 'what we want from place;' the abstract, comparative scan of geography and lifestyle—as a lens on our encounters with place, the QOL gaze promises an exciting and liberating experience for the most banal of activities, like tourism and shopping. That residential mobility has become an emblem for *self-actualization through place* signals a set of social shifts that are hardly an inevitable consequence of modernization. Looking backwards, we see the accumulated force of several historical developments—most relevant here, industrial urbanization, post-industrial suburbanization, and genuine advances in civil rights and human emancipation—that have stripped place of its primordial, ascriptive force in the reproduction of social structure. Parallel background developments impose greater burdens of social reproduction on us as individuals and household: the institutional disintegration of the welfare state, the corporation, the labor union, and other modern organizations that once provided total worlds for their subjects. Closer into the present era, we see the influence of consumer research and urban consulting on marketing places and making palatable, even attractive, the need for places to market themselves for business, population growth, and tourism. These shifts have brought forth the worldview in which the market reigns supreme as the legitimate distributor of the good, in place and other external realms as well, and in which the legitimacy of redistributions by the state and other collective institutions is questioned.

An insight to draw from the critique of placelessness and the thirst for 'authenticity' that perhaps unhelpfully dominate the rhetoric on place-based QOL is that the language of QOL strives to *resist* the market's rationalizing thrust, giving voice to human expressions far richer than the instrumental, desocialized pursuits of *homo economicus*. Expanding on Danbom's thesis that agrarianism offers Americans a "comfortable" frame for criticizing their industrial, urban way of life, we might consider how QOL migration to rural or 'attractive' areas offers a practical opportunity to critique the monotony and alienation of our extant locales and situations. Yet paradoxically, if New Urbanists and creative workers (to name just two iconic figures in this heroic quest for place-based QOL) loathe the corporate franchises and impoverished public space promulgated by rationalized urban development, their resistance nonetheless occurs through the markets for place and labor. "Voting with your feet," their gesture is sometimes called—a useful phrase to highlight the *exit* that QOL migrations mark in physical geography and from whatever world exists outside the market (cf. Hirschman 1970). The 'irrational' location of new economy firms in quality-of-life districts far from the geographical centers of industry attests, quite literally, to how far today's flexible capitalism can accommodate such rarefied market demands.

In sum, place throws into sharp relief the contradictory QOL pursuits that can be observed throughout all the domains covered in this book. Through its material infrastructure, place seems to link people's fates together and promises a means by which to enhance everyone's QOL. Yet its promise is undermined by the context in which people pursue place-based QOL: a geography of competing localities that parallels (and indeed serves) the 'flexible' organization and individualized risk of today's economy. How this moral philosophy that pervades today's dominant QOL outlook is manifest in political participation and discourse is the subject to which I now turn.

7 Politics

> Orgies of mathematics and science are held in defence of nature. Whole battalions of high-powered economic calculations advance, flanked on either side by dissidents from the natural sciences who wish to invert the formulae from which the hazards have escaped and make possible their recapture . . . . Yet it must be said that all of these efforts are only a substitute, a strained way of saying, 'We do not want to live thus!'
>
> (Ulrich Beck 1995:42)

Many of the contemporary pursuits of QOL that I have examined to this point have rather obvious political aspects. Consumption taxes and public subsidies for child daycare, to name just two issues touched upon in Chapters 3 and 4, exemplify policies designed to enhance QOL; they are also political insofar as their advocates enter legislative and electoral arenas to endorse their views of the greater good as worthier than competing views and legislation. Many individual and household decisions made for non-political reasons also comprise a kind of politics, insofar as they embody a tacit policy of institutional non-decisionmaking (Crenson 1971). From the last chapter, the decision to relocate to a rural amenity destination represents a form of "voting with your feet." When multiplied en masse by other households with similar aspirations and opportunities, this market-based redistribution of population and growth pressure absolves governments from dealing with the effects of urban growth and infrastructure strain in the sending regions—or at least the demands of affluent voters, who apparently indicate their view of the costs and benefits of the "rat race" by either 'getting away from it all' or consenting to stay put (cf. Peterson 1981; Tiebout 1956).

In this chapter, I take up these three aspects of politics—policies proposed to enhance QOL, the interests of the constituencies who advocate them, and the institutional legitimacies that their advocacy symbolizes—as I investigate how political action and discourse in the name of QOL reflect and drive the contemporary development of the idea and its pursuits. The discussion here consolidates and makes explicit the political implications of many points and examples from earlier in the book, such as the social divisions and status pursuits that motivate concerns for collective QOL (Chapter 3); the emancipations and responsibilities assigned to individuals under the Anglo-American welfare regime (Chapter 4) and the 'new world of work' (Chapter 5); and the pursuits of lifestyle and community in the market of place (Chapter 6). The issue for this chapter is, quite simply, the contributions of QOL pursuits to *democratic visions of the common good.* In contests over legislation designed to promote the well-being of 'us all,' political movements raising the banner of 'QOL' put forth normative accounts how we relate to one another in democratic polities. The questions I ask are, first, how do these assorted views of the common good legitimate certain frameworks for making political claims? And, second, what alternate visions of the common good get lost in the process?

One way to assess the validity of the common good is in terms of how widely its ideals are held within the polity. On this issue, many commentators have discerned in QOL politics the activism of a 'new class'—a constituency whose position within the economy and state gives it a practical interest in advocating issues that sustain and further advance the trajectories of those spheres. From Chapters 5 and 6, the "creative class" who pursues work- and place-based QOL is an obvious candidate for the new class, although commentators have also nominated "professionals," "knowledge workers," and other post-industrial groups for this role (Bell 1999; Brint 1994). Interpreted more generously, the new class concept highlights the role of other possible vanguards: generations, new social movements, and the like. For some, this suggests that QOL politics lie at the forefront of social progress, an historical avant-garde bringing about changes that benefit the whole of society and drive the march of civilization. Others see the new class in more Machiavellian terms, as a dominant group that tramples over different values and interests (see King and Szelényi 2004). Exemplifying the latter view, David Brooks discerns in the voluntary simplicity movement, the new urbanism, and other usual suspects of QOL movements evidence of an ascendant status group, which he colorfully calls "bourgeois bohemians" or alternately the "liberal gentry" (Brooks 2003), who opportunistically asserts 'QOL' to promote its own worldview and well-being:

> Today, America once again has a dominant class that defines the parameters of respectable opinion and taste—a class that determines conventional wisdom, that promulgates a code of good manners, that establishes a pecking order to give shape to society, that excludes those who violates its codes, that transmits its moral and etiquette codes down to its children, that imposes social discipline on the rest of society so as to improve the "quality of life," to use the contemporary phrase.
>
> (Brooks 2000:46)

These examples suggest there is critical value in undertaking a class or interest-group analysis of whose values and goals are promoted and who subsequently benefits. However, such a method is insufficient for expressions of QOL politics that do not clearly map along class divides, such as the right-to-die movement in the field of health-related QOL. Furthermore, the emphasis on a particular group's interests and efforts in the political arena overlooks how the consequences of QOL politics manifest more broadly. Opponents of particular QOL advocates also contribute to the broader formulation of 'QOL,' for instance, by granting the idea's value and elaborating its underlying framework in certain regards, even as they reject specific goals or values. More generally, we might anticipate a political autonomy to QOL the idea. Following Max Weber, political praxis can be constrained more powerfully by the domains and expressions of political concern that 'QOL' connotes and the legitimacies the idea marshals than by conventional divides of class and power.

A review of QOL politics that strives to be definitive is almost certainly doomed to failure, considering how the subject involves potentially as many political developments and groups as can invoke 'QOL.' I proceed more strategically in this chapter. After reviewing two key theories for the ascendance of QOL politics in contemporary societies, I look at three case studies; two are international in scope (environmentalism and the right-to-die movement), while the third is specific to a particular nation (Britain's rural conflict). Keeping in mind the diversity of values and pursuits that people can attribute to 'QOL,' I avoid privileging particular movements or ideologies as somehow embodying a genuine QOL agenda. Instead, I use these three cases as sites to investigate the surrounding *conflicts* related to QOL—in particular, the underlying contexts for the political praxis and discourse that emerges on both sides, if indeed such an easy dividing line can be drawn.

Modernization and QOL Politics

A central theme in the QOL scholarship is that the idea informs a specific set of political issues, values, and modes of participation that sustain the ongoing process of societal modernization. We have already encountered strands of the two scholarly perspectives that support this contention in Ronald Inglehart's postmaterial thesis of modernization theory (Chapter 2) and Ulrich Beck's theory of individualization (Chapter 6). Here, I sharpen this earlier discussion by elaborating these theories of how politics serves as the vehicle of modernization to promote QOL concerns. Interestingly, both perspectives are ensconced in debates with 'postmodern' cultural relativists who are far more skeptical about the 'rational' legitimacy of the body politic today and about the possibility of articulating a common good.[1] This chapter is not the setting to reopen debates over postmodernism, but their themes inform two issues at heart in the politics of QOL. First, does the political advocacy of QOL really advance civilization? Do societies become more responsible for their social and environmental sustainability, more responsive to the needs and rights of their citizens—in short, more *rational* in the optimistic, modernist sense of the term—when their polities incorporate the demands to sustain or enhance QOL? And second, what is the nature of social relations, of solidarity or "morality" (Durkheim [1893] 1997), in the politics of QOL? Does the latter represent a consensual social good of the kinds idealized during the Enlightenment (like reason and progress), or does it instead open the floodgate to a cacophony of irreconcilable views about how we should live? And how can a QOL politics fall under the formal auspices of the state, with its legitimate authority to represent and command the polity?

The New Political Culture

To recap from Chapter 2, the postmaterial thesis put forth by political scientist Ronald Inglehart and his many colleagues contends that the social and economic conditions for modernization give rise to "emancipative orientations" in the values of a society's members. Those who take for granted the security that modern nation-states and industrial development can provide—particularly the young, the affluent, and the educated—begin to adopt and promote values that challenge tradition and authority; emphasize economic and political freedoms; give priority to environmental integrity, public health, and amenity development; and enshrine civil rights, personal autonomy, and self-actualization. The broad relevance for political change is obvious; this value shift, Inglehart contends, is how democratic regimes initially emerge and eventually embrace more postmaterial agendas. A more detailed account of how such changes materialize in electoral politics comes from Inglehart's collaborations with sociologists Seymour Martin Lipset and Terry Clark on the realignment of left–right issues and constituencies in postindustrial societies. They theorize that the rise of material security and affluence in many market and socialist democracies does not usher in the 'end of politics' as some political theorists predicted (Lipset 1981:509; Inglehart 1979:210–11). Rather, political values evolve away from the working class-left/propertied class-right binaries that drove political systems in scarcity-oriented industrial countries:

> Political issues shift with more affluence: as wealth increases, people take the basics for granted: they grow more concerned with lifestyle and amenities. Younger, more educated and more affluent persons in more affluent and less hierarchical societies should move furthest from traditional class politics.
>
> (Clark and Lipset 1991:403)

Clark and Inglehart (1998) have elaborated the political shifts and consequences of postmaterialism into an ambitious theory of the *new political culture* (NPC), by which they mean the new "rules of the game" that inform changes in politics as well as family and business culture. Table 7.1 lists the 22 hypotheses that form the basis of Clark and Inglehart's NPC theory.

Three tenets of the NPC are especially germane to the discussion of QOL politics. First, the NPC *divorces economic from social and cultural issues*. Emblematically, political advocates operating from a premise of material security fuse the ideologies of fiscal conservatism—i.e., a criticism of hierarchical

Table 7.1 The New Political Culture—22 Propositions

1. The Scarcity Hypothesis. An individual's priorities reflect the socioeconomic environment: One places the greatest subjective value on those things in relatively short supply.
2. The Socialization Hypothesis. Value priorities do not adjust immediately to the socioeconomic environment; a substantial time lag is involved since basic values largely reflect the conditions of one's pre-adult years.
3. The broad shift toward market/individualism in economic policy by many political parties would have been impossible without the concomitant introduction of social issues to complement traditional fiscal/economic issues.
4. The Hierarchy Principle. The more hierarchical the social institutions, the more likely powerful opposition groups are to emerge, challenging the hierarchies and pressing for egalitarian reforms.

4a. As hierarchy declines, it is harder to mobilize against it.

4b. Decline in hierarchy has in turn brought a decline in traditional left and right allegiances of citizens to political parties.

5. Demographic growth of a sector increases its legitimacy and power. The more persons in a political system who support a policy, the more likely it is to succeed.
6. The Consensus-Market Principle. The greater the value consensus among citizens, and the more that public policies reflect these values, the less citizens turn out to vote, support organized groups, parties, and a (hierarchical) bureaucratic state pressing for change.
7. The more ideologically coherent and structurally hierarchical the political parties are, the less likely the emergence of the New Political Culture.
8. New social movements organize locally and nationally in extra-party organizations more often when established party and elected leaders are perceived as unresponsive to movement concerns.

8a. Multiparty systems discourage new social movements by permitting many parties to address more specific issues. New social movements are stronger and more pervasive in systems with few parties.

8b. More centralized national governments, and higher population concentrations in larger cities, generate parties that are stronger, more centralized, less ideologically adaptable, and less citizen-responsive. Party centralization correspondingly encourages protests and various forms of extra-party movements, including new social movements.

9. Markets, ceteris paribus, grow in relevance as income rises.
10. The more advanced the technology and knowledge base, the harder it is to plan in advance and control activities administratively, both within a large firm, and still more by central government planners.
11. Smaller firms are less subject to state regulation and controls and thus are more nimble.
12. The higher the level of income and the more continuous the rate of economic growth, the less powerful are political parties, and the less salient are radical programs like fundamental economic redistribution.
13. The higher the level of income and the more steady the economic growth of a society, and the more stable and affluent each individual, the more fiscally conservative they are.

Table 7.1 Continued

14. The more extensive and complete the adoption of welfare state-type programs, the less the pressure for continued growth of these programs and of government in general.
15. If government grows more rapidly than the private sector economy, support for reduction in government programs is more likely.
16. Younger, more highly educated persons support more socially liberal issues. Although they support the output of many welfare state programs, they also prefer increased efficiency in service delivery and the corresponding lower costs and taxes. These changes in fiscal/administrative preferences are largest (a) among more affluent persons, and (b) in affluent societies with extensive welfare state programs, and (c) among younger persons.
17. The higher the education of an individual, or average level of a social unit (country, city), the greater the support for classic issues of civil rights, civil liberty, and tolerance.
18. The family and intimate personal relations have increasingly become characterized by more egalitarian relations, more flexible roles, and more tolerance for a wider range of behavior.
19. The New Political Culture is more likely to emerge in political contexts stressing issues rather than clientelism.
20. Nonstate religions, such as Protestantism in Catholic countries and nonconformist Protestants in Protestant countries, tend to emphasize individualism, which leads to more abstract issue politics, whereas state religions and Catholicism stress more personalistic ties, encouraging clientelistic politics.
21. The more professionalized and bureaucratized the national welfare state, the more issue politics are likely to prevail over personalistic or clientelistic politics.
22. The more important are mass media, the less important are clientelistic patterns.

Source: Clark and Inglehart (1998:17–64).

control over collective resources (by government bureaucracy, party bosses, or "old boy" business networks) that does not effectively serve citizens' concerns—with social liberalism on civil rights, lifestyle expression, and environment. This ideological realignment spells trouble for conventional political parties and institutions unable to adapt. Seymour Lipset (1981) initially discerned the impact of postmaterial liberalism in the right's electoral victories in the U.S. and Britain of the 1980s:

> Thus, there are now two Lefts, the "materialist" and the "postmaterialist", which are rooted in different classes. A conflict of interest has emerged between them with respect to the consequences of policies that affect economic growth. The materialist Left wants an ever growing pie so that the less privileged can have more, while the postmaterialists are more interested in the quality of life.
>
> (p. 510)

The 1990s offer further evidence for the NPC thesis with the rise of "Third Way," culturally liberal yet pro-market governments under Bill Clinton in the

U.S., Tony Blair in the UK, Lionel Jospin in France, and Gerhardt Schroeder in Germany, to name prominent examples (Lipset 2001; Giddens 1998). Political parties that seek to represent NPC supporters pay an electoral cost, however: "They tend to lose working-class voters" (Clark and Inglehart 1998:46).

Second, the attention to parties misstates the characteristic expression of the NPC in the electoral and policy sphere, which supporters advocate largely on *an issue by issue basis*. An important historical factor here is that "Success is the main problem of the welfare state," which has achieved a basic level of economic security that gives rise to the diverse and politically unmanageable demands of a postmaterial citizenry (Clark and Inglehart 1998:53). On both left and right, groups that advocate particular causes or collective identities—social movement organizations, new social movements, and, in nations with multiparty systems, single-issue parties such as the Greens—have replaced multi-issue class-based parties and labor unions for citizen's participation and allegiance. Mayoralties and local governments are especially responsive to the NPC, since many of these are formally constituted along non-partisan lines and thus amenable to the hybrid left–right agenda of NPC supporters.

Third, even the focus on politics per se overlooks how *the market becomes the preeminent platform for the NPC's expression*. Because economic affluence simultaneously increases demand for personal autonomy, provides consumers greater choice, and weakens the class basis in voters' values, materially secure citizens can better pursue their specialized preferences for household necessities, public services, and lifestyle/self-actualization amenities by buying them in the markets for goods, services, jobs, and places of residence. In contrast, advocating for the provision of such refined preferences through hierarchical, lower-common-denominator institutions like the welfare state, political parties, or corporate employers is much less effective.

More than one commentator has criticized the NPC theory as an apology for neoliberal celebrations of the market and attacks on the welfare state that conservatives initiated in the late 1970s and that Third Way liberals conceded by the 1990s. Although credible, this critique slights the almost Marxist orientation by which NPC theorists view the connection between a new class situation and postmaterial values. Inglehart and his colleagues stress the economic relations that give rise to material security and affluence, although given their multinational focus, they do not specify occupational and sectoral changes as do Daniel Bell or Richard Florida (both of whom are sympathetically cited by postmaterial theorists). Such theoretical generality lets NPC theory incorporate any number of explanations for the new sources of wealth generation (e.g., the new economy) and livelihoods (e.g., the creative class). As a corollary, postmaterialism and the NPC do not materialize without a hitch, given their basis in a material security that can be undermined by war or economic downturn. Nor do postmaterial values diffuse evenly within societies, given the resilience of working and lower classes accustomed to scarcity, the benefits of economic growth, and other material values. Still, if NPC theory and the broader postmaterial thesis cannot be reduced to a crude pro-capitalist ideology of the kind that tarnished the original modernization theory, they nonetheless articulate a sociological vision of the future that resonates for optimists who believe that market development enhances QOL for ever more people, if not exactly lifting all boats evenly. In this vision, the postmaterial 'new class' diffuses concern for QOL in its many manifestations (individual self-actualization, civil rights, amenities) throughout the market until their agenda comprises the dominant values of the body politic. In this way, postmaterial politics frames the horizon toward which civilization marches.

Reflexive Modernization

A second school of thought regarding QOL politics centers on *reflexive modernization*, the dynamic that characterizes the still-emerging "second modernity" in which we now live. This historical epoch overlaps roughly with the shift from modern to postmodern values that Inglehart theorizes (see Chapter 2), but the nature and cause of reflexive modernization are quite different. As explained by Ulrich Beck, the first modernity, corresponding to the period between the Industrial Revolution and the twentieth-century heyday of the welfare state, oriented societies' economic capacities, political priorities, and scientific gaze to controlling nature, material scarcity, and other forces external to society. By contrast, the second, reflexive modernity redirects these capacities and priorities *inward* toward modern society, its institutions, and its characteristic values and forms of legitimacy.[2] As the institutional contradictions or "latent side effects" (Beck, Bonss, and Lau 2003:8; Beck 1992:13) of industrial society manifest in the form of environmental, economic, technological, and social risks, the identification, attribution, distribution, and legitimation of risk become central concerns in the "risk society." Reflexive modernization is set into motion when citizens confront risk-generating institutions and challenge the legitimacy of their proclaimed scientific/economic/political/bureaucratic rationalities as well as the essential themes of modernity: progress, growth, and the accumulation of wealth.

The cultural questioning and institutional challenges of the kind that Beck describes surfaced in the U.S. as early as the late 1950s with the civil rights movements; crystallized in the 1960s Great Society programs, such reflexivity fortified the U.S. welfare state to its greatest and most ambitious capacity. However, Beck locates reflexive modernization's seminal moment in the 1970s and 1980s and casts environmental movements, of the kinds he observed in West Germany, as its symbolic protagonist for two reasons. First, they epitomize how social movements direct critical reason toward the 'rational' authorities of first modernity: myopic research scientists, unresponsive politicians, polluting corporations, intrusive government planners, obfuscating bureaucrats, public relations apologists, and so on, all of whom went as unquestioned and habitually accepted in the first modernity as the traditional authorities of church and nobility were in pre-modernity (Beck 1995, 1994, 1992). Second, environmental movements characteristically operate in the arenas outside the formal polity. Because industrial pollution, nuclear toxicity, food contamination, and other side effects of industrial society obey no boundaries of national territory, bureaucratic jurisdiction, scientific-technological field, or (with their unpredictable shelf-life) even history, environmental movements must not only contest the negative findings of scientists but also the more general relegation of growth and 'progress' to the hybrid and unlegitimated sphere of *sub-politics*. Before the culprits and domains of risk can be politically regulated, they must first and more fundamentally be socio-technically *constituted*: chains of culpable and injured parties, scientific cause-and-effect, techno-economic intentions and externalized outcomes, and political and legal standing—more and more, an international affair—must be identified and legitimately established before states can impose redress or policy from the formally political sphere (Beck 2005; Lash 2003:54).

In one sense, such reflexivity and the political advocacy that embodies it uphold the Enlightenment ideal of advancing human progress through reason even as they radicalize it. However, Beck theorizes that reflexivity, once unbound, infiltrates cultural codes and institutional logics elsewhere; with this theoretical opening, the concept of reflexive modernization resonates strongly in the work of other scholars. Anthony Giddens (1991) observes that in modern lives, self-identity is no longer an existential given, ascribed by tradition. Autobiographical narratives have become reflexive projects in which self-help experts, fitness and cosmetic enhancing services, and media images and ideals help individuals cobble together a mutable and fragile understanding of themselves. The personal work of reflexivity is also visible in today's family forms, the growing variety of which truly challenges the norm of the nuclear family on a number of fronts. The permutations made possible by divorce, cohabitation, remarrying, childless marriages, adoption, intercultural unions, blended families, long-distance households, and the legalization of gay marriage and adoption allow individual family members to elect the kin, surnames, rituals, living arrangements, residential locations, and household expectations of the 'family' they choose to identify with. Children experience the "normal chaos of love" most acutely, since the decline of traditional parental authority in the face of divorce and romantic reaffiliation gives them a space to assemble their imagined family to suit their emotional and material needs (Beck and Beck-Gernsheim 2002). Perhaps unexpectedly, reflexivity is also found at the other end of the power spectrum, in the cutting-edge forms and processes of flexible capitalism. Corporations have turned the reflexive gaze toward the top-down hierarchical rationalities that previously committed them to vertical integration, geographical agglomeration, and economies of scale. The results are economies of signs and space: corporate outsourcing and geographic peripheralization of labor-intensive processes; flexible agglomerations of networked firms in First-World cities and high-tech districts; the value-added shift to advanced business services and technical-aesthetic design activities; and the growth of tourism, entertainment, and other consumer services in regions formerly dominated by primary and secondary sectors (Lash and Urry 1994).

The broader context for these developments in rationality is the legitimacy crisis and organizational disintegration of collective institutions, which give rise to the structural trend Beck calls *individualization*. The very name points to how social relations are constituted—and who shoulders the greatest risks—under reflexive modernization. In the first modernity, an individual's life story was effectively ascribed by dominant institutions like the welfare state, corporatist institutions (big business for white-collar workers, trade unions for blue), class cultures, and the nuclear family, which were regulated by political values (maximum labor force participation, the male breadwinner, lifelong employment) and social hierarchies (such as sexual and racial-ethnic divisions of labor). Altogether, these served to stabilize, if not especially equalize, individuals' life chances and social relations en masse in both broad and minute ways; hence "the old idea that, by knowing someone was a Siemens apprentice, you also knew the things he said, the way he dressed and enjoyed himself, what he read and how he voted" (Beck and Beck-Gernsheim 2002: xxiv; see also Sennett 2006, 1998). In the second, reflexive modernity, these collective institutions and their regulatory frameworks have lost their direct causal power over individuals' biographies—in many cases precisely because the welfare state has succeeded, for instance, in maximizing employment (which undermines the patriarchal family as women enter the workforce) and subsidizing the growth of its national industries (thereby unleashing the technological and political powers of global corporations) (Beck et al. 2003). Whereas in the first modernity the biographical decisions individuals make—to marry (when, to whom), get an education (of what kind, for how long), bear children (when, how many, to keep), take jobs (for how long, for which employer, with what earnings, benefits, and opportunities for advancement), find a residence (where, with what public services, among what kind of neighbors), and so on—served to converge their biographies together under modern society's venerable categories (class, nation, race, gender, and so on), in the second modernity *these choices effectively differentiate their biographies from one another*.

Beck and other theorists of reflexive modernization tend to treat 'QOL' lightly if at all, but their ambivalence toward the thrust of reflexivity is telling. On the one hand, individualization offers unprecedented opportunities to enhance personal and household QOL through the reflexive "do-it-yourself biographies" (Beck and Beck-Gernsheim 2002; Hitzler 1988) it enrolls us in. With individualization, not only do people come closer to the modern pole in sociologists' binary of social ascription/achievement (cf. Parsons 1951), but they can find emancipation from alienating mass identities imposed by class, nationality, ethnicity and gender. New categories and milieus of people's choosing become the venues for human aspirations, identification, and self-actualization, to be inflected aesthetically and emotionally much like an artist paints her canvas: "The more post-traditional the settings in which an individual moves, the more lifestyle concerns the very core of self-identity, its making and remaking" (Giddens 1991:81). On the other hand, individualization accompanies a failure of institutional, economic, political, and technological capacities that exposes us to new and greater risks; the threats to objective QOL and (particularly when risk is psychologically anticipated and internalized) subjective QOL are clear. Moreover, if individualization in the second modernity "is characterized by choice," Scott Lash (2003) observes, "this choice must be *fast*[;] we must—as in a reflex—make *quick* decisions" (p. 51; emphasis in original). Most significantly, the 'freedom' that individualization bestows is one few of us ever agreed to by vote. "What is historically new is that something that was earlier expected of a few—to lead a life of their own—is now being demanded of more and more people and, in the limiting case, of all" (Beck and Beck-Gernsheim 2002:8; quoted in Archer 2007:38).

Herein lies the problem of legitimacy—stated differently, of *public morality*—in reflexive modernization. Social movements and other political agents who experience risk and challenge the legitimacy of modern institutions and principles must wade in the murky realms of sub-politics where "[p]rogress replaces voting" (Beck 1992:184); democratic deliberation in a genuinely political realm becomes another concern, alongside the direct impact of risk, to which political agents must attend. In some regards this becomes an ever more futile task since, as part and parcel of the scrutiny cast upon the welfare state, individualization by default tends to draw the specific issues of risk and the general confronting of social relations into the sub-political realm (Beck and Beck-Gernsheim 2002:29; Beck 1994:18). Legal standing, public debate, political deliberation, *reflexive acknowledgement* of risk's cause and effect and of the broader solidarities risk highlights in principle yet obscures in practice—these steps towards a common good become increasingly difficult to ascend in the rising sub-political tide of reflexive modernization.

Constituting QOL Politics

The theories of the new political culture and reflexive modernization both emphasize how the politics of QOL are characteristically located outside the nation-state's formal political sphere—in the market, civil society, the realm of science and technology, the sub-national municipality, and other non-political domains. From this common premise, however, the two modernization theories differ in their 'so what?' conclusion. NPC theory gives primacy to individuals and their values, and its proponents tend to be sanguine about the eclipse of formal politics, at least as the vehicle for civilization's progress. If the market most effectively provides the specialized goods, services, and opportunities people seek to fulfill their diverse self-actualization goals, NPC theorists see this as a breakthrough in the provision of QOL and find little reason to decry the failure of political institutions. By contrast, reflexive modernization theorists inherit the emphasis on rationality and legitimacy from German sociologists like Max Weber and Jürgen Habermas. In this tradition, rationality secures the rights and obligations that democratic societies confer upon their citizens, which means the formal political sphere remains the key site to legitimate the common good, even if the state and its institutional delegates are now subject to the critical gaze of reflexivity. Consequently, reflexive modernization theorists highlight the tenuous nature of political legitimacy in contemporary society and express some ambivalence about the personal gains and opportunities that individualization promises.

Stated as such, these competing views leave unanswered certain questions about *how* the common good is constituted in the (sub-)politics of QOL. How is QOL envisioned by political advocates of environmental and cultural integrity? And whose QOL? That is, do the politically ascendant QOL values benefit 'us all' or just a particular interest group? Finally, how does rationality inform the political claims we make to preserve and enhance QOL—or does it at all? To explore answers, I now turn to two illustrative case studies, the environmental movement and Britain's rural conflict.

The Localization of Environmental Politics

As we have seen throughout this book, environmentalism looms large in scholarship and public thought as an emblematic mode of QOL politics in all its connotations. As a sustained, self-conscious "environmental movement," ecological critiques and social protest appeared in the 1960s, around the same time that social analysts discerned the postindustrial shift in Western economies and citizens began challenging traditional economic and political priorities. The critique of modern industrialism and authority has informed ecological thought and environmentalist protest since at least *Silent Spring*, Rachel Carson's exposé of synthetic pesticides' contamination of the natural and human chain of life. Many observers now regard Carson's book as the first shot by the environmentalist movement: "The publication of *Silent Spring* in 1962 and the ensuing controversy that made it an epochal event in the history of environmentalism can also be seen as helping launch a new decade of rebellion and protest in which the idea of Nature under stress also began to be seen as a question of the quality of life," argues environmental historian Robert Gottlieb (1993:81). Environmentalism is not all protest, of course, and its impulse has never been solely political. Insofar as it involves the first-hand or even arm-chair appreciation of wilderness, wildlife, and natural 'beauty,' a much older tradition of environmentalism illustrates various modes of self-actualization: restorative and creative leisure, deep sympathy for others (in this case, non-humans), and emotional/aesthetic registers of unity with the world. Such figurations of collective identity and cosmology have led many scholars to recognize the environmental movement as a paradigmatic "new social movement" (Eyerman and Jamison 1991; Melucci 1989). In any case, precisely because it encompasses collective issues of ecological integrity and public health as well as individual expressions of personal well-being, the environment resonates as an object of myriad human concerns across a broad constituency. This is evinced by a 2005 poll finding that 77 percent of voters in the U.S.—hardly a stronghold of green politics, particularly in that post-

9/11 year—agreed with the statement, "This country should do whatever it takes to protect the environment" (Pew Research Center 2005:17). This and other statements like it are admittedly vague in meaning and prescription, but they nevertheless suggest a wide consensus around the environment and its integrity as a public good that can stir convictions of moral obligation.

However, as the environmental movement has developed into a savvy and well-financed political institution, national policies in developed countries (particularly the U.S.) and international consensus about what to do have moved slowly on urgent global environmental problems like climate change, resource consumption, and biodiversity loss. In many regards, the movement, at least in the U.S., has been most successful in constituting environmental politics at the *local* level, enacting legislation and crafting remedies aimed at municipalities and regions. In the name of the environment, local activists have drawn significant levels of citizen participation and established innumerable policies on issues like open space and nature preservation, the containment of urban and suburban development, and environmentally sustainable resource consumption.[3] Perhaps this is fitting, given the movement credo, "Think globally, act locally." A more practical reason, anticipated by NPC theorists, why environmentalists have achieved so many victories in local arenas is because of the simpler means with which local elections and laws are influenced, compared to national and international campaigns that invariably inject more stakeholders, legal complexities, and practical obstacles to derail legislative success.[4] The proliferation of community indicators projects (see Chapter 2) and other local initiatives that incorporate scientific forms of risk documentation have certainly played an important role in establishing legal challenges to unregulated development and urban sprawl. Local environmentalism's flourishing also reflects demographic shifts as places grow homogeneous and regions more segregated (Bishop 2008; Florida 2002). Electoral majorities if not widespread consensus for environmental policies become easier to establish, *ceteris paribus*, when post-material electorates dominate localities:

> Growth controls are more common in cities where citizens are younger, are more highly educated, and include professionals working in high-tech fields. Such citizens support a distinct set of preferences, a new political culture that stresses more consumption and lifestyle than traditional workplace and economic production issues. They value amenities and pursue them in activist manner: in garbage recycling, bicycle paths, and growth control.
>
> (Clark 2000:17)

Local environmental politics' basis in post-material class structure is evident in this passage by NPC theorist Terry Clark. Perhaps this should not surprise us. In the composition of their active participants and financial supporters, formal environmental organizations draw disproportionately from an educated and professional population—as, it should be noted, do other formal social movement organizations across the political spectrum (e.g., Buttel 1987; Morrison and Dunlap 1986). Considering the importance of class in urban inequality, it should come as little surprise that local activism against growth, an advocacy for a kind of postmaterial urban fortune, is shaped by the interests of residents of higher socioeconomic status (Clark and Goetz 1994; Logan and Molotch 1987; see Chapter 6). Tellingly, urban growth and suburban sprawl have been challenged more widely and effectively in municipalities—and spawned a greater constellation of grassroots organizations, local nonprofits, policy consultants, and research institutes—than the often starker, more life-and-death issues of, say, environmental contamination and neighborhood safety. What perhaps merits greater attention in Clark's statement is the idea that environmentalism legislation is driven by preferences for amenities rather than principles of ecological integrity. In citing this familiar QOL initiative of the postmaterial cohort, Clark implies that growth controls reflect an interest-group demand in local politics, analogous to lower taxes or improved services. Accordingly, growth controls reveal a moral fault line within environmental politics and QOL politics more generally: Does environmentalism serve interest-group selfishness or collective concern for earth's well-being?

Practically speaking, environmental opponents of urban growth do not have to choose sides as crassly as this question might suggest. My discussion of voluntary simplicity in Chapter 3 reminds us that explicitly collective, objective QOL motivations (e.g., reducing consumption) can be compatible with the cultural pursuit of individual, subjective QOL (e.g., the status-based gratification that comes with being a "simple liver"). More to the point, in municipal politics the local *is* the common good. The pattern in which growth controls draw support from multiple constituencies—open space and wildlife advocates, community and agricultural preservationists, but also homeowners defending their viewshed assets (recall here the example of California's Central Coast from Chapter 1)—underscores the extent to which the common good has been effectively achieved, at least from a majoritarian perspective. However, the moral fault line within environmental politics reappears when we shift scale to the larger geography of localities where environmental policies and initiatives have been established: what is ecologically sound at one scale can perpetuate environmental hazard and social inequality at a larger scale. This is a point voiced by left-wing critics of the U.S. growth control movement, who note that the federal "home rule" tradition prevents a just, centralized allocation of growth, preservation, costs, and benefit across regions; consequently, "a 'Not in My Back Yard' attitude pushes development away from areas resisting growth, increasing rather than containing sprawl" (Krieger 2005:49; see also Leo et al. 1998). Thus, the localization of the environmental movement does not escape the dynamics of residential migrations, place consumption, and counterurbanization that have transformed the global geography into markets of place, amenities, and policy climates (see Chapter 6); indeed, it depends upon such market transformations. Electoral achievements notwithstanding, the localization of the environmental movement confirms the subpolitical nature of QOL politics.

Not surprisingly, the specter of "culture war" is frequently cited in this context. This has been a nagging problem for the anti-sprawl movement, leaving activists vulnerable to charges of cultural elitism: "It turns out it is also not so easy to state, in a satisfying way, what is wrong with sprawl," land-use professor and activist Matthew J. Kiefer (2005) explains.

> Of course it is ugly . . . but the Smart Growth movement struggles mightily to overcome the suspicion that it is an effort by urban aesthetes and environmentalists to impose their lifestyle choices on the majority, who generally prefer a suburban lifestyle (they just don't want so many others to like to so much too).
>
> (p. 37)

Steeped in the traditional critique of placelessness and the demographic sorting into amenity destinations and other lifestyle enclaves, the support for growth controls often betrays an aesthetic impulse of 'how I *want* to live' that is hard to express in terms of the common good—that is, in the normative language, subject to collective consideration and rational deliberation, of 'how we *should* live' (see Bellah et al. 1996; Lash 1994:135). Such dynamics trouble our optimism in the quality of rationality that reflexive social movements embody; at least, they underscore the distance that must be covered before the environment can be made amenable to legitimate political deliberation.

Reflexive Conflicts in the Countryside

Along these lines, a development unanticipated by both NPC and reflexive modernization theory appears in the contemporary British countryside, where a culture war (if I may import the American phrase) has erupted over rural lifestyles and the QOL their pursuit affords. The broader context here is again counterurbanization. Over the last two to three decades, urban Britons have increasingly toured, relocated, purchased second homes, and opened businesses in the English, Welsh, and Scottish countryside, largely in pursuit of natural amenities and the lifestyle activities enshrined in the "rural idyll" (Halfacree 2004:295). In short, the countryside has become a popular site to pursue individual and household QOL—that is, to live out a reflexive critique of the ways of life and work left behind in British cities and suburb—through the market for place. Predictably, this counterurbanization has brought population growth, rising real estate values, and demands on public services in its wake, leading to an acute crisis of rural housing affordability as well as economic pressures on agriculture, fishing, and forestry sectors.

Within national debate, however, the socioeconomic impacts of counterurbanization seem to take a back seat to a far more visible and heated controversy over what has come to be known as Britain's "rural way of life." This subject steps into morally fraught terrain in British discourse, since the countryside is central to Britain's national mythology. As middle-class counterurbanizers settle in, many take up the mantle of "rural preservation," participate in local "amenity societies" (the British term for groups advocating the preservation of historical and environmental landscapes of all kinds), and voice long-standing criticisms of countryside pastimes and values. Country sports such as hunting and shooting; the rural deference accorded to estate owners; and farmers' stewardship of their land and its species are especially denounced. Amplified by the national efforts of ecological organizations and anti-hunting activists, these criticisms culminated in the Labour Party's passage of two national laws: the 2000 Countryside and Rights of Ways Act (phased in by 2005) that granted nature-hikers and other outdoor recreationalists a legal "right to roam" on privately-owned countryside,[5] and the 2004 Hunting Act that effectively criminalized the traditional practice of fox-hunting by prohibiting hunting with hounds.

Although country dwellers have long reacted negatively to the incursions of 'town' on 'village,' by the turn of the millennium they saw a "rural movement" emerge to challenge the claims of rural preservationists. Three mass protests (including the dramatically named Livelihood March of 2002) brought hundreds of thousands of country dwellers into the streets of London, and a "rural lobby established itself as the most vocal source of opposition to the Blair government" (Woods 2002:207). Significantly, the rural movement has depicted its cause as one of *cultural* preservation and argued that any legal or political constraint upon fox-hunting and landowners' authority essentially destroys "the rural way of life." These two issues of contention are quite related in the eyes of rural advocates. Recounting a long history of "public access" to the British landscape, they emphasize how the traditional custom of roaming is observed by countryside denizens whose livelihoods and pastimes involve a first-hand, material relationship to the land, and whose worldviews are shaped by the local values and social hierarchies of the rural village. "In the early days, those walking would often have links with the land; they had relatives working on estates and farms, and many had considerable knowledge of wildlife," explains farmer, television host, and countryside advocate Robin Page (Page and Shoard 2000:20). In the traditional custom, a hunter politely asks for permission to enter privately owned land, which the landowner would grant based on the credibility of the request (to screen for poaching or insensitive habitat usage) and the requester's standing within community networks. According to rural advocates, hunting and other traditional occasions for accessing private land have thereby maintained civility, stewardship of the land, and an important measure of cross-class respect in the countryside (Marvin 2007).[6] By contrast, respect for and validation of the rural way of life are gallingly absent in the contemporary call for a universal "right" to roam the countryside.

Considering the magnitude of the recent tide of migration into Britain's countryside, which was already experiencing turmoil due to political and structural changes to rural sectors like agriculture (especially after the UK joined the European Commonwealth in 1973), it is useful to understand the recent conflict over the rural way of life as in some regards a manifestation of long-simmering economic conflicts between town and country. This being Britain, class antagonism perhaps unsurprisingly lies just below the surface of this so-called culture war. Since the nineteenth century, British radicals have inveighed against "landlordism," a target that aims at the rural elite who employ the majority of country-dwellers and receive local deference in turn. Despite the complicating roles of urban landowners and agrarian radicals in the nation's history, town and country continue to be understood politically through two opposing classes and their respective parties: the urban proletariat who supports Labour, and the rural landed gentry and its supporting population who support the Conservatives (Woods 2002; but see Heath et al. 1990). Amidst these historic antagonisms, the rural renaissance has further consolidated two classes in post-industrial Britain, one whose productive livelihood depends on the material use of the land, and another whose consumption activities depend on a post-material aesthetic use of the landscape (Urry 2007:78–80; Halfacree 2004; Murdoch et al. 2003; Woods 2003:312). It is not hard to discern laments over rural restructuring, or to identify Britain's ascendant creative class with their recreational "incubation" and self-absorption, in country dwellers' screeds against "ramblers." Rural advocate Robin Page (Page and Shoard 2000) again:

> Now, when I walk the fields around our small Cambridgeshire farm, I usually see nobody. When I meet others, they are usually not 'walking'; they are 'exercising' their dogs, off leads and out of control, and they see fields as dog latrines and footpaths as doggie exercise areas. The only other people I see are joggers . . . . In the Pennines, a gamekeeper has shown me the dangers of roaming without supervision. In the spring, when lapwings were incubating, he took me to one of their most important breeding areas. A rambler had left the footpath for a picnic, despite signs saying 'Please remain on the footpath'. He approached the rambler and politely pointed out the two female lapwings he had forced off their nests, exposing them to cold and to predators. The rambler was equally polite, apologised and went back to the path. 'That was good,' the gamekeeper informed me. 'Nine times out of 10, I would just have got a stream of abuse.'
>
> (p. 20)

On the other hand, as the state intervenes on behalf of the counterurbanizing classes, neither is it hard to suspect country landowners' efforts to lend property rights the veneer of tradition. As land-use professor and roaming advocate Marion Shoard (Page and Shoard 2000) asks Robin Page,

> Do you really believe it is right that ordinary families seeking only to walk in the countryside should have to do so in fear of an ugly confrontation with a quite possibly armed man, bawling at them to leave if they wish to explore those countless parts of their homeland where they are classed as trespassers?
>
> (p. 21)

Helpful as a class analysis of the town and country divide is, it fails to illuminate how the legitimacy of various QOL discourses have shaped the terms and trajectory of the rural conflict, beginning with the scientific rationality of environmental management. As British conservation groups protest the loss of bird and insect species on British farmland, rural advocates have found themselves compelled to defend "country sports," agricultural practices, and land-owning customs as modes of environmental management. Frequently, they cite the agrarian stewardship of the land, arguing it provides farmers a moral incentive to sustain the land's ecological balance and a personalized expertise with the terrain (cf. Berry 1977)—a "practical conservationism" superior to the abstract evaluations of "deskbound conservationists." Rural advocates' scientific attempts to legitimate traditional customs and beliefs have been difficult to maintain persuasively, however, given the alterations of agriculture ushered in by Britain's post-World War II export emphasis as well as contemporary wildlife advocates' access to more robust, if more abstract, measures of species wellbeing. As Shoard (Page and Shoard 2000) explains to Page after reciting scientifically quantified declines in bird species across British farmland,

> It is the job of 'deskbound conservationists' to form overall assessments of the threats actually confronting wildlife. You cannot blame them for concluding that in comparison with damage of the kind being caused by factors such as agricultural intensification, any conceivable damage caused by walkers hardly registers on the scale.
>
> (p. 22)

In the case of fox-hunting, rural advocates deployed an environmental management discourse of 'vermin control' that seems to have backfired, since the Hunting Act now forbids hunting foxes with hounds but not the killing of foxes *per se*, thereby defeating the intent to preserve the specific ritual of fox-hunting (Marvin 2007).

Other, more obviously value-laden QOL values have been consistent elements in counterurbanizers' concerns in these issues. As cultural scholars Mike Storry and Peter Childs (2002) observe, "Unsurprisingly for a people who are statistically more likely to give to animal charities than to the homeless, the British have long fashioned themselves as a nation of animal lovers" (p. 64). The postmaterial values of tolerance and the antipathy toward animal "cruelty" and human "barbarism" motivate much of the movement against fox-hunting and other rural "blood sports," although these too have been tempered by environmental management rationality; presumably, fox-hunting with firearms is a more humane form of vermin control, but it does not satisfy the demands of more radical wildlife advocates. In the case of the right to roam, proponents regularly cite the individual health, recreational, and self-actualization benefits of nature walking; "more and more people long to escape the stresses of urban life," Shoard (Page and Shoard 2000) tells Page, "to enjoy the same kind of rural refreshment which you so obviously appreciate yourself." Countryside roaming is also seen to benefit the conservation of rural nature. "The more people get to know and love our wildlife, the more they will not just support, but positively insist upon, its conservation," Shoard adds. "This effect is likely to be far more significant for the long-term well-being of our wildlife than the odd bit of disturbance that some walkers may cause" (p. 21). Insofar as supporters of the right to roam and the fox-hunting ban voice themes of conservation science (hardly a traditional authority within British agriculture), landscape amenities, and civil tolerance (here extended to non-human species), their agenda appears to illustrate the kinds of QOL values endorsed by the post-material class and social movements, according to NPC and reflexive modernization theory, respectively.

However, the picture of a familiar ideological divide between a postmaterial new class and a material class becomes less clear when we look at the opposing rural movement, particularly the political praxis of its leaders and organizations. In contrast to what the movement's "conservative" and "traditional" designations might suggest, the forging of a collective identity and a critique of modern progress—i.e., reflexive modes of political praxis thought to characterize new social movements—have been central to the movement's appeal and growth.[7] The rural movement has even articulated a civil rights discourse that would not be out of place in an Amartya Sen lecture. On its website, the Countryside Alliance, the major pro-hunting group behind the mass rallies on London—and which has since expanded its agenda to cover rural economic, housing, public service, and "environmental" issues—announces its unwavering defense of "country pursuits, whose participants should be free from prejudice and discrimination" (Countryside Alliance 2006). A high point of this civil rights discourse came in 2005 when the Countryside Alliance invoked the European Convention of Human Rights in its (ultimately unsuccessful) legal challenge of the fox-hunting ban.

Countryside Alliance's human rights challenge to the 2004 Hunting Act

Substance of the Challenge

It is argued that a number of rights guaranteed by the European Convention of Human Rights are infringed by the Hunting Act 2004. In order to show that there is an infringement it must first be shown that an article of the Convention is "engaged". This means that the Hunting Act has an impact on the subject matter protected by that article. If the article is engaged, the Court must then assess whether or not the restrictions imposed by the Hunting Act have a legitimate purpose and whether they are proportionate to the aim of the legislation.

It is argued that the following articles of the Convention are engaged:

- **Article 8: the right to respect for private and family life.** We argue that this right includes the right to develop relationships with others, it protects the social and community lifestyle and business interests of individuals and it safeguards cultural diversity. We argue that the ban on hunting restricts all of these aspects of life.
- **Article 11: freedom of assembly and association.** The Hunting Act does not prevent individuals from assembling (i.e. meeting together in the countryside) and forming associations (hunts). However, we argue that freedom of assembly and association is restricted because the Hunting Act bans the purpose for which individuals meet and form hunts.
- **Article 1 of Protocol 1: protection of property.** We argue that the Hunting Act deprives individuals of property or controls their use of property in a variety of different ways. We have grouped these matters under three headings: (1) land – restricting a landowner's right to hunt/course on his own land and permit others to do so, loss of value, and various costs associated with changing land from hunting/coursing use to other uses; (2) livelihoods – loss of rights for employees and employers under employment contracts and loss of goodwill built up in businesses associated with hunting; (3) other property – dogs, horses, vehicles and other equipment will become redundant.
- **Article 14: prohibition of discrimination.** We argue that, in relation to all the matters set out above, the Hunting Act discriminates against hunting people in comparison to other relevant groups, in particular people who wish to control wild mammals by other methods.
- **Article 6: right to a fair trial.** We argue that the Act is founded on the false presumption that hunting is cruel and thus does not allow a defendant to show that his actions were not cruel as a defence to prosecution.
- **Article 7: no punishment without law.** We argue that because it is unclear what constitutes unlawful hunting there is no certainty as to the law.

It is further argued that the restrictions imposed by the Hunting Act cannot be justified. It is argued that no legitimate aim has been clearly identified by the proponents of a ban. If the aim is to prevent unnecessary suffering, it is argued that there is no evidence that hunting and coursing cause 'unnecessary suffering' and indeed the ban may result in more suffering. If the aim is to protect morals (because hunting and coursing are considered immoral by Parliament) it is argued that this is not legitimate without evidence of 'unnecessary suffering'. Lastly, it is argued that even if the Hunting Act has a legitimate aim, it is not a necessary or proportionate measure for achieving that aim.

Source: Countryside Alliance, "Update on the Legal Challenges, 24 February 2005."

Significantly, Britain's rural movement, which exemplifies a number of similarly 'reactionary' movements across the west (see Castells 1997), embodies the characteristic modes and themes of QOL politics that NPC and reflexive modernization theories assert to be the province of post-material classes and movements. Geographer Michael Woods (2003) explains:

> Thus, the rural movement has appropriated the language and ideas of environmentalism and the anti-globalisation movement, as well as the values of liberal consumerist society. The 'preservation' of rural lifestyle is hence equated with the preservation of the environment; rural identity is equated with local identity, as threatened by globalization; and the movement's rhetoric encoded with the language of 'rights', 'liberty' and freedom from bureaucracy and state interference. Most strikingly, a rural movement that is largely led by a one-time paternalistic elite has sought to represent itself as an 'oppressed minority'.
>
> (p. 317)

To date, the legal right to roam stands, although the fate of the 2004 Hunting Act seems legally precarious—and, of course, Tony Blair's New Labour Party has suffered electoral defections much wider than the rural opposition. But the new collective identity based on 'rural tradition' seems likely to figure in British politics much longer. Questions remain about whether rural advocates represent the rural populace and can thus offer a legitimate vision of its common good. On the one hand, anthropologists and fox-hunting sympathizers Italo Pardo and Giuliana Prato (2005) speak for many defenders of the "rural way of life" when they argue that the fox-hunting ban "jeopardizes the coexistence of different moralities in civil society, as it denies moral weight and legitimacy to the motivations and way of life of a large part of the population basically because they fail to meet the project and morality of a dominant elite" (p. 152). On the other hand, Woods (2002) doubts the regional voice that the rural movement purports:

> There are no 'rural' constituencies that can be identified as exhibiting distinctive patterns of voting behaviour. Instead, there is a small minority group of voters who define themselves as 'rural' by their participation in hunting, farming, and other traditionally 'rural' activities, and whose primary political motivation is to defend these interests.
>
> (p. 226)

If such questions again underscore the difficulties in QOL politics of establishing a normative vision for the common good that can be the basis for a legitimate democratic politics, what Britain's rural conflict nonetheless highlights is how the characteristic praxis and language of QOL politics—the defense of locality and way of life, the assertion of communitarian consensus, the aesthetic impulse, the invocation of civil rights—are hardly monopolized by a postmaterial class.

Deferring the Social from the Common Good

These examples of how the politics of QOL is constituted also hint at a complication in how it is substantively articulated. Namely, in striving to address the common good through formal political discourse, QOL concerns do not apparently involve the social per se. Recalling the last chapter, whereas place-based QOL reimagines social relations as an individual, 'private' concern (e.g., the migratory question, "where do I want to live?"), QOL politics reveals a similar reification in the collective problem of how we should live. In this section, I examine how QOL politics tends to obscure social relations by projecting people's mutual dependence and moral obligations to one another onto material and abstract things, which then 'dictate' the particular issues, underlying frameworks, and political stakes of their collective decisions. The nineteenth-century technocrat's dream that politics might be transcended through science and rational management seems to hover around this issue, but as we will see, a QOL discourse of things hardly dims the heat of human conflict. Indeed, the solutions and underlying contexts for problems may well be obfuscated by this discursive impulse within QOL politics.

Speaking for Nature

Environmentalism is an obvious example of the significant role that things occupy in the discourses of QOL politics. With my analysis here, I do not seek to resurrect academic debates whether 'nature' and 'wilderness' are social constructions and not objective, imminent realities. Nor do I wish to revisit the ideological differences between social ecologists and deep ecologists who view preserving the environment's integrity as the means to important human ends (from relatively consensual goals like safekeeping the environment for future generations, to more controversial ones like sustaining economic growth) versus an intrinsic value irreducible to human concerns, respectively. I focus instead on the clearly 'human' realm of policy to examine how references to species, nature, and biological states influence motives for political action. Very practical implications are evident if we return to the U.S. and look at the case of national policy to respond effectively to climate change. Its current standstill can be attributed partly to the difficulties of coordinating stakeholders across fragmented legislative and institutional domains; as well, the entrenched resistance of corporate interests and other policy opponents are undeniably responsible. However, some environmentalists have identified a failure of political imagination among the U.S. movement's leading organizations, who have let the resolution of climate change become yet another "special interest" that fails to stir public convictions of consensus and moral obligation.

This view was forcefully expressed in the 2004 meeting of the Environmental Grantmakers Association, where environmental organizers Michael Shellenberger and Ted Nordhaus lobbed an intellectual bombshell with their direly-titled paper, "The Death of Environmentalism: Global Warming Politics in a Post-Environmental World."[8] Arguing that "[p]rotecting the environment is indeed supported by a large majority—it's just not supported very strongly," the authors attributed the loss of key policy battles to the leading environmental organizations' failure to draw potential allies like trade unions and campaign reform groups who could have leveraged swing legislative votes on bills like the unsuccessful McCain-Lieberman Climate Stewardship Act (a carbon emission cap-and-trade bill) and recurring attempts to ratchet up auto fuel emission standards in the Clean Air Act. The failure resulted not from their ignorance of or lack of access to either potential allies or swing legislators, Shellenberger and Nordhaus (2005) argued, but rather their narrow and restrictive conception of environmental issues:

> It is a hallmark of environmental rationality to believe that we environmentalists search for "root causes" not "symptoms." What, then, is the cause of global warming?
>
> For most within the environmental community, the answer is easy: too much carbon in the atmosphere. Framed this way, the solution is logical: we need to pass legislation that reduces carbon emissions. But what are the obstacles to removing carbon from the atmosphere?
>
> Consider what would happen if we identified the obstacles as:
>
> - The radical right's control of all three branches of the U.S. government.
> - Trade policies that undermine environmental protections.
> - Our failure to articulate an inspiring and positive vision.
> - Overpopulation.
> - The influence of money in American politics.
> - Our inability to craft legislative proposals that shape the debate around core American values.
> - Poverty.
> - Old assumptions about what the problem is and what it isn't.
>
> The point here is not just that global warming has many causes but also that the solutions we dream up depend on how we structure the problem.

Conservative interest groups, Shellenberger and Nordhaus note, have been masterful in setting the terms of the debates around values and visions that resonate with broader public convictions; eager to link particular anti-environmental initiatives to potential allies' apparently unrelated goals, "never do they say, 'that's not my issue.'" Yet in their exclusive focus on scientific explanations and policy technicalities, environmental organizations regularly avoid such opportunities to reframe debates around widely held liberal values—an avoidance still viewed as politically necessary by many environmental leaders. "We need to remember that we're the environmental movement and that our job is to protect the environment," says the Sierra Club's Global Warming Director, Dan Becker:

> If we stray from that, we risk losing our focus, and there's no one else to protect the environment if we don't do it. We're not a union or the Labor Department. Our job is to protect the environment, not to create an industrial policy for the United States.
>
> (quoted in Shellenberger and Nordhaus 2005)

Such a viewpoint blithely ignores the reality that "[e]nvironmentalists are in a culture war whether we like it or not," Shellenberger and Nordhaus (2005) argue. "It's a war over our core values as Americans and over our vision for the future, and it won't be won by appealing to the rational consideration of our collective self-interest."

In important ways, this critique of mainstream environment groups' insistence that "carbon emissions" be the exclusive focus for their work on global warming, and the necessity for a broader constituency and public-minded vision for the environmental movement, echo criticisms leveled more than a decade earlier at the "Group of Ten" environmental organizations by the environmental justice movement (Meyer 2005). In 1991, at the First National People of Color Environmental Leadership Summit, Dana Alston of the Panos Institute, a global development organization, voiced the environmental justice critique of the orthodox focus on conservation and wilderness issues:

> For us, the issues of the environment do not stand alone by themselves. They are not narrowly defined. Our vision of the environment is woven into an overall framework of social, racial, and economic justice. The environment, for us, is where we live, where we work, and where we play . . . . We refuse narrow definitions. It is not just ancient forests; it is not just saving the whales or saving other endangered species. These are all very important. We understand the life cycle and the inter-connectedness of life. But our communities and our people are endangered species, too.
>
> (quoted in Pezzullo and Sandler 2007:7)

Both the "Death of Environmentalism" paper and the environmental justice movement criticize the view of the environment as an objective entity external to humanity that can be known through human knowledge, be it empirical science or spiritual connection, but which should not be linked to human 'political' interest. Their criticism has not gone unchallenged from within the movement; some wilderness advocates charge that the environmental justice emphasis on social equity and neighborhood well-being issues seems more pertinent to a non-wild, human context. The environmental justice movement "is better conceived as the human justice movement," argues communication professor Kevin DeLuca (2007), who laments the "infinite self-absorption of humans": "Human justice is a fine goal, but it is not environmental justice" (p. 27). Instead, the job of the environmental movement proper is to advocate for the interests of nature.[9]

But what are the interests of nature? A halt to any further incursions on its intact spaces of wilderness? The remediations of climate change, species loss, and genetically modified organisms—at what rate of reversal? Human withdrawal from its settlements, leaving them to the takeover of untamed nature (currently illustrated in radioactive toxic zones like Chernobyl)? Beyond the problem that many of these options are currently political non-starters, just how 'nature'—which, as ecologists acknowledge, will endure in some perhaps unfamiliar form regardless of climactic or geological scenario—needs human intervention is unclear. The increase in the species extinction and earth's temperature can be observed, and its 'solutions' identified, by science, but nature does not demand its equilibrium; *humans* do, at this particular historical moment. Thus, the advocacy of global environmental sustainability raises the question of what social meanings and interests this value represents for its human advocates—a question that, by going unanswered, has helped bring climate change policy to its present standstill.

If climate change seems too daunting a problem even to comprehend fully, the issue of species rights could perhaps be more politically manageable. Yet again, the focus on animals' 'interests' obscures the human interests of its advocates. While activists against animal hunting, vivisection, and fur farming seek to extend civil rights to animals, their opponents sometimes also claim to "speak for" animals. Fox-hunting advocates, for instance, contend that the elaborate pageantries involved in hunting with hounds, far from symbolizing animal cruelty, actually raise the fox's status in the rural worldview, elevating it above other predatory animals unceremoniously killed as vermin. When traditional fox-hunting is banned, a fox-hunting master of hounds asks (quoted in Marvin 2007), "Who then is going to value the fox, who's going to speak for it, who's going to be concerned about its welfare?" (p. 341). Science takes no clear position in this debate, with its complicating issues of animal population control, species' probable fates were they left to their natural habitat, and the 'unnatural' histories via breeding and domestication of animal varieties (particularly dogs and cats) and subspecies (e.g., *Bos primigenius Taurus*, the modern domesticated cow).

The understanding and evaluation of environmental well-being is complex and ambiguous; it takes human values and worldviews to impose a coherency that lends itself to political advocacy. In turn, such values and worldviews have foundations in specific social relations. *Which* social relations are relevant is an empirical question, of course, depending on the QOL political issue at hand, but we might anticipate them to be multiple, contradictory, and imbricated at different sites and scales of social, economic, and geographical foundation. Crucial to any such political analysis is identifying the social contexts for the new classes and new movements that NPC and reflexive modernization theorists emphasize in broad, unspecified ways. That such a fine-tuned analysis may reveal the contradiction of "self-serving" material interests in advocating collective well-being does not preempt a vision of the public good. Quite likely, it is a starting point for pursuing a consensual politics; as conservatives' electoral success in recent decades reminds us, weaving a coalition of complementary plural interests behind a resonant, encompassing vision of 'how we should live' is the essence of good politicking.

Reifying Life

Admittedly, with this book I have devoted paltry discussion to the domain of health, which dominates the attention of most professional and academic literature on the subject of QOL. It may seem a stretch, even an insult, that I only now turn to this domain, no less to bring the dying and suffering of individuals into a discussion of politics, but the issues of low health-related QOL and voluntary euthanasia shed further light on the social foundations for the value positions and material interests that inform the discourse of things. Thanks to rising standards of living and medical advances that have extended the average lifespan, in developed nations elderly people have come to suffer more debilitating diseases and experience levels of frailty and pain unprecedented in the history of a humanity more likely to encounter an earlier and quicker death (Kellehear 2007). Add to this the powers of modern medicine to keep people alive along a spectrum of insentience—from the groggy confusion induced by heavy painkillers, to the continuing physical 'functionality' that accompanies the mental deterioration of an Alzheimer's patient, to the complete "vegetative" state—and one can appreciate how "death with dignity" has for many become a value more important than preserving a life of low quality. Since the 1960s, a movement championing the "right to die" has surfaced in a quintessentially sub-political domain of hospitals, patient–doctor relationships, families wracked by private suffering, the media, professional associations, and, occasionally, courtrooms and legislative bodies where—with some exceptions, most notably the Netherlands and the American state of Oregon—the state's formal position on the issue has developed in a piecemeal, case-by-case fashion (see Petrinovich 1998; Singer 1994).

The right-to-die argument invokes and extends the natural law of individual rights, emphasizing individuals' autonomy to evaluate and manage their well-being, as well as their agency in initiating their deaths (Brock 1992:11). The latter becomes a crucial issue insofar as the patient's initiative (i.e., a request for death given in a state of mental clarity not under duress) and, if others must help him or her die, the patient's consent can absolve the medical caregiver of culpability for the cessation of life—the legal distinction between voluntary and involuntary euthanasia (Kamm 1998). Typically, to the extent that it specifies social relations, the argument for the right to die identifies a conflict between, on the one hand, the autonomous individual seeking a dignified death and, on the other, the medical establishment and conventional morality. By following the commandments of Hippocratic oath and the traditional Western ethic to sanctify and preserve life at all costs, the medical profession and the state join the specters of helplessness and pain in alienating the living from life itself (Singer 1994).

The right-to-die argument, it should be noted, is generally propounded from the perspective of the terminally ill who are inflicted by incurable diseases (e.g., cancer, AIDS, motor neuron diseases) and set on a slow, painful, yet anticipated course into death. Less clearly does it speak to the conundrums faced by caregivers and families of patients who face "profoundly diminished life" due to unanticipated diseases or traumas (from accidents, surgery complications, etc.) that render them in a vegetative state and dependent upon life-prolonging technologies; some evidence suggests that in these cases medical professionals, with their secondary status as patients' agents and executors, may be more likely than families to propose an end to aggressive treatment (e.g., Morreim 1994). Since the 1990s, living wills with advance directives and, for patients entering hospital care of terminal illnesses or high-risk surgery, DNR ("do not resuscitate") orders legally enforce patients' requests to refuse the unwanted prolonging of life. However, at least in the U.S., most adults do not prepare living wills even when they support patients' right to die as a principle; furthermore, when they have living will in hand, medical practitioners can find them too vague, or the medical situation insufficiently dire, to execute patients' premeditated request to die (Fagerlin and Schneider 2004).

Most significantly, the right-to-die argument ignores the *frail elderly* who have become incapable of caring for themselves yet do not have specific terminal illnesses. This group often experiences a despair and loss of dignity with their condition and, according to some studies (summarized in Emanuel 1997), may be more likely to request physician-assisted suicide. To be sure, there are compelling legal and ethical reasons for right-to-die advocates to exclude the frail elderly from the moral claims of the right to die, since physician-assisted suicide to treat "old age" raises the slippery slope concern motivating many legal prohibitions of the practice. Nonetheless, it is instructive to note the different narratives that distinguish Western societies' views of the terminally ill and the 'merely' frail elderly. The terminally ill, we often imagine, are stationed in hospitals or homes redesigned as terminal care units, surrounded by expensive life-prolonging technologies, partaking of painful treatments ("cures worse than the disease") and cognizance-impairing painkillers. These patients may be imagined as challenging the resistance of medical administrators and religious clergy; enlisting the assistance of caregivers, lawyers, clergy, and perhaps political and medical campaigners; and having final, heartbreaking conversations with friends and family as they pursue their right to die. This heroic narrative strikes a powerful chord among citizens at large, in the media, and in many courtroom juries, but it differs remarkably from the settings where far more elderly people find themselves—in nursing homes where "assisted slow dying" (Kellehear 2007:231) is the order of the day, where the acknowledgement of mortality by caregivers and patients alike is ambiguous, and where the merely old and frail are disempowered, infantilized, and isolated from public view daily (Adler 1991). Like those dying from AIDS in developing societies, the frail elderly in developed societies suffer secondarily from withdrawal of institutional resources, public respect, and often families and friends, many of whom have been outlived in any case. This, argues sociologist Allan Kellehear (2007), is the "shameful death" of modern society, illustrated by this 87-year-old resident of an Australian nursing home:

> Marion's chief suffering—aside from her collapsed hips, failing sight and hearing—is her despair. She has lost her privacy ('Good God, you've got no privacy, although they put curtains around you before they do anything'); her much loved possessions ('I gave that all away. You just shed life, you do'); her autonomy and dignity ('Now the only thing that I can still do is wipe my bottom! That's my one little independence'); and especially her desire to have her dying recognized by others . . . . Marion's slow dying (she died some months after I interviewed her) was never recognized, spoken about or openly shared with residents or staff. Her comments were always greeted with weak smiles and embarrassed silence. And these reactions despite the fact that she was never backward in expressing her views about death or dying ('Every day I hope that I won't wake up in the morning. I want to die. Sorry, I do. This will be the end.' And again, 'I know I'll never get back. I don't believe in miracles—I'm here for life. I'm here till I die, which I hope won't be too long in coming').
>
> (pp. 226–7)

The frail elderly too often resolve the stigma of the shameful death through banal methods of suicide that rarely invoke the legal protections or public respect accorded to the right-to-die argument. Elderly suicide is alarmingly frequent in developed nations, particularly among men (who as a rule commit suicide more frequently than women). In 1998 and 1999, U.S. and Canadian men aged 75 and older outpaced all other age groups with suicide rates of 41.7 and 31.6 per 100,000, respectively; the rate is higher absolutely in nations where men aged 75 and older are proportionally edged out by other male cohorts (Howarth 2007:62). Suicide lets the elderly wrest control over the timing of their death: "The theme that repeatedly emerges from doing the numbers game in ageing and dying is that timing is everything," Kellehear (2007) writes. "Outlive your money, your friends and family, or your health, and institutionalised dying will be your future. One option for many has been to cancel that future by taking their own lives" (p. 233). In a sense, elderly suicide mirrors the growing practice of remaining in the workforce long past retirement age; whereas the latter affirmatively demonstrates one's 'productivity' to family, community, and society and keeps one connected to social situations, the former removes one's 'burden' to family, community, and society and effectively ends one's shameful isolation.

This discussion of the dying's connections to others returns us to the larger social relations that encompass death and dying in modern societies. Death ends our lives, but it need not extinguish our relationships to society; through their memories, legacies, and contributions, the dead can sustain and be acknowledged by the collective today, as they have done in traditional societies. This was the function of the Protestant *ars moriendi*, or "art of dying," which brought community into the deathbed scene to witness and aid the dying's final "victory" against death. Sociologist Shai J. Lavi (2005) explains that in the *ars moriendi*, the despair and pain associated with a "bad death" were viewed as mortal temptations by the devil at the gates of death; these were overcome in an act that ennobled the dying before the eyes of God and fellowship. This "good death," the literal translation and traditional meaning of the term *euthanasia*, eventually moved to the province of the medical and legal realms, where it became redefined as "the use of anaesthetics to guarantee a swift and painless death" (p. 3). In the process, euthanasia transformed dying from *art*—in the Heideggerian sense, a practice which "is known by its power to make the fullness of a lifeworld visible through one being in that world"—to *technique*, in which mastery becomes an end in itself and its objects "appear only through their potential to be ordered and lose any characteristic that stands in the way of regulation" (Lavi 2005:9, 11). Lavi's history of dying stops at the 1960s, a telling cut-off date. Already by this point, before debilitating diseases of old age and life-prolonging technologies became popular symbols of the right-to-die movement, the modern hospital had ushered technique into the life-world:

> In the modern hospital, people are treated as patients. They are hospitalized for the purpose of managing their health, which entails more than just being cured. The patient's medical condition and health is examined and diagnosed, measured and prognosed, experimented on and compared, stabilized as much as cured, assessed as much as healed. As patients enter the hospital, they lose their identity as individuals who belong to a particular life world and assume a new identity—that of a patient. Patients are stripped of any distinct identity that they have outside of the hospital, as family members, as experts in their own field, as individuals with particular customs, clothing, and food. Within the hospital context, patients are regarded only through the lens of health management. Medical personnel may care for the patient's emotional well-being as well as physical condition, but only because this is acknowledged to be an important aspect of health management. Hence the patient's place within the domain of the modern hospital manifests the rule of technique more decisively than does the development of medical machinery or scientific method.
>
> (Lavi 2005:11)

Lavi's argument casts a shadow over the conventional language and practice of health-related QOL. Certainly, it joins the strong concerns that medical ethicists have for bureaucratic conceptions of QOL, such as the calculation of QALYs (quality-adjusted life years) that lets caregivers compare and optimize the allocation of scarce treatment resources among patients in a high-technology, high-cost medical care regime (Phillips 2006; Rapley 2003). Yet even the patient-centered field of palliative medicine—defined as "the study and management of patients with active, progressive, far-advanced disease for whom the prognosis is limited and the focus of care is the quality of life" (Field 1996:113)—illustrates how 'QOL' abstracts the individuality of patients even as it genuinely advances the level of care they receive. Is 'health-related QOL' itself a suspect category? An opponent of voluntary euthanasia who calls it "self-determination run amok" points to larger issues in the conceptions of health-related QOL today:

> The acceptance of euthanasia would sanction a view of autonomy holding that individuals may, in the name of their own private, idiosyncratic view of the good life, call upon others, including such institutions as medicine, to help them pursue that life, even at the risk of harm to the common good. This works against the idea that the meaning and scope of our own right to lead our own lives must be conditioned by, and be compatible with, the good of the community, which is more than an aggregate of self-directing individuals.
>
> (Callahan 1992:52)

My point here is not to argue against voluntary euthanasia, but to shed light on the rock and hard place that the contemporary moment of dying puts us between. If we should recoil from the traditional sentiment that physical suffering is somehow "ennobling," we might nonetheless consider how right-to-die advocates have advanced technique in the *individualized context of dying* today. The hospital is a stronghold of individualized society—the final one, for many of us. Through it, diseases are treated yet causes are too often personalized; care is given so that family and community may withdraw, thereby further placing the burden of social reproduction on the shoulders of individuals. Individuals and families may even wield medical technique themselves in their do-it-yourself biographies, as cosmetic surgery, the medicating of children diagnosed with ADHD, and assisted reproductive technologies illustrate; although these admittedly lie on quite different moral planes than euthanasia, in practice they erode the human solidarities that the sanctity of life traditionally symbolizes. Medical mastery of death, as well as the failures it invariably sets up for itself, reify these fundamentally collective relations. The right to die, framed as it generally has been so far, defers crucial questions of social relations—the authority of science; the unplanned trajectory of market-based innovation; the distribution of scarce resources in health-care; the eclipse of family and community by more voluntary and impermanent associations—by projecting them onto objective things, such as the capacities of technologies to extend life or the scientific consensus on what constitutes acceptable pain and "life itself." While its support among many suggests the right-to-die argument may approach the majoritarian status required by democratic polities, by obscuring the very context of individualization that has made it so necessary for a dignified life, it makes more critical discussions of the common good less likely.

Conclusion

As I write, war, economic turmoil, famine, and other horsemen of material scarcity still ride on the world's political stage. Nonetheless, postmaterial concerns—the man-made risks seen to threaten human well-being, but also the laws and amenities thought to advance it—have clearly entered this stage and, considering how the global environment hovers at the precipice of long-term disequilibrium, will probably not leave any time soon. We also see the ascendance of a generation or two that has only known the recent accomplishment of affluence; a post-industrial class for whom creativity, amenities, and self-actualization are the stuff of work and life; and a cadre of advocacy organizations and new social movements that articulate and promote progressive values in and behind the scenes of today's political structures. The theoretical accounts and conceptual vocabulary that modernization theorists give us are useful in identifying and anticipating these broad historical patterns. What is less clear at this moment, however, is whether the ascendance of QOL politics has further developed reason and civilization in the straightforward direction imagined by modernization theorists or others who seek an unambiguous measure of progress in humanity's future. Instead, the issues, values, and modes of participation that pervade QOL politics to date seem only to complicate our understanding of what the direction of history might be.

Not that QOL politics is immune to heated conflict or even violence, but 'QOL' ushers in a peculiar civility within political discourse, dimming the deliberation of social relations in two ways. First and most obviously, 'QOL' has become an almost unassailable political rhetoric. Who can legitimately object to enhancing human well-being, at least as an abstract ideal? For this reason, postmaterial movements and causes have lost any monopoly on 'QOL' as the idea is seized by regressive, 'material' initiatives like the criminalization of public behavior thought to offend middle-class sensibilities (as in the "QOL paradigm" of New York City's community policing strategy [Vitale 2008]); the advocacy of deportation and other stringent measures against undocumented global migrants (illustrated in the moniker adopted by a Long Island, New York anti-illegal immigrant group: "Sachem Quality of Life");[10] and the opposition to health-care reform in the U.S. (a commenter on Georgia's Tax Day Tea Party website fears "[o]ur livelyhood [sic] and our children and grandchildrens [sic] … quality of life is at stake!").[11] To dismiss these conservative references to 'QOL' as cynical ploys is, I think, to fail to appreciate how the concept's tensions and contradictions have made it such an ambiguous yet resonant idea.

It also ignores the success that postmaterial liberals and progressives have had in establishing the legitimacy of the QOL discourse, and in demonstrating the effectiveness of its characteristic modes of political protest and participation.

Second and perhaps unexpectedly, the political emphasis on 'QOL' can defer the political deliberation or, to invoke Beck, the reflexivity of social relations in deliberations over the greater good. Competition and accommodation of social interests may be the rule of the day in democratic legislative bodies, but QOL often displaces an explicitly social language in favor of an object-centric discourse on the elements and mechanisms of QOL. Readers will note this same reifying thrust in the concerns for QOL technology, family, work, and place; this dynamic comprises a central feature of the dominant QOL outlook. What goes missing in this outlook is the acknowledgment of the social foundations for particular value positions and political interests regarding the objects (like climate) and evaluative standards (like sustainability) associated with 'QOL.' What might these social foundations be? Like all other political issues, the issues of QOL draw upon, and have significant consequences for, our evolving relationships of competition, antagonism, dependence, and reciprocity with one another. Admittedly, in a world where people's collective fates become untethered from one another, such connections are difficult to perceive; little wonder, then, that the language of personal values and lifestyle seems to offer a more primordial, authentic basis for social affiliation (cf. Bellah et al. 1996). 'QOL' does nothing to illuminate this state of affairs when added to the political dialogue. More likely, as our review of local environmentalism, Britain's rural conflict, and the right-to-die movement suggest, the idea uncritically conveys the solipsistic imaginations and normative visions of the worlds that our self-interpretations and aspirations would create. Thus is the common good conceived within QOL politics.

These are not inevitable shortcomings of 'QOL' as a political ideal. In part, they reflect a historical failure in the science and policy of QOL; since the heyday of the affluent society, scholars and public thinkers have frequently backed off from using 'QOL' and its accompanying science to support controversial yet far-sighted initiatives on behalf of the common good. Another reason is undoubtedly the subpolitical origins of many QOL concerns that inhibit the formal politicization of conflict and deliberation. Consider the topics covered in this chapter. Climate change, environmental amenities, the integrity of rural ways of life, species rights, the institutional authority to deny death with dignity: all of these emerge in arenas where 'efficiency,' 'tradition,' and other perspectives ill suited for political deliberation have a first-mover advantage in setting the terms, language, and frameworks for conflict. In this regard, reflexive modernization theorists correctly identify the task ahead; the ultimate challenge lies in constituting QOL as a formally political matter.

Given the dismal inertia of government and legislation today, entrenched in the paradigms of nation-state and other "zombie categories" of the first modernity (Beck 2005), it is not clear that a political will exists to introduce a multiple-issue, multiple-constituency concern for 'QOL'—really, an all-encompassing framework on the order of 'security' or 'prosperity'—into current political systems. Yet the failure to do so leaves QOL politics to express itself partially and unevenly across polities—a geographical patchwork of legislation and planning here and there but not everywhere. Such a political terrain may well further naturalize the individualized, subpolitical pursuit of QOL and further consign modern hopes for justice and common good to history's dustbin.

8 Futures

So what can ultimately be said about the idea of quality of life? Conceptually, it offers a framework for evaluating human welfare against explicit or implicit points of reference, such as conventional measures of 'progress' (economic growth, technological advance, extension of life) and historical or counterfactual positions—how one *did* live in the past, *could* live under alternate conditions, *shall* live in the future. As we have seen, 'QOL' can fit over any number of human and environmental domains and be charged with diverse standards and preferences regarding well-being. Yet to be meaningful, defining, evaluating, and pursuing 'QOL' within any one domain or concern requires we semantically fix the idea along what I have called four conceptual tensions: between objective and subjective conditions, individual and collective attributions, the production and distribution of well-being, and universalist and relativist understandings. This connotative activity invariably imports certain paradigmatic baggage into the 'QOL' evaluation, but that hardly dooms the idea to incoherence. Just the opposite—such latent signification is an important basis for the idea's utility, as 'QOL' fits into the going concerns and background assumptions for any particular evaluative undertaking.

Beyond these conceptual properties, the idea exerts a particular force upon its beholders and those influenced by their claims. This book's emphasis on the pursuits of QOL highlights the ways that 'QOL' is a *mobilizing idea*. As a comparative evaluation that crystallizes our hopes and concerns for well-being, the idea exceeds our cognitive interiority to intervene symbolically in our relationship with the world around us. At minimum, the reconsideration of how we might live extends beyond its initial site or association to color other domains and potentials for QOL; at maximum, the idea legitimates practical action to make our hopes and potentials a reality. Evidence of the mobilizing force of 'QOL' appears, most obviously, in its intellectual history. For Aristotle, 'QOL' anchored the philosophical enterprise to endow man (no point in gender-neutralizing Aristotle's male-centered point of view) with agency over the fate assigned by the gods and fortune. The nineteenth-century welfare economics tradition deployed the idea, if not the actual phrase, for much the same undertaking, thereby shattering feudal values of traditional authority with a secularizing, Enlightenment-era thrust. As inherited from Abraham Maslow's ideas of self-actualization and the hierarchy of needs, 'QOL' signaled humanity's refusal of industrial rationality's determinisms, exemplified during his life by world war and genocide. With the same sense of historical possibility, the post-World War II affluent-society critique of developed societies deployed 'QOL'—by this point, a specific expression in popular circulation—to highlight the unprecedented opportunity to lift up the whole of society and recognize our mutual dependence upon one another.

Perhaps all of this is to say that 'QOL' is the latest development in an ongoing reflexive articulation of the common good. This prospect resonates with the familiar modernization narrative in which humanity redirects the Enlightenment legacy of critical reason away from age-old specters of scarcity and death toward the socially constructed world of hierarchical assent and the alienation of everyday life. While appealing, this story as it is usually told presumes reflexivity corresponds to logical-cognitive reason and the identification of universal principles for the common good—the gold standards for critical reason since the Enlightenment and most recently the affluent society critique. However, the contemporary QOL pursuits examined in this book reveal two contrasting dynamics. First, they characteristically embody an *aesthetic* thrust in the exercise of reflexivity. Here, reflexive evaluation critiques the universal—from instrumental rationality and bureaucratic hierarchy, to market forces that propagate affluenza and placelessness—through an expressive interpretation of the particular: a lifestyle, an idiosyncratic 'career' through work and life, a place 'to get away from it all' (see Lash 1994, 1993). Second, the enunciation of 'QOL' rests decreasingly upon a stable and legible foundation of social relationships, life courses, and political orders of the kind emphasized by Jürgen Habermas (1990) and other optimistic rationalists. Instead 'QOL' is shaped by, and in turn comes to represent, contingencies of social, personal, and political situation: what 'works,' 'should work,' or 'will work' as understood in the transitory here and now.

In this aestheticized and illegible social world, the very act of evaluating QOL—of asking, "How is my QOL? Yours? Ours?"—that ostensibly began in classic Greece and anchored a potent post-World War II critique, calls forth the prospects of flourishing, happiness, or other aspirations that always seem out of reach. Few seem content with their given QOL; the idea hails comparisons and further criteria that can unsettle the taken-for-granted specificity of their QOL experience. When QOL frames our evaluations, few seem willing to 'lower my QOL' for other considerations. Perhaps there is no need to, when increasingly we can enlist traditional reasons to constrain or sacrifice our well-being—familial obligation, war, and so on—into the service of 'QOL.' ("I'm doing this so my children can have a better quality of life.") And even when our QOL aspirations and assessments do not spur us to change the world, they nonetheless remake our environment symbolically, highlighting those forces that benefit or impair the support systems of the good life. One result is the cultural invisibility of more nuanced and complex webs of human connection—a simplification of the social world in which we live. Having forgone a vocabulary to express our relations with one another, we come to view groups, activities, and institutions as either 'with us or against us' (individuals and communities both) through their affinities with our aspirations and their impacts on our well-being. Through such frames, we instrumentalize our connections, commonalities, and differences with one another as means or impediments to the goal of supporting our 'way of life,' be that real or imagined. We fall prey to reifying social relations into seemingly fixed, discrete phenomena: an individual's 'core' values, for instance, or an environment's 'intrinsic' beauty.

As this suggests, 'QOL' is more than a modern phrase with which to state otherwise venerable visions of the greater good. The contemporary QOL pursuits examined in this book underscore how the dominant QOL outlook we find today *displaces and erases alternate understandings of the greater good* from our social vocabulary in specific ways. To begin, 'QOL' is characteristically self-directed in the moral object it invokes. Unlike 'faith,' 'duty,' 'solidarity,' or other older values to articulate the common good, 'QOL' does not conceive the good as primarily constituted by external others, be that a god, nation, family, or collectivity. Rather, the idea imagines its beneficiaries as first-person subjects, an 'I' or a 'we,' whose own experience and evaluation of their well-being determine the validity of any QOL claim—even when that claim is made by a proxy like a planner or doctor. 'QOL' is not alone here, of course; 'liberty,' 'happiness,' and 'growth' come to mind as other self-directed visions of the common good. Yet in contrast to these, 'QOL' does not place the subject's specific wants or pursuits of the good into a procedural black box, removed from deliberation. Far from it—the idea is meaningful and actionable precisely to the extent that it explicitly foregrounds specific dynamics and experience of well-being, notwithstanding the facts that any diversity of these can be used to give the idea its substance, and that it is social contexts, not QOL the idea itself, that make particular conditions and dynamics salient.

The Dominant QOL Outlook

Having acknowledged the great variety of human endeavors and concerns for which the idea resonates, I modestly invoke the theorist's privilege to highlight now the most significant trajectories of the dominant QOL outlook, as observed in the contemporary pursuits of QOL. I offer these pointed, possibly overgeneralized statements in the spirit of theoretical provocation, leaving it to skeptical readers to identify counterexamples and develop counterexplanations that refute or qualify the stark depictions and troubling implications of the dominant QOL outlook. As I begin, it is worth restating my premise that the critical inquiry into 'QOL' ultimately takes aim at broad social contexts that appear to have little to do with the idea itself. Indeed, therein lies the possibility for recognizing and rehabilitating the idea from the myriad currents that have subtly yet powerfully stripped 'QOL' of its affluent society promise.

Fixing the Conceptual Tensions

Although its conceptual tensions endow the idea with semantic breadth and remarkable possibility, the dominant QOL outlook tends to fix it around a convergent set of semantic positions. In the tension between objective and subjective conditions, *'QOL' is treated as a subjective property*. Here we can refer to the idea's many psychological expressions, such as the field of positive psychology with its research on happiness, optimism, and other mindstates; or the concept of self-actualization with its focus on idiosyncratic dynamics of developmental becoming. The welfare economics tradition contends that 'QOL' is instead derived from things and activities, yet by consigning the great diversity of such objective sources and conditions for QOL to a conceptual black box, the perspective similarly foregrounds the operational dynamics of cognition and behavior that motivate our pursuits (illustrated most clearly in behavioral economics, the academically thriving hybrid of economics and psychology). Outside the ivory tower, the subjective orientation of 'QOL' is manifest in how we pursue work–life balance and the quality-of-life district. On the one hand, objective properties like hours worked or place amenities are emphasized—indeed, they are characteristically fetishized—for their material support of QOL. On the other hand, the ways we allocate the great diversity of work–life and work–residence 'supply and demand' reveal the utilitarian calculus of the market to be the primary language of QOL today. Especially when viewed against other ways we could provide ourselves work-based and place-based QOL—such as collective negotiations over the features of work or regional planning to allocate job locations, residence, and amenities justly—it is clear how subjective preferences are the organizing principle.

These examples are better understood when we examine how, in the tension between individual and collective attributions, *'QOL' is viewed as an individual property*. This is not a critical individual orientation that calls attention to the QOL inequalities within collectives like families or nations, but rather the taken-for-granted individualism of a market framework. The many markets within which we pursue QOL constitute us as individual actors seeking subjective satisfactions and personal expressions; as I have put the point, they enroll us into a consumer orientation toward QOL. What does this mean? Obviously, someone may profit from the goods, services, jobs, and properties that aid us in our pursuits! Yet even when enhancing QOL involves refraining from consumption, the pursuit of such QOL status distinctions involves the exercise of choice by *a priori* individuals—or at least we believe such ontological individualism to be the case and accordingly hold others individually accountable for their QOL values and aspirations. In 1985, sociologist Robert Bellah and his colleagues (1996) put forth an argument that still pertains to the U.S. and, by now, probably other societies where ontological individualism has become ascendant. "In a world of potentially conflicting self-interests, no one can really say that one value system is better than another," they wrote (p. 7), presaging the culture wars we see around us.

> But to what or whom do our ethical and moral standards commit us if they are "quite independent of other people's standards and agenda"? . . . It should be clear by now that "values" . . . are in themselves no answer. "Values" turn out to be the incomprehensible, rationally indefensible thing that the individual chooses when he or she has thrown off the last vestige of external influence and reaches pure, contentless freedom . . . . The language of "values" as commonly used is self-contradictory precisely because it is not a language of value, or moral choice. It presumes the existence of an absolutely empty unencumbered and improvisational self. It obscures personal reality, social reality, and particularly the moral reality that links person and society.
>
> (Bellah et al. 1996:80)

In the dominant QOL outlook, the "lifestyle enclave" that Bellah and his colleagues first identified comprises the predominant form of social affiliation. Here we join others in affinities and solidarities based on common 'values' and 'lifestyles' that are self-consciously chosen and adhered to—the creation myth of ontological individualism. Such 'community,' however, rarely corresponds to the holistic social structures that sociologists would call community; nor does it involve relations of production of the kind that gave us class solidarity.

In the conceptual tension between production and distribution of well-being, *celebration of QOL's production obscures the unequal distribution of QOL opportunities and pursuits*. 'Production' here means the well-being thought to be generated by, indeed intrinsic to, the thing or activity affecting QOL. In this sense, the only real questions are what kinds of QOL-enhancing things and activities are out there, whether we want them, and how we go about getting them; thus we discover and try on different kinds and experiences of QOL as one might slip on a new coat or paint a room a different color. It is not at all inconsistent that the subjective, individualistic orientations that characterize the dominant QOL outlook give emphasis to the externality or (in this sense) 'objectivity' of QOL; such is the very essence of ideological reification, in which we project the social relations that make possible the experience of QOL onto the apparent carrier of QOL. Technologies, families, work, places—these and other totems of QOL are embedded within concrete social relations of production, consumption, and citizenship that market frameworks too often render invisible, as the consumer orientation becomes natural and the object we pursue preoccupies our vision. As a result, we lose sight of how others fare in terms of the same wants and how unequal, even unjust systems of material and subjective well-being arise.

Finally, in the tension between universalist and relativistic understandings, *'QOL' promotes a moral relativism that ushers in an acute historical amnesia*. The economist's admonition against intertemporal comparisons, the psychologist's insights into subjective adaptation: such principles are useful when an individualized orientation is the norm, but they point us away from our recent past when affluent societies wrestled with moral questions about QOL—questions, ironically, that these perspectives seek to answer. Are all QOL pursuits equally worthy? What roles and responsibilities do societies have to enhance the opportunities for everyone's flourishing? And, most generally, what are the legitimate rights and duties that bind democratic polities to their citizens? Such questions incant older visions of the common good that are not the last word on how we should live—their reassessment was of course the very starting point of the affluent society concern for 'QOL'—but which were perhaps more likely to keep the debate trained on the morality of societies' self-understanding and vision for the future. Certainly, today's QOL pursuits do not lack for universalist themes, such as the "march of civilization" theme that pervades many optimistic views of modernization or (in the opposite direction) the register of alienation that sounds through contemporary diagnoses of our "affluenza." Yet whether a triumphalist's proclamation of the individual's emancipation ("How Life Gets Better While People Feel Worse" [Easterbrook 2003]) or a pessimist's proposal to retrieve what had been lost ("Finding Real Wealth in a Sustainable Lifestyle" [Wann 2007]), these QOL assertions serve as uncritical post hoc rationalizations of a world where moral solidarities are dissolving and the affluent society promise of collective QOL has faded from view.

The Compulsion of Individualization

The broader social context in which we have lost sight of QOL's collective promise is the still-unfolding structural shift we can understand as *individualization* that appeared alongside the affluent society's effervescence but has since eclipsed it. In this social world, people carry out, by themselves or in other micro units, the work of social reproduction once performed by institutions and institutionalized social relations. Individualization does not achieve the ideal of "individualism" if that term implies people are genuinely free and responsible for pursuing the goals they set for themselves. Collective institutions have hardly left the scene, sociologically speaking; rather, they have abandoned the work of social reproduction for other concerns, including their own adaptation and survival. As a result, they make their influence felt on individuals through the integrative void they leave behind and the social risks that this void engenders. This is the world in which 'QOL' guides our sense of agency.

As modernization theorists remind us, individualization first became significant with modernization's fullest institutional developments. Through the full employment policies of the welfare state, women entered the workforce and challenged sexual divisions of labor with their paychecks. Faced with environmental and social risk, social movements marshaled scientific rationality and new laws supporting risk assessments and citizen complaints to challenge the authority of industrial rationality—corporate polluters, co-opted scientists, and quiescent governments. With economic affluence, markets became the primary social mechanisms for pursuing wants and needs more specific than the lowest common denominator provided by public entitlements or communities of birth. These and other developments, however much they destabilized prior trajectories and the taken-for-granted experience of social reproduction, seemed to fulfill the emancipation of individuals and the unfolding of progress that have always been modernity's promise. Tellingly, at the apex of these institutional developments, Duane Elgin (1981), the guru of voluntary simplicity, could foresee a world of environmental crisis populated by optimizing, mobile individuals when he predicted "[c]ontinued population migration as people search for geographic areas more favored with resources such as fresh water and a warm climate" (p. 182). His is but one vision of the Enlightenment's reflexive agent, responding to the unanticipated challenges of modernity with a quintessentially modern set of rational capacities and sense of empowerment.

The structural shift toward individualization, particularly after the 1970s, has also benefited from developments in a number of scholarly disciplines and professions. Psychology's cognitive and experimental fields have pushed aside the humanistic and clinical traditions from the discipline's center, giving rise to individualist inquiries ever more divorced from social relations or (in much neuroscience research) the *homo sapiens* species. In the U.S. at least, the economics profession has largely fended off the heterodox challenge issued by John Kenneth Galbraith and others, thereby consolidating the orthodox, market-based paradigm that inform today's global finance sectors, international development policy, and organizational analysis, among other fields. The trends in psychology and economics illustrate the production of knowledges that, at minimum, lend a 'scientific' credibility to our individual QOL pursuits. More ominously, their contextless focus on the autonomous dynamics of individual and subjective QOL fuel criticisms of 'inefficient' collective interventions. Even what might seem to be antithetical intellectual perspectives give an uncritical, instrumental support for individualization. Perhaps the most alarming example is the field of urban planning, where the wisdom of Jane Jacobs has been rehabilitated to shape fields like the New Urbanism, transportation-oriented development, and creative city planning. The problem is not that practitioners of these fields necessarily misunderstand Jacobs' insights into the holistic, systemic dynamics of urban QOL, nor that the plans they generate necessarily make for bad QOL—far from it. Rather, by training their capacities on individual cities and regions, they naturalize the locality divorced from broader geographic contexts of QOL inequality. The city's 'collective QOL' is too often cultivated and enjoyed as a market good without consideration of how our political frameworks distribute QOL unevenly across places (Zukin 2010).

These institutional and intellectual trends find their fullest elaboration in *neoliberalism*, which most forcefully organizes the social context for individualization today. The inclusive 'social capitalism' embraced by social democratic governments (Scandinavia, for example) and ambitious welfare policies (e.g., the U.S. War on Poverty) may have best epitomized the affluent society's collective, distributionist vision, but these political forms are no longer ascendant. The retrenchment of the welfare state; the ideological rejection of public entitlements in favor of individualist ethics of entrepreneurialism and "workfare" responsibility; the privatization and contractualization of social institutions and activities (corporate bureaucracy, government services, family care-giving, etc.); the acceleration of flows of capital, goods, services, ideas, and people to their 'most efficient' location—such neoliberal tenets liquidate the social forms and relationships that previously bound individuals into durable solidarities. Besides extending the ever-dynamic market to provide all our needs, these tenets enshrine individual choice and, even more, the 'freedom' from tradition, loyalty, and other social regulations that would inhibit the incessant calculations and transactions of the market actor. In this way, neoliberalism offers an uncritical worldview well suited for the do-it-yourself biography. Here, 'QOL' articulates an expressive utilitarian calculus of *homo economicus* as we scrutinize our lives, relationships, jobs, and communities for ways to stabilize, improve, and—why not?—even beautify them. Greed and acquisition are not the *sine qua non* of the neoliberal actor, as voluntary simplicity and other QOL-inspired status restrictions illustrate, so much as the incessant reinvention of self, daily rounds, and worldview—the "discontinuous reinvention of institutions" (Sennett 1998:47) applied to the self.

We can view the apparently anti-individualist strain of communitarianism in QOL discourse in this light. Neoliberalism is hardly incompatible with 'community,' despite its general hostility toward *gemeinschaft*, i.e., the traditional commitment to particular social relations ('my' family, place of origin, vocation, etc.). Indeed, neoliberalism encourages us to view 'community' as an individual utility as equally worthy of desire and pursuit as any other object; hence the centrality of shared ways of life, common values, and collective identity in contemporary discourses of QOL. Yet these are communities of choice that presume the ontological priority of neoliberalism's restless, optimizing, mobile subject. Some may find it meaningful and beneficial to submit to the community's values, but such justification, unnecessary in the *gemeinschaft* proper, draws upon the comparative, reflexive gaze of the market actor. In this regard, 'QOL' is less hostile to 'community' than it is to civil libertarianism—not the aesthetic attraction to ethnic diversity and neighborhood variety thought to animate the creative city (cf. Florida 2002), but tolerance for the marginalized Other who lacks choice in community membership and values (Vitale 2008; Bauman 2007b).

Significantly, neoliberalism pushes us forward into a brave new *sub-political* world. Originally, modernization's promise was most formally voiced, however tentatively and uneasily, in the sphere of the polity as the basis of the politically "liberal" social contract between welfare states and their citizens. By contrast, neoliberalism displaces the formal political sphere for reasons both punitive (to halt the redistribution of wealth and other state interventions into the private sector) and generative (to create new opportunities for institutional reinvention and commercial transactions). 'QOL' accommodates the displacement of the formally political in its worldview; even more, it naturalizes, embellishes, *enchants* this displacement. The historical reason is not hard to discern; too often, the authoritarian state (of both Western and non-Western varieties) has been a source of our personal alienation and political oppression. Yet the necessity of the political—to deliberate, legitimate, and coordinate collective mobilizations toward the greater good—has hardly disappeared in the present era. While neoliberal policies augur in a regressive and anti-democratic transfer of wealth back to the wealthy (Harvey 2005), the embrace of everyday life and "civil society" in a world where interactions and reciprocities with the Other are on the wane deprives 'QOL' of a genuinely *moral* political vocabulary.

QOL after Neoliberalism?

If the drift of 'QOL' from its affluent society promise is not an inevitable development of the idea itself but rather a historic consequence of the social conditions in which QOL has been pursued of late, then perhaps major changes to those conditions could revive a critical, collective understanding of QOL. As I write, we seem to stand on the precipice of such a historical break, with the global economic downturn appearing to have deflated popular enthusiasm and political support for neoliberal policies once and for all. In debates over how to fix the ailing global capitalist system, some voices have urged we use this moment to stem the material unsustainability and cultural debasement that neoliberalism ushered in over the prior 40 years. "The crisis in global capitalism demands a revolution in spirit—fundamental change in attitudes and behavior," argues political theorist Benjamin Barber (2009). "Reform cannot merely rush parents and kids back into the mall; it must encourage them to shop less, to save rather than spend." Reciting a broad set of proposals—national policies to incentivize saving, penalize carbon use, promote production of real human needs, regulate exploitative marketing, and redirect the social costs and risks that capital would externalize back onto the private sector—Barber (2009) articulates a bold challenge:

> And Barack Obama? We elected a president committed in principle to deep change. Rather than try to back out of the mess we are in, why not find a way forward? What if Obama committed the United States to reducing consumer spending from 70 percent of GDP to 50 percent over the next ten years, bringing it to roughly where Germany's GDP is today? The Germans have a commensurate standard of living and considerably greater equality. Imagine all the things we could do without having to shop: play and pray, create and relate, read and walk, listen and procreate—make art, make friends, make homes, make love.
>
> Sound too soft? Too idealistic? If we are to survive the collapse of the unsustainable consumer capitalism that has possessed our body politic over the past three decades, idealism must become the new realism. For if

> the contest is between the material body defined by solipsistic acquisitiveness and the human spirit defined by imagination and compassion, then a purely technical economic response is what will be too soft, promising little more than a restoration of that shopaholic hell of hyper-consumerism that occasioned the current disaster.

Similarly revolutionary QOL aspirations can be discerned in countercultural predictions of our corporate-dominated market society's collapse:

> Remember the upside, though: We're all gonna have more free time as jobs grow scarcer and the three-day work week finally becomes a reality. The greedheads, vampires and middlemen are fading out, which means we labor-of-lovers are finally gonna have some real breathing space to do our thing(s)—you've probably already noticed this happening around you. People with better, brighter, more beautiful, and more fundamentally sound ideas about how we can be living with each other on this planet are gaining the space, time and energy we need to put our ideas into real play. What we're gonna see is: more autonomy, more sharing, more health, more fun.
>
> (Babcock 2009)

These calls for a proactive and self-consciously postmaterial embrace of material scarcity revive a venerable affluent society critique, albeit under economic conditions probably not seen in developed societies since World War II (see Horowitz 2005). They also raise central questions for a QOL politics after neoliberalism. First, how does material scarcity enhance QOL? Economists and psychologists have shown that increases in earnings and spending ultimately reach a ceiling in boosting individual, subjective well-being (summarized in Myers 2003; Frank 2003); possibly, an involuntarily lowering of the ceiling on everyone will achieve a positive effect. Yet the affluent society endorsement of simple living originally reflected an interest in collective, objective QOL. In particular, voluntarily curtailing consumption in a prosperous economy would conserve a material surplus that could be distributed to the less fortunate—"live simply so others may simply live"—in the form of concrete investments in human infrastructure, services, and amenities. How similar investments can be made under deflated economic circumstances will be a thorny issue in the future. Civil society and local initiative will undoubtedly be crucial in initiating such efforts, but in the absence of a greater solidarity that acknowledges and constitutes all citizens in a body politic, they risk reproducing the social inequalities and geographical segregations that neoliberalism fueled.

Thus the second question, more abstract yet arguably more urgent: how does a postmaterial politics of material scarcity conceive of 'us'? That is, how does it constitute the societal collective? Reaping voluntary simplicity's individual benefits may establish the greater good by utilitarian standards, chalking up individual welfares into an aggregate that more or less represents 'society,' but it does little to address the problem of how we are connected to and interdependent upon each another. Simple living may very well save the earth in ecological terms, yet morally it can lapse into the same solipsism and self-segregation found in any affluenza-ridden exurb. The question of how 'QOL' constitutes the social is hardly an esoteric one, particularly once policy comes into the picture. Currently, the Anglo-American liberal welfare regime leaves individuals to secure their well-being through the market. In this political terrain, radical proposals to share sacrifices (which is how a three-day work week will be felt for most) and tax ourselves for collective investments will find a hostile reception among electorates unless these proposals explicitly highlight and convincingly inveigh against the ways that market individualism has eroded collective solidarity since the heyday of the affluent society. No one expects that to be an easy struggle, but the alternate—slipping in a major redistributional policy change under the cover of the political status quo—is no guarantee for success either, as the present battles to establish health-care reform and bold energy policy in the U.S. suggests. Perhaps a libertarian anarchy of individuals and affinity groups pursuing their own well-being, never mind the rest, is all we can hope for in a future of material scarcity. But then we will have hardly abandoned the ontological individualism that the neoliberal market has bequeathed to our pursuits of QOL.

And finally, what are words good for? Can 'QOL' be rehabilitated, given the material force of the many social shifts that have generated our multiplicity of QOL understandings and pursuits? I have doubts that a semantic politics alone can revive the moral commitments that were dreamed of during the affluent society era, but certainly we could articulate 'QOL' and its associated terms to delineate better the potentials and obstacles to the solidarities that genuine change after neoliberalism will require. We might make clearer the dimensions that we connote with 'QOL' and take greater responsibility for their distinctions. Happiness is not the same as family caregiving policy, nor are local amenities equivalent to collective governance over the conditions of work; to convene these or any other QOL dimensions under the same idea misleads us about what is at stake with 'QOL' even as it mobilizes our moral investments. We might also finally take seriously the social divisions and political differences that 'QOL' too often obscures. The civility of 'QOL' that the reification of social relations makes possible is, I would contend, a dead end for the sober, collective, and rational political deliberation that the future demands. In this book, I have situated my view of QOL politics in the perspective of the affluent society critique, which aspired to enhance human well-being in its objective, collective, and distributional conditions, and which acknowledged the historic achievement of modern affluence through an optimistically universalist view of rational progress (put another way, a critical universalist belief in *humane* progress). Readers may have other starting points for 'QOL' that I may differ with; such is the reality of democratic politics. However, without explicating what our distinct premises and goals are and how these conceive our conflicts, sympathies, and dependence with each other, a legitimate politics of QOL will remain unlikely.

As I conclude, it is worth recalling the optimism of Abraham Maslow, or the post-World War II challenge to conventional growth standards. In their own ways, not only did these refuse the dark sociotechnical determinisms that threatened humanity, but more importantly, they critically negated the world as it was ideologically received by its beholders. It is fairly easy to find a spirit of refusal in QOL pursuits today, but do we still seek to negate the ontological categories and social structures of the world that "impair our QOL" *and* also our planet and the justice of our social relations? Too often, 'QOL' means the opposite: accommodating and finding satisfaction from the choices and constraints presented by the world before us. These may be meaningful personal strategies, but they do little to promote the greater good. Perhaps soon, 'QOL' will be reenlisted toward this forgotten goal.

Notes

2 Intellectual History

1 Although this method is indeterminately imprecise, its value derives from the sheer size of the Google Book Search database: over 7 million publications as of January 6, 2009, the date on which I conducted the search. By this time, Google's book database included the out-of-print collections of 13 English-speaking university libraries (Columbia University, Cornell University, Harvard University, Oxford University, Princeton University, the University of California, the University of Michigan, the University of Texas-Austin, the University of Virginia, and the University of Wisconsin-Madison) plus the New York Public Library. Also, at the time of my search the Google corporation had just settled a class action lawsuit brought by the Authors Guild, the Association of American Publishers and a handful of authors and publishers, which allowed the full online display and search of many in-print publications (Rich 2009). My search method underestimates the actual publications of the phrase "quality of life" by excluding frequent modifications (e.g., "quality of adolescent life") and variations (e.g., "qualities of life"). On the other hand, the method overestimates these publications with its occasional miscodings of publication years and multiple citations of the same publication in the same year (generally a result of multiple publishers and, for scholarly publications, multiple publication venues).

2 A detailed intellectual history of the affluent society is beyond the scope of this chapter; I instead refer the reader to Daniel Horowitz's excellent 2005 book, *The Anxieties of Affluence: Critiques of American Consumer Culture, 1939–1979*.

3 My edition of Aristotle's *Nicomachean Ethics* (2002, trans. Christopher Rowe) states it slightly differently: "If one's activities are what determines the quality of one's life, as we have said, no one who is blessed will become miserable . . ." (I.10).

4 Family

1 Customarily, the scholarship on the welfare state reserves the concept to nation-states (1) with developed economies from which wealth can be redistributed sustainably, even if that is a subject of political contention, and (2) with primary footing in some sort of capitalist system, reflecting those nations' social compact with their citizens that emerged in the Cold War against communism. These criteria thereby include most of North America (except Mexico), most of Europe (except the former socialist nations), Japan, Australia, and New Zealand. Conversely, they exclude developing nations and socialist polities—i.e., the rest of the world where people, needless to say, also worry about QOL! Still, I hope readers familiar with the

political and economic trajectories of nations in this excluded category can analyze other nations through one of the welfare 'regimes' described here.

2 There are of course limits to how the public provision of childcare facilities enhances the work–life balance of mothers—or fathers, for that matter. Survey researchers Harald Bielenski and Alexandra Wagner (2004: 152) observe:

> In Denmark, France, and Norway, the public provision of childcare facilities means that the conditions for combining paid work and family responsibilities are good. Nevertheless, parents in these countries would prefer to work significantly shorter hours than men and women without children. This shows that a good supply of public childcare facilities does not in itself create the optimal conditions for combining paid work and childrearing. Parents would also like to work shorter hours in order to reduce their heavy burden of paid and unpaid work or simply to have more time for their children.

3 However, Esping-Andersen (1999) also identifies an important gendering of the social democratic welfare regime's emphasis on women's participation in the workplace: its "massive apparatus of collective social services has created an essentially female, occupational hierarchy in the welfare state," thereby producing "the unintended side-effect of unusually strong job sex-segregation". This suggests that although women in Scandinavia have more resources to support their full-time employment, their self-determination may be constrained in terms of *where* they work.

4 Political and legal traditions in France discourage the kind of gender equality in the public sphere that the American women's movement has fought to establish. French law has no tradition of civil rights and identity politics to produce legislation that identifies women or other groups as deserving special protection from discrimination. Sexual harassment is viewed as a problem of sexual violence but not sexual discrimination; thus, women in the workplace lack legal protections from a 'hostile environment' of sexist jokes, touching, unwelcome solicitations, pornography, or other harassing behavior that falls short of a workplace ultimatum (Saguy 2004).

5 Work

1 In this chapter, I refer to "work-based QOL" instead of the slightly less unwieldy "quality of working life" in order to reserve the latter expression for the historically specific corporate movement of the 1970s and 1980s described in the section, "The Quality of Working Life Initiative."

6 Place

1 I thank my student Daniel McPhee for bringing this newspaper column to my attention.

2 I thank my student Julia Fiore for drawing this quotation to my attention.

3 The exceptions to this group—migrants of necessity who make long-distance moves, such as immigrant laborers (Portes 1995)—often rely in their own ways upon the institutions of *gemeinschaft* from their home community. Family, neighborhood, and other community networks typically precede the long-distance migrant via chain migration, thereby making the migratory decision and destination more likely (Massey 1990; Stack 1974).

7 Politics

1 Postmodernists' positions in this debate are distinct from Ronald Inglehart's confusing reference to the "postmodern" (i.e., postmaterial) shift in values and institutions; see Chapter 2.

2 Ulrich Beck acknowledges that his account of reflexive modernization's force upon the welfare state and its citizenry is specific to the developed world:

> Since this theory posits first modern society as a prerequisite for second modern society, there are groups of countries it doesn't apply to, for example, parts of Africa or Asia. … It takes for granted that the institutions that second modern society dissolves or transforms are there in the first place: a nation-state, a welfare state (a rudimentary one at least), highly developed institutions of science and technology, and the institutionalized expectation of full employment.
>
> (Beck et al. 2003:7)

3 Almost certainly, the localization of environmentalism has not been an explicit strategy of the Big Ten or any other hierarchic conception of the 'environmentalist movement,' even though many local environmentalists hail from this movement and view their activism as its logical legacy. The charge of "NIMBYism" (not in my backyard) leveled at local environmentalist groups has long rested uneasily with the leading environmental organizations seeking their seat at the table of national political and legislative power—an important backdrop to the Big Ten's initial resistance to the environmental justice movement (Gottlieb 1993:190).

4 Significantly, reflexive modernization theory views the 'local' as distinctly subpolitical: "Those decision-making areas which had been protected by the political in industrial capitalism—the private sector, business, science, *towns*, everyday life and so on—are caught in the storms of political conflict in reflexive modernity" (Beck 1994:18; emphasis added).

5 Britain's movement to establish a legal right to roam has centered on private lands because the state has no public lands designated for recreational and access purposes. Before the focus on the demands of recreational "ramblers," Britain's policies of public access embodied less than fully public goals: to diversify agriculture in the context of "politically embarrassing and financially unsustainable" food surpluses in the mid-1980s; to curtail development in the early 1990s via greenways and "pocket parks"; and to provide revenue for the expansion of the National Forestry Estate throughout the 1990s (Curry 2001:401–3).

6 This account of the traditional custom of roaming probably overstates the historic exclusivity of the rural *gemeinschaft*. Since at least the Victorian era, when the railway connected the countryside to Britain's cities and towns, hunting enthusiasts and nature lovers from the city have entered the countryside, its social milieu, and (for some social climbers among the urban bourgeoisie) their families and properties through intermarriage (George 1999). From this long ago, many country dwellers resented urban hunters' "lack of riding manners and unwillingness 'to obey the rules' and, above all, their reluctance to understand the countryside and the problems of farmers" (Pardo and Prato 2005:146). Nevertheless, even urban pretensions to live the country life appeared to bestow an interest and participation in the rural order of things, if not a deep sympathy. In the traditional custom of roaming, then, outsiders generally validated the rural way of life, according to many rural advocates.

7 It is a complex question to what extent reflexivity pervades the rural way of life itself. Anthropologist Garry Marvin is skeptical, contending that the fox-hunting community is pointedly not motivated by heritage, by which he means "not just habit but conscious choice" in following tradition (cf. Lowenthal 1998:34; Lash

and Urry 1994). He quotes one huntsman's reluctance to emphasize fox-hunting's long history:

> This is here and now to me. This is your life. This is what you do. This is the proper way to do it. The whole idea of tradition to me is the way I do my job. It's not saying, "Oh, they did this 250 years ago." . . . It's an ongoing thing, . . . It's everyday life while we are hunting that maintains the tradition. You don't have to think about it because the way we do things . . . is the tradition.
>
> (Marvin 2007:354)

In any case, Marvin's view underscores the need to distinguish between *practitioners of rural tradition* in the countryside, such as the fox-hunters he studies, and the undoubtedly smaller and more politically active group of *rural advocates in the public realm*.

8 Shellenberger and Nordhaus have elaborated this argument in *Break Through: From the Death of Environmentalism to the Politics of the Possible* (2007) and subsequent writings found at http://www.thebreakthrough.org/.

9 To the dismay of DeLuca and others, mainstream environmental groups have since begun incorporating demands from the environmental justice movement, expanding the social diversity of the Big Ten's governing boards and emphasizing social, cultural, and environmental sustainability issues in protests against NAFTA and other world trade agreements.

10 I thank my students Lauren Jacobson and Melanie Lin for calling Sachem Quality of Life to my attention. See the Center for Individual Rights' brief: http://www.cir-usa.org/cases/perez_v_posse.html.

11 Posted March 18, 2009, at http://taxdayteaparty.com/teaparty/georgia/.

Permissions

Table 1.1	Domains and terms of QOL from Comprehensive Quality of Life Scale. Source: Robert A. Cummins, "The Domains of Life Satisfaction: An Attempt to Order Chaos," *Social Indicators Research*, Vol. 28, No. 3 (1996), pg. 309. Copyight © 1996 Kluwer Academic Publishers. Reprinted with permission of Springer, via Copyright Clearance Center.
Table 1.2	Residual terms of QOL from Comprehensive Quality of Life Scale. Source: Robert A. Cummins, "The Domains of Life Satisfaction: An Attempt to Order Chaos," *Social Indicators Research*, Vol. 28, No. 3 (1996), pg. 309. Copyright © 1996 by Kluwer Academic Publishers. Reprinted with permission of Springer, via Copyright Clearance Center.
Table 1.3	QOL assessments based on objective and subjective factors. Source: Mark Rapley, Figure 2.1, "Categories of individual welfare" in *Quality of Life Research: A Critical Introduction* (London, UK: Sage), pg. 31. © 2003 Mark Rapley. Originally printed in Wofgang Zapf, "Individuelle Wohlfahrt: Lebensbedingungen und Wahrgenommene Lebensqualität in der Bundesrepublik" from *Lebensqualität in der Bundesrepublik*, edited by W. Glatzer and W. Zapf (Frankfurt, Germany: Campus). Reprinted by permission of Sage.
Table 2.2	Materialism and postmaterialism. Source: Inglehart, Ronald; *Modernization and Postmodernization*. © 1997 Princeton University Press. Reprinted by permission of Princeton University Press.
Table 3.1	Diffusion rate of selected household appliances in the U.S. and Britain. Source: Avner Offer, Table 8.1, "Diffusion rate of selected household appliances in the United States and Britain" in *The Challenge of Affluence* (New York: Oxford University Press), pp. 174–5. © 2006 Avner Offer. Reprinted by permission of Oxford University Press.
Table 4.1	Family leave—maternity and parental leave provisions, approximately 2000. Source: Gornick, Janet C. and Marcia

	K. Meyers. Table 5.1, "Family Leave – Maternity and Parental Leave Provisions, Approximately 2000." In *Families That Work: Policies for Reconciling Parenthood and Work*. © 2003 Russell Sage Foundation, 112 East 64th Street, New York, NY 10065. Reprinted with permission.
Table 4.3	Households of men and women married or living together – Europe, 1998. Source: Table 6, "The Distribution of Paid Work Between Men and Women in Two-Adult Households with at Least One Economically Active Person with Respect to the Existence of Children (in %)." Reprinted from *Advances in Life Course Research*, Vol 8, Harald Bielenski and Alexandra Wagner, "Employment Options of Men and Women in Europe," pp. 137–62, © 2004, with permission from Elsevier.
Figure 5.1	Flyer from the Take Back Your Time Day campaign. Source: Jennifer Akre, "Medieval Peasants Worked Less Than You," in John De Graaf, *Take Back Your Time* San Francisco, CA: Berrett-Koehler. © 2003 John De Graaf. Reprinted by permission of author.
Figure 6.1	Residential mobility of Americans, 1948–2008. Source: Claude S. Fischer, "The myth that never moves," March 23, 2010 http://madeinamericathebook.wordpress.com. © 2010 Claude S. Fischer. Reprinted by permission of author.
Figure 6.2	Examples of multiple residence by life course phase. Source: Kevin E. McHugh, Timothy D. Hogan and Stephen K. Happel, Figure 1, "Examples of Multiple Residence by Life Course Phase," in "Multiple Residence and Cyclical Migration: A Life Course Perspective," *Professional Geographer* Vol. 47, No. 3 (1995), pg. 253. © 1995 Association of American Geographers. Reprinted with permission of Taylor & Francis, via Copyright Clearance Center.
Table 7.1	The New Political Culture—22 propositions. Source: Terry Nichols Clark and Ronald Inglehart. 1998. "The New Political Culture: Changing Dynamics of Support for the Welfare State and other Policies in Postindustrial Societies." in *The New Political Culture*, edited by T.N. Clark and V. Hoffmann-Martinot (Boulder, CO: Westview Press), pp. 9–72. © 1998 Westview Press, via Copyright Clearance Center.
Extract: 373 words of Page & Shoard	Source: Robin Page and Marion Shoard, "Should We Have a Right To Roam?" This article first appeared in the October 2000 issue of *The Ecologist* Vol. 30, No. 10 www.theecologist.org. © 2000 The Ecologist. Reprinted with permission.
Extract: 278 words of Shellenberger and Nordhaus	Source: Ted Shellenberger and Michael Nordhaus, "The Death of Environmentalism: Global Warming Politics in a Post-Environmental World" *Grist*, January 13, www.grist.org. © 2005 Ted Shellenberger and Michael Nordhaus. Reprinted with permission of authors.

References

Abramson, Paul and Ronald Inglehart. 1995. *Value Change in Global Perspective*. Ann Arbor, MI: University of Michigan Press.

Adler, Ursula. 1991. *A Critical Study of the American Nursing Home*. New York: Edwin Mellon Press.

Agacinski, Sylviane. 2001. *Parity of the Sexes*. Translated by Lisa Walsh. New York: Columbia University Press.

Aksoy, Sahin. 2000. "Can the 'Quality of Life' Be Used as a Criterion in Health Care Services?" *Bulletin of Medical Ethics* October (162): 19–22.

Amin, Ash. 1994. *Post-Fordism*. Cambridge, MA: Blackwell.

Anderson, Benedict. 1991. *Imagined Communities: Reflections on the Origin and Spread of Nationalism*. London: Verso.

Andrews, Cecile. 1997. *The Circle of Simplicity*. New York: Harper Collins.

Andrews, Frank M. and Stephen B. Withey. 1976. *Social Indicators of Well-Being*. New York: Plenum Press.

Apter, David E. 1965. *The Politics of Modernization*. Chicago, IL: University of Chicago Press.

Archer, Margaret S. 2007. *Making Our Way Through the World*. Cambridge, UK: Cambridge University Press.

Aristotle. 2002. *Nicomachean Ethics*, trans. Christopher Rowe. Oxford, UK: Oxford University Press.

Aron, Cindy S. 1999. *Working at Play: A History of Vacations in the United States*. New York: Oxford University Press.

Aronowitz, Stanley. 2001. *The Last Good Job in America*. Lanham, MD: Rowman & Littlefield.

Babcock, Jay. 2009. "Command Performance." *The Arthur Magazine Email Bulletin* No. 00134, February 3. Retrieved October 28, 2009 (http://www.arthurmag.com/2009/02/07/arthur-email-bulletin-no-00134).

Badinter, Elisabeth. 1981. *Mother Love*. New York: Macmillan.

Bahrami, Homa and Stuart Evans. 2000. "Flexible Recycling and High-Technology Entrepreneurship," pp. 165–89 in *Understanding Silicon Valley: The Anatomy of an Entrepreneurial Region*, edited by M. Kenney. Stanford, CA: Stanford University Press.

Barber, Benjamin R. 2009. "The Economic Crisis Isn't All Bad; It's a Chance for Us and Obama to Reimagine How We Live Our Lives." *The Nation*, January 28. Retrieved October 28, 2009 (http://www.alternet.org/story/123157/).

Bauman, Zygmunt. 2007a. *Consuming Life*. Cambridge, UK: Polity Press.

Bauman, Zygmunt. 2007b. *Liquid Times*. Cambridge, UK: Polity Press.

Bauman, Zygmunt. 1998. *Work, Consumerism and the New Poor*. Buckingham, UK: Open University Press.

Bean, Lowell J. and Charles R. Smith. 1978. "Gabrielino," pp. 538–49 in *Handbook of North American Indians*, vol. 8, *California*, edited by R. F. Heizer. Washington, DC: Smithsonian Institution.

Beck, Ulrich. 2005. *Power in the Global Age*. Cambridge, UK: Polity Press.

Beck, Ulrich. 1995. *Ecological Politics in an Age of Risk*. Cambridge, UK: Polity Press.

Beck, Ulrich. 1994. "The Reinvention of Politics: Towards a Theory of Reflexive Modernization," pp. 1–55 in *Reflexive Modernization*, edited by U. Beck, A. Giddens and S. Lash. Stanford, CA: Stanford University Press.

Beck, Ulrich. 1992. *Risk Society*. Thousand Oaks, CA: Sage.

Beck, Ulrich and Elizabeth Beck-Gernsheim. 2002. *Individualization*. Thousand Oaks, CA: Sage.

Beck, Ulrich, Wolfgang Bonss and Christoph Lau. 2003. "The Theory of Reflexive Modernization: Problematic, Hypotheses and Research Programme." *Theory, Culture and Society* 20(2): 1–33.

Becker, Gary. 1991. *A Treatise on the Family*. Rev. ed. Cambridge, MA: Harvard University Press.

Bell, Daniel. 1999. *The Coming of Post-Industrial Society*. Special anniversary ed. New York: Basic Books.

Bellah, Robert N., Richard Madsen, William M. Sullivan, Ann Swidler and Steven M. Tipton. 1996. *Habits of the Heart*. Updated ed. Berkeley, CA: University of California Press.

Benjamin, Walter. 1999. *The Arcades Project*. Cambridge, MA: Belknap.

Berger, Leslie. 2000. "What Children Do When Home and Alone." *New York Times*, April 11.

Berk, Sarah Fenstermaker. 1985. *The Gender Factory: The Apportionment of Work in American Households*. New York: Plenum Press.

Berry, Wendell. 1977. *The Unsettling of Agriculture*. San Francisco, CA: Sierra Club Books.

Besleme, Kate, Elisa Maser and Judith Silverstein. 1999. *A Community Indicators Case Study: Addressing the Quality of Life in Two Communities*. San Francisco, CA: Redefining Progress.

Bianchi, Suzanne M., John P. Robinson and Melissa A. Milkie. 2006. *Changing Rhythms of American Family Life*. New York: Russell Sage Foundation.

Bielenski, Harald and Josef Hartmann. 2000. *Combining Family and Work: The Working Arrangements of Women and Men*. Dublin, Ireland: European Foundation for the Improvement of Living and Working Conditions.

Bielenski, Harald and Alexandra Wagner. 2004. "Employment Options of Men and Women in Europe." *Advances in Life Course Research* 8: 137–62.

Bihan, Blanche and Claude Martin. 2005. "Atypical Working Hours: Consequences for Childcare Arrangements," pp. 9–33 in *Overstretched: European Families Up Against the Demands of Work and Care*. Malden, MA: Blackwell.

Bills, David B. 2004. *The Sociology of Education and Work*. Malden, MA: Blackwell.

Bishop, Bill. 2008. *The Big Sort: Why the Clustering of Like-Minded America is Tearing Us Apart*. Boston, MA: Houghton Mifflin.

Bittman, Michael, James Mahmud Rice and Judy Wajcman. 2004. "Appliances and their Impact: The Ownership of Domestic Technology and Time Spent on Household Work." *British Journal of Sociology* 55: 401–23.

Blair-Loy, Mary. 2003. *Competing Devotions*. Cambridge, MA: Harvard University Press.

Blanchard, Ian. 1994. "Introduction," pp. 9–38 in *Labour and Leisure in Historical Perspective, Thirteenth to Twentieth Centuries*. Stuttgart, Germany: Franz Steiner Verlag.

Blau, Francine D., Marianne A. Ferber and Anne E. Winkler. 2002. *The Economics of Women, Men, and Work*. Upper Saddle River, NJ: Prentice-Hall.

Bluestone, Irving. 1983. "Labor's Stake in Improving the Quality of Working Life," pp. 33–41 in *The Quality of Working Life and the 1980s*, edited by H. Kolodny and H. van Benium. New York: Praeger.

Boisvert, Maurice Philippe. 1977. "The Quality of Working Life: An Analysis." *Human Relations* 30: 155–60.

Bonner, Kieran. 1997. *A Great Place to Raise Kids*. Montreal and Kingston, Canada: McGill-Queen's University Press.

Bosch, Gerhard. 2004. "Toward a New SER in Western Europe." *British Journal of Industrial Relations* 42: 617–36.

Bourdieu, Pierre. 1984. *Distinction: A Social Critique of the Judgment of Taste*. Cambridge, MA: Harvard University Press.

Brazelton, T. Berry. 1983. *Infants and Mothers*. New York: Delacorte.

Brende, Eric. 2004. *Better Off: Flipping the Switch on Technology*. New York: Harper Collins.

Brint, Steven. 1994. *In an Age of Experts: The Changing Role of Professionals in Politics and Public Life*. Princeton, NJ: Princeton University Press.

Brock, Dan W. 1992. "Voluntary Active Euthanasia." *Hastings Center Report* 22: 10–22.

Brooks, David. 2004. *On Paradise Drive*. New York: Simon & Schuster.

Brooks, David. 2003. "Conspicuous 'Simplicity,'" pp. 175–82 in *Voluntary Simplicity: Responding to Consumer Culture*, edited by D. Doherty and A. Etzioni. Lanham, MA: Rowman & Littlefield.

Brooks, David. 2000. *Bobos in Paradise*. New York: Simon & Schuster.

Brown, David L. 2002. "Migration and Community: Social Networks in a Multilevel World." *Rural Sociology* 67: 1–23.

Brown, David L., Glenn V. Fuguitt, Tim B. Heaton and Saba Waseem. 1997. "Continuities in Size of Place Preferences in the United States, 1972–1999." *Rural Sociology* 62: 408–24.

Brown, Patricia Leigh. 2008. "For 'EcoMoms,' Saving Earth Begins at Home." *New York Times*, February 16.

Budig, Michelle J. and Paula England. 2001. "The Wage Penalty for Motherhood." *American Sociological Review* 66: 204–25.

Buss, David M. 2000. "The Evolution of Happiness." *American Psychologist* 55: 15–23.

Buttel, Frederick H. 1987. "New Directions in Environmental Sociology." *Annual Review of Sociology* 13: 465–88.

Buttel, Frederick H., G. A. Wilkening and Oscar B. Martinson. 1977. "Ideology and Social Indicators of the Quality of Life." *Social Indicators Research* 4: 353–69.

Calhoun, Craig. 1998. "Community without Propinquity Revisited: Communications Technology and the Transformation of the Urban Public Sphere." *Sociological Inquiry* 68: 373–97.

Calhoun, Craig. 1995. *Critical Social Theory*. Malden, MA: Blackwell.

Callahan, Daniel. 1992. "When Self-Determination Runs Amok." *Hastings Center Report* 22(2): 52–55.

Callenbach, Ernest. 1975. *Ecotopia: The Notebooks and Reports of William Weston*. Berkeley, CA: Banyan Tree Books.

Campbell, Angus and Philip E. Converse, eds. 1972. *The Human Meaning of Social Change*. New York: Russell Sage Foundation.

Carnoy, Martin. 2002. *Sustaining the New Economy*. New York: Russell Sage Foundation.

Carson, Rachel. 1962. *Silent Spring*. Boston, MA: Houghton Mifflin.

Castells, Manuel. 1997. *The Power of Identity*. Malden, MA: Blackwell.

Castells, Manuel. 1996. *The Rise of the Network Society*. Malden, MA: Blackwell.

Champion, Anthony G. 1994. "Population Change and Migration in Britain since 1981: Evidence for Continuing Deconcentration." *Environment and Planning* A 26: 1501–20.

Champion, Anthony G., ed. 1989. *Counterurbanization*. London: Edward Arnold.

Childe, V. Gordon. 1925. *The Dawn of European Civilization*. New York: A.A. Knopf.

Chouinard, Yvon and Nora Gallagher. 2004. "Don't Buy This Shirt Unless You Need It." Ventura, CA: Patagonia. Retrieved September 20, 2010 (http://www.patagonia.com/us/patagonia.go?assetid=2388).

Cipolla, Carlo M. 1976. *Before the Industrial Revolution*. New York: W.W. Norton.

Ciulla, Joanne B. 2000. *The Working Life*. New York: Three Rivers Press.

Claritas Inc. 2008. "MyBestSegments." San Diego, CA: Nielsen Claritas. Retrieved February 3, 2008 (http://www.claritas.com/MyBestSegments/Default.jsp).

Clark, David A. 2005. "The Capability Approach: Its Development, Critiques and Recent Advances." Working Paper GPRG-WPS-032, Global Poverty Research Group, San Francisco, CA.

Clark, David E. and James C. Cosgrove. 1991. "Amenities Versus Labor Market Opportunities: Choosing the Optimal Distance to Move." *Journal of Regional Science* 31: 311–28.

Clark, Kim. 1999. "Why it Pays to Quit." *U.S. News and World Report* 127, November 1.

Clark, Terry Nichols. 2004. "Urban Amenities: Lakes, Operas, and Juice Bars: Do They Drive Development?" pp. 103–40 in *The City as an Entertainment Machine*, edited by T. N. Clark. *Research in Urban Policy*, vol. 9. Amsterdam, Netherlands: Elsevier.

Clark, Terry Nichols. 2000. "Old and New Paradigms for Urban Research: Globalization and the Fiscal Austerity and Urban Innovation Project." *Urban Affairs Review* 36: 3–45.

Clark, Terry Nichols and Edward G. Goetz. 1994. "The Anti-Growth Machine," pp. 105–45 in *Urban Innovation*, edited by T. N. Clark. Newbury Park, CA: Sage.

Clark, Terry Nichols and Vincent Hoffmann-Martinot, eds. 1998. *The New Political Culture*. Boulder, CO: Westview Press.

Clark, Terry Nichols and Ronald Inglehart. 1998. "The New Political Culture: Changing Dynamics of Support for the Welfare State and other Policies in Postindustrial Societies," pp. 9–72 in *The New Political Culture*, edited by T. N. Clark and V. Hoffmann-Martinot. Boulder, CO: Westview Press.

Clark, Terry Nichols and Seymour Martin Lipset. 1991. "Are Social Classes Dying?" *International Sociology* 6: 397–410.

Clifford, Catherine. 2006. "Mother Superior," pp. 71–86 in *Mommy Wars*, edited by L. M. Steiner. New York: Random House.

Coates, Ken S., Robert Healy and William R. Morrison. 2002. "Tracking the Snowbirds: Seasonal Migration from Canada to the U.S.A. and Mexico." *American Review of Canadian Studies* 32: 433–51.

Cobb, Clifford W. 2000. *Measurement Tools and the Quality of Life*. San Francisco, CA: Redefining Progress.

Communitarian Network. 1990. “Responsive Communitarian Platform: Rights and Responsibilities.” Retrieved July 20, 2006 (http://www.gwu.edu/~ccps/platformtext.html).

Conley, Valerie Martin. 2005. “Career Paths for Women Faculty: Evidence from NSOPF:99,” pp. 25–39 in *New Directions for Higher Education*, vol. 130, *The Challenge of Balancing Faculty Careers and Family Work*, edited by J. W. Curtis. San Francisco, CA: Jossey-Bass.

Cooper, Cary L. and Ronald J. Burke, eds. 2002. *The New World of Work: Challenges and Opportunities*. Cambridge, MA: Blackwell Business.

Cooper, Simon. 2002. *Technoculture and Critical Theory*. London: Routledge.

Countryside Alliance. 2006. “10 Policy Pieces for a Better Countryside.” September 12. Retrieved August 6, 2008 (http://www.countryside-alliance.org.uk/our-campaigns/our-policy-jigsaw/10-policy-pieces-for-a-better-countryside).

Cowan, Ruth Schwartz. 1979. “From Virginia Dare to Virginia Slims: Women and Technology in American Life.” *Technology and Culture* 20: 51–63.

Cox, Kevin R. and Andrew Mair. 1988. “Locality and Community in the Politics of Local Economic Development.” *Annals of the Association of American Geographers* 78: 307–25.

Craver, Charles B. 1993. *Can Unions Survive?* New York: NYU Press.

Crenson, Matthew A. 1971. *The Un-Politics of Air Pollution: A Study of Non-Decision-making in the Cities*. Baltimore, MD: Johns Hopkins Press.

Crittenden, Ann. 2001. *The Price of Motherhood*. New York: Owl Books.

Cronon, William. 1991. *Nature's Metropolis*. New York: W.W. Norton.

Cross, Gary. 2004. *The Cute and the Cool: Wondrous Innocence and Modern American Children's Culture*. New York: Oxford University Press.

Csikszentmihalyi, Mihaly. 1990. *Flow: The Psychology of Optimal Experience*. New York: Harper Perennial.

Cubbon, J. 1991. “The Principle of QALY Maximisation as the Basis for Allocating Health Care Resources.” *Journal of Medical Ethics* 17: 181–4.

Culyer, Anthony J. 1990. “Commodities, Characteristics of Commodities, Characteristics of People, and the Quality of Life,” pp. 9–27 in *Quality of Life: Perspectives and Policies*, edited by S. Baldwin, C. Godfrey, and C. Propper. London: Routledge.

Cummins, Robert A. 2003. “Normative Life Satisfaction: Measurement Issues and a Homeostatic Model.” *Social Indicators Research* 64: 225–56.

Cummins, Robert A. 1997. “Assessing Quality of Life,” pp. 116–50 in *Quality of Life for People with Disabilities*, edited by R. I. Brown. 2nd ed. Cheltenham: Stanley Thornes.

Cummins, Robert A. 1996. “The Domains of Life Satisfaction: An Attempt to Order Chaos.” *Social Indicators Research* 28: 303–28.

Cummins, Robert A. and Anna L. D. Lau. 2005. “Personal Wellbeing Index – School Children (PWI-SC).” Draft 3rd ed. Retrieved October 12, 2010 (http://www.deakin.edu.au/research/acqol/instruments/wellbeing-index/pwi-school.pdf).

Cummins, Robert A., Elonora Gullone and Anna L. D. Lau. 2002. “A Model of Subjective Well-Being Homeostasis: The Role of Personality,” pp. 7–46 in *The Universality of Subjective Well-Being Indicators*, edited by E. Gullone and R. A. Cummins. Dordrecht, Germany: Kluwer Academic.

Curry, Nigel. 2001. “Access for Outdoor Recreation in England and Wales: Production, Consumption and Markets.” *Journal of Sustainable Tourism* 9: 400–16.

Dale, Jennifer and Peggy Foster. 1986. *Feminists and State Welfare*. London: Routledge and Kegan Paul.

Dallimore, Elise and Amy Mickel. 2006. "Quality of Life: Obstacles, Advice, and Employer Assistance." *Human Relations* 59: 61–103.

Danbom, David P. 1996. "Why Americans Value Rural Life." *Rural Development Perspectives* 12: 15–18.

Darrah, Charles N., James M. Freeman, and J. A. English-Lueck. 2007. *Busier Than Ever!* Stanford, CA: Stanford University Press.

Darton, Nina. 1990. "Mommy vs. Mommy." *Newsweek*, June 4, p. 66.

Davis, Louis E. 1983. "Learnings from the Design of New Organizations," pp. 65–86 in *The Quality of Working Life and the 1980s*, edited by H. Kolodny and H. van Benium. New York: Praeger.

Deal, Terrence E. and Allan A. Kennedy. 1999. *The New Corporate Cultures: Revitalizing the Workplace After Downsizing, Mergers, and Reengineering*. Reading, MA: Perseus Books.

Deal, Terrence E. and Allan A. Kennedy. 1982. *Corporate Cultures: The Rites and Rituals of Corporate Life*. Reading, MA: Addison-Wesley.

De Graaf, John, ed. 2003. *Take Back Your Time*. San Francisco, CA: Berrett-Koehler.

De Graaf, John, David Wann and Thomas H. Naylor. 2005. *Affluenza: The All-Consuming Epidemic*. 2nd ed. San Francisco, CA: Berrett Koehler.

DeLuca, Kevin. 2007. "A Wilderness Environmentalism Manifesto: Contesting the Infinite Self-Absorption of Humans," pp. 27–55 in *Environmental Justice and Environmentalism*, edited by R. Sandler and P. C. Pezzullo. Cambridge, MA: MIT Press.

Desai, Megnhad. 1991. "Human Development: Concepts and Measurement." *European Economic Review* 35: 350–7.

Deutsch, Francine M. 1999. *Halving It All: How Equally Shared Parenting Works*. Cambridge, MA: Harvard University Press.

Dewey, John. 1916. *Democracy and Education: An Introduction to the Philosophy of Education*. New York: Macmillan.

Diener, Ed. 2000. "Subjective Well-Being: The Science of Happiness and a Proposal for a National Index." *American Psychologist* 55: 34–43.

Dizard, Jan and Howard Gadlin. 1990. *The Minimal Family*. Amherst, MA: University of Massachusetts Press.

Domhoff, G. William. 1996. *State Autonomy or Class Dominance?* Hawthorne, NY: Aldine de Gruyter.

Drew, Eileen. 1998. "Re-conceptualising Families," pp. 11–26 in *Women, Work and the Family in Europe*, edited by E. Drew, R. Emerek and E. Mahon. London: Routledge.

Duany, Andres, Elizabeth Plater-Zyberk and Jeff Speck. 2000. *Suburban Nation*. New York: North Point Press.

Duesenberry, James Stemble. 1949. *Income, Saving, and the Theory of Consumer Behavior*. Cambridge, MA: Harvard University Press.

Du Gay, Paul. 1996. *Consumption and Identity at Work*. Thousand Oaks, CA: Sage.

Duncan, James S. and Nancy G. Duncan. 2004. *Landscapes of Privilege: The Politics of the Aesthetic in an American Suburb*. New York: Routledge.

Duneier, Mitchell. 1999. *Sidewalk*. New York: Farrar, Straus and Giroux.

Durkheim, Emile. 1997 [1893]. *The Division of Labor in Society*. New York: Free Press.

Easterbrook, Gregg. 2003. *The Progress Paradox: How Life Gets Better While People Feel Worse*. New York: Random House.

Eco, Umberto. 1993. *Misreadings*. New York: Harvest.

Edin, Kathryn and Laura Lein. 1997. *Making Ends Meet*. New York: Russell Sage Foundation.

Edwards, Paul and Judy Wajcman. 2005. *The Politics of Working Life*. Oxford, UK: Oxford University Press.

Ehrenreich, Barbara and Deirdre English. 1973. *Complaints and Disorders: The Sexual Politics of Sickness*. New York: Feminist Press.

Elgin, Duane. 1981. *Voluntary Simplicity: Toward a Way of Life that is Outwardly Simple, Inwardly Rich*. New York: William Morrow & Co.

Elias, Norbert. 2000. *The Civilizing Process*. Rev. ed. Malden, MA: Blackwell.

Emanuel, Ezekiel. 1997. "Whose Right to Die?" *The Atlantic Monthly*, March. Retrieved August 17, 2009 (http://www.theatlantic.com/past/issues/97mar/emanuel/emanuel.htm).

England, Paula. 2001. "Toward Gender Equality: Progress and Bottlenecks," pp. 245–64 in *The Declining Significance of Gender?*, edited by F. D. Blau, M. C. Brinton and D. B. Brusky. New York: Russell Sage Foundation.

Erikson, Robert. 1993. "Descriptions of Inequality: The Swedish Approach to Welfare Research," pp. 67–83 in *The Quality of Life*, edited by M. Nussbaum and A. Sen. Oxford, UK: Clarendon Press.

Esping-Andersen, Gøsta. 1999. *Social Foundations of Postindustrial Economies*. Oxford and New York: Oxford University Press.

Esping-Andersen, Gøsta. 1990. *The Three Worlds of Welfare Capitalism*. Princeton, NJ: Princeton University Press.

Etzioni, Amitai. 2003. "Introduction," pp. 1–25 in *Voluntary Simplicity: Responding to Consumer Culture*, edited by D. Doherty and A. Etzioni. Lanham, MA: Rowman & Littlefield.

Etzioni, Amitai, ed. 1998. *The Essential Communitarian Reader*. Lanham, MD: Rowman & Littlefield.

Evans, Page. 2006. "Sharks and Jets," pp. 21–36 in *Mommy Wars*, edited by Leslie Morgan Steiner. New York: Random House.

Eyerman, Ron and Andrew Jamison. 1991. *Social Movements: A Cognitive Approach*. University Park, PA: Pennsylvania State University Press.

Fagerlin, Angela and Carl E. Schneider. 2004. "Enough: The Failure of the Living Will." *Hastings Center Report* 34: 30–42.

Fagnani, Jeanne. 1998. "Recent Changes in Family Policy in France," pp. 58–65 in *Women, Work and the Family in Europe*, edited by E. Drew, R. Emerek and E. Mahon. London: Routledge.

Faludi, Susan. 1991. *Backlash: The Undeclared War Against American Women*. New York: Crown.

Farb, Peter. 1978. *Humankind*. Boston, MA: Houghton Mifflin.

Fenwick, Rudy and Mark Tausig. 2004. "The Health and Family-Social Consequences of Shift Work and Schedule Control: 1977 and 1997," pp. 77–110 in *Fighting for Time: Shifting Boundaries of Work and Social Life*, edited by C. F. Epstein and A. L. Kalleberg. New York: Russell Sage Foundation.

Field, David. 1996. "Terminal Care Education for Doctors," pp. 111–23 in *Contemporary Issues in the Sociology of Death, Dying and Disposal*, edited by G. Howarth and P. C. Jupp. New York: St. Martin's.

Field, John. 2003. *Social Capital*. London: Routledge.

Fischer, Claude S. 2010. "The Myth that Never Moves." *Made in America* (blog),

March 23. Retrieved July 6, 2010 (http://madeinamericathebook.wordpress.com/2010/03/23/the-myth-that-never-moves/).

Fischer, Claude S. 2002. "Ever More Rooted Americans." *City and Community* 1: 177–98.

Fischer, Claude S. 1994. *America Calling: A Social History of the Telephone to 1940*. Berkeley, CA: University of California Press.

Fischer, Claude S. and Michael Hout. 2006. *Century of Difference: How America Changed in the Last One Hundred Years*. New York: Russell Sage Foundation.

Fishman, Robert. 1987. *Bourgeois Utopias*. New York: Basic Books.

Florida, Richard. 2008. *Who's Your City? How the Creative Economy is Making Where to Live the Most Important Decision of Your Life*. New York: Basic Books.

Florida, Richard. 2005a. *Cities and the Creative Class*. New York: Routledge.

Florida, Richard. 2005b. *The Flight of the Creative Class*. New York: HarperBusiness.

Florida, Richard. 2002. *The Rise of the Creative Class: And How It's Transforming Work, Leisure, Community and Everyday Life*. New York: Basic Books.

Foderaro, Lisa W. 2006. "Working Mothers Find Some Peace on the Road." *New York Times*, November 1.

Frank, Robert H. 2003. "Achieving Collective Well-Being through Greater Simplicity: A Simple Proposal," pp. 83–98 in *Voluntary Simplicity: Responding to Consumer Culture*, edited by D. Doherty and A. Etzioni. Lanham, MA: Rowman & Littlefield.

Franzen, Axel and Reto Meyer. 2009. "Environmental Attitudes in Cross-National Perspective: A Multilevel Analysis of the ISSP 1993 and 2000." *European Sociological Review* 26: 1–16.

Fraser, Jill Andrewsky. 2001. *White-Collar Sweatshop: The Deterioration of Work and its Rewards in Corporate America*. New York: W.W. Norton.

Frey, William H. 2004. "The Fading of City–Suburb and Metro–Nonmetro Distinctions in the United States," pp. 67–88 in *New Forms of Urbanization*, edited by T. Champion and G. Hugo. Burlington, VT: Ashgate.

Frey, William H. 2003. "Melting-Pot Suburbs: A Study of Suburban Diversity," pp. 155–79 in *Redefining Urban and Suburban America*, edited by B. Katz and R. E. Lang. Washington, DC: Brookings Institution Press.

Friedman, Thomas L. 2005. *The World is Flat*. New York: Farrar, Straus & Giroux.

Galbraith, John Kenneth. 1998 [1958]. *The Affluent Society*. 40th anniv. ed. Boston, MA: Houghton Mifflin.

Gans, Herbert. 1967. *The Levittowners*. New York: Pantheon.

Gans, Herbert. 1962. "City Planning and Urban Realities." *Commentary* 33: 170–5.

Garfinkel, Simson. 2001. *Database Nation: The Death of Privacy in the 21st Century*. Cambridge, MA: O'Reilly.

Gauthier, Anne H., Timothy M. Smeeding and Frank F. Furstenberg, Jr. 2004. "Are Parents Investing Less Time in Children?: Trends in Selected Industrialized Countries." *Population and Development Review* 30: 647–71.

George, Janet. 1999. *A Rural Uprising*. London: J.A. Allen.

Gershuny, Jonathan. 2000. *Changing Times: Work and Leisure in Postindustrial Society*. Oxford, UK: Oxford University Press.

Gerson, Elihu M. 1976. "On 'Quality of Life.'" *American Sociological Review* 41: 793–806.

Giannarelli, Linda and James Barsimantov. 2000. *Child Care Expenses of America's Families*. Washington, DC: Urban Institute.

Giddens, Anthony. 1998. *The Third Way*. Malden, MA: Polity.

Giddens, Anthony. 1991. *Modernity and Self-Identity*. Stanford, CA: Stanford University Press.

Giddens, Anthony. 1984. *The Constitution of Society*. Berkeley, CA: University of California Press.

Giele, Janet Zollinger and Elke Holst. 2004. "New Life Patterns and Changing Gender Roles," pp. 3–22 in *Changing Life Patterns in Western Industrial Societies*, edited by J. Z. Giele and E. Holst. Amsterdam, Netherlands: Elsevier.

Gilder, George. 2000. *Telecosm: The World After Bandwidth Abundance*. New York: Free Press.

Gilman, Nils. 2004. *Mandarins of the Future: Modernization Theory in Cold War America*. Baltimore, MD: Johns Hopkins University Press.

Gintis, Herbert. 1972. "A Radical Analysis of Welfare Economics and Individual Development." *The Quarterly Journal of Economics* 86: 572–99.

Glaeser, Edward L. and Jesse M. Shapiro. 2003. "City Growth: Which Places Grew and Why," pp. 13–32 in *Redefining Urban and Suburban America*, edited by B. Katz and R. E. Lang. Washington, DC: Brookings Institution Press.

Glendinning, Chellis. 1994. *My Name Is Chellis and I'm in Recovery from Western Civilization*. New York: Random House.

Goffman, Erving. 1961. *Asylums*. New York: Doubleday.

Goldscheider, Frances K., Dennis Hogan, Susan Short and Berna Mille. 2002. "The Growing Isolation of Parenthood in the Life Course and in the Family, 1880–1990." Presented at the annual meeting of the American Sociological Association, August 16–19, Chicago, IL.

Goodman, Paul. 1960. *Growing Up Absurd*. New York: Random House.

Goodman, Percival and Paul Goodman. 1947. *Communitas: Means of Livelihood and Ways of Life*. Chicago, IL: University of Chicago Press.

Gore, Al. 1992. *Earth in the Balance: Ecology and the Human Spirit*. Boston, MA: Houghton Mifflin.

Gornick, Janet C. and Marcia K. Meyers. 2004. "Welfare Regimes in Relation to Paid Work and Care," pp. 45–67 in *Changing Life Patterns in Western Industrial Societies*, edited by J. Z. Giele and E. Holst. Amsterdam, Netherlands: Elsevier.

Gornick, Janet C. and Marcia K. Meyers. 2003. *Families that Work*. New York: Russell Sage Foundation.

Gottlieb, Robert. 1992. *Forcing the Spring*. Washington, DC: Island Press.

Greenhouse, Steven. 2008. *The Big Squeeze: Tough Times for the American Worker*. New York: Knopf.

Grigsby, Karen. 2004. *Buying Time and Getting By: The Voluntary Simplicity Movement*. Albany, NY: State University of New York Press.

Gustafsson, Siv. 1999. "Childcare and Types of Welfare States," pp. 45–61 in *Gender and Welfare State Regimes*, edited by D. Sainsbury. Oxford, UK: Oxford University Press.

Haase, Joan E., Sue P. Heiney, Kathleen S. Ruccione and Cynthia Stutzer. 1999. "Research Triangulation to Derive Meaning-Based Quality-of-Life Theory: Adolescent Resilience Model and Instrument Development." *International Journal of Cancer* 12(supplement): 125–31.

Habermas, Jürgen. 1990 [1983]. *Moral Consciousness and Communicative Action*. Cambridge, MA: MIT Press.

Hacker, Andrew. 2003. *Mismatch: The Growing Gulf between Women and Men*. New York: Scribner.

Hagerty, Michael R., Robert A. Cummins, Abbott L. Ferriss, Kenneth Land, Alex C. Michalos, Mark Peterson, Andrew Sharpe, Joseph Sirgy and Joachim Vogel. 2001. "Quality of Life Indexes for National Policy: Review and Agenda for Research." *Social Indicators Research* 55: 1–96.

Haq, Mahbub ul. 1995. *Reflections on Human Development*. Oxford, UK: Oxford University Press.

Halebsky, Stephen. 2004. "Superstores and the Politics of Retail Development." *City and Community* 3: 115–34.

Halfacree, Keith. 2004. "Rethinking 'Rurality,'" pp. 285–304 in *New Forms of Urbanization: Beyond the Urban–Rural Dichotomy*, edited by T. Champion and G. Hugo. Burlington, VT: Ashgate.

Hannigan, John. 1998. *Fantasy City*. New York: Routledge.

Harrington, Michael. 1962. *The Other America*. New York: Macmillan.

Harvey, David. 2005. *A Brief History of Neoliberalism*. Oxford, UK: Oxford University Press.

Harvey, David. 1989a. *The Condition of Postmodernity*. Cambridge, MA: Blackwell.

Harvey, David. 1989b. "From Managerialism to Entrepreneurialism: The Transformation in Urban Governance in Late Capitalism." *Geografiska Annaler B* 71: 3–18.

Hays, Sharon. 1996. *The Cultural Contradictions of Motherhood*. New Haven, CT: Yale University Press.

Head, Simon. 2003. *The New Ruthless Economy*. New York: Oxford University Press.

Heath, Anthony, Roger Jowell, John Curtice and Geoff Evans. 1990. "The Rise of the New Political Agenda?" *European Sociological Review* 6: 31–48.

Heidegger, Martin. 1977 [1954]. *The Question Concerning Technology, and Other Essays*. New York: Harper & Row.

Heschel, Abraham Joshua. 1952. *The Sabbath: Its Meaning to Modern Man*. New York: Farrar, Straus.

Hirsch, Fred. 1976. *Social Limits to Growth*. Cambridge, MA: Harvard University Press.

Hirschman, Albert O. 1970. *Exit, Voice, and Loyalty*. Cambridge, MA: Harvard University Press.

Hitzler, Ronald. 1988. *Kleine Lebenswelten*. Opladen, Germany: Westdeutscher Verlag.

Hochschild, Arlie. 1997. *The Time Bind: When Work Becomes Home and Home Becomes Work*. New York: Metropolitan Books.

Hochschild, Arlie. 1989. *The Second Shift*. New York: Viking.

Hodge, Johanna. 1990. "The Quality of Life: A Contrast Between Utilitarian and Existentialist Approaches," pp. 42–54 in *Quality of Life: Perspectives and Policies*, edited by S. Baldwin, C. Godfrey and C. Propper. London: Routledge.

Hofferth, Sandra L. 1996. "Child Care in the United States Today." *Future of Children* 6: 41–61.

Hogan, Timothy D. and Donald N. Steinnes. 1994. "Toward an Understanding of Elderly Seasonal Migration Using Origin-Based Household Data." *Research on Aging* 16: 463–75.

Holliday, Charles O., Jr., Stephan Schmidheiny and Philip Watts. 2002. *Walking the Talk: The Business Case for Sustainable Development*. San Francisco, CA: Berrett-Koehler.

Honoré, Carl. 2008. *Under Pressure: Rescuing Our Children from the Culture of Hyper-Parenting*. New York: Harper Collins.

Honoré, Carl. 2004. *In Praise of Slowness: How a Worldwide Movement is Challenging the Cult of Speed*. San Francisco, CA: Harper San Francisco.

Hook, Jennifer L. 2010. "Gender Inequality in the Welfare State: Sex Segregation in Housework, 1965–2003." *American Journal of Sociology* 115: 1480–523.

Horowitz, Daniel. 2005. *The Anxieties of Affluence: Critiques of American Consumer Culture, 1939–1979*. Amherst, MA: University of Massachusetts Press.

Howarth, Glennys. 2007. *Death and Dying*. Cambridge, UK: Polity.

Hudnut, William H., III. 2003. *Halfway to Everywhere*. Washington, DC: Urban Land Institute.

Hummon, David M. 1990. *Commonplaces*. Albany, NY: State University of New York Press.

Iggulden, Conn and Hal Iggulden. 2007. *The Dangerous Book for Boys*. New York: Collins.

Inglehart, Ronald. 1997. *Modernization and Postmodernization: Cultural, Economic, and Political Change in Societies*. Princeton, NJ: Princeton University Press.

Inglehart, Ronald. 1990. *Culture Shift in Advanced Industrial Society*. Princeton, NJ: Princeton University Press.

Inglehart, Ronald. 1979. "Value Priorities and Socioeconomic Change," pp. 305–43 in *Political Action*, edited by S. H. Barnes, M. Kaase, and K. R. Allerbeck. Beverly Hills, CA: Sage.

Inglehart, Ronald and Christian Welzel. 2005. *Modernization, Cultural Change and Democracy: The Human Development Sequence*. Cambridge, UK: Cambridge University Press.

Jackson, Kenneth T. 1985. *Crabgrass Frontier*. New York: Oxford University Press.

Jacobs, Jane. 1961. *The Death and Life of Great American Cities*. New York: Pantheon.

Jacobs, Jerry A. 2003. "The Faculty Time Divide." Presidential Address, Eastern Sociological Society, Philadelphia, PA.

Jacobs, Jerry A. and Kathleen Gerson. 2004a. "Understanding Changes in American Working Time: A Synthesis," pp. 25–45 in *Fighting for Time: Shifting Boundaries of Work and Social Life*, edited by C. F. Epstein and A. L. Kalleberg. New York: Russell Sage Foundation.

Jacobs, Jerry A. and Kathleen Gerson. 2004b. *The Time Divide: Work, Family, and Gender Inequality*. Cambridge, MA: Harvard University Press.

Jenkins, David. 1983. "Quality of Working Life: Trends and Directions," pp. 1–32 in *The Quality of Working Life and the 1980s*, edited by H. Kolodny and H. van Benium. New York: Praeger.

Jenson, Jane and Mariette Sineau. 1995. *Mitterrand et les Francaises*. Paris, France: Presse de Sciences Po.

Jones, Robert Emmett and Riley E. Dunlap. 2010. "The Social Bases of Environmental Concern: Have They Changed Over Time?" *Rural Sociology* 57: 28–47.

Jones-Lee, M., M. Hammerton and P. R. Phillips. 1985. "The Value of Safety: Results of a National Sample Survey." *Economic Journal* 95: 49–72.

Jordan, Sarah. 2003. *The Anxieties of Idleness: Idleness in Eighteenth-Century British Literature and Culture*. Lewisburg, PA: Bucknell University Press.

Judis, John B. and Rudy Teixeira. 2002. *The Emerging Democratic Majority*. New York: Scribner.

Kamm, Frances M. 1998. "Physician-Assisted Suicide, Euthanasia, and Intending Death," pp. 28–62 in *Physician-Assisted Suicide*, edited by M. P. Battin, R. Rhodes and A. Silvers. New York: Routledge.

Karasik, Sherry. 2000. "Experts: More Latchkey Kids Means More Trouble." APB News Service, April 14.

Keeble, David and Lilach Nachum. 2002. "Why do Business Service Firms Cluster? Small Consultancies, Clustering and Decentralisation in London and Southern England." *Transactions of the Institute of British Geographers* NS 27: 67–90.

Keeble, David and Peter Tyler. 1995. "Enterprising Behavior and the Urban–Rural Shift." *Urban Studies* 32: 975–97.

Kellehear, Allan. 2007. *A Social History of Dying*. Cambridge, UK: Cambridge University Press.

Kelling, George L. and Catherine M. Coles. 1996. *Fixing Broken Windows*. New York: Martin Kessler.

Kennett, Douglas J. 2005. *The Island Chumash: Behavioral Ecology of a Maritime Society*. Berkeley, CA: University of California Press.

Keyes, Corey L. M. and Jonathan Haidt, eds. 2003. *Flourishing: Positive Psychology and the Life Well-Lived*. Washington, DC: American Psychological Association.

Kiefer, Matthew J. 2005. "Suburbia and its Discontents: Notes from the Sprawl Debate," pp. 34–43 in *Sprawl and Suburbia*, edited by W. S. Saunders. Minneapolis, MN: University of Minnesota Press.

King, Lawrence Peter and Iván Szelényi. 2004. *Theories of the New Class*. Minneapolis, MN: University of Minnesota Press.

Knight, Richard V. 1989. "City Development and Urbanization: Building the Knowledge-Based City," pp. 223–42 in *Cities in a Global Society*, ed. R. V. Knight and G. Gappert. Newbury Park, CA: Sage.

Knox, Paul. 2005. "Vulgaria: The Re-Enchantment of Suburbia." *Opolis: An International Journal of Suburban and Metropolitan Studies* 1(2): 33–46. Retrieved May 14, 2010 (http://repositories.cdlib.org/cssd/opolis/vol1/iss2/art3).

Koch, Tom. 2000. "Future States: The Axioms Underlying Prospective, Future-Oriented, Health Planning Instruments." *Social Science and Medicine* 52: 453–65.

Kolodny, Harvey and Hans van Beinum. 1983. "Preface," pp. vii–x in *The Quality of Working Life and the 1980s*, edited by H. Kolodny and H. van Benium. New York: Praeger.

Kossek, Ellen Ernst, Brenda A. Lautsch and Susan C. Eaton. 2006. "Telecommuting, Control, and Boundary Management: Correlates of Policy Use and Practice, Job Control, and Work–Family Effectiveness." *Journal of Vocational Behavior* 68: 347–67.

Kotkin, Joel. 2003. "Paths to Prosperity." *American Enterprise*, July/August, pp. 32–35.

Kotkin, Joel. 2000. *The New Geography: How the Digital Revolution is Reshaping the American Landscape*. New York: Random House.

Kravdal, Øystein and Ronald R. Rindfuss. 2008. "Changing Relationships between Education and Fertility: A Study of Women and Men Born 1940 to 1964." *American Sociological Review* 73: 854–73.

Krieger, Alex. 2005. "The Costs—and Benefits?—of Sprawl," pp. 44–56 in *Sprawl and Suburbia*, edited by W. S. Saunders. Minneapolis, MN: University of Minnesota Press.

Kronman, Anthony T. 2007. *Education's End: Why Our Colleges and Universities Have Given Up on the Meaning of Life*. New Haven, CT: Yale University Press.

Kunstler, James Howard. 1998. *Home From Nowhere*. New York: Simon & Schuster.

Kurz, Demi. 2002. "Caring for Teenage Children." *Journal of Family Issues* 23: 748–67.

Laclau, Ernesto and Chantal Mouffe. 1985. *Hegemony and Socialist Strategy: Towards a Radical Democratic Politics*. London: Verso.

Ladd-Taylor, Molly. 1994. *Mother-Work*. Urbana, IL: University of Illinois Press.

Lancy, David F. 2007. "Accounting for Variability in Mother–Child Play." *American Anthropologist* 109: 273–84.

Landen, Delmar. 1981. "Transforming Organizations: Principles and Strategies." Presented at the QWL and the 1980s conference, August, Toronto, Canada.

Lareau, Annette. 2003. *Unequal Childhoods: Class, Race, and Family Life*. Berkeley, CA: University of California Press.

Larabee, Eric and Rolf Meyersohn, eds. 1958. *Mass Leisure*. Glencoe, IL: Free Press.

Lash, Scott. 2003. "Reflexivity as Non-Linearity." *Theory, Culture and Society* 20(2): 49–57.

Lash, Scott. 1994. "Reflexivity and its Doubles: Structure, Aesthetics, Community," pp. 110–73 in *Reflexive Modernization*, edited by U. Beck, A. Giddens and S. Lash. Stanford, CA: Stanford University Press.

Lash, Scott. 1993. "Reflexive Modernization: The Aesthetic Dimension." *Theory, Culture and Society* 10: 1–23.

Lash, Scott and John Urry. 1994. *Economies of Signs and Space*. London: Sage.

Latham, Michael E. 2000. *Modernization As Ideology*. Chapel Hill, NC: University of North Carolina Press.

Lavi, Shai J. 2005. *The Modern Art of Dying*. Princeton, NJ: Princeton University Press.

Leach, Penelope. 1986. *Baby and Child: From Birth to Age Five*. New ed. London: Penguin.

Lear, Jonathan. 2000. *Happiness, Death, and the Remainder of Life*. Cambridge, MA: Harvard University Press.

Leo, Christopher, Mary Ann Beavis, Andrew Carver and Robyne Turner. 1998. "Is Urban Sprawl Back on the Political Agenda? Local Growth Control, Regional Growth Management, and Politics." *Urban Affairs Review* 34: 179–212.

Lesnard, Laurent. 2008. "Off-Scheduling within Dual-Earner Couples: An Unequal and Negative Externality for Families." *American Journal of Sociology* 114: 447–90.

Letablier, Marie-Thérèse. 2004. "Work and Family Balance: A New Challenge for Policies in France," pp. 189–209 in *Changing Life Patterns in Western Industrial Societies*, edited by J. Z. Giele and E. Holst. Amsterdam, Netherlands: Elsevier.

Levinson, David. 2003. "Community Indicators," pp. 272–75 in *Encyclopedia of Community*, edited by K. Christensen and D. Levinson. Thousand Oaks, CA: Sage.

Librado, Fernando, John Peabody Harrington and Travis Hudson. 1977. *The Eye of the Flute: Chumash Traditional History and Ritual*. Santa Barbara, CA: Santa Barbara Museum of Natural History.

Lipset, Seymour Martin. 2001. "The Decline of Class Ideologies: The End of Political Exceptionalism?" pp. 249–72 in *The Breakdown of Class Politics*, edited by T. N. Clark and S. M. Lipset. Washington, DC: Woodrow Wilson Center Press.

Lipset, Seymour Martin. 1981. *Political Man*. Expanded ed. Baltimore, MD: Johns Hopkins University Press.

Little, Arthur D. 2006 [1924]. "Life As We Know It." *The Atlantic Monthly*, website archive. Retrieved August 13, 2006 (http://www.theatlantic.com/ideastour/technology/little-full.mhtml).

Lloyd, Richard D. 2003. *Neo-Bohemia: Art and Commerce in the Post-Industrial City*. New York: Routledge.

Logan, John and Harvey Molotch. 1987. *Urban Fortunes*. Berkeley, CA: University of California Press.

Longino, Charles F., Jr. and Don E. Bradley. 2006. "Internal and International

Migration," pp. 76–93 in *Handbook of Aging and the Social Sciences*, 6th ed., edited by R. H. Binstock and L. K. George. San Diego, CA: Elsevier.

Loomes, Graham and Lynda McKenzie. 1990. "The Scope and Limitations of QALY Measures," pp. 84–102 in *Quality of Life: Perspectives and Policies*, edited by S. Baldwin, C. Godfrey and C. Propper. London: Routledge.

Loudoun, John Claudius. 2006. "British Horticulturalist J. C. Loudoun Lays the Foundation for a Suburban Ideal, 1838," pp. 16–18 in *The Suburb Reader*, edited by B. M. Nicolaides and A. Wiese. New York: Routledge.

Lowenthal, David. 1998. *The Heritage Crusade and the Spoils of History*. Cambridge, UK: Cambridge University Press.

Lundberg, Shelly and Elaina Rose. 2000. "Parenthood and the Earnings of Married Men and Women." *Labor Economics* 7: 689–710.

Lynd, Robert S. and Helen Merrell Lynd. 1929. *Middletown*. New York: Harcourt, Brace and Company.

Mander, Jerry. 1991. *In the Absence of the Sacred: The Failure of Technology and the Survival of the Indian Nations*. San Francisco, CA: Sierra Club.

Mann, Michael. 1986. *The Sources of Social Power. Vol. I: A History of Power from the Beginning to A.D. 1760*. Cambridge, UK: Cambridge University Press.

Marchand, Roland. 1985. *Advertising the American Dream*. Berkeley, CA: University of California Press.

Marcuse, Herbert. 1998 [1941]. "Some Social Implications of Modern Technology," pp. 39–65 in *Technology, War and Fascism: Collected Papers of Herbert Marcuse, Vol. 1*, edited by D. Kellner. London: Routledge.

Marcuse, Herbert. 1964. *One-Dimensional Man*. Boston, MA: Beacon Press.

Marcuse, Peter. 2003. "Review of *The Rise of the Creative Class* by Richard Florida." *Urban Land* 62: 40–1.

Marsh, Jan. 1982. *Back to the Land*. London: Quartet Books.

Marvin, Garry. 2007. "English Foxhunting: A Prohibited Practice." *International Journal of Cultural Property* 14: 339–60.

Marx, Karl. 1978 [1844]. "Economic and Philosophic Manuscripts of 1844," pp. 66–125 in *The Marx-Engels Reader*, 2nd ed., edited by R. C. Tucker. New York: W.W. Norton.

Marx, Karl. 1972 [1845]. "The German Ideology: Part I," pp. 110–64 in *The Marx–Engels Reader*, edited by R. C. Tucker. New York: W.W. Norton.

Marx, Karl. 1906 [1867]. *Capital: A Critique of Political Economy*. Reprint. New York: Modern Library.

Maslow, Abraham. 1987. *Motivation and Personality*. 3rd ed. New York: Harper and Row.

Massey, Douglas. 1990. "Social Structure, Household Strategies and the Cumulative Causation of Migration." *Population Index* 56: 3–26.

Mattingly, Marybeth J. and Suzanne M. Bianchi. 2003. "Gender Differences in the Quantity and Quality of Free Time: The U.S. Experience." *Social Forces* 81: 999–1030.

McCann, Eugene J. 2007. "Inequality and Politics in the Creative City-Region: Questions of Livability and State Strategy." *International Journal of Urban and Regional Research* 31: 188–96.

McClelland, David. 1961. *The Achieving Society*. Princeton, NJ: Van Nostrand.

McEvoy, Arthur F. 1986. *The Fisherman's Problem*. New York: Cambridge University Press.

McHugh, Kevin E., Timothy D. Hogan and Stephen K. Happel. 1995. "Multiple

Residence and Cyclical Migration: A Life Course Perspective." *Professional Geographer* 47: 251–67.

McIntyre, Norman. 2006. "Introduction," pp. 3–14 in *Multiple Dwelling and Tourism*, edited by N. McIntyre, D. Williams and K. McHugh. Oxfordshire, UK: CABI.

McIntyre, Norman, Joseph W. Rogenbuck and Daniel R. Williams. 2006. "Home and Away: Revisiting 'Escape' in the Context of Second Homes," pp. 114–28 in *Multiple Dwelling and Tourism*, edited by N. McIntyre, D. Williams and K. McHugh. Oxfordshire, UK: CABI.

McMahon, Darrin M. 2006. *Happiness: A History*. New York: Atlantic Monthly Press.

Megone, Chris B. 1990. "The Quality of Life: Starting from Aristotle," pp. 28–41 in *Quality of Life: Perspectives and Policies*, edited by S. Baldwin, C. Godfrey and C. Propper. London: Routledge.

Melucci, Alberto. 1989. *Nomads of the Present: Social Movements and Individual Needs in Contemporary Society*. Philadelphia, PA: Temple University Press.

Menzies, Heather. 2005. *No Time: Stress and the Crisis of Modern Life*. Vancouver, BC: Douglas & McIntyre.

Merton, Robert K. 1957. *Social Theory and Social Structure*. Glencoe, IL: Free Press.

Meštrovi, Stjepan Gabriel. 1998. *Anthony Giddens*. London: Routledge.

Meyer, John M. 2005. "Does Environmentalism Have a Future?" *Dissent* Spring: 69–75.

Michener, James A. 1970. *The Quality of Life*. Philadelphia, PA: Girard Bank.

Mieszkowski, Katharine. 2003. "Americans are Not Going Broke Over Lattes!" *Salon.com*, October 13. Retrieved January 9, 2008 (http://dir.salon.com/story/tech/feature/2003/10/13/bankrupt_parents).

Miles, Ian. 1985. *Social Indicators for Human Development*. New York: St. Martin's.

Mills, C. Wright. 1956. *The Power Elite*. New York: Oxford University Press.

Mills, C. Wright. 1951. *White Collar*. New York: Oxford University Press.

Mings, R. C. 1997. "Tracking 'Snowbirds' in Australia: Winter Sun Seekers in Far North Queensland." *Australian Geographical Studies* 35: 168–82.

Mintz, Steven. 2004. *Huck's Raft: A History of American Childhood*. New York: Belknap.

Moen, Phyllis. 2003. *It's About Time: Couples and Careers*. Ithaca, NY: ILR Press.

Molotch, Harvey. 2003. *Where Stuff Comes From: How Toasters, Toilets, Cars, Computers, and Many Other Things Come to Be As They Are*. New York: Routledge.

Molotch, Harvey. 1976. "The City as a Growth Machine." *American Journal of Sociology* 82: 309–30.

Molotch, Harvey and William Freudenburg. 1996. *Santa Barbara County: Two Paths*. OCS Study MMS 96-0036, under Contract No. 14-35-001-30663. Camarillo, CA: U.S. Department of Interior, Minerals Management Service, Pacific Outer Continental Shelf Region.

Molotch, Harvey, William Freudenburg and Krista E. Paulsen. 2000. "History Repeats Itself, But How? City Character, Urban Tradition, and the Accomplishment of Place." *American Sociological Review* 65: 791–823.

Moore, A. M. T. 1982. "Agricultural Origins in the Near East: A Model for the 1980s." *World Archaeology* 14: 224–36.

Morreim, E. Haavi. 1994. "Profoundly Diminished Life: The Casualties of Coercion." *Hastings Center Report* 24: 33–42.

Morris, Douglas E. 2005. *It's a Sprawl World After All*. Gabriola Island, BC: New Society.

Morrison, Denton E. and Riley E. Dunlap. 1986. "Environmentalism and Elitism: A Conceptual and Empirical Analysis." *Environmental Management* 10: 581–89.

Morse, Rob. 2001. "The Cesspool that is the Streets of San Francisco." *San Francisco Chronicle*, July 16, p. A-2.

Moss, Lawrence A. G., ed. 2006a. *The Amenity Migrants: Seeking and Sustaining Mountains and Their Cultures*. Oxfordshire, UK: CAB International.

Moss, Lawrence A. G. 2006b. "The Amenity Migrants: Ecological Challenge to Contemporary Shangri-La," pp. 3–25 in *The Amenity Migrants: Seeking and Sustaining Mountains and their Cultures*, edited by L. A. G. Moss. Oxfordshire, UK: CAB International.

Mumford, Lewis. 1934. *Technics and Civilization*. New York: Harcourt, Brace and Co.

Murdoch, Jonathan, Philip Lowe, Neil Ward and Terry Marsden. 2003. *The Differentiated Countryside*. London: Routledge.

Murdoch, Lydia. 2002. "Review of *Unknown London: Early Modernist Visions of the Metropolis, 1815–45*, ed. John Marriott." *Victorians Institute Journal* 30: 179–89.

Myers, David G. 2003. "Wealth and Happiness: A Limited Relationship," pp. 41–51 in *Voluntary Simplicity: Responding to Consumer Culture*, edited by D. Doherty and A. Etzioni. Lanham, MA: Rowman & Littlefield.

Myrdal, Alva and Viola Klein. 1956. *Women's Two Roles, Home and Work*. London: Routledge & Paul.

Myrdal, Gunner. 1963. *Challenge to Affluence*. New York: Pantheon.

Nadeau, Jean-Benoît and Julie Barlow. 2003. *Sixty Million Frenchmen Can't Be Wrong: Why We Love France But Not the French*. New York: Sourcebooks.

Nassaw, David. 1993. *Going Out*. New York: Harper Collins.

Nelson, Andrew and Stephanie Corley. 2005. "Showdown in Marfa." *Salon.com*, August 1. Retrieved August 1, 2005 (http://www.salon.com/news/feature/2005/08/01/marfa/index.html).

Nevarez, Leonard. 2003. *New Money, Nice Town: How Capital Works in the New Urban Economy*. New York: Routledge.

Nevarez, Leonard. 1999. "Working and Living in the Quality-of-Life District." *Research in Community Sociology* 9: 185–215.

Noll, Herbert-Heinz. 2000. "Social Indicators and Social Reporting: The International Experience." Canadian Council on Social Development, unpublished paper. Retrieved June 8, 2006 (http://www.ccsd.ca/noll1.html).

Nordhaus, William D. and James Tobin. 1973. "Is Growth Obsolete?" *The Measurement of Economic and Social Performance, Studies in Income and Wealth* 38: 509–32.

Norman, Donald A. 1994. *Things that Make Us Smart: Defending Human Attributes in the Age of the Machine*. New York: Basic Books.

Nussbaum, Martha. 2000. *Women and Human Development: The Capabilities Approach*. Cambridge, UK: Cambridge University Press.

Nussbaum, Martha. 1993. "Non-Relative Virtues: An Aristotelian Approach," pp. 242–73 in *The Quality of Life*, edited by M. Nussbaum and A. Sen. Oxford, UK: Clarendon Press.

Nussbaum, Martha. 1988. "Nature, Function and Capability: Aristotle on Political Distribution." *Oxford Studies in Ancient Philosophy* Supl. vol.: 145–84.

Offer, Avner. 2006. *The Challenge of Affluence: Self-Control and Well-Being in the United States and Britain since 1950*. Oxford, UK: Oxford University Press.

O'Harrow, Robert O., Jr. 2005. *No Place to Hide: Behind the Scenes of Our Emerging Surveillance Society*. New York: Free Press.

Olson, Mancur. 1965. *The Logic of Collective Action: Public Goods and the Theory of Groups*. Cambridge, MA: Harvard University Press.

Otero, Adriana, Lia Nakayama, Susana Marioni, Elisa Gallego, Alicia Lonac, Andrés Dimitria, Rodrigo González and Claudia Hosid. 2006. "Amenity Migration in the Patagonian Mountain Community of San Martín de los Andes, Neuquén, Argentina," pp. 200–11 in *The Amenity Migrants: Seeking and Sustaining Mountains and Their Cultures*, edited by L. A. G. Moss. Oxfordshire, UK: CAB International.

O'Toole, Randal. 2007. *The Best-Laid Plans: How Government Planning Harms Your Quality of Life, Your Pocketbook, and Your Future*. Washington, DC: Cato Institute.

Packard, Vance O. 1960. *The Waste Makers*. New York: D. McKay Co.

Packard, Vance O. 1959. *The Status Seekers*. New York: D. McKay Co.

Page, Robin and Marion Shoard. 2000. "Should We Have a Right To Roam?" *The Ecologist* 30 (October): 20–3.

Papadopoulos, Theodoros N. 1998. "Greek Family Policy from a Comparative Perspective," pp. 47–57 in *Women, Work and the Family in Europe*, edited by E. Drew, R. Emerek and E. Mahon. London: Routledge.

Pardo, Italo and Giuliana B. Prato. 2005. "The Fox-Hunting Debate in the United Kingdom: A Puritan Legacy?" *Human Ecology Forum* 12: 143–55.

Park, Robert E. 1925. "Community Organization and Juvenile Delinquency," pp. 99–112 in *The City*, edited by R. E. Park, E. W. Burgess, and R. D. McKenzie. Chicago, IL: University of Chicago Press.

Parsons, Talcott. 1951. *The Social System*. Glencoe, IL: Free Press.

Paulsen, Krista. 2004. "Making Character Concrete: Empirical Strategies for Studying Place Distinction." *City and Community* 3: 243–62.

Pavot, William and Ed Diener. 1993. "Review of the Satisfaction with Life Scale." *Psychological Assessment* 5: 164–72.

Peck, Jamie. 2005. "Struggling with the Creative Class." *International Journal of Urban and Regional Research* 29: 740–70.

Perna, Laura. 2005. "The Relationship Between Family and Employment Outcomes," pp. 5–24 in *New Directions for Higher Education*, vol. 130, *The Challenge of Balancing Faculty Careers and Family Work*, edited by J. W. Curtis. San Francisco, CA: Jossey-Bass.

Peters, Thomas J. and Robert H. Waterman, Jr. 1982. *In Search of Excellence: Lessons from America's Best-Run Companies*. New York: Harper & Row.

Petersen, William. 1964. "A General Typology of Migration," pp. 271–90 in *The Politics of Population*, edited by W. Petersen. Garden City, NY: Doubleday.

Peterson, Christopher. 2000. "The Future of Optimism." *American Psychologist* 55: 44–55.

Peterson, Paul E. 1981. *City Limits*. Chicago, IL: University of Chicago Press.

Petrinovich, Lewis. 1998. *Living and Dying Well*. Cambridge, MA: MIT Press.

Pew Research Center. 2005. *Trends 2005*. Washington, DC: Pew Research Center. Retrieved May 14, 2010 (http://pewresearch.org/assets/files/trends2005.pdf).

Pezzullo, Phaedra C. and Ronald Sandler. 2007. "Introduction: Revisiting the Environmental Justice Challenge to Environmentalism," pp. 1–24 in *Environmental Justice and Environmentalism*, edited by R. Sandler and P. C. Pezzullo. Cambridge, MA: MIT Press.

Philipson, Ilene. 2002. *Married to the Job*. New York: Free Press.

Phillips, David. 2006. *Quality of Life: Concept, Policy and Practice*. London: Routledge.

Pink, Daniel H. 2001. *Free Agent Nation*. New York: Warner Books.

Piore, Michael J. and Charles F. Sabel. 1984. *The Second Industrial Divide*. New York: Basic Books.

Plantinga, Andrew J. and Stephanie Bernell. 2007. "The Association Between Urban Sprawl and Obesity: Is it a Two-Way Street?" *Journal of Regional Science* 47: 857–79.

Portes, Alejandro. 1995. "Economic Sociology and the Sociology of Immigration: A Conceptual Overview," pp. 1–41 in *The Economic Sociology of Immigration*, edited by A. Portes. New York: Russell Sage Foundation.

Porter, Eduardo. 2006. "Stretched to Limit, Women Stall March to Work." *New York Times*, March 2.

Postman, Neil. 1992. *Technopoly: The Surrender of Culture to Technology*. New York: Knopf.

Presser, Harriet B. 2004. "Employment in a 24/7 Economy: Challenges for the Family," pp. 46–76 in *Fighting for Time: Shifting Boundaries of Work and Social Life*, edited by C. F. Epstein and A. L. Kalleberg. New York: Russell Sage Foundation.

Presser, Harriet B. 2003. *Working in a 24/7 Economy: Challenges for American Families*. New York: Russell Sage Foundation.

Qizilbash, M. 1998. "The Concept of Well-Being." *Economics and Philosophy* 14: 51–73.

Quinn, Bernadette. 2004. "Dwelling Through Multiple Places: A Case Study of Second Home Ownership in Ireland," pp. 113–30 in *Tourism, Mobility and Second Homes*, edited by C. M. Hall and D. K. Müller. Clevedon, UK: Channel View Publications.

Rainwater, Lee. 1974. "Work, Well-Being, and Family Life," pp. 361–78 in *Work and the Quality of Life*, edited by J. O'Toole. Cambridge, MA: MIT Press.

Rapley, Mark. 2003. *Quality of Life Research: A Critical Introduction*. London: Sage.

Rasker, Ray and Ben Alexander. 2003. *Getting Ahead in the Greater Yellowstone*. Bozeman, MT: Sonoran Institute.

Reed, Isaac. 2008. "Justifying Sociological Knowledge: From Realism to Interpretation." *Sociological Theory* 26: 101–29.

Reich, Robert B. 1998. "Broken Faith: Why We Need to Renew the Social Compact." *The Nation*, February 16, pp. 11–17.

Reich, Robert B. 1992. *The Work of Nations*. New York: Vintage.

Relph, E. C. 1976. *Place and Placelessness*. London: Pion.

Renfrew, Colin. 1972. *The Emergence of Civilisation*. London: Methuen.

Renshaw, Patrick. 1991. *American Labor and Consensus Capitalism, 1935–1985*. Jackson, MI: University Press of Mississippi.

Rich, Motoko. 2009. "Google Hopes to Open a Trove of Little-Seen Books." *New York Times*, January 4.

Riesman, David. 1964. *Abundance for What?* Garden City, NJ: Doubleday.

Riesman, David. 1950. *The Lonely Crowd: A Study of the Changing American Character*. New Haven, CT: Yale University Press.

Rifkin, Jeremy. 1995. *The End of Work*. New York: J.P. Tarcher.

Rifkin, Jeremy. 1987. *Time Wars: The Primary Conflict in Human History*. New York: Henry Holt.

Ritzer, George. 2004. *The Globalization of Nothing*. Thousand Oaks, CA: Pine Forge.

Ritzer, George. 1993. *The McDonaldization of Society*. Newbury Park, CA: Sage.

Rivera, Amaad, Brenda Cott-Escalera, Anisha Desai, Jeannette Huezo and Dedrick Muhammad. 2008. *Foreclosed: State of the Dream 2008*. Boston, MA: United for a Fair Economy. Retrieved July 22, 2009 (http://www.faireconomy.org/files/pdf/StateOfDream_01_16_08_Web.pdf).

Robinson, Bryan E., Bobbie H. Rowland and Mick Coleman. 1989. *Home-Alone Kids:*

The Working Parent's Complete Guide to Providing the Best Care for Your Child. Lexington, MA: Lexington Books.

Robinson, Joe. 2003. *Work to Live*. New York: Perigree.

Robinson, John P. and Geoffrey Godbey. 1997. *Time For Life: The Surprising Ways Americans Use Their Time*. University Park, PA: Pennsylvania University Press.

Rockefeller, Nelson Aldrich. 1969. *Quality of Life in the Americas: Report of a U.S. Presidential Mission for the Western Hemisphere*. Washington, DC: Agency for International Development.

Rogerson, Robert J. 1999. "Quality of Life and City Competitiveness." *Urban Studies* 36: 969–85.

Rones, Phillip, Randy Ilg and Jennifer Gardner. 1997. "Trends in Hours of Work Since the Mid-1970s." *Monthly Labor Review* April: 3–14.

Rose, Michael. 1985. *Re-Working the Work Ethic*. New York: Schocken.

Roseman, Curtis C. 1992. "Cyclical and Polygonal Migration in a Western Context," pp. 33–45 in *Community, Society, and Migration*, edited by P. C. Jobes, W. F. Stinner and J. M. Wardwell. Lanham, MD: University Press of America.

Rosenfeld, Alvin and Nicole Wise. 2000. *The Over-Scheduled Child*. Formerly published as *Hyper-Parenting*. New York: St. Martin's.

Ross, Andrew. 2009. *Nice Work If You Can Get It: Life and Labor in Precarious Times*. New York: NYU Press.

Ross, Andrew. 2003. *No Collar: The Humane Workplace and its Hidden Costs*. New York: Basic Books.

Ross, Andrew. 1999. *The Celebration Chronicles: Life, Liberty, and the Pursuit of Property Value in Disney's New Town*. New York: Ballantine.

Rostow, Walt W. 1960. *The Stages of Economic Growth: A Non-Communist Manifesto*. Cambridge, UK: Cambridge University Press.

Roth, Louise Marie. 2006. "Because I'm Worth It? Understanding Inequality in a Performance-Based Pay System." *Sociological Inquiry* 76: 116–39.

Saguy, Abigail. 2004. "National Specificity in an Age of Globalization: Sexual Harassment Law in France." *Contemporary French and Francophone Studies* 8: 425–40.

Sahlins, Marshall. 1972. *Stone Age Economics*. Chicago, IL: Aldine-Atherton.

Sainsbury, Diane. 1999. "Women's and Men's Social Rights: Gendering Dimensions of Welfare States," pp. 151–69 in *Gender and Welfare State Regimes*, edited by D. Sainsbury. Oxford, UK: Oxford University Press.

Sassen, Saskia. 2006. *Cities in a World Economy*. 3rd ed. Thousand Oaks, CA: Pine Forge.

Saunders, Clare. 2008. "Double-Edged Swords? Collective Identity and Solidarity in the Environment Movement." *British Journal of Sociology* 59: 227–53.

Savage, Mike, James Barlow, Peter Dickens and Tony Fielding. 1992. *Property, Bureaucracy and Culture: Middle-Class Formation in Contemporary Britain*. London: Routledge.

Schachter, Jason. 2001. "Why People Move: Exploring the March 2000 Current Population Survey." *U.S. Census Bureau, Current Population Report*, May.

Schmitt, Peter J. 1969. *Back to Nature: The Arcadian Myth in Urban America*. New York: Oxford University Press.

Schor, Juliet B. 2003. "The Problem of Overconsumption: Why Economists Don't Get It," pp. 65–82 in *Voluntary Simplicity: Responding to Consumer Culture*, edited by D. Doherty and A. Etzioni. Lanham, MA: Rowman & Littlefield.

Schor, Juliet B. 1999. *The Overspent American*. New York: Basic Books.

Schor, Juliet B. 1991. *The Overworked American*. New York: Basic Books.

Schumacher, E. F. 1973. *Small is Beautiful: A Study of Economics As If People Mattered*. London: Blond and Briggs.

Schwartz, Barry. 2004. *The Paradox of Choice: Why Less is More*. New York: CCCO/Harper Collins.

Schwartz, Michael. 1976. *Radical Protest and Social Structure*. New York: Academic Press.

Sealander, Judith. 2003. *The Failed Century of the Child: Governing America's Young in the Twentieth Century*. New York: Cambridge University Press.

Seligman, Martin E. P. and Mihaly Csikszentmihalyi. 2000. "Positive Psychology: An Introduction." *American Psychologist* 55: 5–14.

Sen, Amartya. 1999. *Development as Freedom*. Oxford, UK: Oxford University Press.

Sen, Amartya. 1993. "Capability and Well-Being," pp. 30–53 in *The Quality of Life*, edited by M. Nussbaum and A. Sen. Oxford, UK: Clarendon Press.

Sen, Amartya. 1985. *Commodities and Capabilities*. Oxford, UK: Elsevier Science Publishers.

Sen, Amartya. 1983. "Development: Which Way Now?" *Economic Journal* 93: 745–62.

Sennett, Richard. 2006. *The Culture of the New Capitalism*. New Haven, CT: Yale University Press.

Sennett, Richard. 1998. *The Corrosion of Character*. New York: W.W. Norton.

Sennett, Richard. 1977. *The Fall of Public Man*. New York: Knopf.

Severson, Kim. 2008. "A Locally Grown Diet with Fuss but No Muss." *New York Times*, July 22.

Shammas, Carole. 2002. *A History of Household Governance in America*. Charlottesville, VA: University Press of Virginia.

Shapiro, Laura. 2004. *Something from the Oven*. New York: Viking.

Sharone, Ofer. 2004. "Engineering Overwork: Bell-Curve Management at a High-Tech Firm," pp. 191–218 in *Fighting for Time*, edited by C. F. Epstein and A. L. Kalleberg. New York: Russell Sage Foundation.

Shea, Lois R. 2006. "Big House, Little House, Back House, Barn," pp. 101–13 in *Mommy Wars*, edited by L. M. Steiner. New York: Random House.

Shellenberger, Michael and Ted Nordhaus. 2007. *Break Through: From the Death of Environmentalism to the Politics of Possibility*. Boston, MA: Houghton Mifflin.

Shellenberger, Michael and Ted Nordhaus. 2005. "The Death of Environmentalism: Global Warming Politics in a Post-Environmental World." *Grist*, January 13. Retrieved August 1, 2008 (http://www.grist.org/news/maindish/2005/01/13/doe-reprint/).

Shenk, David. 1997. *Data Smog: Surviving the Information Glut*. Revised and updated ed. San Francisco, CA: HarperEdge.

Singer, Peter. 1994. *Rethinking Life and Death*. New York: St. Martin's.

Sirgy, M. Joseph. 1996. "Strategic Marketing Planning Guided by the Quality-of-Life (QOL) Concept." *Journal of Business Ethics* 15: 241–59.

Sirgy, M. Joseph. 1986. "A Quality-of-Life Theory Derived from Maslow's Developmental Perspective: 'Quality' Is Related to Progressive Satisfaction of a Hierarchy of Needs, Lower Order and Higher." *The American Journal of Economics and Sociology* 45: 329–42.

Sloane, Lauren. 2005. "Brand Appeal Analysis of *Organic Gardening Magazine*."

Department of Sociology, Vassar College, unpublished fieldwork paper.
Smith, Adam. 1904 [1776]. *An Inquiry into the Nature and Causes of the Wealth of Nations*. 5th ed. London: Methuen. Retrieved July 20, 2006 (http://www.econlib.org/LIBRARY/Smith/smWN.html).
Smith, Cyril Stanley. 1981. *A Search for Structure: Selected Essays on Science, Art, and History*. Cambridge, MA: MIT Press.
Smith, Kristin E. and Amaru Bachu. 1999. "Women's Labor Force Attachment Patterns and Maternity Leave: A Review of the Literature." U.S. Bureau of the Census, Population Division Working Paper No. 32. Retrieved February 4, 2008 (http://www.census.gov/population/www/documentation/twps0032/twps0032.html).
Smith, Michael D. and Richard S. Krannich. 2000. "'Culture Clash' Revisited: Newcomer and Longer-Term Residents' Attitudes Toward Land-Use, Development, and Environmental Issues in Rural Communities in the Rocky Mountain West." *Rural Sociology* 65: 396–421.
Smith, Paul, Chris Berry and Alan Pulford. 1999. *Strategic Marketing Communications*. London: Kogan Page.
Smith, Stanley K. 1989. "Toward a Methodology for Estimating Temporary Residents." *Journal of the American Statistical Association* 84: 430–6.
Snyder, C. R. and Shane J. Lopez. 2007. *Positive Psychology*. Thousand Oaks, CA: Sage.
Solomon, Deborah. 2008. "Corporate Giver." *New York Times Magazine*, March 9, p. 13.
Spalter-Roth, Roberta and William Erskine. 2006. "Resources or Rewards? The Distribution of Work–Family Policies." American Sociological Association Research Brief, May 2006. Washington, DC: American Sociological Association.
Sperling, Bert and Peter Sandler. 2007. *Cities Ranked and Rated*. 2nd ed. Hoboken, NJ: Wiley.
Spock, Benjamin M. 1946. *The Pocket Book of Baby and Child Care*. New York: Pocket Books.
Stack, Carol. 1974. *All Our Kin*. New York: Harper & Row.
Starr, Kevin. 1990. *Material Dreams: Southern California through the 1920s*. New York: Oxford University Press.
Stearns, Peter N. 2003. *Anxious Parents: A History of Modern Childrearing in America*. New York: NYU Press.
Stedman, Richard C. 2006. "Places of Escape: Second-Home Meanings in Northern Wisconsin, USA," pp. 129–44 in *Multiple Dwelling and Tourism*, edited by N. McIntyre, D. Williams and K. McHugh. Oxfordshire, UK: CABI.
Steiner, Leslie M., ed. 2006. *Mommy Wars: Stay-at-Home and Career Moms Face Off on Their Choices, Their Lives, Their Families*. New York: Random House.
Stier, Haya, Noah Lewin-Epstein and Michael Braun. 2001. "Welfare Regimes, Family-Supportive Policies, and Women's Employment Along the Life-Course." *American Journal of Sociology* 106: 1731–60.
Storry, Mike and Peter Childs. 2002. *British Cultural Identities*. 2nd ed. London: Routledge.
Stone, Clarence N. 1993. "Urban Regimes and the Capacity to Govern: A Political Economy Approach." *Journal of Urban Affairs* 15: 1–28.
Strasser, Susan. 1989. *Satisfaction Guaranteed*. Washington, DC: Smithsonian Books.
Strecher, Victor G. 1968. *Police–Community Relations, Urban Riots, and the Quality of Life in Cities*. St. Louis, MO: Washington University.
Streeten, Paul P. S.J. Burki, Mahbub ul Haq, Norman Hicks and Frances Stewart. 1981.

First Things First: Meeting Basic Human Needs in Developing Countries. New York: Oxford University Press.

Sulloway, Frank J. 2001. "Sibling-Order Effects," pp. 14058–63 in *International Encyclopedia of Social and Behavioral Sciences*, edited by N. J. Smelser and P. B. Baltes. Oxford, UK: Elsevier Science.

Sumner, L.W. 1996. *Welfare, Happiness and Ethics*. Oxford, UK: Clarendon Press.

Swain, David and Danielle Hollar. 2003. "Measuring Progress: Community Indicators and the Quality of Life." *International Journal of Public Administration* 26: 789–814.

Sykes, Charles. 1999. *The End of Privacy*. New York: St. Martin's.

Thatcher, Margaret. 1987. Interview for *Woman's Own*, September 23. Retrieved October 13, 2010 (http://www.margaretthatcher.org/document/106689).

Therborn, Göran. 2004. *Between Sex and Power*. London: Routledge.

Thistle, Susan. 2006. *From Marriage to the Market*. Berkeley, CA: University of California Press.

Thompson, E. P. 1967. "Time, Work-Discipline and Industrial Capitalism." *Past and Present* 36: 57–97.

Tiebout, Charles M. 1956. "A Pure Theory of Local Expenditures." *Journal of Political Economy* 64: 416–24.

Twitchell, James B. 1999. *Lead Us Into Temptation*. New York: Columbia University Press.

United States Department of Health, Education, and Welfare. 1969. *Towards a Social Report*. Washington, DC: US Government Printing Office.

Urry, John. 2007. *Mobilities*. Cambridge, UK: Polity.

Urry, John. 2000. *Sociology Beyond Societies*. London: Routledge.

Urry, John. 1995. *Consuming Places*. New York: Routledge.

Urry, John. 1990. *The Tourist Gaze*. London: Sage.

Vachon, Marc and Amy Vachon. 2010. *Equally Shared Parenting: Rewriting the Rules for a New Generation of Parents*. New York: Penguin.

Vallance, Aylmer. 1939. *Hire-Purchase*. New York: Thomas & Sons.

Vanek, Joanne. 1974. "Time Spent in Housework." *Scientific American* 11: 116–20.

Veblen, Thorstein. 1994 [1899]. *The Theory of the Leisure Class*. Reprint. New York: Penguin.

Veenhoven, Ruut. 2001. "Quality-of-Life and Happiness: Not Quite the Same," pp. 67–95 in *Health and Quality of Life*, edited by G. DeGirolamo et al. Torino, Italy: Centro Scientifico Editore.

Vitale, Alex. 2008. *City of Disorder*. New York: NYU Press.

Waldfogel, Jane. 1998. "Understanding the 'Family Gap' in Pay for Women with Children." *Journal of Economic Perspectives* 12: 137–56.

Waldfogel, Jane. 1997. "The Effect of Children on Women's Wages." *American Sociological Review* 62: 209–17.

Walkowitz, Judith R. 1992. *City of Dreadful Delight*. Chicago, University of Chicago Press.

Walton, John. 2001. *Storied Land: Community and Memory in Monterey*. Berkeley, CA: University of California Press.

Wann, David. 2007. *Simple Prosperity: Finding Real Wealth in a Sustainable Lifestyle*. New York: St. Martin's.

Warner, Judith. 2005. *Perfect Madness: Motherhood in the Age of Anxiety*. New York: Riverhead.

Warner, Judith. 2001. "Who Knew? The French Got Femininity Right." *Washington Post*, June 3, p. B1.

Warr, Mark and Christopher B. Ellison. 2000. "Rethinking Social Reactions to Crime: Personal and Altruistic Fear in Family Households." *American Journal of Sociology* 106: 551–78.

Warren, Elizabeth and Amelia Warren Tyagi. 2003. *The Two-Income Trap*. New York: Basic Books.

Webber, Melvin. 1963. "Order in Diversity: Community without Propinquity," pp. 25–54 in *Cities and Space*, edited by L. Wingo, Jr. Baltimore, MD: Johns Hopkins Press.

Weber, Max. 2005a. [1914]. "The Distribution of Power within the Group: Class, Status, Party," pp. 151–62 in *Max Weber: Readings and Commentary on Modernity*, edited by S. Kalberg. Cambridge, MA: Blackwell.

Weber, Max. 2005b [1905]. *The Protestant Ethic and the Spirit of Capitalism*. Reprint, New York: Routledge.

Weber, Max. 2005c [1920]. "The Separation of the Worker from the Means of Production, the Spread of Officialdom, and Organizational Discipline in the Factory," pp. 130–7 in *Max Weber: Readings and Commentary on Modernity*, edited by S. Kalberg. New York: Blackwell.

Weil, Elizabeth. 2007. "When Should a Kid Start Kindergarten?" *New York Times Magazine*, June 3, pp. 46–51.

Welch, Jack. 2001. *Straight from the Gut*. New York: Warner Business Books.

Wellman, Barry, ed. 1999. *Networks in the Global Village*. Boulder, CO: Westview.

Welzel, Christian, Ronald Inglehart and Hans-Dieter Klingemann. 2003. "The Theory of Human Development: A Cross-Cultural Analysis." *European Journal of Political Research* 42: 341–79.

White, L., Jr. 1963. "What Accelerated Technological Progress in the Western Middle Ages?" pp. 279–91 in *Scientific Change*, edited by A. C. Crombie. New York: Basic Books.

Whyte, William H. 1980. *The Social Life of Small Urban Spaces*. New York: Project for Public Spaces.

Whyte, William H. 1956. *Organization Man*. New York: Simon & Schuster.

Williams, Anne S. and Patrick C. Jobes. 1990. "Economic and Quality-of-Life Considerations in Urban–Rural Migration." *Journal of Rural Studies* 6: 187–94.

Williams, Bernard. 1987. "The Standard of Living: Interests and Capabilities," pp. 94–102 in *The Standard of Living*, edited by G. Hawthorn. Cambridge, UK: Cambridge University Press.

Williams, Joan. 2000. *Unbending Gender: Why Family and Work Conflict and What to Do About It*. New York: Oxford University Press.

Williams, Raymond. 1975. *The Country and the City*. Oxford, UK: Oxford University Press.

Wilson, Andrew. 1991. *The Culture of Nature*. Toronto, Canada: University of Toronto Press.

Wilson, Elizabeth. 1991. *The Sphinx in the City*. Berkeley, CA: University of California Press.

Wilson, John Oliver. 1969. *Quality of Life in the United States: An Excursion Into the New Frontier of Socio-economic Indicators*. Kansas City, MO: Midwest Research Institute.

Wilson, William J. 1997. *When Work Disappears*. New York: Knopf.

Wirth, Louis. 1938. "Urbanism as a Way of Life." *American Journal of Sociology* 44: 1–24.

Wohl, Anthony S. 1983. *Endangered Lives: Public Health in Victorian Britain*. Cambridge, MA: Harvard University Press.

Woodburn, J. 1981. "The Transition to Settled Agriculture." Presented at the Patterns of History Seminar, London School of Economics, November 17, London.

Woodburn, J. 1980. "Hunters and Gatherers Today and Reconstruction of the Past," pp. 95–117 in *Soviet and Western Anthropology*, edited by E. Gellner. London: Duckworth.

Woods, Michael. 2003. "Deconstructing Rural Protest: The Emergence of a New Social Movement." *Journal of Rural Studies* 19: 309–25.

Woods, Michael. 2002. "Was There a Rural Rebellion? Labour and the Countryside Vote in the 2001 General Election." *British Elections and Parties Review* 12: 206–28.

Zapf, Wolfgang. 1984. "Individuelle Wohlfahrt: Lebensbedingungen und Wahrgenommene Lebensqualität in der Bundesrepublik," pp. 13–26 in *Lebensqualität in der Bundesrepublik*, edited by W. Glatzer and W. Zapf. Frankfurt: Campus.

Zaretsky, Eli. 1976. *Capitalism, the Family, and Personal Life*. London: Pluto Press.

Zelizer, Viviana A. 1985. *Pricing the Priceless Child: The Changing Social Value of Children*. New York: Basic Books.

Zorbaugh, Harvey. 1929. *The Gold Coast and the Slum*. Chicago, IL: University of Chicago Press.

Zukin, Sharon. 2010. *Naked City: The Death and Life of Authentic Urban Places*. New York: Oxford University Press.

Index